Literature *for* Lively Lessons

The Month-by-Month, Week-by-Week, Day-by-Day Guide to
Great Picture Books That Will Help You Plan Your Lessons!

Sheila Edwards, Ed.D.

McGraw·Hill

New York   Chicago   San Francisco   Lisbon   London   Madrid   Mexico City
Milan   New Delhi   San Juan   Seoul   Singapore   Sydney   Toronto

Library of Congress Cataloging-in-Publication Data

Edwards, Sheila H.
    Literature for lively lessons : the month-by-month, week-by-week, day-by-day guide to great picture books
that will help you plan your lessons / by Sheila Edwards.
        p.   cm.
    ISBN 0-07-144410-6
    1. Children's literature—Study and teaching (Primary)—United States.   2. Lesson planning—United
States.   3. Children—Books and reading—United States.   4. Calendars—United States.   5. Picture
books for children—United States.   I. Title.

LB1527.E39   2005
372.64—dc22   2005043757

This book is dedicated to all the wonderful mentors who
fueled my passion for children's literature and to all the
children who ask me, "Read it again!"

1 2 3 4 5 6 7 8 9 0   DOC/DOC   0 9 8 7 6 5

ISBN 0-07-144410-6

McGraw-Hill books are available at special quantity discounts to use as premiums and sales promotions, or for
use in corporate training programs. For more information, please write to the Director of Special Sales,
Professional Publishing, McGraw-Hill, Two Penn Plaza, New York, NY 10121-2298. Or contact your local
bookstore.

This book is printed on acid-free paper.

Introduction

In my thirty years of experience as a reading specialist in the public schools and in my work with parent groups and new teachers, I have always emphasized that reading good stories to children is a key ingredient to their success in school. This guide for children aged four to eight explores the wonderful world of picture books. Did you know that picture books often contain the great American novel in thirty-two pages?

The "teacher" in me always wants to share my passion for the joy that reading can bring to all children. Hundreds of selections with myriad themes are presented here, along with project suggestions to help teachers set up lesson plans with various curriculum connections.

I'd like to acknowledge Joanne Bell for helping to make this book a reality. She helped me in the research and editing. But most importantly, she was my encouraging right hand through the entire writing process. We make a great team!

How to Use This Book

The book is divided into twelve chapters—one for each month of the year. Each chapter begins with a "Month at a Glance" section that contains interesting quotations; helpful reading tips; and monthly designations such as National Hot Tea Month, Keep America Beautiful Month, National Bike Month, Fire Prevention Month, and so on. Each designation includes a reading suggestion or website for further information. The balance of this section outlines the information presented in the chapter.

Weekly Themes and Curriculum Connections

Each month contains four weekly themes with several possible curriculum connections. The lists of reading suggestions include fiction as well as nonfiction and were chosen based on the following criteria:

- A tie-in to a particular month. For example, April is National Poetry Month, so poetry picture books are one of the themes for April.
- An abundance of quality picture books on the theme.
- New and refreshing books or ideas.

- Cross-curricular selections for kindergarten through fourth grade. Most early elementary curriculum is interrelated, and weekly theme books can be used in a variety of ways during the month.
- A theme that is broad enough to span the interest and age levels of kindergarten through fourth grade.
- A theme that lends itself to both fiction and nonfiction titles.
- Positive presentation of the theme. The themes are offered in an upbeat and constructive approach.
- Correlation to the standards in the curricula for kindergarten through fourth grade. For instance, understanding weather is a standard science topic for early elementary students in many states.

And finally, is the topic fun to read about, and will students and teachers relate positively to the theme and the books?

Featured Monthly Birthdays and Special Events
This section is divided into sixteen days with two or more event themes per day. Types of events include the following:

- Presidential proclamations, such as National Teacher Day
- Religious holidays, such as Easter
- Sponsored events, such as National Sandwich Day
- Ethnic and international observations, such as Kwanzaa
- Historic anniversaries, such as Independence Day
- Important birthdays, such as those of children's authors and other famous people

Reading Strategies
Each chapter concludes with a detailed reading strategy that includes instructions and suggestions to implement the strategy in the classroom.

Indexes
The indexes provide easy access to the hundreds of outstanding children's picture book suggestions. You can access books alphabetically by title, author, and subject.

And now, I invite you to explore all the wonderful books just waiting to be discovered by children and the teachers who are helping them become lifelong lovers of the written word.

January at a Glance

The greater part of our happiness depends on our disposition and not on our circumstances.
—Martha Washington

January Reading Tip: When reading aloud, be sure you are modeling the fluency you want from the children. Remember to vary the pitch, tone, and volume of your voice so that it is interesting for the children to listen to you read.

JANUARY HIGHLIGHTS
National Hot Tea Month
The Tiger Who Came to Tea (2002), written and illustrated by Judith Kerr, is a funny story about a tiger who comes to tea at Sophie's house and eats and drinks everything in the house.

National Mentoring Month
President Bush issued a proclamation designating January as National Mentoring Month to focus national attention on youth mentoring—how it benefits young people, adults, and society as a whole.

Oatmeal Month
The Magic Porridge Pot (1996) retold by Harriet Ziefert, illustrated by Emily Bolam, is about a poor family who discovers that cooking with a magic porridge pot is easy—the hard part is getting it to stop.

Walk Your Pet Month
New Year's resolutions aren't just for humans. Most of our four-legged friends need to watch their weight and begin an exercise program too. So grab that leash and walk!

Soup Month
Celebrate one hundred years of the Campbell Soup Kids with their ABC book *Campbell Kids' Alphabet Soup* (2004) that's "M'm! M'm! Good!"

January Reading Strategy: Retelling

WEEKLY THEMES AND CURRICULUM CONNECTIONS
Week One: Alaska (Social Studies and Geography)
Week Two: Fairy Tales/Folktales (Language Arts)
Week Three: Pirates (Social Studies)
Week Four: Elephants (Science)

Special Events in January

Ellis Island Anniversary	Jan. 1
Alaska Admitted to the Union	Jan. 3
Bird Day	Jan. 5
Answer Your Cat's Question Day	Jan. 22
National Compliment Day	Jan. 28

FEATURED JANUARY BIRTHDAYS

Paul Revere....................Jan. 1	Ina Friedman ....Jan. 6	Katharine Holabird ....Jan. 23
Betsy Ross ....Jan. 1	Michael Bond ....Jan. 13	Wolfgang Amadeus
Alma Flor Ada.................Jan. 3	Martin Luther King, Jr. ..Jan. 15	Mozart..........................Jan. 27
Joan Walsh Anglund ....Jan. 3	Benjamin Franklin..........Jan. 17	Harry Allard ....Jan. 27
Louis Braille ....Jan. 4	A. A. Milne ....Jan. 18	Laura Kvasnosky ....Jan. 27
Jacob Grimm ....Jan. 4	Arthur Ransome ....Jan. 18	Vera Williams ....Jan. 28
George Washington	Paul Cézanne ....Jan. 19	Rosemary Wells ....Jan. 29
Carver ....Jan. 5	Pat Mora ....Jan. 19	Jackie Robinson ....Jan. 31
Lynn Cherry ....Jan. 5	Blair Lent ....Jan. 22	Denise Fleming.............Jan. 31
Carl Sandburg ....Jan. 6	John Hancock ....Jan. 23	Gerald McDermott........Jan. 31

Week One: Alaska

🏛 🌐 Curriculum Connection: Social Studies and Geography

Primary students are fascinated by geographic areas that are different than where they live. They are also very interested in the people and animals from those areas. The resources listed here whet the students' appetites for more knowledge of the native peoples and animals of the far north. If you spend some time studying Alaska, it would be great to have someone who has lived or visited there to talk to your class about life in the frozen North.

Akiak: A Tale From the Iditarod (1997) written and illustrated by Robert Blake. Ten-year-old sled dog Akiak has raced the 1,151 miles of the Iditarod sled dog race before but has never won. With her age and an injured paw working against her, will she be able to win this year?

Alaska ABC Book (1988) by Charlene Kreeger, illustrated by Shannon Cartwright. This delightful ABC book uses animals of Alaska to interest children in learning the basics of reading.

Alaska Brown Bear (1997) by Jason Cooper. The physical characteristics and habits of the large bears that live on the southern coast of Alaska are described.

Alaska Facts and Symbols (2003) by Muriel L. Dubois, illustrated by Linda Clavel. This interesting, easy-to-read text on major state symbols includes a "fast facts" section listing such details as the capital city, physical size, population, and natural resources.

Alaska (2004) by Su Tien Wong. This introduction to Alaska focuses on each region and its geographical features.

Alaska's 12 Days of Summer (2003) by Pat Chamberlin-Calamar, illustrated by Shannon Cartwright. This book uses the rhythm of "The Twelve Days of Christmas" to introduce interesting facts about Alaskan animals, includ-

ing bears, swans, caribou, moose—and even mosquitoes.

Andy: Alaskan Tale (1992) by Susan Welsh-Smith, illustrated by Rie Munoz. This lively story of an old English sheepdog that comes to live in a remote Eskimo village follows his adventures and acceptance by the native community.

Arctic Adventure: Inuit Life in the 1800s (1997) by Dana Rau, illustrated by Peg Magovern. Readers can travel back in time with Tomas as he becomes an Inuit boy living in the Arctic regions in the nineteenth century.

Arctic Peoples (1999) by Mir Tamim Ansary. This book describes various elements of the traditional life of Arctic people and how that life changed as Europeans arrived.

Circle of Thanks (2001) by Susi Fowler, illustrated by Peter Catalanotto. The illustrations and story explore the lives of the animals and people of the isolated region known as the Alaskan tundra.

Denali National Park and Preserve (1996) by David Petersen. The author describes the scenery, wildlife, and fun things for visitors to do at Alaska's Denali National Park.

The Giant Cabbage: An Alaska Folktale (2003) by Chérie B. Stihler, illustrated by Jeremiah Trammell. Moose wants to enter his enormous cabbage in the fair, but he can't carry it. Can he and his friends get it there? A delicious recipe for cabbage soup is included.

Groucho's Eyebrows (2003) by Tricia Brown, illustrated by Barbara Lavallee. Because of his silly eyebrows, Kristie names her snow-white cat Groucho. One wintry night in Alaska, during a game of hide-and-seek, Groucho slips outside into the snow and disappears. Will Kristie be able to find her white cat in all that snow?

How Raven Stole the Sun (2001) by Maria Williams, illustrated by Felix Vigil. In this traditional Tlingit tale, Raven transforms himself to bring light to the dark earth.

Kumak's Fish (2004) by Michael Bania. While ice fishing with his family, Kumak hooks what he thinks is an enormous fish—and the entire village pitches in to help pull it out.

Meet Lydia: A Native Girl from Southeast Alaska (2004) by Miranda Belarde-Lewis, with photographs by John Harrington. Insightful and educational, *Meet Lydia* explores Native American life by offering a rare glimpse into the modern culture of Alaska's Tlingit tribe.

North American Animals of the Arctic (1997) by Colleayn Mastin, illustrated by Jan Sovak. This is a nature lover's tour of the frozen North and the animals that live there.

River of Life (2000) by Debbie S. Miller, illustrated by Jon Van Zyle. This depiction of a river in Alaska explores the life that it supports and the plants and animals that are dependent on it for their survival.

The Salmon Princess: An Alaska Cinderella Story (2004) written and illustrated by Mindy Dwyer. Loosely based on the original *Cinderella* story, this Alaskan version features a fairy godmother who is an eagle spirit, and a unique "glass slipper": a heavy rubber boot—left behind at the Silver Salmon Festival.

This Place Is Cold (1994) by Vicki Cobb, illustrated by Barbara Lavallee. Imagine living in this cold and distant place. The gorgeous illustrations provide a peek at the land, animals, plants, and climate of Alaska.

Three River Junction: A Story of an Alaskan Bald Eagle Preserve (1997) by Saranne Burnham, illustrated by Tom Antonishak. A hungry bald eagle searching for food joins other eagles at an Alaskan preserve.

Togo (2002) written and illustrated by Robert J. Blake. Togo, a feisty and independent Siberian husky, works hard to become a great sled dog. In 1925, he leads a team that rushes the diphtheria antitoxin from Anchorage to Nome, Alaska, saving people's lives.

Very Last First Time (2002) by Jan Andrews, illustrated by Ian Wallace. In search of mussels while the tide is out, a young Eskimo girl searches alone on the seabed under a thick shelf of ice. What happens when her candle goes out?

Whale Snow (2003) by Debby Dahl Edwardson and Shelley Gill, illustrated by Annie Patterson. At the first whaling feast of the season, a young Inupiat boy learns about the whaling traditions of his people.

January 1

ELLIS ISLAND ANNIVERSARY
Ellis Island opened in the port of New York on this day in 1892. By 1924, more than twenty-two million immigrants had passed through this portal, which became a museum in 1990. Resources for primary students include *Ellis Island Christmas* (1994) by Maxinne Leighton and *Watch the Stars Come Out* (1994) by Riki Levinson.

PAUL REVERE: BIRTHDAY
Paul Revere, the famous American patriot, was born January 1, 1735, and died in 1818. A member of the Sons of Liberty, he took part in the Boston Tea Party in 1773. On April 18, 1775, he made his famous ride to warn the citizens that the British were coming to Concord. *Paul Revere: Patriot* (2003) by Carin Ford and *The Midnight Ride of Paul Revere* (2001) by Henry Wadsworth Longfellow, illustrated by Christopher Bing, provide further information for primary students.

BETSY ROSS: BIRTHDAY
Betsy Ross was born on January 1, 1752. The book *Betsy Ross* (1998) by Alexandra Wallner introduces the life of this Philadelphia seamstress who is credited with sewing the first American flag.

January 3

ALMA FLOR ADA: BIRTHDAY
Children's author Alma Flor Ada was born on January 3, 1938. She grew up in Cuba and says she writes to share some of the feelings of joy, excitement, and surprise she had as a child. Knowing two languages, Spanish and English, has made the world richer for her. *The Gold Coin* (1994), illustrated by Neil Waldman, and *Dear Peter Rabbit* (1997), illustrated by Leslie Tryon, are two of her books.

JOAN WALSH ANGLUND: BIRTHDAY
Joan Walsh Anglund was born on this day in 1926. She became a success with her first book, *A Friend Is Someone Who Likes You* (1983). *In a Pumpkin Shell: A Mother Goose ABC* showcases her use of charm and whimsy.

ALASKA ADMITTED TO THE UNION
On January 3, 1959, Alaska became our forty-ninth and largest state. The thematic list on Alaska provides a wealth of resource books on this very interesting state. Did you know that your hair could freeze and break off in some parts of Alaska?

January 4

LOUIS BRAILLE: BIRTHDAY

Louis Braille was born on January 4, 1809, and died in 1852. He became blind at the age of three from an infection and was twelve when he devised the system of raised dots that became the Braille system of reading for blind people. The first Braille book was published in 1829. *A Picture Book of Louis Braille* (1998) by David A. Adler, illustrated by John and Alexandra Wallner, is a good resource for more information about this incredible man.

JACOB GRIMM: BIRTHDAY

Jacob Grimm, half of the famous fairy tale author team of the Brothers Grimm, was born on January 4, 1785, and died in 1863. With his brother, Wilhelm, he collected fairy tales and folktales from several countries in Europe. Some of the Brothers Grimm stories are included in the thematic listing for Week Two and are classics that should be shared with children. Many of these books are also beautifully illustrated and foster children's appreciation of different art forms.

January 5

GEORGE WASHINGTON CARVER: BIRTHDAY

George Washington Carver, an agricultural chemist, was born January 5, 1864, and died in 1943. He did research on peanuts and other plants. He devised more than three hundred products from peanuts and more than one hundred products from sweet potatoes. Not wanting to profit from his research, he never applied for patents. He taught himself through observing others, questioning, and experimenting. *A Weed Is a Flower: The Life of George Washington Carver* (1991), written and illustrated by Aliki, provides further information on this very interesting man.

LYNNE CHERRY: BIRTHDAY

Lynne Cherry, children's author and nature lover, was born on January 5, 1952. She wants her books to encourage children to explore the world around them. *How Groundhog's Garden Grew* (2003) is written for the 4–7 age group.

BIRD DAY

January 5 is Bird Day. Do the wild birds in your area need some help finding food during the winter? A class bird feeder would be a good science project. *Wild Birds* (2003) by Joanne Ryder, illustrated by Susan Estelle Kwas, is a great science read-aloud.

Week Two: Fairy Tales/Folktales

📖 Curriculum Connection: Language Arts

Once upon a time . . . Those magic words let the reader or listener know that the story that follows is not based in the current time. The title of folktale or fairy tale also lets the reader or listener know that the tale is not true but will be entertaining and instructive in some way. The following list of books is just the tip of the iceberg for this genre of children's literature. Books were chosen for their endurance as classics and for their richness of illustrations and language.

Beauty and the Beast (1990) retold and illustrated by Jan Brett. A kind, loving, and beautiful maid releases a handsome prince from the spell that turned him into an ugly beast.

Daisy Comes Home (2002) written and illustrated by Jan Brett. Daisy, an unhappy hen in China, floats down the river in a basket and has an adventure that teaches her how to stand up for herself.

The Dancing Pig (1999) by Judy Sierra, illustrated by Jesse Sweetwater. After being snatched by a terrible ogress who locks them in a trunk, two sisters are rescued by a dancing pig, a talking mouse, and an amusing frog band.

Fritz and the Beautiful Horses (1987) written and illustrated by Jan Brett. A pony named Fritz becomes a hero when he rescues some children from a walled city.

Gingerbread Baby (2003) written and illustrated by Jan Brett. Here is another wonderful version of the Gingerbread Man with delightful illustrations and an enjoyable twist at the end.

Goldilocks and the Three Bears (2003) retold by Jim Aylesworth, illustrated by Barbara McClintock. A little girl wandering in the woods comes upon the house of three bears and explores their belongings. One of *Publishers Weekly*'s Best Children's Picture Books of

2003. The back cover features a yummy recipe for porridge cookies.

Hansel and Gretel (1994) retold by Rika Lesser, illustrated by Paul O. Zelinsky. When a poor woodcutter abandons his children in the forest, they come upon a house made of cookies, cakes, and candy, which is occupied by a wicked witch.

How the Guinea Fowl Got Her Spots: A Swahili Tale of Friendship (1991) written and illustrated by Barbara Knutson. This folktale offers an explanation for how the black guinea fowl got white spots, which helps it to hide from the lion.

It Couldn't Be Worse (2003) written and illustrated by Vlasta van Kampen. A farmer, his wife, their six children, and their grandparents live together in a tiny house with only one room. They always get in each other's way. It couldn't be worse! How can they make things better?

Joseph Had a Little Overcoat (2000) written and illustrated by Simms Taback. When Joseph's coat got too old and shabby, he made it into a jacket. But what did he make it into after that? And after that? This was the winner of the 2000 Caldecott Medal.

Juan Bobo Goes to Work: A Puerto Rican Folk Tale (2000) retold by Marisa Montes, illustrated by Joe Cepeda. Although he tries hard to follow instructions, foolish Juan Bobo keeps getting things all wrong.

The Legend of the Bluebonnet: An Old Tale of Texas (1996) retold and illustrated by Tomie dePaola. This retelling of the Comanche Indian legend explains how the flower called bluebonnet came to be the state flower of Texas.

Little Red Riding Hood (2002) retold by Candice Ransom, illustrated by Tammie Lyon. While visiting her grandmother, Little Red Riding Hood wonders why she's reminded of the sly wolf she met along the way.

A Little Story About a Big Turnip (2004) retold by Tatiana Zunshine, illustrated by Evgeny Antonenkov. This is an adaptation of the Russian children's folktale about a family that must work together to harvest a very large turnip.

Mufaro's Beautiful Daughters: An African Tale (1987) written and illustrated by John Steptoe. Mufaro has two beautiful daughters—one bad-tempered, one kind and sweet. Which one will the king choose for a wife?

Parrott: An Italian Folktale (1997) retold and illustrated by Lászlóand Raffaella Gál. Children love this story of a beautiful princess, an evil king, sneaky kidnappers, foul witches, and a handsome prince.

The Princess and the Pea (1982) adapted from Hans Christian Andersen, illustrated by Janet Stevens. To prove she is a real princess, a young girl passes the queen's test when she is able to feel a pea through twenty mattresses and twenty featherbeds.

The Princess Mouse: A Tale of Finland (2003) by Aaron Shepard, illustrated by Leonid Gore. This is a retelling of the Finnish folktale about a young man who searches for a wife in the deep, dark woods.

Rapunzel (1997) retold and illustrated by Paul O. Zelinsky. This is an enchanting retelling of the story about a young prince rescuing a beautiful golden-haired girl who is unfairly imprisoned in a lonely tower.

Tops and Bottoms (1995) adapted and illustrated by Janet Stevens. Hare and Bear farm together, but Bear is very lazy. Read how Hare cleverly harvests the crops to get the largest share. This was a 1996 Caldecott Honor Book.

The Trial of the Stone: A Folk Tale (2000) retold by Richardo Keens Douglas, illustrated by Stéphane Jorisch. When a thief steals some money that a young boy hid under a stone, the stone is blamed and must stand trial for theft.

Two Greedy Bears: Adapted from a Hungarian Folk Tale (1998) by Mirra Ginsburg, illustrated by Jose Aruego and Ariane Dewey. In this adaptation, a clever fox teaches two quarrelsome bears a lesson about sharing.

Rumpelstiltskin (1986) retold and illustrated by Paul O. Zelinsky. When the king demands that the miller's daughter spin straw into gold, she seeks help from a strange little man who asks that in return she give him her firstborn child. How does she get out of this predicament? This was a 1987 Caldecott Honor Book.

January 6

CARL SANDBURG: BIRTHDAY

The famous poet Carl Sandburg was born on January 6, 1878, and died in 1967. Most famous for his poetry for adults, he also wrote some wonderful titles for children. *Carl Sandburg: Adventures of a Poet* (2003) by Penelope Niven traces his life and details his winning of the Pulitzer Prize for both poetry and history. Sandburg's *From Daybreak to Good Night: Poems for Children* (2001), illustrated by Lynn Smith-Ary, is a treat for children who hear these poems read aloud.

INA FRIEDMAN: BIRTHDAY

Ina Friedman was born on this day in 1926. She holds a master of arts degree in storytelling from Lesley College. Her book *How My Parents Learned to Eat* (1987), illustrated by Allen Say, is a humorous story of how an American father learns to use chopsticks as a Japanese mother practices with a knife, fork, and spoon. This book received a Christopher Award for promoting cultural understanding. She believes that every person has the right to participate in the American dream.

January 13

MICHAEL BOND: BIRTHDAY

Michael Bond was born January 13, 1926, in England. He is most famous for his Paddington Bear books. His first book, *A Bear Called Paddington*, was published in 1958. Since then he has written more than 150 books for children and adults, and Paddington's adventures have been published in twenty countries. There is even a Paddington corner in the London Toy Museum. The official Paddington website at paddingtonbear.co.uk is user-friendly for children.

January 15

MARTIN LUTHER KING, JR.: BIRTHDAY

Martin Luther King, Jr., was born January 15, 1929, and was assassinated on April 4, 1968. He entered college at age fifteen and was ordained a Baptist minister at seventeen. He made his now-famous speech, "I Have a Dream," in 1963 and was awarded the Nobel Peace Prize in 1964.

In 1983, the third Monday in January was designated a federal holiday in honor of Dr. King. His birthplace in Atlanta and his gravesite have been made into national historic sites. More information about this peace-loving man can be found at thekingcenter.com.

Several books can provide additional information: *A Picture Book of Martin Luther King, Jr.* (1991) by David A. Adler, illustrated by Robert Casilla; *My Brother Martin: A Sister Remembers Growing Up with the Rev. Dr. Martin Luther King, Jr.* (2002) by Christine King Farris, illustrated by Chris Soentpiet; and *I Have a Dream* (1997) by Martin Luther King, Jr., illustrated by Kathleen A. Wilson.

January 17

BENJAMIN FRANKLIN: BIRTHDAY

Benjamin Franklin—a scientist, inventor, diplomat, and philosopher—was born January 17, 1706, and died in 1790.

He was the oldest person to sign both the Declaration of Independence and the U.S. Constitution. He is best remembered as a patriot and inventor. There are many books about this amazing man. *The Ben Franklin Book of Easy and Incredible Experiments* (2003) by the Franklin Institute Science Museum, edited by Lisa Jo Rudy, is an appealing collection of easy science projects. All of the activities are either actual experiments tried by Franklin or variations on his research. What better way to celebrate Ben Franklin's birthday than by doing one of his experiments?

A Picture Book of Benjamin Franklin (1991) by David A. Adler, illustrated by John and Alexandra Wallner, provides a brief biography.

After learning about Ben Franklin and the many things he did during his life, you might want to have the students write about the most important thing that Ben Franklin did.

Week Three: Pirates

♊ Curriculum Connection: Social Studies

Ahoy, mates! How about a fantasy trip across the bounding main to the world of pirates? January can be a dull, boring, and cold month, but with a little imagination and the resources listed here, you and your students can be transported off across the seven seas to a land of enchantment, excitement, and warm weather. This realm has lots of avenues to explore. What would it be like to live on a pirate ship? What would you do if you found a pirate's buried treasure? Are the characters in these pirate stories good or bad? Would you want to be a pirate?

Bubble Bath Pirates (2003) written and illustrated by Jarrett J. Krosoczka. Readers will love this spirited adventure set on the high seas of the bathtub. Who won't want to take a bath when it's this fun?

Captain Abdul's Pirate School (2004) written and illustrated by Colin McNaughton. Do you think it would toughen you up if your dad decided to send you to pirate school? Maybe you would have the most fun of your life.

Captain Slaughterboard Drops Anchor (2001) written and illustrated by Mervyn Peake. A pirate captain finds an island full of unusual animals and makes friends with one he calls Little Yellow Creature.

Do Pirates Take Baths? (1997) by Kathy Tucker, illustrated by Nadine Bernard Westcott. This cute and amusing book of rhymes provides answers to the eleven important questions about the lives of pirates.

Edward and the Pirates (1997) written and illustrated by David McPhail. Learning to read opens up a whole new world of adventure for Edward.

The Erie Canal Pirates (2002) by Eric A. Kimmel, illustrated by Andrew Glass. A folk song inspired this rhyming tale of a boat captain and his crew battling pirates on the Erie Canal.

Everything I Know About Pirates (2003) written and illustrated by Tom Lichtenheld. This is a humorously illustrated collection of entertaining tidbits about pirates.

How I Became a Pirate (2003) by Melinda Long, illustrated by David Shannon. When Jeremy Jacob joins a pirate crew, he discovers what pirates do and what they *don't* do.

Jonah and the Pirates Who (Usually) Don't Do Anything (2004) by Erick Metaxas and Cindy Kenney, illustrated by Robert Vann and Ron Eddy. Pa Grape, who belongs to the crew known as The Pirates Who Don't Do Anything, describes the crew's one and only adventure.

Little Badger, Terror of the Seven Seas (2001) by Eve Bunting, illustrated by LeUyen Pham. With a little bit of imagination, a young badger becomes a pirate.

Lucy and the Pirates (1997) by Glen Petrie, illustrated by Matilda Harrison. One of the few books with a female main character on an exciting adventure, this book has great illustrations and a lively story.

Matthew and the Midnight Pirates (1998) by Allen Morgan, illustrated by Michael Martchenko. Matthew is worried about a library fine on a long-overdue pirate book. That night, he dreams that pirates arrive and join forces with the librarians to save the city's books.

Mrs. Honey's Dream (1993) written and illustrated by Pam Adams. A group of fearsome pirates are no match for Mrs. Honey and her cat, Thomas.

Pirate Jam (2003) written and illustrated by Jo Brown. What can Fredbeard and Little Jim do after they fail pirate school? You can't be a pirate if you get seasick!

Pirate Pete Sets Sail (2003) by J. Allison James and J. Jaggi, illustrated by Alan Clarke. Young sailors and landlubbers alike will enjoy this humorous story of a young boy moving to a new home who imagines he is a pirate heading to a new hideout.

Pirate Pete (2002) by Kim Kennedy, illustrated by Doug Kennedy. Children will love the funny and exciting adventures of Pirate Pete in this gorgeously illustrated story.

The Pirate, Pink (2001) by Jan Day, illustrated by Janeen Mason. Pink is the daughter of the fierce pirate Red Beard, so how does she become a different sort of pirate?

Pirates: Robbers of the High Seas (1999) written and illustrated by Gail Gibbons. Simple text and illustrations describe the lives and activities of pirates.

Pirates (1997) by Dina Anastasio, illustrated by Donald Cook. Learn about life on the high seas as well as interesting facts about real-life pirates, including Blackbeard and Captain Kidd.

Rabbit Pirates: A Tale of the Spinach Main (1999) by Judy Cox, illustrated by Emily Arnold McCully. Two rabbits (retired pirates) own a restaurant in France called the Spinach Main. What happens when Monsieur Reynard (the fox) walks in?

Tough Boris (1998) by Mem Fox, illustrated by Kathryn Brown. Maybe Boris the pirate isn't as mean, greedy, and scary as they say.

Uncle Pete's Pirate Adventure (2003) by Susannah Leigh, illustrated by Brenda Haw. Join Mary and her friend, Zac, on board Uncle Pete's pirate boat and help them look for missing pirate pals.

January 18

A. A. MILNE: BIRTHDAY

A. A. Milne, creator of Winnie the Pooh, was born on January 18, 1882, and died in 1956. He was inspired in all of his writing by his son, Christopher Robin Milne. His stories have been printed in more than twenty-five languages and more than seventy million copies have been sold since they were first published in 1926. Much more information on A. A. Milne and Winnie the Pooh can be found at pooh-corner.com and worldkids.net/pooh.

When We Were Very Young (1976), illustrated by Ernest H. Shepard, is a wonderful collection of poems for young children. Be sure you introduce children to the classic Winnie the Pooh as well as the modern Walt Disney version.

ARTHUR RANSOME: BIRTHDAY

Arthur Ransome was born January 18, 1884, and died in 1967. He is most remembered for his version of the Russian folktale The Fool of the World and the Flying Ship: A Russian Tale (1987), illustrated by Uri Shulevitz, which won the Caldecott Medal in 1969.

January 19

PAUL CÉZANNE: BIRTHDAY

Paul Cézanne, a French painter, was born on January 19, 1839, and died in 1906. He was the forerunner of modern painting in that he didn't sketch or draw his subject before he put the brush to the canvas. The website expo-cezanne.com is a permanent museum showing more than two hundred of Cézanne's paintings.

Paul Cézanne (1998) by Mike Venezia describes Cézanne's work and the new ideas he tried in his paintings.

PAT MORA: BIRTHDAY

Pat Mora was born on January 19, 1942, and grew up in Texas. She has won many awards for her poetry both for adults and children. Raised in a bilingual home, she feels that if a person can speak two languages, their value is doubled. A Birthday Basket for Tía (1997), illustrated by Cecily Lang, and The Gift of the Poinsettia: El Regalo de la Flor de Nochebuena (1995), written with Charles Ramírez Berg, illustrated by Daniel Lechón, are two of her most-loved books. This Big Sky (2002), illustrated by Steve Jenkins, is a book of poetry for children.

January 22

BLAIR LENT: BIRTHDAY
Blair Lent, illustrator of children's books, was born on January 22, 1930. He won a Caldecott Medal in 1973 for *The Funny Little Woman* (1972), a Japanese folktale retold by Arlene Mosel. He has illustrated books for several authors such as *Tikki Tikki Tembo* (1995), also retold by Arlene Mosel, and *Why the Sun and the Moon Live in the Sky* (1990) by Elphinstone Dayrell.

ANSWER YOUR CAT'S QUESTION DAY
January 22 is designated as Answer Your Cat's Question Day. If you look at a cat, you will find that the cat is looking at you with a serious question—think about it and then answer it. This idea can be turned into a terrific creative writing assignment.

January 23

JOHN HANCOCK: BIRTHDAY
John Hancock, the first signer of the Declaration of Independence, was born on January 23, 1737, and died in 1793. His flamboyant signature is the most easily recognized of all those on the document. That's why when you sign a document, it is known as giving your John Hancock. Discuss with students the need to have a legible signature—you never know when a signature might be as important as John Hancock's. Among many other important things, Hancock was instrumental in creating a navy for the United States.

Will You Sign Here, John Hancock? (1997) by Jean Fritz, illustrated by Trina Schart Hyman, provides a biography that outlines the many things Hancock did for Massachusetts and his new nation.

KATHARINE HOLABIRD: BIRTHDAY
Katharine Holabird, the author of the Angelina Ballerina series, was born on this day in 1948. She lives in England and has written fourteen books about Angelina since 1983. Check out her wonderful website, angelinaballerina.com, which has games, coloring pages, and much more for students to enjoy.

Week Four: Elephants

✳ Curriculum Connection: Science

Elephants in both fact and fiction provide the basis for this thematic unit. Children are interested in all animals but especially those that are the biggest, smallest, fastest, or in some other way unusual. Be sure to include some nonfiction reading on elephants for those of your students who are curious about real life and are hungry for information. This could be a good topic for fact or fiction trivia after exposing your students to many of the resources listed here.

The African Elephant (1996) by Ellen Weiss. Did you know the African elephant is as tall as a one-story house and as heavy as five station wagons?

The Ant and the Elephant (1980) written and illustrated by Bill Peet. The mighty elephant rescues lots of animals, but only the tiny ant returns the favor.

Eight Enormous Elephants (2002) by Penny Dolan, illustrated by Leo Broadley. A brave mouse makes eight enormous elephants clean up after themselves after they rampaged through the house.

Elephant Rescue (1990) by Terua Teramura, adapted by Jill Barnes, illustrated by Tsutomu Murakami. One day a poor little elephant falls into a deep hole. How will his animal friends rescue him?

Elephants (2000) by Martin Schwabacher. The physical characteristics and behavior of elephants, their family groups, food habits, and threats to their existence are described here.

Elephants: Life in the Wild (2000) by Monica Kulling, illustrated by Michael Maydak. Did you know an elephant can weigh as much as fifteen thousand pounds? Or that elephants eat for twenty hours a day?

Elephants on Board (1999) written and illustrated by Suse MacDonald. Elephant per-formers on their way to a show have a flat tire that leads to big trouble and lots of fun.

The Elephant's Pillow (2003) by Diana Reynolds Roome, illustrated by Jude Daly. Sing Lo, a wealthy boy living in Peking, visits the late emperor's imperial elephant and discovers he has trouble sleeping. What can he do to help the elephant get a good night's sleep?

Eleven Elephants Going Up! (1996) by Bethany Roberts and Patricia Hubbell, illustrated by Minh Uong. Eleven elephants riding the elevator create havoc on each floor of a department store.

Ella (1978) written and illustrated by Bill Peet. Ella the elephant still thinks of herself as a famous circus star but gets a lesson in humility when she has to work on a farm.

Elmer (1991) written and illustrated by David McKee. Elmer elephant, who is a patchwork of brilliant colors, has trouble blending in with a herd of gray elephants. What does he do?

Elympics (1999) written by X. J. Kennedy, illustrated by Graham Percy. These fun poems tell about elephants who compete in their own Olympics.

Five Minutes' Peace (1999) written and illustrated by Jill Murphy. Will Mrs. Large ever have five minutes' peace from her energetic "children"?

Grandma Elephant's in Charge (2003) by Martin Jenkins, illustrated by Ivan Bates. This is a description of the behavior of elephants in a family group, especially the role older female elephants play.

Growing Up in Africa's Elephant Kingdom: The Story of Little Bull (2001) by Ellen Foley James, photographed by Karl Ammann. Through photographs and poetic text, follow an elephant's life from birth to adulthood in Africa.

Hansa, the True Story of an Asian Elephant Baby (2002) by Clare Hodgson Meeker, illustrated by Linda Feltner. This is a true story about the birth of a baby elephant at Seattle's Woodland Park Zoo and the first months of her life there.

Horton Hatches the Egg (1976) written and illustrated by Dr. Seuss. What are the animals in the jungle saying when they hear that an elephant hatches an egg?

How to Catch an Elephant (2001) written and illustrated by Amy Schwartz. This book provides instructions for using some very odd tools to catch an elephant.

I Love My Mama (2003) by Peter Kavanagh, illustrated by Jane Chapman. This gentle picture book shows how a baby elephant and his mother spend their days together.

Jumbo: The Most Famous Elephant in the World! (2001) by Bonnie Worth, illustrated by Christopher Santoro. Here's the history of Jumbo, the famous elephant star of Barnum and Bailey's Greatest Show on Earth.

Just a Little Bit (1996) by Ann Tompert, illustrated by Lynn Munsinger. When Mouse and Elephant decide to go on the seesaw, many animals must join Mouse before they can go up and down.

Oliver (2000) written and illustrated by Syd Hoff. When Oliver the dancing elephant finds out the circus already has enough elephants, he looks elsewhere to achieve his dream.

Otto's Trunk (2003) written and illustrated by Sandy Turner. Otto the elephant doesn't fit in with the other elephants because he has a very small trunk. But one day he discovers a unique talent!

The Right Number of Elephants (1992) by Jeff Sheppard, illustrated by Felicia Bond. This counting book tells about a little girl who must decide how many elephants are needed for various tasks.

The Saggy Baggy Elephant (2003) by Kathryn and Byron Jackson, illustrated by Gustaf Tenggren. Don't miss this charming tale of this unique elephant who is trying to find his special place in the jungle.

17 Kings and 42 Elephants (1987) by Margaret Mahy, illustrated by Patricia MacCarthy. Seventeen kings and forty-two elephants make their joyous way through the jungle. What will they find?

"Stand Back," Said the Elephant, "I'm Going to Sneeze!" (1991) by Patricia Thomas, illustrated by Wallace Tripp. The animals don't want the elephant to sneeze. They remember what happened last time!

January 27

WOLFGANG AMADEUS MOZART: BIRTHDAY

Mozart, one of the greatest composers who ever lived, was born January 27, 1756, and died in 1791. He showed a gift for music at a very young age; he began composing music at the age of five. He could write musical notes before he could write words. *Mozart* (1992) by Ann Rachlin, illustrated by Susan Hellard, focuses on his childhood and early musical training.

HARRY ALLARD: BIRTHDAY

Harry Allard was born January 27, 1928. He is the author of *Miss Nelson Is Missing* (1985), *Miss Nelson Is Back* (1986), and *Miss Nelson Has a Field Day* (1991)—all illustrated by James Marshall. The illustrations add greatly to the humor in the text.

LAURA KVASNOSKY: BIRTHDAY

Laura Kvasnosky was born on this day in 1951 and has considered herself a writer since she was a little girl. She says creating books for children is her dream job. She is most loved for her book *Zelda and Ivy* (2002), which tells the exploits of two fox sisters. Visit her website at lmkbooks.com for more information.

January 28

VERA WILLIAMS: BIRTHDAY

Vera Williams was born January 28, 1927. She didn't write for publication until she was in her midforties and her children were all grown. She often writes in the first person as she did in *A Chair for My Mother* (1984). This book won the Caldecott Honor in 1983 along with the Boston Globe Horn Book Award.

Her book *Three Days on a River in a Red Canoe* (1984) is the closest to an autobiography that she has written and is based on real events. Some of her other books include *Cherries and Cherry Pits* (1991) and *Something Special for Me* (1986).

NATIONAL COMPLIMENT DAY

The fourth Wednesday in January is National Compliment Day. Not only does the receiver appreciate compliments, but they also lift the spirits of the giver. Discuss with your students what compliments are and what makes a good compliment. Challenge your students to give one compliment to at least five different people today.

January 29

ROSEMARY WELLS: BIRTHDAY

Rosemary Wells was born on this day in 1943. She began to draw at the age of two. She has published more than sixty books, and in most of them she uses animals rather than people for her characters. She gets most of her ideas from real-life experiences.

Noisy Nora (2000), *Morris's Disappearing Bag* (2001), and *Yoko* (1998) are children's favorites. She also has written many stories about Ruby and Max. These two characters are siblings modeled after Wells's own children.

The website rosemarywells.com is an interactive site for children.

January 31

JACKIE ROBINSON: BIRTHDAY

Jackie Robinson, a symbol of hope to millions of Americans, was born on January 31, 1919, and died in 1972. He broke the color barrier in baseball in 1947 and led the way for generations of black athletes. There are many great resources for information about Jackie Robinson: *A Picture Book of Jackie Robinson* (1998) by David A. Adler, illustrated by Robert Casilla, and *Teammates* (1992) by Peter Golenbock, illustrated by Paul Bacon, are just a couple.

DENISE FLEMING: BIRTHDAY

Children's author and illustrator Denise Fleming was born on this day in 1950. Her website at denisefleming.com has information about her, as well as information on the craft of papermaking. *Count!* (1992), *Buster* (2003), and *Alphabet Under Construction* (2002) are some of her books.

GERALD MCDERMOTT: BIRTHDAY

Gerald McDermott, who writes books based on folklore and mythology, was born on January 31, 1941. He has created more than twenty-five books and films for children.

Anansi the Spider (1987), *Arrow to the Sun* (1977), and *Raven* (2001) have all won Caldecott awards.

January Reading Strategy

Retelling

Literacy comprehension begins with listening to a selection and builds as the independent reading skills of the child increase. The child's comprehension is often assessed by asking questions orally and later by having the answers written. There are other ways of assessing comprehension besides questioning. Retelling of the plot points or character development is one of the best ways to check for comprehension.

Retelling of the plot points is best done in small groups, with partners, or one-on-one with the adult leading the retelling. The reader (or listener) is asked to retell the story using no more than three of the main plot points. This is relatively easy for the student if previous work has been done on the beginning, middle, and end of the selection. Prompts such as the following may be used: In the beginning of the story, the characters were _____. The main problem of the story was _____. In the middle, _____ happened, and the problem was solved by _____. At the end of the story, _____. These prompts can help the student focus on main ideas. As the child's literary skills increase, the retellings can include more plot points and more details. By third grade, children should be very skilled at retellings with four main ideas or events and a supporting detail for each one. Retellings should never be so extensive that every plot point and detail is mentioned.

Character development retelling is a variation that is beneficial both for comprehension and creative writing. Before a selection is read to children, they are asked to pay attention to the main character and how that character changes during the story. After the selection is read, the children are asked to discuss the character in relationship to the events of the story. The focus of the discussion is on the character's actions or thoughts at the beginning, middle, and end of the story. When the children are writing stories of their own, the retelling formats become writing structures or outlines for their own work. In this case, the prompts change somewhat: At the beginning of my story, the family is _____; then _____ happens; and at the end, the family decides _____. With these prompts filled in, the writer can put in details and minor events, and the story will have a backbone focus from which the child can write.

Another variation of retelling is to start reading a selection and stop after two or three pages to have the children tell a partner what has happened so far in the story, what the setting is, or details they know so far about the main characters. This is an excellent strategy for teaching children to be more effective listeners. It increases listening comprehension of primary students and more fully engages those who might be having difficulty listening attentively. In all language arts lessons, it is imperative that all four of the elements of reading, writing, listening, and speaking be fostered as much as possible. Retelling is a strategy that does that with minimal preplanning on the teacher's part.

February at a Glance

If you can imagine it, you can create it. If you can dream it, you can become it.
—William Arthur Ward

February Reading Tip: Remember to allow time for reflection after reading to children. Give them time to discuss the text and form opinions about the experience.

FEBRUARY HIGHLIGHTS
Black History Month
Portraits of African-American Heroes (2003) by Tonya Bolden, illustrated by Ansel Pitcairn, is a beautiful book that contains portraits in pictures and words of twenty outstanding African Americans from the sciences, the arts, politics, literature, sports, education, and adventure.

Library Lover's Month
Mr. Wiggle's Library (2003) by Carol Thompson and Paula Craig, illustrated by Bobbie Houser, explains the organization of a library by following a sweet inchworm, Mr. Wiggles.

National Bird Feeding Month
Birds in Your Backyard (2001) by Barbara Herkert describes how fun and easy watching birds can be, especially in your own backyard!

Valentine's Day (February 14)
The Story of Valentine's Day (1999) by Clyde Robert Bulla, illustrated by Susan Estelle Kwas, explains how Valentine's Day evolved from its beginning in Roman times. Cookie recipes are included.

Presidents' Day (third Monday in February)
Presidents' Day (2002) by David Marx, Katharine Kane, and Nanci Vargus discusses the achievements of two of our most honored presidents, George Washington and Abraham Lincoln.

February Reading Strategy: Use of Why Questions

WEEKLY THEMES AND CURRICULUM CONNECTIONS
Week One: Black History (Social Studies)
Week Two: Friendship (Social Studies)
Week Three: Birds (Science)
Week Four: Sports—Basketball, Football, and Soccer (Social Studies)

Special Events in February

Groundhog Day	Feb. 2
Weather Forecasters' Day	Feb. 5
100 Billionth Crayola Crayon Anniversary	Feb. 6
Mardi Gras (Dates Vary Yearly)	Feb. 8
International Table Manners Week	Feb. 13
Valentine's Day	Feb. 14
Presidents' Day	Feb. 20
Grand Canyon National Park Anniversary	Feb. 26

FEATURED FEBRUARY BIRTHDAYS

Langston Hughes............Feb. 1	Jane Yolen ....Feb. 11	Norman Bridwell ....Feb. 15
Judith Viorst ....Feb. 2	Abraham Lincoln ....Feb. 12	Galileo Galilei ....Feb. 15
Charles Lindbergh ....Feb. 4	David Small ....Feb. 12	Ansel Adams ....Feb. 20
Russell Hoban ....Feb. 4	Jacqueline Woodson ....Feb. 12	Frederick Douglass ......Feb. 20
Patricia Lauber................Feb. 5	Grant Wood ....Feb. 13	George Washington......Feb. 22
David Wiesner ....Feb. 5	Simms Taback ....Feb. 13	Wilhelm Grimm............Feb. 24
Babe Ruth ....Feb. 6	Paul O. Zelinsky............Feb. 14	William Cody................Feb. 26
Anne Rockwell................Feb. 8	Phyllis Root ....Feb. 14	Donna Jo Napoli ....Feb. 28
Thomas Edison ....Feb. 11	Susan B. Anthony..........Feb. 15	Megan McDonald ....Feb. 28

Week One: Black History

🏛 Curriculum Connections: Social Studies

February has been designated Black History Month since 1976. This thematic unit focuses on picture books that enhance the study of the black experience in America. Contributions of African Americans are presented in many of the books listed here, and the lives of famous black Americans are also profiled. Many other resources are available.

African-American Holidays (1996) by Faith Winchester. Learn about special African American celebrations occurring throughout the year, including Black History Month, Mardi Gras, Juneteenth, Harambee, Junkaroo, and Kwanzaa.

Ashanti to Zulu: African Traditions (1980) by Margaret Musgrove, illustrated by Diane and Leo Dillon. This 1977 Caldecott Medal winner uses the alphabet and compelling illustrations to introduce traditions and customs of various sub-Saharan African tribes.

Black Cowboys (2003) written and illustrated by Ryan Randolph. This inspiring book for primary children explores the little-known but valuable contribution of African American cowboys who helped build the American West.

Carter G. Woodson: The Father of Black History (2002) by Patricia McKissack, illustrated by Fredrick McKissack. Woodson, an author, editor, publisher, and historian who earned a Ph.D. in history from Harvard in 1912, was instrumental in founding Black History Month.

Frederick Douglass (2002) written and illustrated by Catherine A. Welch. This book about Frederick Douglass, a former slave who escaped, worked for the abolition of slavery, and had the honor of meeting President Abraham Lincoln in the White House, is for older primary students.

Freedom River (2000) by Doreen Rappaport, illustrated by Bryan Collier. The author surrounds her telling of an incident in the life of John Parker with a biography about this ex-slave who bought his freedom and worked tirelessly to help runaway slaves escape on the Underground Railroad.

Goin' Someplace Special (2001) by Patricia McKissack, illustrated by Jerry Pinkney. In the segregated 1950s, the public library in Nashville was one of the few integrated places in town. Winner of the Coretta Scott King Illustrator Award.

Ida B. Wells-Barnett: A Voice Against Violence (2001) by Patricia McKissack, illustrated by Fredrick McKissack. Starting as a teacher, this black woman became a journalist who championed the civil rights of women. In 1909, she founded the National Association for the Advancement of Colored People (NAACP).

If I Only Had a Horn: Young Louis Armstrong (2002) by Roxane Orgill, illustrated by Leonard Jenkins. Find out how a poor boy in New Orleans became a famous jazz trumpeter in this wonderfully illustrated primary biography.

Jesse Jackson: A Rainbow Leader (1987) by Patricia Stone Martin, illustrated by Bernard Doctor. This book, from the Reaching Your Goal series, tells about the life and activities of this well-known black leader and civil rights worker.

Mary McLeod Bethune: A Great American Educator (2001) by Patricia McKissack, illustrated by Fredrick McKissack. Mary

McLeod Bethune was not only a black teacher who devoted her life to educating African Americans, but she also was an advisor to many U.S. presidents and a committed advocate to equality. Black and white photos are included in this biography.

Moja Means One: Swahili Counting Book (1976) by Muriel Feelings, illustrated by Tom Feelings. This richly illustrated primary book offers information about Eastern African culture as well as how to count to ten in Swahili. It is a 1972 Caldecott Honor Book.

Momma, Where Are You From? (2000) by Marie Bradby, illustrated by Chris K. Soentpiet. Momma tells her children through words and delightful illustrations about her childhood at a time when all the children at school were brown. This book is for primary readers.

A Picture Book of Harriet Tubman (1996) by David A. Adler, illustrated by Samuel Byrd. Harriet Tubman began life as a slave, escaped, hid out, and eventually became a well-known conductor on the Underground Railroad. Rich illustrations bring this story to life.

A Picture Book of Martin Luther King, Jr. (1991) by David A. Adler, illustrated by Robert Casilla. The beautiful illustrations in this book complement Adler's text highlighting the life and legacy of this famous civil rights leader.

A Picture Book of Rosa Parks (1997) by David A. Adler, illustrated by Robert Casilla. This biography of the Alabama black woman who helped launch the civil rights movement by refusing to give up her seat on a bus offers lessons that we all can learn from.

Ragtime Tumpie (1993) by Alan Schroeder, illustrated by Bernie Fuchs. This gorgeously illustrated book tells about the childhood of a young black girl who grows up to become the famous dancer, Josephine Baker.

Virgie Goes to School with Us Boys (1999) by Elizabeth Fitzgerald Howard, illustrated by E. B. Lewis. After the Civil War a young black girl is determined to get an education. This book won the Coretta Scott King Illustrator Honor Book Award in 2001.

A Voice of Her Own: The Story of Phillis Wheatley, Slave Poet (2003) by Kathryn Lasky, illustrated by Paul Lee. This is a beautifully illustrated biography (for older primary students) of an African slave girl who became the first published black female poet in America.

Working Cotton (1997) by Sherley Anne Williams, illustrated by Carole Byard. This 1993 Caldecott Honor Book for best illustration in a book for children describes a typical day in the life of an African American girl's migrant cotton-picking family. The gorgeous illustrations and use of dialect bring the story to life for primary readers.

Young Thurgood Marshall: Fighter for Equality (1996) by Eric Carpenter, illustrated by James Watling. This short biography for primary readers tells the story of the first black man appointed to be an associate justice of the Supreme Court.

February 1

LANGSTON HUGHES: BIRTHDAY

Langston Hughes, one of America's great poets, was born February 1, 1902, and died in 1967. His *The Sweet and Sour Animal Book* (1997) is an alphabet book with illustrations by first through third graders in Harlem. It contains twenty-six short poems introducing animals for each letter of the alphabet. *Carol of the Brown King: Nativity Poems* (1998), illustrated by Ashley Bryan, is a collection of simple poems about Christmas containing vivid color illustrations.

February 2

GROUNDHOG DAY

The official website for Groundhog Day is groundhog.org. The book *Groundhog Day* (2003) by Michelle Becker, illustrated by Don Curry, introduces the history of Groundhog Day and explains how it is observed today. *Gretchen Groundhog, It's Your Day!* (1998) by Abby Levine, illustrated by Nancy Cote, and *It's Groundhog Day* (1991) by Steven Kroll, illustrated by Jeni Bassett, provide additional material for this day.

JUDITH VIORST: BIRTHDAY

Judith Viorst was born on this day in 1931. Her *The Tenth Good Thing About Barney* (1975), illustrated by Erik Blegvad, is a special book to read whenever a pet dies. *Alexander and the Terrible, Horrible, No Good, Very Bad Day* (1976), illustrated by Ray Cruz, is Viorst's most popular book. Several creative-writing projects could use this book as a starting point. Ask the students to write about a bad day they have experienced, or pick a place they would like to go (besides Australia) if they were having a bad day.

February 4

CHARLES LINDBERGH: BIRTHDAY
American aviator Charles Lindbergh was born on February 4, 1902, and died in 1974. He was the first person to fly solo across the Atlantic in 1927. His plane was called the *Spirit of St. Louis*. For more information, the website charleslindbergh.com can be a wonderful resource. The books *Flight: The Journey of Charles Lindbergh* (1998) by Robert Burleigh, illustrated by Mike Wimmer, and *Good-bye, Charles Lindbergh: Based on a True Story* (1998) by Louise Borden, illustrated by Thomas Allen, will provide more information on this American hero.

RUSSELL HOBAN: BIRTHDAY
Russell Hoban was born on this day in 1925. He has written more than fifty books for children and is best known for his Frances books. Of the six books in that series, two of the most popular are *Bread and Jam for Frances* (1986) and *Best Friends for Frances* (1976). Both books were illustrated by his wife, Lillian Hoban.

February 5

PATRICIA LAUBER: BIRTHDAY
Patricia Lauber, who has written more than eighty books for children, was born February 5, 1924. Many of her books explain things in the natural world like hurricanes, floods, and dinosaurs. In her book *You're Aboard Spaceship Earth* (1996), illustrated by Holly Keller, she portrays the earth as a spaceship in orbit. *An Octopus Is Amazing* (1996), also illustrated by Holly Keller, is an introduction to the octopus and the amazing things it can do.

DAVID WIESNER: BIRTHDAY
David Wiesner was born on February 5, 1957. He has written more than twenty books for children and won the Caldecott Medal twice—in 1992 for *Tuesday* (which is almost wordless) and in 2002 for *The Three Pigs* (which is like no other rendition of this tale).

WEATHER FORECASTERS' DAY
February 5 is Weather Forecasters' Day. Two resources are *Weather Forecasting* (1993), written and illustrated by Gail Gibbons, and *Geoffrey Groundhog Predicts the Weather* (1998), written and illustrated by Bruce Koscielniak. Watching the forecasters on television would be a good homework assignment for today.

Week Two: Friendship

🏛 Curriculum Connection: Social Studies

Friendship can be portrayed in a variety of ways. Primary children often need guidance in making and keeping friends. Many of these resources will be invaluable in the social growth of a primary class.

Amos and Boris (1977) written and illustrated by William Steig. This tender yet comical story tells of a friendship between Amos the mouse and Boris the whale.

And to Think That We Thought That We'd Never Be Friends (2003) by Mary Ann Hoberman, illustrated by Kevin Hawkes. In rhyming verse, a brother and sister learn that friendship is better than fighting.

The Best Friends Book (2000) written and illustrated by Todd Parr. This book presents a humorous look at how best friends treat each other.

Best Friends for Frances (1976) by Russell Hoban, illustrated by Lillian Hoban. Fun songs, easy-to-understand language, and cute illustrations explore lessons about friendship.

Best Friends: Stories and Pictures (1990) written and illustrated by Steven Kellogg. Kathy is very lonely when her best friend goes away for the summer. What does she do?

Emily and Alice, Best Friends (2001) by Joyce Champion, illustrated by Sucie Stevenson. Alice and Emily are good friends, but they learn that each must sometimes do what the other wants.

Frank and Izzy Set Sail (2004) written and illustrated by Laura McGee Kvasnosky. Opposites make good friends in this uplifting story.

A Friend Is Someone Who Likes You (1983) written and illustrated by Joan Walsh Anglund. Text and illustrations describe what a friend is in this very popular book.

Friends (1986) written and illustrated by Helme Heine. Three inseparable friends discover that there are times when they just can't do things together.

How to Be a Friend: A Guide to Making Friends and Keeping Them (2001) by Laurie Krasny Brown and Marc Brown. Precise language and humorous illustrations offer good advice on how to be a friend.

How to Lose All Your Friends (1997) written and illustrated by Nancy Carlson. This vividly illustrated book offers six easy steps to success if you want to lose your friends.

Hunter's Best Friend at School (2002) by Laura Malone Elliott, illustrated by Lynn Munsinger. If your best friend acts up at school, should you follow along?

I Like You (1976) by Sandol Stoddard Warburg, illustrated by Jacqueline Chwast. This longtime favorite book expresses the true meaning of friendship—and not only for the little ones.

Little Bear's New Friend (2002) by Else Minarik, illustrated by Heather Green. Little Bear meets a bear cub living alone and helps him find his missing parents.

Loki and Alex: The Adventures of a Dog and His Best Friend (2001) written and photographed by Charles R. Smith, Jr. Alex and his dog, Loki, are best friends, but they don't always see things from the same perspective!

Lottie's New Friend (2002) written and illustrated by Petra Mathers. Can Herbie the duck still be friends with Lottie the chicken after a new bird moves in nearby?

Make New Friends (2003) by Rosemary Wells, illustrated by Jody Wheeler. When Juanita moves to a new school, her classmates help her feel welcome.

Making Friends (1996) by Fred Rogers, photographed by Jim Judkis. Making friends is fun, but it's not always easy!

May I Bring a Friend? (1974) by Beatrice Schenk De Regniers, illustrated by Beni Montresor. In this 1965 Caldecott Medal winner, a little boy is often invited to visit the king and queen. When he asks to bring a friend, they are surprised when the friend turns out to be an animal.

My Best Friend: A Book About Friendship (2001) written and illustrated by Heather Feldman. Sometimes it is easy to be best friends, and sometimes it is very challenging.

My Friend John (2000) by Charlotte Zolotow, illustrated by Amanda Harvey. This pleasantly illustrated story reveals what happens when two friends think they know "everything" about each other.

A Rainbow of Friends (2001) written and illustrated by P. K. Hallinan. This brightly colored book teaches children that you can still be friends even when people are different.

Tara and Tiree, Fearless Friends: A True Story (2003) by Andrew Clements, illustrated by Ellen Beier. When Jim falls through the ice on a lake in Canada, how are his two dogs able to rescue him?

That's What a Friend Is (2001) written and illustrated by P. K. Hallinan. This bestseller has been teaching children the true meaning of friendship since first being published more than twenty years ago.

We Are Best Friends (1991) written and illustrated by Aliki. When Robert's best friend moves away, they discover they can still be best friends even as they make new friends.

Where Are You Going? To See My Friend! (2003) by Kazuo Iwamura, illustrated by Eric Carle. Bestselling U.S. and Japanese authors Carle and Iwamura combine their talents to create a story of friendship, culture, and fun in one of *Publishers Weekly*'s Best Children's Picture Books of 2003.

Will I Have a Friend? (1971) by Miriam Cohen, illustrated by Lillian Hoban. This more "old-fashioned" story for young children tells about Jim's happiness when he makes a new friend on his first day of school.

February 6

100 BILLIONTH CRAYOLA CRAYON ANNIVERSARY

The 100 billionth Crayola crayon was produced on this day in 1996. How many crayons have been produced by now? This is a great question for estimation and large number use. Crayons were first invented in 1903 and are now made in 120 colors. The website crayola.com has several different activities for children as well as facts about the crayon. *Crayons: From Start to Finish* (1999) by Samuel Woods, photographed by Gale Zucker, illustrates how crayons are made at the Binney and Smith Company where about twelve million crayons are produced every day.

GEORGE HERMAN "BABE" RUTH: BIRTHDAY

Babe Ruth was born February 6, 1895, and died in 1948. *The Babe and I* (1999) by David A. Adler, illustrated by Terry Widener, is about a newspaper boy meeting Babe Ruth. *The Girl Who Struck Out Babe Ruth* (2000) by Jean L. S. Patrick, illustrated by Jeni Reeves, tells of a seventeen-year-old female professional player who struck out both Babe Ruth and Lou Gehrig in an exhibition game in 1931.

February 8

ANNE ROCKWELL: BIRTHDAY

Anne Rockwell was born on February 8, 1934. She has always loved books and drawing. Sometimes she illustrates her own books, and sometimes she has another illustrator work with her. *Morgan Plays Soccer* (2001), illustrated by Paul Meisel, is the first in a series of books about what it means to be a "good sport." *Bugs Are Insects* (2001), illustrated by Steve Jenkins, shows why children are taken with the beauty and variety they see in the insect world.

MARDI GRAS

Mardi Gras is a traditional holiday that is celebrated in many states. The websites holidays.net/mardigras and mardigras.com provide additional resources for this holiday. Mardi Gras (Fat Tuesday) falls on the day prior to Ash Wednesday, which is forty-seven days before Easter. The date changes each year. *Mimi's First Mardi Gras* (1991) by Alice Couvillon and Elizabeth Moore, illustrated by Marilyn Carter Rougelot, details many of the traditional aspects of the celebration. *Mardi Gras: A City's Masked Parade* (2003), written and illustrated by Lisa Gabbert, describes the origins and symbols of Mardi Gras.

February 11

THOMAS ALVA EDISON: BIRTHDAY

Thomas Edison was born on February 11, 1847, and died in 1931. He held more than twelve hundred patents during his life for such things as the lightbulb, the phonograph, and parts for the movie camera. The books *Thomas Edison* (2002) by Lola Schaefer and *Thomas Edison* (2004) by Lucia Raatma provide biographical information on this fascinating man.

JANE YOLEN: BIRTHDAY

Jane Yolen was born on this date in 1939. Two of the books she wrote—*The Emperor and the Kite* (1968), illustrated by Ed Young, and *Owl Moon* (1988), illustrated by John Schoenherr—won Caldecott awards for the illustrations. *Color Me a Rhyme: Nature Poems for Young People* (2000), photographed by Jason Stemple, is a wonderful collection of poems about the colors of the rainbow.

February 12

ABRAHAM LINCOLN: BIRTHDAY

Abraham Lincoln was born on February 12, 1809, and assassinated in April 1865. He won the respect of people worldwide with honesty, common sense, and a sense of humor. The following books provide a wealth of information on our sixteenth president: *Mr. Lincoln's Whiskers* (1999), written and illustrated by Karen B. Winnick, and *A Picture Book of Abraham Lincoln* (1990) by David A. Adler, illustrated by Alexandra and John Wallner.

DAVID SMALL: BIRTHDAY

David Small was born on this day in 1945. He won the Caldecott Award in 2001 as illustrator for *So You Want to Be President?* by Judith St. George. He often illustrates what his wife, Sarah Stewart, writes, including titles such as *The Library* (1999) and *The Journey* (2001).

JACQUELINE WOODSON: BIRTHDAY

Jacqueline Woodson was born February 12, 1964. She often shares experiences she had as a child. *We Had a Picnic This Sunday Past* (1998), illustrated by Diane Greenseid, shows love and humor within a contemporary African American family.

Week Three: Birds

✳ Curriculum Connection: Science

Primary children are fascinated by anything that flies. Birds are present in most children's environments and peak children's curiosity and wonderment. The resources listed here range from the fantastic to the factual. Birds have been characters in myths, legends, fairy tales, and other kinds of stories for centuries. Several of these resources are beautiful art books that can be enjoyed by adults as well as children.

About Birds: A Guide for Children (1997) by Cathryn Sill, illustrated by John Sill. Children will learn the basics about birds in this watercolor-illustrated book.

The Baby Beebee Bird (2003) by Diane Redfield Massie, illustrated by Steven Kellogg. The baby beebee bird likes to sleep during the day and make lots of noise at night. The animals at the zoo aren't getting any sleep!

Bird (1997) written and illustrated by David Burnie. The diversity of birds, from the fluffy chick to the brilliantly colored to the big-beaked and the long-legged, is revealed in this richly illustrated and photographed book.

Birds in Your Backyard (2001) written and illustrated by Barbara Herkert. Watching birds is easy and lots of fun, and you can even do it in your own backyard! This book deals with various North American birds.

Birds, Nests, and Eggs (1998) by Mel Boring, illustrated by Linda Garrow. This book provides descriptions of birds, their nests, their eggs, and locations where they can be found.

Blue Sky Bluebird (2004) written and illustrated by Rick Chrustowski. This book introduces the life cycle of the bluebird.

Cat and Canary (2004) written and illustrated by Michael Foreman. A city cat wishes he could fly like his best friend, the canary.

Crows! Strange and Wonderful (2004) by Laurence Pringle, illustrated by Bob Marstall. Learn all about this clever and fascinating bird in this lively, illustrated book perfect for reading aloud.

Eagles (2001) by Laura Evert, illustrated by John McGee. Interesting information is presented on the lives of the two kinds of eagles living in North America: bald eagles and golden eagles.

Fine Feathered Friends: All About Birds (1998) by Tish Rabe, illustrated by Aristides Ruiz. Sally and Dick meet a variety of birds, from the ten-foot ostrich to the two-inch hummingbird.

Have You Seen Birds? (1988) by Joanne Oppenheim, illustrated by Barbara Reid. This is a wonderful picture book on a wide variety of birds seen throughout the year in various locations.

House Sparrows Everywhere (1992) by Caroline Arnold, photographed by Richard Hewett. Older primary students will enjoy this book containing a multitude of facts and vivid pictures of the common house sparrow.

How Do Birds Find Their Way? (1996) by Roma Gans, illustrated by Paul Mirocha. Read and explore the mysteries of bird migration, including theories on how birds find their way.

How to Draw Birds (1999) written and illustrated by John Green. This easy-to-follow guide helps artists create recognizable drawings of a variety of avian creatures.

It's a Hummingbird's Life (2003) written and illustrated by Irene Kelly. This story of a year in the life of a hummingbird provides a close look into this tiny bird's busy days.

Just Plain Fancy (1994) written and illustrated by Patricia Polacco. Naomi, an Amish girl who knows the importance of adhering to the simple ways of her people, is worried when one of her hen eggs hatches into a peacock!

The Lion and the Little Red Bird (1996) written and illustrated by Elisa Kleven. In this sweet book, a little bird wonders why a lion's tail changes color each day.

The Mountain That Loved a Bird (2000) by Alice McLerran, illustrated by Eric Carle. A lonely, lifeless mountain is transformed into a garden of trees, flowers, and streams.

A Nest Full of Eggs (1995) by Priscilla Belz Jenkins, illustrated by Lizzy Rockwell. Follow a robin's full year of growth and change: how it develops, how it matures, how it learns to fly, and how it migrates to warmer climates in winter only to return and start all over when spring comes around again.

Rainforest Birds (1997) by Bobbie Kalman, illustrated by Barbara Bedell. This is an excellent book for older primary students, introducing rainforest birds, forest-floor dwellers, middle-layer fliers, and raptors.

Richard Scarry's The Early Bird (1999) written and illustrated by Richard Scarry. Early Bird finds a friendly worm in a funny hat to play with.

Subway Sparrow (1997) written and illustrated by Leyla Torres. The passengers of the D train speak different languages and are all different ages, but together they rescue a frightened bird.

What Makes a Bird a Bird? (1995) by May Garelick, illustrated by Trish Hill. Packed with detailed pictures, this nonfiction book leads the reader to discover what makes a bird a bird.

Woodpeckers (1998) written and illustrated by Lynn Stone. This book provides information on different kinds of woodpeckers, including the flicker, Gila, and red-bellied varieties.

February 13

GRANT WOOD: BIRTHDAY
American artist Grant Wood was born on February 13, 1892, and died in 1942. His most famous painting is *American Gothic*. More information can be obtained from *Artist in Overalls: The Life of Grant Wood* (1996) by John Duggleby and *Grant Wood* (1996) by Mike Venezia.

SIMMS TABACK: BIRTHDAY
Simms Taback, author and illustrator, was born on this date in 1932. He has written and illustrated more than thirty-five books for children and also designed the first McDonald's Happy Meal box. He won the Caldecott Honor for *There Was an Old Lady Who Swallowed a Fly* in 1998. In 2000, he won the Caldecott Medal for *Joseph Had a Little Overcoat*.

INTERNATIONAL TABLE MANNERS WEEK
The third week in February is International Table Manners Week. Everyone can use a refresher in table manners. The book *What You Never Knew About Fingers, Forks and Chopsticks* (2002) by Patricia Lauber, illustrated by John Manders, describes eating customs through history and the origins of table manners.

February 14

VALENTINE'S DAY
Valentine's Day is perhaps the most widely celebrated unofficial holiday in the United States. The following books offer resources for the classroom: *It's Valentine's Day* (1996) by Jack Prelutsky, illustrated by Yossi Abolafia, and *Valentine's Day* (1989), written and illustrated by Gail Gibbons.

PAUL O. ZELINSKY: BIRTHDAY
Paul O. Zelinsky, author and illustrator, was born on this day in 1953. His version of *Rapunzel* won the 1998 Caldecott Medal, while *Hansel and Gretel* (1985), *Rumpelstiltskin* (1987), and *Swamp Angel* by Anne Isaacs (1995) all won Caldecott Honor awards. Zelinsky also illustrates for other authors, such as with Jack Prelutsky's *Awful Ogre's Awful Day* (2001).

PHYLLIS ROOT: BIRTHDAY
Phyllis Root was born February 14, 1949. She has written more than twenty books for children. She writes rollicking stories that beg to be read aloud; *Kiss the Cow* (2003), illustrated by Will Hillenbrand, fits that description. *Rattletrap Car* (2004), illustrated by Jill Barton, and *If You Want to See a Caribou* (2004), illustrated by Jim Meyer, are two of her books that have become favorites.

February 15

SUSAN B. ANTHONY: BIRTHDAY
Susan B. Anthony, born in 1820 and died in 1906, was an American reformer and advocate of women's suffrage. She was the first American woman to have her picture on a coin—the Susan B. Anthony dollar, which was minted in 1979. See the website susan banthonyhouse.org for more information on this famous lady.

NORMAN BRIDWELL: BIRTHDAY
Norman Bridwell, creator of *Clifford the Big Red Dog* and dozens of other books about the beloved character, was born February 15, 1928. The website pbskids.org/clifford is great for younger primary readers. Bridwell also illustrates books for other writers; *Magic Matt and the Skunk in the Tub* (2003) by Grace Maccarone is a good example.

GALILEO GALILEI: BIRTHDAY
Galileo (1564–1642) was a famous mathematician and astronomer. The book *Starry Messenger* (2000), written and illustrated by Peter Sis, traces Galileo's life and won a Caldecott Honor in 1997.

February 20

ANSEL ADAMS: BIRTHDAY
Ansel Adams was born February 20, 1902, and died in 1984. He is one of the most famous photographers in America. *Eye on the Wild: A Story About Ansel Adams* (1995) by Julie Dunlap, illustrated by Kerry Maguire, details his life and work.

FREDERICK DOUGLASS: DEATH ANNIVERSARY
Frederick Douglass died on this day in 1865. Two good books—*Frederick Douglass: Leader Against Slavery* (2002) by Patricia and Fredrick McKissack and *A Picture Book of Frederick Douglass* (1993) by David A. Adler, illustrated by Samuel Byrd—provide background biographical information about this man who escaped slavery to become an orator, writer, and leader.

PRESIDENTS' DAY
To honor Abraham Lincoln and George Washington, Presidents' Day is officially the third Monday in February. More information and activities for this day can be found at alpha bet-soup.net. Another good resource is *Presidents' Day* (1998) by Mir Tamim Ansary, which explains the historical events behind it, how it became a holiday, and how it is observed.

Week Four: Sports—Basketball, Football, and Soccer

🏛 Curriculum Connection: Social Studies

The thematic listing for sports includes stories, game rules, and heroes from the world of sports. Primary students need guidance in learning how to play on a team, exhibit good sportsmanship, and admire the right values in their heroes. Sports statistics make a great foundation for all kinds of math lessons. The sports section of the newspaper can often motivate a reluctant reader.

BASKETBALL

Allie's Basketball Dream (1998) by Barbara E. Barber, illustrated by Darryl Ligasan. A special friend helps a young African American girl learn to play basketball.

Basketball ABC: The NBA Alphabet (1996) by Florence Cassen Mayers, photographed by the NBA. Done in brilliant color, this book is perfect fun for basketball fans learning to read.

Count to 100 with the NBA! (2001) written and illustrated by Scholastic, Inc., and the NBA. This colorful book teaches young children to count to ten and then, using groups of ten, to count to one hundred.

The Illustrated Rules of Basketball (2001) by Frank Bennett, illustrated by Paul Zuehlke. This is an introduction for young players to the basic rules of basketball.

Let's Play Basketball (2004) by Charles R. Smith, Jr., illustrated by Terry Widener. This picture book tells the story of a basketball that wants to go outside to play.

My Basketball Book (2000) written and illustrated by Gail Gibbons. This informative but clearly worded book uses a fun story to explain the game of basketball to youngsters.

Salt in His Shoes: Michael Jordan in Pursuit of a Dream (2003) by Deloris Jordan with Roslyn M. Jordan, illustrated by Kadir Nelson. Young Michael Jordan learns that determination and hard work are more important than size when playing the game of basketball.

Swish! (1997) by Bill Martin Jr. and Michael Sampson, illustrated by Michael Chesworth. This fast-paced book features a close and intense game of basketball between two girls' teams.

FOOTBALL

Doug Flutie: International Football Star (1999) written and illustrated by Rob Kirkpatrick. Readers will learn about the quarterback for the Buffalo Bills, Doug Flutie.

Football (2003) by Cynthia Klingel and Robert B. Noyed. Simple text for young children explains how football is played and what equipment is needed.

Football for Fun (2003) written and illustrated by Kenn Goin. Here's an informative book about the basic rules and skills needed to have fun playing football.

The Football That Won (1999) by Michael Sampson, illustrated by Ted Rand. This cumulative tale follows a Super Bowl game from kickoff to winning touchdown.

The History of Football (2003) by Diana Helmer, illustrated by Thomas Owens. This book follows the development of football including improvements in the rules and equipment.

The Illustrated Rules of Football (2001) by R. L. "Buddy" Patey, illustrated by Patrick T. McRae. Using watercolor illustrations and clear language, young players are introduced to football, including the rules, positions, history, officiating, and sportsmanship.

My Football Book (2000) written and illustrated by Gail Gibbons. This colorful, football-shaped boardbook is an excellent introduction to the game of football.

SOCCER

Franklin Plays the Game (1995) by Paulette Bourgeois, illustrated by Brenda Clark. Franklin discovers it is fun to play soccer even if you don't win.

Game Time! (2000) by Stuart J. Murphy, illustrated by Cynthia Jabar. Calendars and clocks are featured in this story of a championship soccer game.

The History of Soccer (2003) by Diane Star Helmer, illustrated by Thomas S. Owens. Large print and colorful photographs explain the history of soccer from its reputed origin to its current level of popularity.

K Is for Kick: A Soccer Alphabet (2003) by Brad Herzog, illustrated by Melanie Rose. Examine the history and lore of soccer from *A* to *Z* while teaching the alphabet.

My Soccer Book (2000) written and illustrated by Gail Gibbons. This picture book offers a clear and easy-to-understand introduction to one of the world's most popular games, soccer.

Rhinos Who Play Soccer (2001) written and illustrated by Julie Mammano. Rhinoceroses play an exciting game of soccer in this vividly illustrated book, which includes soccer vocabulary words.

Soccer (1996) written and illustrated by Paul Joseph. This book for older primary students explains in great detail how to play the game of soccer.

Soccer (1999) written and illustrated by Kirk Bizley. This amusingly illustrated introduction to the game of soccer features tips on safety for beginners.

Soccer Counts! (2003) by Barbara Barbieri McGrath and Peter Alderman, illustrated by Pau Estrada. This introduction to counting uses the history, rules, and interesting facts about soccer.

Soccer for Fun (2003) written and illustrated by Kenn Goin. Everything you need to know about soccer is included in this book. Good for coaching both girls and boys.

Soccer Mom from Outer Space (2002) written and illustrated by Barney Saltzberg. Lena learns how her mother seemed to turn into an alien when she watched soccer games.

February 22

GEORGE WASHINGTON: BIRTHDAY

The celebration honoring our first president, who was born in 1732 and died in 1799, has moved around in the month from the eleventh to the twenty-second and now to the third Monday. Along with celebrating the birth and deeds of this man, the monument that bears his name could also be studied at this time. *The Washington Monument* (2003) by Kristin L. Nelson is an introduction to its purpose, structure, and history. Two good resources on the man and his life are *Picture Book of George Washington* (1995) by David A. Adler, illustrated by Alexandra and John Wallner, and *Crossing the Delaware: George Washington and the Battle of Trenton* (2004) by Arlan Dean.

February 24

WILHELM CARL GRIMM: BIRTHDAY

Wilhelm Grimm—born in 1786—was half of the Brothers Grimm (Jacob was the other half) who collected more than two hundred classic fairy tales such as *Hansel and Gretel, Sleeping Beauty, Snow White and Rose Red*, and *Cinderella*. First compiled in 1812 and revised to the form we know in 1857, these tales include magic, communication between animals and humans, moral values, and the teachings of right and wrong that still delight and teach children of today. Wilhelm Grimm died in 1859.

February 26

WILLIAM "BUFFALO BILL" CODY: BIRTHDAY

William Cody was born on February 26, 1846, and died in 1917. He had many careers during his life. He was a Pony Express rider, Indian fighter, scout, and star of his own Wild West show. The following books provide information and stories about this famous cowboy: *The Sweetwater Run: The Story of Buffalo Bill Cody and the Pony Express* (1996) by Andrew Glass, and *Buffalo Bill Cody* (2001) by Charles J. Shields.

GRAND CANYON NATIONAL PARK ANNIVERSARY

The Grand Canyon National Park was established on this date in 1919. It is the most spectacular natural phenomenon in the world. *Grand Canyon: A Trail Through Time* (2000) by Linda Vieira, illustrated by Christopher Canyon, has breathtaking illustrations and illuminating prose. *G Is for Grand Canyon: An Arizona Alphabet* (2002) by Barbara Gowan, illustrated by Katherine Larson, is a very unusual alphabet book that uses the people, places, and other characteristics of Arizona to illustrate the alphabet.

February 28

DONNA JO NAPOLI: BIRTHDAY

Donna Jo Napoli was born on February 28, 1948. She writes both picture books and young adult novels. Her books have been translated into at least six languages and cover a wide range of topics from math to contemporary fiction to science to books geared toward helping deaf people learn to read. Her book with Richard Tchen, *How Hungry Are You?* (2001), illustrated by Amy Walrod, introduces simple division and could easily be turned into a reader's theater presentation. Another popular book is *Rocky, the Cat Who Barks* (2002), written with Marie Kane and illustrated by Tamara Petrosino; Rocky the dog has a difficult life when he first moves into a house with five cats.

MEGAN MCDONALD: BIRTHDAY

Megan McDonald, born on this date in 1959, has her own website at meganmcdonald.net. Two of her noteworthy picture books are *Insects Are My Life* (1997), illustrated by Paul Brett Johnson, and *Penguin and Little Blue* (2003), illustrated by Katherine Tillotson.

February Reading Strategy

The Use of Why Questions

Many students want to know "why" for every event or action that they are asked to participate in or learn. Why should I _____? Why do I have to _____? Why did the story _____? Why did the characters _____? Why did the author _____? Setting up the language arts lesson to increase every child's comprehension will actively engage students and have them answer all their own why questions regarding that particular reading.

In introducing a new book to be shared, a new theme to be explored, a new topic to be researched, a new person to read about, or a new topic to write about, the student needs to be engaged. Discussing the teacher's rationale for using the book, assigning the topic, or delving even further to discover the author's purpose helps children comprehend the selection. Why do we need to know about _____? is a great opening for a thematic unit. This can also be phrased as, What do you know or think you know about _____, and how did you learn that? Why do you think we should read about _____? Why is it important that we know about _____?

The why question to ask for individual self-selections is, Why did you choose to read this book over others? Why do you think the author wrote this story? Understanding the purpose behind choosing and reading a selection is a great engagement tool as well as a great motivator. If the students know why they are doing something, they can better relate to it and become more interested. Intellectual curiosity is a wonderful attribute of primary students. What was the author's purpose? is a question often asked on standardized tests. The more practice students have at choosing and discussing an author's purpose, the better they will do with this question when seeing it in a test format. Children need lots of time to discuss why the author chose a particular story for a particular point. Is there a life lesson in the story, or is it pure entertainment? Why is it funny to the reader? Why did the author have the main character do _____? Why did the author use animals instead of people (or vice versa)?

Class discussions need not always focus on plot. Setting, character development, details, and time elements, as well as the author's purpose and craft, have their place in both discussion about reading selections and in children's writing about literature. The strategic use of why questions will increase everyone's understanding of the text.

March at a Glance

*Even a minor event in the life of a child is an event of that
child's world, and thus a world event.*
—Gaston Bachelard

March Reading Tip: Read at a slow enough pace for the listener to form mental images of characters, settings, and events.

MARCH HIGHLIGHTS
Irish-American Heritage Month
The St. Patrick's Day Shillelagh (2002) by Janet Nolan, illustrated by Ben F. Stahl, captures a part of Irish heritage and the importance of family tradition and roots.

Music in Our School Month
Froggie Went A-Courtin' (2002), adapted and illustrated by Iza Trapani, is a fun adaptation of the folk song about a frog in search of a wife.

National Craft Month
The Colossal Book of Crafts for Kids and Their Families (1997) by Phyllis and Noel Fiarotta offers a variety of projects using items from around the house and from nature.

National Umbrella Month
The Umbrella Thief (1987) by Sybil Wetta-singhe and Cathy Hirano shows how umbrellas become an item of exotic fascination in Sri Lanka.

Women's History Month
Mae Jemison: Out of This World (2002) by Corinne J. Naden and Rose Blue is an inviting biography featuring Mae Jemison, the first African American woman in space. It's both readable and colorful.

Youth Art Month
When Pigasso Met Mootisse (1998) by Nina Laden is a delightful tale of modern artists—a porky Pigasso and a bullish Mootisse.

Deaf History Month
Moses Goes to a Concert (2002) by Isaac Millman relates how the attendance of a class of deaf children at an orchestral concert leads to the revelation that the ability to hear is not a prerequisite for enjoying music.

March Reading Strategy: The Venn Diagram

WEEKLY THEMES AND CURRICULUM CONNECTIONS
Week One: Pigs (Language Arts)
Week Two: Weather (Science)
Week Three: Magical People (Language Arts and Geography)
Week Four: Caldecott Award Winners (Fine Arts)

Special Events in March

National Agriculture Week	Mar. 14
St. Patrick's Day	Mar. 17
Spring	Mar. 20
UN World Day for Water	Mar. 22
Make Up Your Own Holiday Day	Mar. 26
Earthquake Strikes Alaska	Mar. 27

FEATURED MARCH BIRTHDAYS

Dr. Seuss ....Mar. 2	Ezra Jack Keats..............Mar. 11	Randolph Caldecott ....Mar. 22
Leo Dillon ....Mar. 2	Wanda Gag ....Mar. 11	Harry Houdini ....Mar. 24
Mem Fox ....Mar. 5	Casey Jones ....Mar. 14	Sandra Day O'Connor ..Mar. 26
Thacher Hurd ....Mar. 6	Douglas Florian ....Mar. 18	Vincent Van Gogh ....Mar. 30
Chris Raschka ....Mar. 6	Mitsumasa Anno ....Mar. 20	Franz Joseph Haydn......Mar. 31
Michelangelo ....Mar. 6	Johann Sebastian Bach..Mar. 21	
Robert Sabuda ....Mar. 8	David Wisniewski ....Mar. 21	

Week One: Pigs

📖 Curriculum Connection: Language Arts

National Pig Day (March 1) is celebrated by pig lovers everywhere. Share some of the books listed here so your children will get into the swing of this fun day.

Choose a nonfiction book such as *Pigs* by Gail Gibbons and a fiction book such as *Swine Divine* by Jan Carr to practice the comprehension skill of comparing and contrasting two different books. Read each book aloud, discuss it, and then lead the children in a discussion of what parts of the two books were the same and which were different. These comparisons can be as broad as the fact that both books were about pigs or as detailed as noting that the pig in one is pink and the pig in the other is black and white.

To practice the writing skill of comparing and contrasting, children can make a list of the things that are the same in each story and another list of things that are different. These lists can be long or short and can be read aloud and the differences discussed. The Venn diagram is very useful here (see p. 54).

Children can also discuss and then draw pictures of what a real pig looks like or can do and contrasting pictures of a make-believe pig or a pig that does unpiglike things from one of the fiction books.

Chester, the Worldly Pig (1978) written and illustrated by Bill Peet. This amusingly illustrated story tells how the road to stardom is often rocky—especially if you are Chester.

Dumpy La Rue (2001) by Elizabeth Winthrop, illustrated by Betsy Lewin. This cutely illustrated story for primary readers shows that good things can happen if you follow your heart and believe in yourself.

The Great Pig Escape (1996) written and illustrated by Eileen Christelow. The pigs overhear the farmer and his wife talking about a plan to sell them, and the trouble—or the fun—begins in this brightly illustrated book.

Hog-Eye (1998) written and illustrated by Susan Meddaugh. A young pig trying to outwit a wolf that intends to eat her uses the dreaded Hog-Eye stare in this delightful book.

Louella Mae, She's Run Away! (2002) by Karen Beaumont Alarcón, illustrated by Rosanne Litzinger. Everyone on the farm is looking for the missing Louella Mae. This is a terrific book to read out loud, and it has a surprise ending.

Oink (1995) written and illustrated by Arthur Geisert. Mama Pig and her eight piglets speak only one word, "oink," in this fun and noisy picture book.

Olivia (2000) written and illustrated by Ian Falconer. In this 2001 Caldecott Honor Book, Olivia, a new and unexpected heroine, is a spunky little pig with an abundance of energy.

Piggie Pie! (1997) by Margie Palatini, illustrated by Howard Fine. Pigs put on a variety of disguises to hide from a witch who wants to eat them for lunch. This book is sure to bring giggles.

Piggins (1992) by Jane Yolen, illustrated by Jane Dyer. Piggins the butler solves the mysterious disappearance of a diamond necklace in this primary story.

Pigs Can't Fly (2002) written and illustrated by Ben Cort. A little pig is bored and looking for adventure. Wouldn't flying be fun?

Pigs from 1 to 10 (1992) written and illustrated by Arthur Geisert. In this unusual and entertaining counting book, ten pigs go on an adventurous quest. Children love to find the industrious pigs and elusive numbers craftily disguised in each illustration.

Pigs from A to Z (1986) written and illustrated by Arthur Geisert. Readers learn about the shapes of the letters by finding them hidden in the intricate artwork.

Pigs on a Blanket: Fun with Math and Time (1998) by Amy Axelrod, illustrated by Sharon McGinley Nally. A group of plump porkers plan a trip to the beach and provide readers with practice in adding, subtracting, and telling time.

Pigs (2000) written and illustrated by Gail Gibbons. This nonfiction book is packed with art and information about pigs.

Suddenly! A Preston Pig Story (1998) written and illustrated by Colin McNaughton. Time after time Preston outwits the wolf who is trying to eat him.

Swine Divine (1999) by Jan Carr, illustrated by Robert Bender. Rosie the pig proves pigs belong in the mud and not dressed up in front of a camera.

Swine Lake (1999) by James Marshall, illustrated by Maurice Sendak. This is a fun tale about a wolf who attends a ballet performed by an all-pig troupe.

The Three Little Pigs (2000) retold and illustrated by James Marshall. Marshall breathes fresh new life into this favorite and classic tale with funny dialogue and cartoon-like illustrations.

The Three Little Pigs (2001) written and illustrated by David Wiesner. We learn to never doubt the power of a pig in this innovative fractured fairy tale that won the 2002 Caldecott Medal.

The Three Little Javelinas (1992) by Susan Lowell, illustrated by Jim Harris. Southwestern pig cousins outsmart a coyote who wants to eat them with red chili sauce.

The Three Little Wolves and the Big Bad Pig (1993) by Eugene Trivizas, illustrated by Helen Oxenbury. This traditional story is cleverly turned upside down and filled with humor.

The True Story of the Three Little Pigs (1995) by Jon Scieszka, illustrated by Lane Smith. In the wrong place at the wrong time, here is the "real" story from the wolf's perspective.

March 2

THEODOR "DR. SEUSS" GEISEL: BIRTHDAY

Theodor Geisel—better known as Dr. Seuss—was born on March 2, 1904, and died in 1991. His books have sold more than 200 million copies. In 1984, he received a Pulitzer Prize "for his contribution over nearly half a century to the education and enjoyment of America's children and their parents."

March 2 is also Read Across America Day, a national campaign connected with the celebration of Dr. Seuss, encouraging all children to read a book this evening. *Green Eggs and Ham* (1976) is a story in which Sam-I-Am keeps trying to get the grumpy grown-up to taste green eggs and ham.

LEO DILLON: BIRTHDAY

Born March 2, 1933, Leo Dillon is a talented illustrator who, with his wife Diane, has won two Caldecott Medals. *Why Mosquitoes Buzz in People's Ears* (1978), with text written by Verna Aardema, is a humorous tale exploring some of the animals that inhabit the rain forest. His other Caldecott title is *Ashanti to Zulu: African Traditions* (1980) by Margaret Musgrove.

March 5

MERRION FRANCES FOX: BIRTHDAY

Merrion Frances (Mem) Fox was born on March 5, 1946, in Australia. She has written many delightful books during her career and is still writing today. Her most famous books are:

The Magic Hat (2002) illustrated by Tricia Tusa. One fine day, from out of town, a magic hat appears and plops down on the head of resident after resident, transforming each person into an animal. And then a wizard arrives. . . .

Possom Magic (1991) illustrated by Julie Vivas. Two Australian bush possums star in this warm and wonderful exploration of Australia.

Koala Lou (1994) illustrated by Pamela Lofts. A young koala enters the Bush Olympics hoping to win her distracted mother's attention.

Hattie and the Fox (1992) illustrated by Patricia Mullins. Hattie, a big black hen, discovers a fox in the bushes, but the other barnyard animals won't listen to her warning. Will they survive?

March 6

THACHER HURD: BIRTHDAY

Thacher Hurd, born in 1949, is both an author and an illustrator. He writes humorous books using almost a cartoon style in his illustrations. For example, *Art Dog* (1997) is the story of when the Mona Woofa is stolen from the Dogopolis Museum of Art, and a mysterious character who calls himself Art Dog tracks down the thieves.

CHRIS RASCHKA: BIRTHDAY

Author and illustrator Chris Raschka was born in 1959 and has written books on many different topics from jazz musicians to the alphabet. *Yo! Yes?* (1993), a 1994 Caldecott Honor Book, is the story of two boys parlaying what could be a confrontation into friendship.

MICHELANGELO: BIRTHDAY

Michelangelo (di Lodovico Buonarroti Simoni)—an artist whose name is recognized by almost everyone—was born March 6, 1475, and was a sculptor as well as a painter. Two of his most famous works are the sculpture *David* and the frescoes in the Sistine Chapel. He died in 1564.

Michelangelo (1992), written and illustrated by Mike Venezia, is a good biography for primary students and describes the life of this Italian Renaissance artist.

March 8

ROBERT SABUDA: BIRTHDAY

Born in 1965, author and illustrator Robert Sabuda is the best-known pop-up book artist working today. He has also created books that use a variety of other media in inventive ways. Examples range from simulated handmade Egyptian papyrus for his book *Tutankhamen's Gift* (1997), to paper cut to look like mosaics in *Saint Valentine* (1998), to paintings that resemble stained glass for *Arthur and the Sword* (1995).

His *The Christmas Alphabet* (1994) is a marvel of paper engineering. This unusual book combines the magic of Christmas with a pop-up alphabet. Letter by letter, each image unfurls to reveal one of twenty-six seasonal surprises.

He also provides illustrations for other authors, such as *The Paper Dragon* (1997) by Marguerite W. Davol. When a fire-breathing dragon threatens to destroy their rice fields, the villagers turn to their humble but famous artist, Mi Fei. The text is printed on the right-hand pages, which open up into triple-page spreads of glorious painted tissue-paper collages.

Week Two: Weather

❋ Curriculum Connection: Science

March can come in like a lion and go out like a lamb; it all depends on things that are out of human control. This week is devoted to the weather—different types of storms, forecasting methods, and fears that some children have.

Children might want to listen to weather forecasts and keep a journal for the week. What caused the forecasts to be accurate or inaccurate? What new words are used in the forecasts? A personal weather words dictionary would be a good writing and vocabulary activity for this week.

Several of the following books also contain simple science experiments.

Can It Rain Cats and Dogs? (1999) by Melvin and Gilda Berger, illustrated by Robert Sullivan. Curious children will uncover the answers they seek about all kinds of weather.

The Cloud Book (1984) written and illustrated by Tomie dePaola. This is an introduction to the ten most common types of clouds and what they tell about weather changes.

Cloudy With a Chance of Meatballs (1982) by Judi Barrett, illustrated by Ron Barrett. In the land of Chewandswallow, meals fall from the sky. This is a good book to spark the imagination. What would your children like to see come down from the sky? What are their favorite foods?

Down Comes the Rain (1997) by Franklyn M. Branley, illustrated by James Graham Hale. This concise and informative look at the water cycle includes easy science activities.

Feel the Wind (1990) written and illustrated by Arthur Dorros. The author defines wind and its uses in a way that children can easily understand.

Flash, Crash, Rumble, and Roll (1999) by Franklyn M. Branley, illustrated by True Kelley. Storms can be scary if you don't know what causes them. Two simple experiments are included.

Heat Wave at Mud Flat (1997) written and illustrated by James Stevenson. Join the Mud Flat gang as they suffer through some problems caused by bad weather.

I Face the Wind (2003) by Vicki Cobb, illustrated by Julia Gorton. This is a good introduction to the concept that air is a real thing even though it can't be seen. The book includes simple experiments.

It Looked Like Spilt Milk (1988) written and illustrated by Charles G. Shaw. Is the white shape on each page a rabbit, a bird, or just spilt milk? Children are kept guessing until the surprise ending. Not only is this a good introduction to clouds, but it can also be used to increase artistic expression.

Lightning (1999) by Seymour Simon. Readers will be fascinated by the spectacular full-color photographs and clear, concise text that explore the natural phenomenon of lightning.

The Magic School Bus Inside a Hurricane (1996) by Joanna Cole, illustrated by Bruce Degen. This book makes a subject like hurricanes fun to learn.

The Magic School Bus Kicks Up a Storm (2000) by Nancy White, illustrated by Art Ruiz and Bruce Degen. Ride the Magic School Bus into the storm clouds and learn a science lesson you'll never forget!

Monsoon (2003) by Uma Krishnaswami, illustrated by Jamel Akib. Rhythmic prose takes the reader on a tour of urban India and the magical clouds that bring their gift of rain to the land.

On the Same Day in March: A Tour of the World's Weather (2001) by Marilyn Singer, illustrated by Frane Lessac. What is the weather like in different parts of the world on the same day?

One Monday (2001) written and illustrated by Amy Huntington. This book is written with the exaggeration of a tall tale—"On Wednesday, it was so windy, carrots and turnips twisted out of the garden beds, and the corn picked itself."

The Reasons for the Seasons (1996) written and illustrated by Gail Gibbons. The author explains the weather and the seasons and the wonders that come with each of them.

Sergio and the Hurricane (2000) written and illustrated by Alexandra Wallner. In San Juan, Puerto Rico, young Sergio discovers how destructive hurricanes can be.

The Storm Book (1988) by Charlotte Zolotow, illustrated by Margaret Bloy Graham. This book starts with the buildup of a big storm and ends with a beautiful rainbow. Make a list of all the things you can do on a rainy day. Wear raincoats and boots indoors just for inspiration. Go outside and practice opening umbrellas safely.

Thunder Doesn't Scare Me! (2001) by Lynea Bowdish, illustrated by John Wallace. A girl and her dog fend off the loud, scary thunder by creating their own noise.

Twister (1999) by Darleen Bailey Beard, photographed by Nancy Carpenter. A rural family faces potential disaster from a tornado in this suspenseful and ultimately reassuring picture book.

Weather Forecasting (1993) written and illustrated by Gail Gibbons. Readers visit a small weather station to see forecasters at work.

Weather Words and What They Mean (1996) written and illustrated by Gail Gibbons. The author illustrates and defines weather terms in easy-to-understand language.

Where Does the Wind Blow? (2002) written and illustrated by Cynthia Rink. Explore the ways in which wind touches people and places around the world and connects them.

March 11

EZRA JACK KEATS: BIRTHDAY
Author and illustrator Ezra Jack Keats was born March 11, 1916, in New York, and died in 1983. One of the first children's authors to use minority children in his stories; many of his characters were either African American or Hispanic. Keats employed the use of collage combined with other techniques to make his intriguing illustrations. His many children's books include the classic *The Snowy Day* (1996). This winner of the 1963 Caldecott Medal captures the magic of a first snowfall and reveals a child's wonder at a new world and the hope of keeping that wonder forever.

WANDA GAG: BIRTHDAY
Millions of Cats author and illustrator Wanda Gag was born March 11, 1893, and died in 1946. *Cats* features a repetitive line that children love to recite: "Hundreds of cats, thousands of cats" will continue echoing throughout the day. The book lends itself well to a group project of producing a mural of the plot line, which develops a deep and lasting comprehension of this classic story.

March 14

CASEY JONES: BIRTHDAY
John Luther "Casey" Jones, the railroad engineer hero, was born in Cayce, Kentucky, on this date in 1864. The book *Casey Jones* (2001), written and illustrated by Allan Drummond, tells of his railroading adventures and provides a great tie-in to American musical history and the joy of singing folk songs.

NATIONAL AGRICULTURE WEEK
National Agriculture Week is celebrated annually during the third week in March. Dedicated to honoring the farmers of America, this week would be a perfect time to invite a farmer to talk to the students about life on the farm. Suggested reading materials include the following:

The Year at Maple Hill Farm (2001) by Alice and Martin Provensen. Through gently humorous text and charming illustrations, this book captures changes on a farm and surrounding countryside throughout the year.

Life on a Crop Farm (2001) by Judy Wolfman, photography by David Lorenz Winston. Learn about life on a farm, and enjoy the happy color photographs that make the text come to life.

March 17

SAINT PATRICK'S DAY

This holiday commemorates the patron saint of Ireland, Bishop Patrick, who lived from A.D. 389 to 461 and introduced Christianity to Ireland in 432. Students can make up several math problems involving St. Patrick. How many years ago was he born? How old was he when he died? How many years ago did he introduce Christianity to Ireland? These questions help children see the value in learning the basics of arithmetic. The following books are helpful in explaining this holiday to younger children:

St. Patrick's Day (1995) by Gail Gibbons. The author provides a basic introduction to the holiday—how it began, the life and works of St. Patrick, and various ways in which the day is celebrated.

Patrick: Patron Saint of Ireland (1994) by Tomie dePaola. The book places a near-mythic religious figure within a historical context, relating the known and not-so-familiar details of his life.

Saint Patrick (1998) by Ann Tompert, illustrated by Michael Garland. Tompert concentrates on facts rather than legend for her text in this appealing look at the life of Ireland's patron saint.

March 18

DOUGLAS FLORIAN: BIRTHDAY

Douglas Florian, poet and illustrator, was born in 1950 and has written many delightful books for children. His brief poems are silly and clever, funny and serious. They make children laugh and can easily stimulate a student's own imaginative attempts with either a pencil or a paintbrush. Among his most popular collections are the following:

Beast Feast (1998) is a hilarious collection of animal poems and paintings.

Insectlopedia (2002) presents twenty-one short poems about such insects as the inchworm, termite, cricket, and ladybug.

Mammalabilia (2000) is a menagerie of twenty-one original poems and paintings. Readers will be laughing out loud at the silliness of Florian's observations about mammals ranging from the howling coyote to the speedy tiger. This collection is an excellent choice for an elementary school unit on either poetry or mammals, or just a fun read for a class or a family.

Week Three: Magical People

📖 ⚙ Curriculum Connection: Language Arts and Geography

The basic question "Are there really magical people such as leprechauns, trolls, the Tooth Fairy, and good witches?" leads to many discussion topics and the development and acceptance of different opinions.

Most of the magical people originated in other countries, and their stories were brought to America by immigrants. Finding the countries of origin as the books are read this week would be a meaningful map activity. It would also be interesting to ask the children if they know of other magical people and where they originated.

Elf Night (2002) by Jan Wahl, illustrated by Peter Weevers. Brief rhymes tell about a young child watching the elf world at play.

The Elves and the Shoemaker (2003) retold and illustrated by Jim LaMarche. This is a retelling of the tale of a poor shoemaker and his wife who are aided by two selfless elves. One or both elves are hidden on each double-page spread, and children enjoy searching for them.

Fluffy Meets the Tooth Fairy (2002) by Kate McMullan, illustrated by Mavis Smith. Fluffy, a class guinea pig, decides there really is a Tooth Fairy.

Franklin and the Tooth Fairy (1996) by Paulette Bourgeois, illustrated by Brenda Clark. Franklin's friends are losing their teeth, but not Franklin (turtles don't have teeth). Franklin learns it's OK to be different.

Good Night, Fairies (2002) by Kathleen Hague, illustrated by Michael Hague. A mother answers her child's questions about what fairies do at nighttime.

Jack and the Leprechaun (2000) by Ivan Robertson, illustrated by Katy Bratun. Jack Mouse is visiting Ireland and is determined to catch a leprechaun.

Jamie O'Rourke and the Big Potato (1997) written and illustrated by Tomie dePaola. Taking the easy way out is sometimes more trouble than it's worth.

Jethro and Joel Were a Troll (1990) written and illustrated by Bill Peet. What happens when the good half of a two-headed troll gets in trouble when he lets the bad side rule for a day? This story is fun and a good read-aloud; it might also assist in a discussion about choices we all have to make.

The Luckiest Leprechaun (2001) by Justine Korman, illustrated by Denise Brunkus. This funny tale is about friendship between a dog named Lucky and a feisty leprechaun.

Nice Try, Tooth Fairy (2003) by Mary W. Olson, illustrated by Katherine Tillotson. Hoping to get back her lost tooth, Emma writes letters to the Tooth Fairy, but the wrong teeth keep coming back.

Quackadack Duck (2003) by Allen Morgan, illustrated by John Beder. A comical tale of how a troll and a duck become friends.

Rumpelstiltskin (1996) retold by Paul O. Zelinsky. A mysterious little man appears out of nowhere to help the miller's daughter spin straw into gold. Outstanding illustrations enliven the story.

Strega Nona Takes a Vacation (2003) written and illustrated by Tomie dePaola. Strega Nona is giving the villagers the wrong remedies; it's time for a vacation!

Strega Nona (1979) written and illustrated by Tomie dePaola. In Italy, Grandma Witch teaches her assistant, Big Anthony, a few lessons about cooking pasta and about life. Visit the pasta aisle in the grocery store and count the many different types of pasta. Pick one you haven't had before and cook it.

Strega Nona's Magic Lessons (1984) written and illustrated by Tomie dePaola. When Big Anthony tries to join Strega Nona's magic class, the results are hilarious.

The Sun Egg (1997) written and illustrated by Elsa Beskow. An elf solves the mystery of a large orange egg that fell into the woods.

The Three Billy Goats Gruff (1990) retold and illustrated by Janet Stevens. This "modern" version offers a new glimpse into how three billy goats outwit an ugly troll.

The Tomten (1997) adapted by Astrid Lindgren, illustrated by Harald Wiberg. A friendly troll leaves soundless tracks in the snow and whispers promises of a coming spring in this tale for youngsters that's comforting to read on a cold, dark winter night.

The Troll-Bridge Troll (2000) by Patricia Rae Wolff, illustrated by Kimberly Bulken Root. A boy and a young troll face off in a series of humorous encounters.

Thumbelina (1985) retold by Amy Ehrlich, illustrated by Susan Jeffers. This thumb-size girl has to brave the huge, dangerous world before she finds happiness with others her size.

Tim O'Toole and the Wee Folk (1992) written and illustrated by Gerald R. McDermott. This is a lighthearted Irish tale of magic, greed, and revenge.

Tooth Fairy (1991) written and illustrated by Audrey Wood. It's hard to fool the Tooth Fairy with a fake tooth!

March 20

SPRING

Each year around March 20, the spring season begins in the Northern Hemisphere with the vernal equinox (the moment the sun crosses directly over the earth's equator). Robert Maass, a gifted photographer, demonstrates the wonders of spring through full-color photos and a simple narrative in his book *When Spring Comes* (1996).

MITSUMASA ANNO: BIRTHDAY

Born in Japan on March 20, 1926, Anno has written and illustrated many books for the education and enjoyment of children all over the world. In 1984, he won the Hans Christian Andersen Medal, the highest honor attainable in the field of children's book illustration. Two of Anno's picture books are wordless delights:

Anno's Journey (1997). Told through brilliant illustrations, this wordless book takes young readers on a wondrous journey through northern Europe.

Anno's Counting Book (1986). This clever and educational book presents the concepts of counting as a village grows, months of the year as the seasons evolve, and time of day as the clock marks the hours.

March 21

DAVID WISNIEWSKI: BIRTHDAY

This popular author and illustrator, who was born in England on March 21, 1953, and died in 2002, spent many years as a circus clown and shadow puppeteer before he began writing and illustrating children's books. His book *Golem*, for older readers, won the 1997 Caldecott Medal. The 4–8 age group will also enjoy *Tough Cookie* (1999), both written and illustrated by Wisniewski. When his friend Chips is snatched and chewed, Tough Cookie sets out from the bottom of the jar to stop Fingers.

JOHANN SEBASTIAN BACH: BIRTHDAY

Born in 1685, Bach was one of the most influential composers in musical history as well as an organist. In her book *Sebastian: A Book About Bach* (1999), writer and illustrator Jeanette Winter combines a spare text and colorful illustrations to capture her subject's personality. The story clearly relates how music dominated Bach's life until his death in 1750.

March 22

RANDOLPH CALDECOTT: BIRTHDAY

Randolph Caldecott, who was born in England in 1846 and died in 1886, is credited with bringing beauty and humor into children's literature. The Caldecott Medal named in his honor is awarded annually in the United States to the illustrator of the most distinguished picture book published in the previous year. This coveted prize was established in 1938, so unfortunately many of the early winners are out of print. Those books earning the award since 1960 should be available in the public library.

What Do Illustrators Do? (1999) by Eileen Christelow helps children understand the work of an illustrator. *A Caldecott Celebration* (1998) by Leonard S. Marcus depicts how six authors earned their Caldecott medals.

UNITED NATIONS: WORLD DAY FOR WATER

This observance is to promote public awareness of how water resource development contributes to economic and social well-being. The book *Water, Water Everywhere* (1995) by Mark J. Rauzon and Cynthia Overbeck Bix does a splendid job of conveying the marvel of our "water planet" and the urgency of protecting our limited resource.

March 24

HARRY HOUDINI: BIRTHDAY

One of the most famous magicians and the most famous escape artist in the world, Ehrich Weisz (Harry Houdini) was born on March 24, 1874, and died on Halloween in 1926. A master showman with a knack for publicity, Houdini was extremely self-confident and always kept himself in the spotlight. Although he has been dead for more than seventy-five years, his name is still instantly recognized throughout the world. Patricia Lakin chronicles Houdini's life in the book *Harry Houdini: Escape Artist* (2002).

Another book that contains both magic and a magician is *Abiyoyo* (1994) by Pete Seeger, illustrated by Michael Hays. Banished from town for making mischief, a little boy and his father are welcomed back when they find a way to make the dreaded giant Abiyoyo disappear. Based on a South African lullaby and folk story, this is a book both children and adults will enjoy.

Week Four: Caldecott Award Winners

🎼 Curriculum Connection: Fine Arts

The Caldecott Medal is awarded annually to the artist of the most distinguished American picture book for children. Discuss the role of illustrators in the picture book process as well as the many different media they use. You might want to set up a reading table with Caldecott Medal winners and Honor Books for the class to skim on their own. Ask the children to bring in their favorite Caldecott winner and discuss why these particular books were chosen for awards.

Illustrations add to a story. Invite children to create their own illustrations for a well-known story such as *The Three Pigs*. Provide several different media from which they can choose—chalk, crayons, colored pencils, watercolors, markers, and so on. Display the results, and discuss why each child chose a specific medium.

A Chair for My Mother (1982) written and illustrated by Vera B. Williams. After losing all of their furniture in a fire, a family saves dimes to buy a comfortable arm chair in this 1983 Caldecott Honor Book.

Freight Train (1978) written and illustrated by Donald Crews. Clear, bright illustrations show all the cars of a train moving through day and night, country and city in this 1979 Caldecott Honor Book.

Hey, Al (1986) by Arthur Yorinks, illustrated by Richard Egielski. Al, a city janitor, and his treasured canine companion, Eddie, are transported on a journey to paradise and discover that home is best in this 1987 Caldecott Medal winning book.

Joseph Had a Little Overcoat (2000) written and illustrated by Simms Taback. Joseph had a little overcoat, but it was full of holes—just like this book. When Joseph's coat got too old and shabby, he made it into a jacket. But what did he make it into after that? Find out in this 2000 Caldecott Medal winning story.

Madeline (1939) written and illustrated by Ludwig Bemelmans. This 1940 Caldecott Honor Book is a classic tale about Miss Clavel

and twelve little girls. The smallest girl, Madeline, is very brave and doesn't even get scared of a lion in the zoo.

Make Way for Ducklings (1941) written and illustrated by Robert McCloskey. This winner of the 1942 Caldecott Medal also won a place in generations of children's hearts for its sense of place, humorous illustration, and the author's description of the ducks' street-crossing adventure.

Mirandy and Brother Wind (1997) by Patricia McKissack, illustrated by Jerry Pinkney. Vibrant illustrations bring to life the historic cakewalk dance in this 1989 Caldecott Honor Book inspired by an old photograph of the author's African American grandparents.

My Friend Rabbit (2003) written and illustrated by Eric Rohmann. In this 2003 Caldecott Medal winner, when Mouse lets his best friend, Rabbit, play with his brand-new airplane, he's asking for trouble.

Owl Moon (1987) by Jane Yolen, illustrated by John Schoenherr. This 1988 Caldecott Medal winner is the gentle story of a young child and her father who take a nighttime stroll to look for owls.

Ox-Cart Man (1979) by Donald Hall, illustrated by Barbara Cooney. This 1980 Caldecott Medal winner describes the life of an early nineteenth-century New England family as the seasons change.

The Relatives Came (1985) by Cynthia Rylant, illustrated by Stephen Gammell. In this lively 1986 Caldecott Honor Book the author shows what types of things a family goes through when relatives come to visit while it teaches children the importance of family.

Seven Blind Mice (1992) written and illustrated by Ed Young. One by one, the seven blind mice investigate the strange "something" by the pond. This 1993 Caldecott Honor Book can be used to teach color, texture, shape, and days of the week.

Snowflake Bentley (1998) by Jacqueline Briggs Martin, illustrated by Mary Azarian. Bentley's patience and determination in photographing snowflakes reveal two important truths: first, that no two are alike and second, that each one is beautiful. No wonder it won a 1999 Caldecott Medal.

Song and Dance Man (1988) by Karen Ackerman, illustrated by Stephen Gammell. Grandpa performs his old vaudeville act for his grandchildren in this beautifully illustrated 1989 Caldecott Medal winner.

Sylvester and the Magic Pebble (1969) written and illustrated by William Steig. In this vividly illustrated 1970 Caldecott Medal winner an unassuming donkey finds a magic pebble that will grant his every wish.

There Was an Old Lady Who Swallowed a Fly (1997) written and illustrated by Simms Taback. Everyone knows the song about the old lady who swallowed a fly, but who's ever seen what happens in the old lady's stomach? This 1998 Caldecott Honor Book might just offer a peek.

Where the Wild Things Are (1963) written and illustrated by Maurice Sendak. This classic 1964 Caldecott Medal winning story shows that the wild things are scary-looking but they are really more funny than scary.

Yo! Yes? (1993) written and illustrated by Chris Raschka. In this 1994 Caldecott Honor book, the author uses only 19 words to tell the story of two boys who meet on the street and become friends.

March 26

MAKE UP YOUR OWN HOLIDAY DAY

This is the day you and your students have been waiting for! Children often have ideas for special days that adults would never think of. Let your imagination run wild, and make up a new holiday as a class. What new holiday have you always wished for? What local hero or heroine deserves a day? What career needs special recognition?

A good starting point might be *Children Just Like Me: Celebrations!* (1997) by Barnabas and Anabel Kindersley. Children will enjoy learning how kids just like them have fun, and in the process they will broaden their cultural horizons.

SANDRA DAY O'CONNOR: BIRTHDAY

O'Connor, who was born in 1930, began her legislative career as Arizona state senator in 1969. She served as a judge in the superior court in Phoenix and the Arizona Court of Appeals and was appointed to the U.S. Supreme Court in 1981.

Sandra Day O'Connor (1997), written by Gini Holland and illustrated by Gary Rees, introduces the life and accomplishments of the first woman named to the country's highest court.

March 27

EARTHQUAKE STRIKES ALASKA

On March 27, 1964, a great earthquake took 125 lives and caused about $311 million in property loss. Anchorage sustained the most severe damage. About thirty blocks of dwelling and commercial buildings in the downtown area were damaged or destroyed. The shock from this quake, with a magnitude of 9.2, generated a tsunami that devastated many towns along the Gulf of Alaska, Canada, the west coast of the United States, and Hawaii.

The following books present facts and pictures to help children understand this kind of phenomenon:

Earthquakes (2002) by Ellen J. Prager, illustrated by Susan Greenstein. This colorful book, which provides basic information about earthquakes, is lively and appealing and lends itself to reading aloud.

Earthquake! (1999) by Bill Haduch. Wacky science writer Bill Haduch combines entertainment and information in this enjoyable book.

Earthquakes (1995) by Seymour Simon. Award-winning author Seymour Simon examines how earthquakes are caused and how they are measured.

March 30

VINCENT VAN GOGH: BIRTHDAY

The Dutch painter Vincent Van Gogh was born in 1853 in the Netherlands and died in France in 1890. He is especially noted for his use of bold colors. During his lifetime, he received little recognition and sold only one painting. There are several good books about this colorful artist:

Camille and the Sunflowers (1994) written and illustrated by Laurence Anholt. This book is based on the true story of a young French boy and his family who befriend the lonely painter and begin to admire his work.

Vincent Van Gogh: Sunflowers and Swirly Stars (2001) by Joan Holub. This clever biography explains Van Gogh's short, sad life and brilliant work in terms that elementary school children can understand.

In the Garden with Van Gogh (2002) by Julie Merberg and Suzanne Bober. Using well-known works by the artist, rhyming text tells a story from the artwork.

March 31

FRANZ JOSEPH HAYDN: BIRTHDAY

Born on March 31, 1732, Haydn's musical abilities developed early. When he was only six, he began studying music in Hainburg, Austria. From 1740 to 1750, he sang in the choir at St. Stephen's Cathedral in Vienna. He then worked as a freelance musician for the next nine years, writing sacred works, music for theater comedies, and chamber music. In 1762, he became director of an ensemble of some fifteen to twenty musicians and was required to compose as his employer, Prince Nikolaus Esterhazy, might command. His work in the 1780s included piano sonatas and symphonies, but his most important work was an oratorio, *The Creation*.

Haydn remained productive nearly to the end of his life and was known in his last years as Vienna's grand old man of music. He died in 1809 at the age of seventy-seven.

Young children will enjoy *Franz Joseph Haydn: Great Man of Music* (1994) by Carol Greene, illustrated by Steven Dobson. This biography has short, easy-to-understand text; historical photos; and eye-catching illustrations.

March Reading Strategy

The Venn Diagram

The Venn diagram is a very easily understood graphic aid used to foster reading comprehension. Once it is introduced, students as young as kindergarten age can benefit from its use.

What is a Venn diagram? Simply stated, it is two intersecting circles with the elements of one piece of writing in one circle and the elements of another piece of writing in the other circle. The elements common to both pieces of writing are written in the intersection of the two circles. Example:

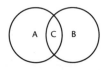

By using a Venn diagram, a comparison/contrast can be made between items that have similarities in some areas while also having some unique qualities. Plots, characters, settings, historical times, values, cultures, celebrations, kinds of literature, and many other items can be compared using this graphic aid.

A sample use of an early primary Venn diagram might be to have the students compare the story of the Three Bears with the story of the Three Pigs. The teacher would lead the class into looking critically at the characters, setting, and plot elements of each, and then list the agreed-upon elements of each story in the circle for that story while putting common elements in the intersection. The Three Bears circle might contain *three bears*, *mother*, *father*, *little girl*, and *house*. The Three Pigs circle might contain *three pigs*, *wolf*, *three houses*, and so on. The intersection of the two circles could contain the number three (both have *three* in their title) and animals (both have animals as main characters).

Critical thinking skills and a deeper comprehension of both stories is the result of this type of discussion. Comparing and contrasting is an important skill in meeting the standards of comprehension of grade-level reading material in elementary school.

April at a Glance

Outside of a dog, a book is man's best friend. Inside a dog, it's too dark to read.
—Groucho Marks

April Reading Tip: Always practice reading a book before you read it out loud. That way you will know where the pitfalls are and how the author uses language to tell the story or impart information.

APRIL HIGHLIGHTS
Animal Cruelty Prevention Month
ASPCA: The American Society for the Prevention of Cruelty to Animals (2003) by Anastasia Suen describes the history and functions of this organization.

Keep America Beautiful Month
The Lorax (1976) by Dr. Seuss is narrated by the Once-ler, who describes how careless actions harm the environment.

Month of the Young Child
Today I Feel Silly and Other Moods That Make My Day (1998) by Jamie Lee Curtis, illustrated by Laura Cornell, helps kids understand their ever-changing moods.

National Child Abuse Prevention Month
The Right Touch (1998) by Sandy Kleven, illustrated by Jody Lynn Bergsma, gently explains how children can protect themselves from improper touching by strangers.

School Library Media Month
Check It Out! (1988), written and illustrated by Gail Gibbons, presents a wealth of information about libraries and the services they provide.

Aquarium Month
My Visit to the Aquarium (1996) by Aliki takes children and adults of various ages, races, and physical abilities on a tour through a public aquarium.

National Humor Month
Crazy Hair Day (2003) by Barney Saltzberg tells the story of Stanley, who is excited about Crazy Hair Day at his school until he learns to his horror that he has the wrong date.

April Reading Strategy: The Art of Questioning

WEEKLY THEMES AND CURRICULUM CONNECTIONS
Week One: Humor (Language Arts)
Week Two: Numbers (Math)
Week Three: Zoo Animals (Science)
Week Four: Poetry (Language Arts)

Special Events in April

April Fool's Day	Apr. 1
National Reading a Road Map Week	Apr. 4
National Week of the Ocean	Apr. 5
National Poetry Month	Apr. 12
Pan American Day	Apr. 14
National Coin Week	Apr. 18
Thank Your School Librarian Day	Apr. 21
Kindergarten Day	Apr. 21
Arbor Day	Apr. 30

FEATURED APRIL BIRTHDAYS

Hans Christian Andersen Apr. 2	Trina Schart Hyman ....Apr. 8	Lee Bennett Hopkins ....Apr. 13
Ruth Heller.....................Apr. 2	Buddha ....Apr. 8	Garth Williams ....Apr. 16
Washington Irving ....Apr. 3	Martin Waddell ....Apr. 10	Ludwig Bemelmans ......Apr. 27
Graeme Base ....Apr. 6	Thomas Jefferson ....Apr. 13	John Burningham..........Apr. 27

Week One: Humor

📖 Curriculum Connection: Language Arts

April is designated National Humor Month. Laughter is one of the greatest stress reducers available to everyone. The joy of sharing laughter with children is one of the perks of teaching.

Primary children are still developing their own unique sense of humor, but almost all children in this age-group enjoy humor that involves characters doing seemingly impossible things, characters with human child–type problems solved in funny ways, and humorous situations involving other children who could easily be them.

One of the real advantages of using humorous books in the classroom is to teach the value of laughing *with* someone and not *at* them and not taking life too seriously. Humorous books help children understand life consequences.

Humorous books can also be used to lighten the load when children become bogged down in the trials of growing up. Using any of the books on the following list can certainly make standardized testing more fun. This list is just a small peek into the world of humorous picture books. The children you work with probably have favorites of their own that they would like to share.

Alexander and the Terrible, Horrible, No Good, Very Bad Day (1976) by Judith Viorst, illustrated by Ray Cruz. When he woke up with gum in his hair, Alexander knew the rest of the day would be horrible. This longtime favorite is sure to bring laughs.

Amelia Bedelia (1983) by Peggy Parish, illustrated by Fritz Siebel. Literally trying to follow instructions causes trouble for Amelia Bedelia in this cutely illustrated story.

Animals Should Definitely Not Wear Clothing (1988) by Judi Barrett, illustrated by Ron Barrett. Humorous pictures point out the problems animals would encounter if they wore clothes.

Are We There Yet? (2003) by Dandi Mackall, illustrated by Shannon McNeill. Every family will be able to see themselves in this hilarious book about a family car trip.

Arnie, the Doughnut (2003) written and illustrated by Laurie Keller. Arnie convinces Mr.

Bing not to eat him in this laugh-out-loud picture book.

A Bad Case of Stripes (1998) written and illustrated by David Shannon. How will Camilla Cream get rid of the stripes on her face?

Big Anthony: His Story (2001) written and illustrated by Tomie dePaola. Big Anthony never pays attention. Will Italy survive his hilarious mishaps?

David Goes to School (1999) written and illustrated by David Shannon. This brightly illustrated story follows David at school and how he manages to get into one predicament after another.

The Giant Jam Sandwich (1987) by John Vernon Lord, illustrated by Janet Burroway. In this nonsense tale four million wasps are trapped in a large strawberry-jam sandwich.

Grandpa's Teeth (1999) written and illustrated by Rod Clement. When Grandpa's teeth disappear from a glass of water near his bed, Inspector Rate starts an investigation. Where could they be?

Green Wilma (1997) written and illustrated by Tedd Arnold. When Wilma awakes one morning to find that she has turned green and craves flies for breakfast, her parents don't know what to do.

I Am Not Going to Get Up Today! (1987) by Dr. Seuss, illustrated by James Stevenson. A very sleepy boy vows nothing will get him out of bed.

Imogene's Antlers (1988) written and illustrated by David Small. Imogene, a young girl, grows huge antlers and her life definitely changes.

Mud Puddle (1996) by Robert Munsch, illustrated by Sami Suomalainen. Whenever July Ann goes outside, Mud Puddle gets her muddy all over. Soon July Ann finds a way to vanquish her opponent.

Old Black Fly (1994) by Jim Aylesworth, illustrated by Stephen Gammell. This delightful, rhyming alphabet book begs to be read aloud.

Old Granny and the Bean Thief (2003) by Cynthia DeFelice, illustrated by Cat Bowman Smith. An odd assortment of talking creatures—a snake, a pecan, a cow patty, a prickly pear cactus, and an alligator—help Old Granny foil her bean thief.

The Old Man Who Loved Cheese (1998) by Garrison Keillor, illustrated by Anne Wilsdorf. Wallace P. Flynn loves smelly cheeses so much that his family threatens to leave him. Will Wallace ever learn to change his ways?

Possum Come a-Knockin' (1992) by Nancy Van Laan, illustrated by George Booth. This story tells in rollicking rhyme about a possum who keeps knocking on a family's door and then disappears.

Rotten Teeth (2002) by Laura Simms, illustrated by David Catrow. Melissa brings a big glass bottle of authentic pulled teeth to school for show-and-tell.

The Secret Knowledge of Grown-Ups (2001) written and illustrated by David Wisniewski. Here's a very funny tale of the real reasons why adults tell children to do things, such as "Don't blow bubbles in your milk."

Soap! Soap! Don't Forget the Soap! (1996) by Tom Birdseye, illustrated by Andrew Glass. This cumulative story tells of a forgetful boy who gets into trouble by repeating what each person he meets on the road says to him.

Stephanie's Ponytail (1996) by Robert Munsch, illustrated by Michael Martchenko. A little girl comes to school every day with a different hairdo, but the other girls always copy her. What happens when she vows to shave her head?

What Are You So Grumpy About? (2003) written and illustrated by Tom Lichtenheld. In this collection of cartoons the author takes various reasons for being grumpy and makes them funny instead.

April 1

APRIL FOOL'S DAY

April Fool's Day has been celebrated somewhere in the world since the sixteenth century. *April Fool's Day* (2003) by Melissa Schiller, illustrated by Don Curry, introduces the history of April Fool's Day and explains how some people celebrate it today. Third and fourth graders can write a quick paragraph on why they think this day continues to be celebrated in the modern world. The students can then share their writings with the rest of the class on a "What We Think" bulletin board.

Mud Flat April Fool (1998) by James Stevenson is another book that students will enjoy on this silly day.

KAREN WALLACE: BIRTHDAY

April 1 is the birthday of Canadian author, Karen Wallace, who wrote *Imagine You Are a Crocodile* (1997), illustrated by Mike Bostock. Each child will want a turn telling which animal they would like to be after they have listened to this book.

April 2

HANS CHRISTIAN ANDERSEN: BIRTHDAY

Hans Christian Andersen was born in Odense, Denmark, in 1805 and died at Copenhagen in 1875. A famous author, he wrote more than 150 fairy tales, many of which are considered classics. Among his stories are *The Princess and the Pea, The Snow Queen*, and *The Ugly Duckling*. *The Ugly Duckling* (1999), illustrated by Jerry Pinkney, is probably the most beautiful version of this favorite.

RUTH HELLER: BIRTHDAY

Ruth Heller, the gifted science author for children, was born on this day in 1924. One of her best books to share with young students is *Chickens Aren't the Only Ones* (1999), a very original book on the subject of eggs. As a good prereading activity, have the children list all the animals they know that lay eggs. When you have finished reading, ask if they learned about any new animals that do this.

April 3

WASHINGTON IRVING: BIRTHDAY

On April 3, 1783, Washington Irving was born in New York City. He wrote many historical and biographical works and is famous for his creation of Rip Van Winkle, a man who sleeps for twenty years in the Catskill Mountains and wakes to a much-changed world. A good version of this classic is *Rip Van Winkle* (2000), illustrated by Arthur Rackham.

Discuss how many events happen during Rip Van Winkle's nap to help children understand the passage of time during a span longer than one year. Also discuss with the students how they will change in twenty years and how they think their parents will change. Are their thoughts accurate?

Irving, who was also an attorney and onetime U.S. minister to Spain died in Tarrytown, New York, in 1859.

April 4

NATIONAL READING A ROAD MAP WEEK

The first week in April is National Reading a Road Map week. Your local automobile association is the place to obtain a map for each child. Students will enjoy having a map of their own to chart the roads from school to their homes. Many students will want to spend time "reading" their map and should be allowed to practice this life skill. Children should be encouraged to discover alternate routes from home to school and to other local areas such as the police station, the post office, and shopping areas. Depending on the students' ages, the skills associated with map reading can be introduced, taught to mastery, or reviewed. The motto for this week is "Happiness is knowing how to read a road map."

A good resource for this week is *As the Crow Flies: A First Book of Maps* (1993) by Gail Hartman, illustrated by Harvey Stevenson.

Week Two: Numbers

🎹 Curriculum Connection: Math

Working with numbers is often frustrating to both teacher and student. The titles provided here are designed to help children explore, understand, and have fun with numbers and number concepts.

Children say they can count, but in reality they count by rote and are fuzzy on the concepts behind counting, especially with large numbers. Third and fourth graders are often confused about the concepts of multiplication and division and their relationship to addition and subtraction. Often, reteaching in a story context helps clear up the confusion.

Mathematical concepts are embedded in almost all daily activities, and many of the following books help students "see" math in everyday activities such as cooking and telling time.

This is by no means an exhaustive list of the books available to help students understand mathematical concepts. Often a contextual introduction of a new concept helps the mathematically challenged student understand when an abstract presentation doesn't help.

Amanda Bean's Amazing Dream (1998) by Cindy Neuschwander and Marilyn Burns, illustrated by Liza Woodruff. In an amazing dream, Amanda realizes that being able to multiply will help her count things faster.

Anno's Counting Book (1986) written and illustrated by Mitsumasa Anno. Anno's beautiful watercolors lead children through number concepts.

Arithme-Tickle (2002) by J. Patrick Lewis, illustrated by Frank Remkiewicz. Eighteen zany riddles use addition, subtraction, and simple multiplication for a variety of math problems.

Bat Jamboree (1998) by Kathi Appelt, illustrated by Melissa Sweet. At an outdoor theater, fifty-five bats perform in a toe-tapping revue, shown in vivid color.

Bunny Money (2000) written and illustrated by Rosemary Wells. Max and Ruby are trying to save money to buy their grandma a birthday present, but things keep happening that require them to spend their money. Will they have enough left for a gift?

The Doorbell Rang (1989) written and illustrated by Pat Hutchins. Each time the doorbell rings, there is someone new who wants to taste Ma's wonderful cookies.

Each Orange Had 8 Slices (1999) by Paul Giganti, illustrated by Donald Crews. This stimulating counting book uses familiar objects to introduce beginning math concepts.

Emily's First 100 Days of School (2000) written and illustrated by Rosemary Wells. This book is chock-full of surprising discoveries, age-appropriate activities, and plenty of humor as readers count from one to a hundred.

Even Steven and Odd Todd (1996) by Kathryn Cristaldi, illustrated by Henry Morehouse. Even Steven and Odd Todd teach basic number concepts in a way that children will enjoy. This book includes an activities and game section.

From One to One Hundred (1995) written and illustrated by Teri Sloat. This ingenious counting book is jam-packed with information as it introduces numbers one through ten and then counting by tens to one hundred.

Get Up and Go! (1996) by Stuart J. Murphy, illustrated by Diane Greenseid. Using rhyme, the author explains the concepts of timeliness and addition as a girl gets ready for school.

How Big Is a Foot? (1991) by Rolf Myller. This clever tale offers a reason why measurements became standardized.

How Much Is a Million? (1993) by David M. Schwartz, illustrated by Stephen Kellogg. Text and pictures are used to visualize the concept of a million, a billion, and a trillion.

I Won't Get Lost (2003) by Martha Lambert, illustrated by Kate Duke. This instructive picture book teaches kids the importance of learning their home address and phone number.

If You Hopped Like a Frog (1999) by David M. Schwartz, illustrated by James Warhola. This book introduces the concept of ratio by comparing what humans would be able to do if they had bodies like different animals.

Let's Count (1999) written and photographed by Tana Hoban. Full-color photographs of objects such as one fat chicken, five smashed cans, and twelve rolls of bathroom tissue encourage children to look at the world around them as they learn numbers from one to a hundred.

Macaroni Math (2000) by Diane C. Ohanesian, illustrated by Jim Connolly. With easy, do-it-yourself projects and activities using pasta and other inexpensive household items, this collection illuminates basic math skills, including counting, sorting, measuring, addition, and subtraction.

Measuring Penny (2000) written and illustrated by Loreen Leedy. Lisa has fun measuring her dog, Penny, with all sorts of units, including pounds, inches, dog biscuits, and cotton swabs.

My Little Sister Ate One Hare (1998) by Bill Grossman, illustrated by Kevin Hawkes. In this very funny counting book, a little sister eats everything from one hare to ten peas.

One Hundred Hungry Ants (1999) by Elinor J. Pinczes, illustrated by Bonnie MacKain. This whimsical story is an enjoyable visual introduction to division.

Pigs Will Be Pigs: Fun with Math and Money (1997) by Amy Axelrod, illustrated by Sharon McGinley-Nally. The Pig family learns about money as they search the house looking for enough money to buy dinner at the local restaurant.

Skittles Math Riddles (2001) by Barbara Barbieri Mcgrath, illustrated by Roger Glass. Using a blend of poetry and riddles, this book makes solving word problems fun.

Ten Little Mummies: An Egyptian Counting Book (2003) by Philip Yates, illustrated by G. Brian Karas. Ten mummies are painting the town red in this refreshingly funny counting book.

12 Ways to Get to 11 (1996) by Eve Merriam, illustrated by Bernie Karlin. This book takes young readers on a counting adventure as they find twelve creative ways to get to eleven.

What Time Is It? (1999) by Sheila Keenan, illustrated by Kayne Jacobs. Through rhyming questions and answers, this book demonstrates how to tell time.

April 5

NATIONAL WEEK OF THE OCEAN

The second full week in April has been designated as National Week of the Ocean, focusing on our interdependence with the sea. A teacher's resource packet is available from Cynthia Hancock, National Week of the Ocean, Inc., PO Box 179, Ft. Lauderdale, FL 33302.

The different environments of the ocean are fascinating to young children. The inhabitants of those environments provide a whole different perspective to explore. All areas of the curriculum also offer perspectives for study of the ocean: from microscopic to overfishing, to poetry, to science report writing. Art projects such as dioramas are a great way for children to display new knowledge about the five oceans of our planet.

Exploring the Deep, Dark Sea (2002) by Gail Gibbons; *Gentle Giant Octopus* (2002) by Karen Wallace, illustrated by Mike Bostock; and *The Magic School Bus on the Ocean Floor* (1994) by Joanna Cole and Bruce Degen are three of the many good books for children in the early grades that explore oceans and their inhabitants.

April 6

GRAEME BASE: BIRTHDAY

Australian Graeme Base is both an artist and a musician. He was born in England on April 6, 1958, and moved to Australia with his family when he was six. He grew up in Melbourne and still lives there today.

In the field of children's literature, Base is best known for his picture book *Animalia* (1986), an alphabet book with very detailed illustrations. This is a book to share in a setting where every child can easily view the pictures. Children as well as adults can spend a lot of entertaining time finding things hidden in the background of each picture. *Animalia* has now sold more than two million copies worldwide.

His most recent book, *The Water Hole* (2001), provides teaching in many ways. It has counting, hidden pictures, geography, and an environmental theme.

April 8

TRINA SCHART HYMAN: BIRTHDAY

Trina Schart Hyman, a famous illustrator, was born on April 8, 1939. She has illustrated several Caldecott Medal–winning books as well as several Caldecott Honor Books. *Little Red Riding Hood* (1987) is one of her best-known projects. Students might enjoy browsing through a display of her books when they have free time. Her books are beautiful! Older students might try enlarging one of her little illustrations and adding details of their own. Students who like tracing will find many wonderful items to trace in the borders around her illustrations.

BUDDHA: BIRTHDAY

April 8 is the most important Buddhist holiday as it is the birthday of the Buddha. It is celebrated in many countries of the world, including Indonesia and Korea. A resource for this day is *Buddha: Father of Buddhism* (2002) by Anna Carew-Miller, a biography of Buddha, who was a prince in India about twenty-five hundred years ago who gave up earthly riches to seek enlightenment about the mysteries of life.

April 10

MARTIN WADDELL: BIRTHDAY

Children's author Martin Waddell was born April 10, 1941, during a bombing raid on Belfast, Ireland, during World War II. He describes his previous jobs as "boiler stoker" and "footballer." Waddell writes all kinds of stories for children, including picture books, and is the author of the well-loved Little Bear stories. The following are two of his best:

Can't You Sleep, Little Bear? (1994) illustrated by Barbara Firth. This book deals gently with the childhood fear of the dark. When bedtime comes, Little Bear is afraid of the dark, so Big Bear brings him a small light, then a larger light, and so on.

Owl Babies (2002) illustrated by Patrick Benson. Three owl babies are frightened when they awake and find their mother has gone out in the night. The repetitive approach in this story encourages children's participation.

Week Three: Zoo Animals

❋ Curriculum Connection: Science

April is National Zoo Month. The following list of zoo-related books provides a good springboard for varied discussions and projects related to the residents of a zoo, their behaviors, and their environments. A science curriculum detailing habitats for different land animals, amphibians, and reptiles will be enhanced by discussions of habitat areas that exist in a zoo.

This is a great month to visit a zoo. Obtain a map of the zoo for each child to enhance reading skills. Lessons can be built around the map and the geographical features built into each of the habitats. Develop discussion questions focusing on the environmental needs of the various animals and how the zoo does or does not meet those needs.

Classifying and sorting the animals by habitat, environmental needs, foods eaten, and many other variables provides critical-thinking practice. This activity can be tailored for individual grades—simple sorting for kindergarten students and more complicated sorting (such as animals whose young are hatched versus those born alive) for fourth graders.

Charting and report-writing skills can be used to classify favorite animals and describe individual preferences.

Career awareness and the world of work can be explored from many different aspects of the zoo experience. Animal caregivers are the primary focus at the zoo, but many other jobs are necessary for the zoo to run successfully. Ask students to list all the workers who have been introduced in the following books.

Animals in the Zoo (2000) written and illustrated by Allan Fowler. Using colorful photographs, the reader gets to examine a variety of zoo animals—including elephants, bears, reptiles, and killer whales—and their housing.

The Baby Beebee Bird (2003) by Diane Redfield Massie, illustrated by Steven Kellogg. The zoo animals are exhausted because the baby beebee bird likes to be awake at night. This delightful story is almost as much fun as a visit to the zoo.

The Baby Zoo (1995) by Bruce McMillan. Featuring photos of sixteen baby zoo animals, this fact-filled book also contains maps showing where the animals came from.

The Biggest Animal on Land (1996) by Allan Fowler. Using full-color photographs, this book features the elephant, the biggest animal in the zoo.

City Zoo Blizzard Revue (2003) written and illustrated by Barbara Crispin. When visitors stay away because of an extremely cold winter, the arctic animals put on a show so the zoo will not have to close.

Good Night, Gorilla (2000) written and illustrated by Peggy Rathmann. After a gorilla steals the zookeeper's keys, all the animals secretly follow him home.

Inside a Zoo in the City (2000) by Alyssa Satin Capucilli, illustrated by Tedd Arnold. Through cumulative rhyme, the various animals in a city zoo wake up and startle each other.

Little Panda: The World Welcomes Hua Mei at the San Diego Zoo (2004) by Joanne Ryder, with photographs by the San Diego Zoo staff. There are fewer than one thousand giant pandas left in the world, making Hua Mei's birth at the San Diego Zoo a cause for celebration. She is the first giant panda cub ever to survive in captivity in the Western Hemisphere.

Mealtime for Zoo Animals (1999) by Caroline Arnold, photographed by Richard Hewett. Describing the wide variety of foods eaten by zoo animals, this book is a perfect visual outing on those days when the zoo is closed.

Mother to Tigers (2003) by George Ella Lyon, illustrated by Peter Catalanotto. This remarkable book tells the story of Helen Martini, founder of the Bronx Zoo's animal nursery in 1944 and its first woman zookeeper.

Our Class Took a Trip to the Zoo (2002) by Shirley Neitzel, illustrated by Nancy Winslow Parker. A young boy has a wonderful day at the zoo, despite a series of mishaps with the animals.

The Painting Gorilla (1997) written and illustrated by Michael Rex. A talented gorilla living in a zoo becomes rich through her creative paintings of the animals and people around her. What can a gorilla do with money?

Polar Bear, Polar Bear, What Do You Hear? (1991) by Bill Martin, Jr., illustrated by Eric Carle. Learn the various sounds that zoo animals make in this fun book.

Sleepytime for Zoo Animals (1999) by Caroline Arnold, photographed by Richard Hewett. Using photographs of adorable animals, this book describes how and where zoo animals sleep.

The Tiger Has a Toothache: Helping Animals at the Zoo (2002) by Patricia Lauber, illustrated by Mary Morgan. This informative book examines the work of zoo veterinarians.

The Zanzibar Zoo (2002) by Jewel Prediletto, illustrated by Delores Messenger. Simple rhymes teach children the alphabet through a visit to the zoo.

Zoo (1990) written and illustrated by Gail Gibbons. Spend an entire day at the zoo in this informative book by a well-known nonfiction author.

Zoo-Looking (1996) by Mem Fox, illustrated by Candace Whitman. The rhythmic text is filled with surprises, and the torn-paper collages bring all the animals to life.

April 12

NATIONAL POETRY MONTH
The Children's Book Council with the Academy of American Poets sponsors National Poetry Month each April. For current information, you can visit the website at cbcbooks.org.

Many resources are listed in the weekly thematic unit on poetry for this month. Other resources include the following:

Old Elm Speaks: Tree Poems (1998) by Kristine O'Connell George, illustrated by Kate Kiesler. This is a collection of short, simple poems relating to trees.

Touch the Poem (2000) by Arnold Adoff, illustrated by Lisa Desimini. These poems address the sense of touch, including peach fuzz on your lip and your forehead against a cold window.

Plan to keep several books of poetry on hand and have children memorize a short poem to share with the rest of the class. Class recitation of poetry makes a great parent night activity, while giving students a chance to speak in front of an audience without being alone.

April 13

THOMAS JEFFERSON: BIRTHDAY
Thomas Jefferson, the third president of the United States, is most noted for being one of the authors of the Declaration of Independence. He was born in Virginia on April 13, 1743, and died in 1826. During his presidency, the United States acquired the Louisiana Territory from Napoleon in 1803.

Thomas Jefferson: A Picture Book Biography (1994) by James Cross Giblin, illustrated by Michael Dooling, is a good resource for third and fourth graders. *Thomas Jefferson: A Photo-Illustrated Biography* (1996) by T. M. Usel is better for younger students.

LEE BENNETT HOPKINS: BIRTHDAY
Lee Bennett Hopkins, noted poet who authored *Blast Off: Poems About Space* (1996), was born on April 13 in 1938. *Blast Off* is a great collection of poems about the moon, stars, planets, and related wonders. His collections of poetry are treasures. Be sure to share *Oh, No! Where Are My Pants?* and *Wonderful Words* with your students.

April 14

PAN AMERICAN DAY

April 14 is, by Presidential Proclamation, Pan American Day. It began in 1948 to celebrate all the peoples and countries of South, Central, and North America. *"De Colores" and Other Latin-American Folk Songs for Children* (1994), by José-Luis Orozco, illustrated by Elisa Kleven, with the lyrics provided in both English and Spanish is a great book to use as you plan a Pan American singing time.

Prepare a class graph detailing how many people from which Pan American countries each child knows or which of the Pan American countries different students have visited. Another graph can be made depicting which languages other than English are spoken in these countries. Children will be surprised to learn that many people in Brazil speak Portuguese.

April 16

GARTH WILLIAMS: BIRTHDAY

April 16, 1912, is the birth date of Garth Williams, one of the most loved and prolific illustrators of children's books. Among his works are many classics, including E. B. White's *Stuart Little* and *Charlotte's Web*, and the Little House series. He also illustrated many of the books written by Margaret Wise Brown, such as *Mister Dog* (2003), *The Little Fur Family* (1984), and *Wait Till the Moon Is Full* (1989).

Initiate a class discussion comparing the illustrations of Garth Williams and those of Trina Schart Hyman: *Little Red Riding Hood* (1987) or *Snow White* (1979). They are very different, but both add depth and richness to the written text they are designed to support.

Week Four: Poetry

📖 Curriculum Connection: Language Arts

April is National Poetry Month, a good time to appreciate many different kinds of poetry and even write some original verse. Many of the books listed for this theme are not true picture books but rather collections of poetry for children. You could spend time each day reading from a favorite collection, or you might select one or two poems from several collections for each day of the week. The books listed here can be used both to inspire appreciation and as springboards for students' creative writing.

The classic *Hailstones and Halibut Bones* (1972) provides a foundation for either a class-created poem about a specific color or individually created poems about a student's favorite color. Many of the books can be the starting point for new poems using the same character or main idea in a different format.

Memorization of a favorite poem in its entirety or lines from a poem can also be a class project or individual assignments. Choral reading of a class favorite is a skill that will help all students with oral fluency.

Antarctic Antics: A Book of Penguin Poems (1998) by Judy Sierra, illustrated by Jose Aruego and Ariane Dewey. Visit the distinguished-yet-waddling emperor penguin of icy Antarctica in these fun poems.

Beneath a Blue Umbrella (1990) by Jack Prelutsky, illustrated by Garth Williams. Here is a collection of short, humorous poems about creatures across the country.

Bow Wow Meow Meow: It's Rhyming Cats and Dogs (2003) written and illustrated by Douglas Florian. If you like dogs and cats, the twenty-one poems and paintings in this collection will surely entertain you.

The Burger and the Hot Dog (2001) by Jim Aylesworth, illustrated by Stephen Gammell. Zany food rhymes will delight young readers.

Commotion in the Ocean (2002) by Giles Andreae, illustrated by David Wojtowycz. Children will enjoy these snappy poems about creatures that live in and around the ocean.

Corn Chowder (2003) written and illustrated by James Stevenson. Although the subjects of these poems are familiar, the author presents them in fresh and funny ways.

Dirty Beasts (2002) by Roald Dahl, illustrated by Quentin Blake. This collection of clever poems is perfect for reading aloud.

The Dragons Are Singing Tonight (1998) by Jack Prelutsky, illustrated by Peter Sis. This irresistible collection of poems is all about dragons. Ask each student to choose his or her favorite poem and make a graph showing how the poems compared.

Flicker Flash (1999) by Joan Bransfield Graham, illustrated by Nancy Davis. This delightful collection of poems is a celebration of light in all its forms.

The Frogs Wore Red Suspenders (2002) by Jack Prelutsky, illustrated by Petra Mathers. This book features poems about people and animals set in places such as Minot, Minneapolis, Tuscaloosa, Tucumcari, and the Grand Canyon.

Good Mousekeeping (2001) by J. Patrick Lewis, illustrated by Lisa Desimini. Where would animals reside if they could decide? This is the theme of these humorous poems.

Hailstones and Halibut Bones (1972) by Mary O'Neill, illustrated by John Wallner. This children's classic, originally published in 1961, presents the colors of the spectrum.

Harlem (1996) by Walter Dean Myers, illustrated by Christopher Myers. This poem captures Harlem—the people, the sights, and the sounds.

Heartland (1992) by Diane Siebert, illustrated by Wendell Minor. The gorgeous illustrations and poetic text offer a joyful celebration of the Midwest.

I Invited a Dragon to Dinner (2002) illustrated by Chris L. Demarest. Silliness reigns supreme in this collection of verses by twenty-three new poets who won a nationwide contest.

K Is for Kissing a Cool Kangaroo (2003) by Giles Andreae, illustrated by Guy Parker-Rees. This wondrously illustrated ABC book is pure pleasure.

My Beastie Book of ABC (2002) written and illustrated by David Frampton. This book featuring real and imaginary animals is not like any alphabet book you've ever seen.

Nothing Beats a Pizza (2001) written and illustrated by Loris Lesynski. Meant to be read aloud, these poems feature an offbeat sense of humor.

Paul Revere's Ride (1996) by Henry Wadsworth Longfellow, illustrated by Ted Rand. "Paul Revere's Ride" is newly interpreted, beautifully illustrated, and never fails to entertain.

Rumble in the Jungle (2001) by Giles Andreae, illustrated by David Wojtowycz. You will meet a lively collection of animals in these entertaining poems.

Timothy Tunny Swallowed a Bunny (2003) by Bill Grossman, illustrated by Kevin Hawkes. These outrageously funny poems and vivid pictures will inspire older kids to read.

Wake Up House! Rooms Full of Poems (2001) by Dee Lillegard, illustrated by Don Carter. In these playful poems, the contents of a house show off their unique personalities.

Zin! Zin! Zin! A Violin (1995) by Lloyd Moss, illustrated by Marjorie Priceman. Ten instruments play one by one in a musical performance. Use this upbeat, introduction to orchestral instruments by having each student pretend to play their favorite instrument from the book and see if the other students can guess which instrument they chose.

April 18

NATIONAL COIN WEEK

The third week in April is National Coin Week. This week promotes the history, love, and collection of coins. The U.S. Mint has a website for children: usmint.gov/kids. This would be a great week to review the introduction of state quarters that began in 1999 and will conclude in 2008. Each state legislature was able to pick the design for that state's quarter, and they are introduced in the order that the states came into the Union. Hawaii (the newest state) will be the last one to introduce its quarter.

Many math problems can be made using coins and state quarters. Money and coins fascinate young students. Capitalize on that fascination to encourage children to make change and familiarize themselves with the values of different coins.

April 21

THANK YOUR SCHOOL LIBRARIAN DAY

This is a day to thank and recognize the work of school librarians. *A Day with a Librarian* (2000) by Jan Kottke provides career awareness for students as to what the librarian does all day. Do librarians ever have a chance to read all those books they have on their shelves?

KINDERGARTEN DAY

Observed on the birthday of Friedrich Froebel (April 21, 1782), who established the first kindergarten in 1837, this is a day to recognize the importance of kindergarten in children's education.

Miss Bindergarten Gets Ready for Kindergarten (2001) by Joseph Slate, illustrated by Ashley Wolff, introduces the letters of the alphabet to new students in Miss Bindergarten's kindergarten.

Miss Bindergarten Celebrates the 100th Day of Kindergarten (2002) by Joseph Slate, illustrated by Ashley Wolff, combines math and reading in a great read-aloud story.

April 27

LUDWIG BEMELMANS: BIRTHDAY

Madeline was created by Ludwig Bemelmans, who was born on April 27, 1898, and died in 1962. Bemelmans was one of the first people to write and illustrate a series of books for children. *Madeline* continues to be a favorite of children all over the world, and the books have been translated into many languages since they were written in the early 1930s.

JOHN BURNINGHAM: BIRTHDAY

Hey! Get Off Our Train (1994) is about how a boy and his stuffed toy dog rescue various endangered animals on a trip aboard a toy train. John Burningham, who was born on April 27, 1936, wrote this book as a perfect backdrop for teaching children about what *endangered* really means. This storybook blends in beautifully with the zoo animal theme from Week Three. The scientific relationships between habitat, environment, and endangered animals will provide many discussion topics for you and your students. Students will also find plenty of paragraph topics as they explore endangered species.

April 30

ARBOR DAY

Arbor Day is traditionally celebrated on the last Friday in April. Although it is not a national day for the celebration of trees, it is observed in over half of the states. Is it observed in yours? This is the first question one of your students can research. Two websites offer great resources for learning about trees: talkabouttrees.org and arbor-day.net. Science, literature, art, and many other tree-related activities can be found on these two sites.

The Tremendous Tree Book (1998) by Barbara Brenner and May Garelick, illustrated by Fred Brenner, combines pictures with interesting science information. *Tell Me, Tree: All About Trees for Kids* (2002) by Gail Gibbons is a perfect book for classroom sharing. In simple text and colorful illustrations, Gibbons explains the life cycle of trees and how to identify some of the more common varieties in North America. *Mighty Tree* (1996) by Dick Gackenbach conveys a timely message about the use and protection of natural resources.

April Reading Strategy

The Art of Questioning

Teachers ask questions of children in class many times a day. The way a question is asked requires different types of thinking. The teacher becomes the facilitator for the thinking, comprehension, and critical analysis of the text.

For younger children, the teacher should model what the thinking processes are that lead to comprehension. Statements similar to wondering aloud help students structure their own thinking about the text. The statement "I wonder why Goldilocks went into the empty cottage" leads children to think about character motivation. "I would be scared if I met a wolf in the woods. I wonder what Red Riding Hood was feeling," leads children to think about character emotions. A statement reflecting the sequence of events leading to the climax of a story enables children to practice the comprehension skills of prediction and logical plot completion.

The use of why questions fosters a deeper level of understanding and whole-story comprehension than does the use of literal questions. "Why do you think the wolf put on Grandmother's nightgown and got in bed?" encourages a deeper level of thinking and understanding than "What did the wolf do next?" In the story of *The Three Little Pigs*, the question "Why couldn't the wolf blow down the house made of bricks?" takes a higher level of thinking and comprehension than does the question "Did the wolf blow down the brick house?" Why questions also invoke more discussion than literal questions. This clarifies the story comprehension for the rest of the class, not just the child who answers the question.

Children using English as a second language will have success answering literal questions much earlier than why questions. Listening to others discussing open-ended questions will help them gain a deeper, more complex understanding of the text.

Questions that go beyond the literal level help all students gain comprehension of text whether it is heard or read independently. Open-ended questions and "what do you think" questions help children grow in their critical thinking and understanding.

May at a Glance

I would be most content if my children grew up to be the kind of people who think decorating consists of building enough bookshelves.
—Anna Quindlen

May Reading Tip: Stop during the reading to wonder out loud so children can learn to model the thinking that goes on while reading. For instance, as the story is building to a climax, the reader might say, "I wonder what is coming next."

MAY HIGHLIGHTS
Asian/Pacific American Heritage Month
The following books give a brief introduction to the customs and traditions Asian/Pacific immigrants brought to America: *Chinese Americans* (2002) by Lucia Raatma, *Japanese Americans* (2002) by Melissa McDaniel, and *Vietnamese Americans* (2002) by C. Ann Fitterer.

National Bike Month
Bicycle Safety (1996) by Nancy Loewen, illustrated by Penny Dann, explains the safe way to ride a bicycle and identifies important equipment such as helmets and reflectors.

Older American Month
Service with a Smile (1994) by Karen O'Conner, illustrated by Glen Meyers, introduces Luke and Laura, who find a way to help senior citizens while they earn money for church camp. The book includes service activity suggestions for home and school.

Mother's Day (second Sunday of May)
Celebrating Mother's Day (1996) by Shelly Nielsen, illustrated by Marie-Claude Monchaux, uses rhyming text to introduce the aspects of this holiday celebrating mothers.

National Nurses Week (May 6–12 annually)
Nurses (2002) by Cynthia Klingel, illustrated by Robert B. Noyed, gives a simple description of the activities, tools, uniforms, training, skills, problems, and importance of nurses.

National Book Month
The National Book Foundation invites everyone in America to "read a good book." More information is available at nationalbook.org.

May Reading Strategy: Into and Through

WEEKLY THEMES AND CURRICULUM CONNECTIONS
Week One: Asian/Pacific American Heritage (Social Studies)
Week Two: Mothers (Social Studies)
Week Three: World of Work (Social Studies)
Week Four: Vehicles/Transportation (Science and Social Studies)

Special Events in May

May Day	May 1
National Teacher Day	May 4
Cinco de Mayo (see May 3)	May 5
Japan Children's Day	May 5
Korea Children's Day	May 5
Lewis and Clark Expedition	May 14
World of Work Week	May 14
Police Officer Memorial Day	May 15
Armed Forces Day	May 15
National Transportation Week	May 20
School Support Staff Week	May 23
Memorial Day	May 31

FEATURED MAY BIRTHDAYS

Leonardo da Vinci (death anniversary) ....May 2	Peter Ilich Tchaikovsky ....May 7	Arnold Lobel ....May 22
Don Wood......................May 4	Edward Lear ....May 12	Margaret Wise Brown ..May 23
Leo Lionni ....May 5	Margaret Rey...............May 16	Sally Ride......................May 26
	Lillian Hoban ....May 18	

Week One: Asian/Pacific American Heritage

🏛 Curriculum Connection: Social Studies

This week's thematic book collection begs to have children use their emerging map and geography skills to locate all the Asian/Pacific countries that are included. The books highlight Japan, China, Korea, Vietnam, and Cambodia and the people who have immigrated from those countries. Children enjoy learning about the cultures of this area. You might want to set out globes and maps to make a geography corner so the students can explore and find these countries on their own.

Be sure to include both fiction and nonfiction in the selections you share with children during this month. Classic stories like *Tikki Tikki Tembo* and *The Seven Chinese Brothers* are fun to share with each generation of children.

A Carp for Kimiko (1996) by Virginia L. Kroll, illustrated by Katherine Roundtree. This story is a fun introduction to the celebration of Children's Day in Japan.

Children of Vietnam (1996) by Marybeth Lorbiecki, photographed by Paul P. Rome. The photo-essays in this book show the daily activities of children in Vietnam as well as tell interesting details of its history and culture.

Colors of Japan (1997) by Holly Littlefield, illustrated by Helen Byers. Explore Japan's history, culture, and landscape through colors.

Count Your Way Through China (1990) by Jim Haskins, illustrated by Dennis Hockerman. Children learn about China and its culture using the numbers one through ten in Chinese.

Count Your Way Through Japan (1988) by Jim Haskins, illustrated by Martin Skoro. Learn about Japan and its culture in this book that presents the numbers one through ten in Japanese.

Count Your Way Through Korea (1993) by Jim Haskins, illustrated by Dennis Hockerman. This book presents concepts about Korea and its culture using the numbers one through ten in Korean.

Crow Boy (1972) written and illustrated by Taro Yashima. This Caldecott Honor Book features a lonely boy in Japan who learns all the calls of the crows on his way to and from school each day.

The Empty Pot (1996) written and illustrated by Demi. Ping wins the emperor's contest by telling the truth.

A Family from Vietnam (1998) written and illustrated by Simon Scoones. The author describes the everyday life of a family of five living in a small village in North Vietnam.

The Funny Little Woman (1977) retold by Arlene Mosel, illustrated by Blair Lent. In this tale set in old Japan, a lively little woman chases a runaway dumpling.

Goodbye, 382 Shin Dang Dong (2002) by Frances and Ginger Park, illustrated by Yangsook Choi. A young Korean girl has a hard time saying good-bye to family and customs when her family moves to America.

Grandfather's Journey (1993) by Allen Say. This autobiographical book describes the author's grandfather, who is torn between love for his native Japan and his adopted home in California where his daughter was born.

Happy Birthday, Mr. Kang (2001) written and illustrated by Susan L. Roth. In this collage-illustrated book about living in two cultures, the author tells the story of a Chinese American retiree, his grandson, and caged birds.

Journey of the Third Seed (2001) by Jane Scoggins Bauld, illustrated by Cynthia G. Darr. In this beautiful book three lotus seeds are found after being lost at sea for a thousand years, and the emperor of Japan sends one to America.

Look What Came from China (1999) by Miles Harvey. The author describes many things, both familiar and unfamiliar, that originally came from China.

Look What Came from Japan (1999) by Miles Harvey. The author describes many things in our lives that originally came from Japan.

A Pair of Red Clogs (2002) by Masako Matsuno, illustrated by Kazue Mizumura. This gorgeously illustrated story tells about a little Japanese girl who breaks her beloved new clogs. What does she do?

The Seven Chinese Brothers (1992) by Margaret Mahy, illustrated by Jean and Mou-Sien Tseng. With humor and wit, the author captures the adventures of seven brothers who use their supernatural gifts against a cruel emperor.

The Story About Ping (1976) by Marjorie Flack, illustrated by Kurt Wiese. This classic story features the adventures of a duckling that lives on a boat on the Yangtze River.

The Story of Chopsticks (2001) by Ying Chang Compestine, illustrated by Yong-Sheng Xuan. Here is a possible explanation of why chopsticks were invented. Notes about the history and use of chopsticks and a recipe for rice pudding are included.

Suki's Kimono (2003) by Chieri Uegaki, illustrated by Stéphane Jorisch. This wonderful story about being yourself also teaches a little about Japanese culture.

Tikki Tikki Tembo (1989) retold by Arlene Mosel, illustrated by Blair Lent. This humorous folktale explains why the Chinese give their children short names.

Two of Everything: A Chinese Folktale (1993) retold and illustrated by Lily Toy Hong. This story with a perfect blend of humor and wisdom describes the adventures of a poor old Chinese farmer who finds a magic pot that doubles or duplicates whatever is placed inside.

May 1

MAY DAY

Since ancient times, people have observed the first of May as the coming of spring with festivals using maypoles and baskets of flowers. In the United States, children often gather spring flowers, place them in handmade paper baskets, and hang them on the doorknobs of relatives and friends. They ring the doorbells and run away, leaving their flowers as a surprise.

Hawaii celebrates this special day as Lei Day, when everyone gives a lei as a gift to another. Some Hawaiian celebrations are complete with pageants, a lei queen, and her court.

Summer (1997) by Gillian Chapman describes some of the holidays that are celebrated around the world in summer, including May Day, and provides instructions for a variety of related craft projects.

Youngsters aged five to eight will enjoy *The Happy Hippopotami* (1992) by Bill Martin, illustrated by Betsy Everitt. This lively, rhyming story about hippopotami dancing around the maypole at the beach makes a perfect read-aloud.

May 2

LEONARDO DA VINCI: DEATH ANNIVERSARY

Leonardo da Vinci, famous artist, scientist, and inventor, died on this day in 1519. He was born in 1452, but the exact date is unknown.

The following books will introduce primary-age children to this famous man: *Leonardo, Beautiful Dreamer* (2003) by Robert Byrd, *Leonardo da Vinci* (2000) by Diane Stanley, *The Life and Work of Leonardo da Vinci* (2001) by Sean Connolly, and *Leonardo da Vinci* (1992) by Ibi Lepscky. Each of these books depicts the many talents of this great man.

Today would be a good time to set up easels and let your students create their own paintings in the style of Leonardo da Vinci. Using *The Last Supper* as a model, the children could try to copy the content.

Since da Vinci had so many talents, your more able students might like to prepare a virtual interview with one student playing da Vinci and another student conducting the interview with a *Sixty Minutes*–type focus.

May 3

PREPARATION FOR CINCO DE MAYO

Use this day to prepare for Cinco de Mayo (May 5). This holiday is more widely celebrated as the Hispanic population grows across the United States. Cinco de Mayo celebrates the defeat of the French army by the Mexican army at Pubela, Mexico, in 1862. The following books will help introduce this holiday to young children: *Cinco de Mayo* (2003) by Aurora Colon Garcia and *Cinco de Mayo* (2001) by Lola M. Schaefer.

Fiesta! (1988) by June Behrens provides songs, poems, and crafts that will help children observe this holiday. There are also recipes and other activities that you can use to have your own Cinco de Mayo celebration.

Today's students are really students of the world and like to learn about other countries. The holidays of those countries provide connections for your social studies curriculum.

May 4

NATIONAL TEACHER DAY

National Teacher Day is celebrated annually on Tuesday of the first full week in May. Use this day to explain to your students why you became a teacher. You may be the one to inspire one or more of them to pursue a teaching career.

DON WOOD: BIRTHDAY

May 4, 1945, is the birthday of Don Wood, best known for his illustrations in books written by his wife, Audrey Wood. *The Napping House* (1984) and *King Bidgood's in the Bathtub* (1985) are two of his best works.

Using *The Napping House* as a model for a cumulative tale, help your students write a class story that involves everyone in the writing and illustration, just like the team of Audrey and Don Wood. Make sure that everyone participates in the project in order to build class pride.

Week Two: Mothers

🏛 Curriculum Connection: Social Studies

In today's society, it takes a great deal of sensitivity to talk with children about their families. A traditional family structure is often not in the majority. Everyone has a mother, but that mother may not live with the child, or some other person may have taken on the mother role. Therefore, it is vital when exploring books about mothers to introduce children to all kinds of mothers in many different situations, both fictional and factual.

Because Brian Hugged His Mother (1999) by David L. Rice, illustrated by K. Dyble Thompson. A chain reaction of kindness spreading through a whole town started because a small boy hugged his mother.

The Best Place to Read (2003) by Debbie Bertram and Susan Bloom, illustrated by Michael Garland. A young child finds that his mother's lap is the perfect place to read his new book.

But Mom, Everyone Else Does (2002) by Kay Winters, illustrated by Doug Cushman. In different languages and households around the world you'll hear children say these words. What's a mom to do?

A Chair for My Mother (1984) written and illustrated by Vera B. Williams. When all their furniture is lost in a fire, a family saves dimes to buy a comfortable armchair.

Come on, Rain! (1999) by Karen Hesse, illustrated by Jon J. Muth. In this beautifully illustrated book, Tess longs for rain to cool the hot summer day in the city.

Even Firefighters Hug Their Moms (2002) by Christine Kole MacLean, illustrated by Mike Reed. An imaginative boy pretends to be a firefighter and other busy people, but takes time to give his mom a hug.

Five Minutes' Peace (1999) written and illustrated by Jill Murphy. Mrs. Large longs for five minutes peace from her energetic family.

George Washington's Mother (1992) by Jean Fritz, illustrated by DyAnne DiSalvo-Ryan. Did you know that George Washington's mother loved to work in her garden and sometimes smoked a pipe?

I Love You Stinky Face (1997) by Lisa McCourt, illustrated by Cyd Moore. A mother assures her son she would still love him even if he were a stinky skunk.

I'll Always Be Your Friend (2001) by Sam McBratney, illustrated by Kim Lewis. A little fox gets angry and tells his mother, "I'm not your friend anymore." But his mother reassures him, "I'll always be your friend."

Just a Minute (2003) by Bonny Becker, illustrated by Jack E. Davis. It seems like days have flown by and months have come and gone as Johnny waits for his mother to finish shopping. How could he spend this time?

Mean Soup (1995) written and illustrated by Betsy Everitt. It has been a bad day for Horace, and he feels very mean until he helps his mother make Mean Soup in this humorous tale.

The Mommy Book (2002) written and illustrated by Todd Parr. With bright colors and funny characters, each page of this delightful picture book describes a mom.

A Mother for Choco (1996) written and illustrated by Keiko Kasza. Choco, a chubby-faced yellow bird with blue-striped feet sets off to find a mother. This is a highly recommended story about adoption for children.

Mother, Mother, I Feel Sick; Send for the Doctor Quick, Quick, Quick (2001) by Remy Charlip and Burton Supree. The doctor cures a stomachache by removing some strange objects from the patient's stomach in this uniquely illustrated book.

Mother's Day Mess (2003) written and illustrated by Karen Gray Ruelle. When Harry and Emily's plans to give their mother a perfect Mother's Day run into some unexpected problems, Dad saves the day.

Mr. Rabbit and the Lovely Present (1977) by Charlotte Zolotow, illustrated by Maurice Sendak. This 1963 Caldecott Honor Book tells how Mr. Rabbit and a little girl find the perfect present for her mother's birthday.

On Mother's Lap (1992) by Ann Herbert Scott, illustrated by Glo Coalson. Mother's lap has room for everyone in this heartwarming and beautifully illustrated story.

31 Uses for a Mom (2003) by Harriet Ziefert, illustrated by Rebecca Doughty. Moms are great at lots of things! Humorous drawings show how children view the world and sing the praises of mothers everywhere.

The Ugly Vegetables (1999) written and illustrated by Grace Lin. A little girl thinks her mother's garden is ugly until she discovers that flowers are pretty, but Chinese vegetable soup is the best of all. A recipe for ugly vegetable soup is included so you can try it for yourself.

What Moms Can't Do (2001) by Douglas Wood, illustrated by Doug Cushman. There are lots of things that moms can't do. They can't wait to wake kids up in the morning, they can't sit very long without someone on their lap, and they can't let go of a hug without a kiss.

May 5

LEO LIONNI: BIRTHDAY

Besides being Cinco de Mayo (see May 3), this day is the birthday of author and illustrator Leo Lionni. He was born in 1910 and died in 1999. During his life, he wrote and illustrated more than thirty books. Two of his works, *Frederick* (1973) and *Inch by Inch* (1994), were Caldecott Honor Books. He is best remembered for *Little Blue and Little Yellow* (1994), which provides the backdrop for lessons on color mixing in art and the color spectrum in science.

CHILDREN'S DAY—JAPAN AND KOREA

May 5 is a national holiday in Japan and Korea. Two good resources are *Japanese Children's Day and the Obon Festival* (1997) by Dianne M. MacMillan, which describes the significance of this holiday and the ways it is celebrated in Japan and the United States, and *Korean Children's Day* (1992) by Ruth Suyenaga, which contains many resources such as foods, songs, and games that are traditional for Korean Children's Day.

May 7

PETER ILICH TCHAIKOVSKY: BIRTHDAY

May 7 is the birthday of both Johannes Brahms and Peter Tchaikovsky. Brahms was born in 1833 and died in 1897, while Tchaikovsky was born in 1840 and died in 1893.

The best resource on Brahms for primary children is a biography of the great German composer with emphasis on his childhood and early musical training: *Brahms* (1993) by Ann Rachlin, illustrated by Susan Hellard.

Tchaikovsky, a Russian composer, is best known to children for his music in the ballet *The Nutcracker*. Ann Rachlin and Susan Hellard also wrote and illustrated a biography about him: *Tchaikovsky* (1993).

Children's books and other language arts resources such as films will foster music appreciation. Music can be used during social studies time to complement the content of your other lessons, but remember to keep the listening time short enough to be enjoyable.

A composer's birthday is a good time to introduce classical music that may be a new experience for your students.

May 12

EDWARD LEAR: BIRTHDAY

Today is the birthday of Edward Lear, an English artist and author who was born in 1812 and died in 1888. He is most remembered for his children's book, *The Owl and the Pussycat*. Written in the mid-1800s, it has become a classic that is still enjoyed today. Lines from this nonsensical romance between an owl and a pussycat are often quoted. The 1996 version, illustrated by Jan Brett, is an instant hit with young children.

Edward Lear is also famous for limericks and other humorous poetry he wrote for primary-age children. His *Poetry for Young People* (2001) has twenty poems that will be enjoyed by third- and fourth-grade students. This book and others from Lear are good models for students to use in creating their own limericks. Because limericks are only five lines long, they make a great individual writing project. How about a limerick about the current topic in math?

May 14

LEWIS AND CLARK EXPEDITION

More than two hundred years ago on this date, the Lewis and Clark expedition set out from St. Louis, Missouri, to find a route to the Pacific Ocean. Many resources have been developed to commemorate this thirty-three-member expedition. One unique resource is *Cooking on the Lewis and Clark Expedition* (1999) of the Exploring History through Simple Recipes series by Mary Gunderson. This book can also be used for other units on early American history or social studies units on pioneer life.

Lewis and Clark for Kids: Their Journey of Discovery with 21 Activities (2000) by Janis Herbert provides several projects that use map skills, botany concepts, and other topics to make the study of American history more interesting to children.

WORLD OF WORK WEEK

During the month of May, many days are set aside to celebrate community workers. *The Work We Do* (2002) by David Conrad is a good introduction to a variety of workers, including teachers, bus drivers, police officers, firefighters, doctors, nurses, veterinarians, writers, scientists, factory and construction workers, and architects.

Week Three: World of Work

🏛 Curriculum Connection: Social Studies

For primary-age children, work is a place Mom, Dad, or both go while they are in school. They have limited knowledge of community workers such as police officers, doctors, postal workers, nurses, and garbage removal personnel. The following books aim at introducing children to the many options open to them as they begin to think about what they want to do when they grow up.

Ask Nurse Pfaff, She'll Help You! (1998) by Alice K. Flanagan, photographs by Christine Osinski. Easy-to-understand text and large full-color photographs help illustrate a nurse's job in a hospital taking care of patients.

The Beeman (2002) by Laurie Krebs, illustrated by Melissa Iwai. This story introduces beekeeping equipment and explains the harvesting of honey to youngsters using rhymes and colorful illustrations.

Big Jimmy's Kum Kau Chinese Take Out (2001) written and illustrated by Ted Lewin. The sights, sounds, and smells of a busy Chinese take-out restaurant are experienced from the viewpoint of the owner's young son.

Community Helpers from A to Z (1997) by Bobbie Kalman, illustrated by Niki Walker. This lavishly illustrated alphabet book includes such community helpers as police officers and veterinarians.

A Day in the Life of a Builder (2001) Jobs People Do series by Linda Hayward. What does a builder concentrate on while working?

A Day in the Life of a Coach (2001) by Mary Bowman-Kruhm, illustrated by Claudine G. Wirths. The author describes Coach Jackson's work as both a gym teacher *and* a football coach.

A Day in the Life of a Doctor (2001) Jobs People Do series by Linda Hayward. A mother brings her little girl in to see Doctor Mills. What is wrong?

A Day in the Life of a Firefighter (2001) Jobs People Do series by Linda Hayward. How does a firefighter begin the day?

A Day in the Life of a Musician (2001) Jobs People Do series by Linda Hayward. Tonight Jane Lee will play a violin solo at the concert hall. Will the audience like it?

A Day in the Life of a Teacher (2001) Jobs People Do series by Linda Hayward. How does a teacher prepare for class?

A Day in the Life of a TV Reporter (2001) Jobs People Do series by Linda Hayward. Will Mark Garcia's story about the river cleanup make the six o'clock news?

Exploring Parks with Ranger Dockett (1997) by Alice K. Flanagan, photographs by Christine Osinski. This typical day of an urban park ranger shows him tending to the plants and animals in his care and teaching people about the park.

Farming (1990) written and illustrated by Gail Gibbons. Simple text and illustrations present real-life activities on a farm through the various seasons.

Fire! Fire! Hurry! Hurry! (2003) by Andrea Zimmerman, illustrated by Karen Barbour. The alarm rings often as the hungry firefighters sit down to eat. It's a busy night at the fire station.

Garbage Collectors (2000) by Paulette Bourgeois, illustrated by Kim LaFave. Children will be fascinated with this in-depth look at the everyday duties of garbage collectors.

I Want to Be an Astronaut (1999) by Stephanie Maze. Filled with excellent photographs, this book describes the education and training required to be an astronaut.

I Want to Be a Chef (1999) by Stephanie Maze. This book describes some of the careers in the culinary arts, such as master chef, executive chef, pastry chef, and prep chef.

I Want to Be a Doctor (2000) by Dan Liebman. Visits to a doctor's office and a hospital are described in this basic introduction to the medical profession.

I Want to Be a Police Officer (2000) by Dan Liebman. The author stresses how police officers enjoy helping people.

I Want to Be a Teacher (2001) by Dan Liebman. With color photographs; this book shows elementary teachers instructing students in actual school settings.

I Want to Be a Truck Driver (2001) by Dan Liebman. Truck driver is the career of choice in this realistic overview of the day-to-day tasks of these hardworking people.

I Want to Be a Zookeeper (2003) by Dan Liebman. Partnering with the Toronto Zoo, the author has produced an excellent book that shows zookeepers interacting with the animals in their daily routines.

If I Were President (1999) by Catherine Stier, illustrated by Dyanne Disalvo-Ryan. This easy-to-read picture book provides a nice introduction to the presidency for primary-age children.

My Dad's Job (2003) by Peter Glassman, illustrated by Timothy Bush. A young boy imagines all the fun his dad must have at work every day.

The Night Worker (2000) by Kate Banks, illustrated by Georg Hallensleben. Alex's father is an engineer who works at night. One night, he has a surprise for Alex—a hard hat. For that night, Alex gets to be a night worker just like Papa.

Richard Scarry's Busy, Busy Town (1994) written and illustrated by Richard Scarry. Welcome to Busytown, where everyone is on their way to work. The author describes jobs and professions that keep this busy town running.

Tonka: Working Hard with the Mighty Loader (1993) by Justine Korman, illustrated by Steven James Petruccio. Steve and his Mighty Loader have a busy week digging ditches, leveling dirt, and building a new road.

Yippee-Yay! A Book About Cowboys and Cowgirls (1998) written and illustrated by Gail Gibbons. This book tells about the work and lifestyle of cowboys and cowgirls in the Old West.

May 15

POLICE OFFICER MEMORIAL DAY
May 15 is celebrated as Police Officer Memorial Day, commemorating the many officers who have died protecting people in every type of community. The week containing May 15 is designated as National Police Week and National Emergency Medical Services Week. The resources in the Week Three thematic listing for World of Work will be of value as your students explore these and other important jobs they may want to pursue.

A Day in the Life of a Police Officer (2001) by Linda Hayward gives a realistic view of the day-to-day work of a police officer.

ARMED FORCES DAY
May 15 has also been designated Armed Forces Day by Presidential Proclamation since 1950. It is dedicated to the men and women who serve in the military. *Pilot Mom* (2003) by Kathleen Benner Duble, illustrated by Alan Marks, is an excellent resource to discuss children's fears when their parents or relatives serve in the armed forces.

May 16

MARGARET REY: BIRTHDAY
Curious George is one of the most beloved characters in children's literature and is known throughout the world. Margaret Rey—who was born on May 16, 1906, and died on December 21, 1996—wrote the Curious George stories, and her husband, H. A. Rey, illustrated them. Children identify with all the trouble that Curious George gets into, while adults identify with the work the monkey creates for the man with the yellow hat.

These books are best read in the original format. The more recent ones by other writers lack the charm of those authored by Margaret Rey. After reading several Curious George stories, your students can discuss what it is about George that makes him so likable. Primary students are developing writers, and with guidance, they should be able to write a character description.

May 18

LILLIAN HOBAN: BIRTHDAY

Lillian Hoban, author and illustrator, was born on May 18, 1925, and died in 1998. Lillian illustrated the popular Frances book series written by her husband, Russell Hoban. She also did illustrations for other authors such as James Howe—*The Day the Teacher Went Bananas* (1987)—and wrote and illustrated many books on her own. A good example of her work is *Joe and Betsy the Dinosaur* (1996).

After reading one of the Frances books, pair up your students to write and illustrate another adventure for Frances. One student might be the illustrator while the other one might be the author, or they may both do part of each job. This project can also be used for enrichment, while connecting the art of illustration with the art of writing a good story. *Bread and Jam for Frances* (1986) is a good resource.

May 20

NATIONAL TRANSPORTATION WEEK

National Transportation Week is reserved for the week that contains the third Friday of May. The thematic listing for Week Four this month has many resources that can be used for studying transportation and vehicles as part of science, social studies, art, westward migration, immigration, history, and inventions. Connections between the books, curriculum, and standards are many and varied. For example, the concept of transportation as getting from one place to another can be introduced to very young students with the book *Bunnies on the Go: Getting from Place to Place* (2003) by Rick Walton, illustrated by Paige Miglio. A bunny family takes a trip using many different types of transportation, including a car, a train, a balloon, a ferry, and a tractor.

The transportation theme can be expanded to encompass more than just the third week in May. Some teachers use transportation as a unifying theme for a summer session or even for a whole year. Thematic teaching can be an exciting way to present all strands of a primary curriculum.

Week Four: Vehicles/Transportation

✳ ⛫ Curriculum Connection: Science and Social Studies

How do goods such as food and paper get from the place they are grown or manufactured to the child in front of you? How do people get from one place to another? These topics are explored in this week's titles. The variety of vehicles and types of transportation lends itself to categorization—vehicles that go on land, transportation for fresh food, emergency vehicles, and so on. In turn, categorizing builds thinking skills, language art skills, and vocabulary skills.

The Airplane Alphabet Book (1999) by Jerry Pallotta and Fred Stillwell, illustrated by Rob Bolster. This alphabet book presents realistic illustrations and interesting facts about different kinds of airplanes.

Ambulances (2001) by Anne E. Hanson. This book describes ambulances and the responsibilities of emergency medical teams who ride in them.

The Best Book of Trains (1999) written and illustrated by Richard Balkwill. With its fast-action text and detailed, full-color illustrations, this lively book introduces trains from all over the world.

Bicycle Book (1995) written and illustrated by Gail Gibbons. In this engaging picture book, the history of bicycles, the science behind the design, descriptions of different types, maintenance, and safety rules are clearly and simply presented.

Big Book of Airplanes (2001) by Caroline Bingham. This book provides a fascinating look at flying machines.

Big Book of Monster Machines (1998) by Caroline Bingham. Large machines such as trucks, jets, supertankers, tractors, bulldozers, and fire engines are described in a way that even the most reluctant reader will enjoy.

Big Book of Rescue Vehicles (2000) by Caroline Bingham. Children will delight in the photographs of these rescue vehicles in action taking care of emergencies.

Big Joe's Trailer Truck (1974) written and illustrated by Joe Mathieu. Simple text and illustrations follow a truck driver through a typical day.

Big Wheels (2003) by Anne Rockwell. This introduction to a variety of large-wheeled vehicles is filled with bright watercolor illustrations and descriptive text.

The Caboose Who Got Loose (1980) written and illustrated by Bill Peet. Katy Caboose hates being on the back of a long freight train. One day when the train hits a bump, Katy's coupling breaks and she is free. Find out what happens to her in this exciting book.

Dirt Movers (1995) by Bobbie D. Kalman, illustrated by Petrina Gentile. Packed with full-color photos of vehicles in action, this book discusses what various construction machines do.

Extreme Machines on Land (1999) by Patricia and David Armentrout. The authors describe some unusual land vehicles, such as all-terrain vehicles, tanks, and solar cars.

Fighting Fires (1999) by Susan Kuklin. Vehicles, equipment, and procedures used by firefighters are presented in this action-packed photo-essay. Tips on fire safety are also included.

Fireboat: The Heroic Adventures of the John J. Harvey (2002) by Maira Kalman. The inspiring, true story of the *John J. Harvey*—a retired New York City fireboat reinstated on September 11, 2001, addresses the tragic events that occurred that day in easy-to-understand language for children.

Green Cars: Earth-Friendly Electric Vehicles (1994) written and illustrated by John Coughlan. This book features exotic and unusual vehicles available today as well as a glimpse of the cars of the future.

I Stink! (2002) by Kate and Jim McMullan. A big-city garbage truck makes its rounds in this lively alphabet book, which was the *New York Times Book Review* Best Illustrated Children's Book of 2002.

I'm Mighty! (2003) by Kate McMullan, illustrated by Jim McMullan. A little tugboat has the big job of bringing large ships into the harbor.

The Little Engine That Could (1990) by Watty Piper, illustrated by George and Doris Hauman. This children's classic tells the story of a little blue engine that pulls a stranded train full of toys over the mountain.

Maybelle, the Cable Car (1997) written and illustrated by Virginia Lee Burton. Maybelle loves to carry people up and down the hilly streets of San Francisco in this story of actual events in the city's effort to keep the cable cars running.

Mike Mulligan and His Steam Shovel (1976) written and illustrated by Virginia Lee Burton. Mike Mulligan proves that his beautiful red steam shovel, Mary Anne, is still useful. Although it was first published in 1939, this classic has never lost its appeal.

1-2-3 Draw Cars, Trucks and Other Vehicles (2001) by Freddie Levin. Starting with simple shapes, children can create cars, trucks, construction equipment, and emergency vehicles using the tips offered in this book.

This Boat (2001) written and illustrated by Paul Collicutt. All kinds of boats are celebrated using full-color renderings of marine vessels from around the world throughout history.

This Is the Way We Go to School (1992) by Edith Baer, illustrated by Steve Björkman. Jaunty rhymed couplets tell the informative story of the many different modes of transportation children all over the world use to get to school.

This Plane (2002) by Paul Collicutt. Simple text and full-color illustrations celebrate different types of airplanes and the work they do.

Trucks: Giants of the Highway (1999) by Ken Robbins. Huge and powerful trucks roar across the pages of this photo-essay.

May 22

ARNOLD LOBEL: BIRTHDAY
Arnold Lobel—who was born on May 22, 1933, and died in 1987—was the author and illustrator of the Frog and Toad series. He also won the Caldecott Medal for his book *Fables*. Several different projects can be based on Lobel's books.

Because his works are a blend of picture book and chapter book, they make a great transitional read from the simpler form to the more complex. The universal appeal of the characters provides discussion points for developing the comprehension skill of characterization and for character-description writing assignments.

The Caldecott winner *Fables* is a definitive work of the genre for young children. It provides opportunities for classroom discussions of morals and their application today. Ask older primary-age children to write modern-day fables to match the morals in Lobel's *Fables*.

May 23

MARGARET WISE BROWN: BIRTHDAY
Margaret Wise Brown—who was born on May 23, 1910, and died in 1952—wrote *Goodnight Moon* (1976) and *The Runaway Bunny* (1977), both illustrated by Clement Hurd. These books have become classics due to the soothing nature of the stories. Most students probably know these books from their preschool days. After a quick review of both books, initiate a discussion about what makes a book a classic. A list of other classics and what classics have in common helps develop student literacy. Critical evaluation of stories is a skill that needs much practice. Students need guidance to become adept at knowing the difference between trash and treasures.

SCHOOL SUPPORT STAFF WEEK
The fourth week in May is school support staff week. This is a perfect time to have your students write letters of appreciation to those who work at your school but are not teachers or administrators.

May 26

SALLY RIDE: BIRTHDAY

The first American woman in space, Sally Ride was born on May 26, 1951. She was a competitive tennis player and astrophysicist before she became famous as a female astronaut on her space trip in 1983. *Sally Ride* (2003) by Pamela Hill Nettleton, illustrated by Jeff Yesh, is a brief biography that highlights some important events in her life.

Dr. Ride has written two books for children herself, *Exploring Our Solar System* (for ages ten to twelve) and *To Space and Back* (for ages seven to eleven).

As a class writing project, ask your students to make a list of questions they would like to ask Dr. Ride or write a paragraph on what they think it would feel like to be in space.

May 31

MEMORIAL DAY

Memorial Day is celebrated on the last Monday in May and is sometimes known as Decoration Day because of the tradition of decorating the graves of servicemen. The flag flies at half-staff until noon and a Presidential Proclamation asks citizens to pray for peace.

There are several books about Memorial Day for primary-age students. *Memorial Day* (2002) by Jacqueline Cotton, Katharine Kane, and Nanci Vargus introduces the history of Memorial Day and describes how it is observed. *Memorial Day* (2000) by Helen Frost explains how and why Memorial Day became a holiday. *Memorial Day Surprise* (2004) by Theresa Golding is about a young boy who is surprised to see his grandfather marching with the veterans in the Memorial Day parade.

As an art project, ask your students to draw what they have learned from these books about Memorial Day.

May Reading Strategy

Into and Through

Into and Through is a two-pronged approach to helping readers understand and appreciate a written literary work. *Into* refers to the connections readers make to their prior knowledge about the topic before reading or listening to it. *Through* refers to the discussions and other comprehension strategies used during the reading of the story (see June Reading Strategy).

The Into phase of this strategy takes place before the literary work is shared. For example, in the book *The Seven Chinese Brothers* (1992) by Margaret Mahy, the adult would direct the children to look at the cover art and then discuss what the book might be about—predicting the characters and setting. Who will be in the story? What will they do? Where will the story take place? Will the story be real or fictional? Follow-up questions should elicit any other information the students have that can connect to that particular book. Has anyone ever been to China? How many brothers do the students have? What do you think might happen to the brothers in this story? Has anyone ever heard this story before?

At this point, the students should have many unanswered questions that form the basis for curiosity and engagement with the story as it is read. This Into step can be expanded depending on the amount of time and background knowledge needed for the children to comprehend the work. This background knowledge increases reading comprehension.

The Into portion of this strategy becomes more important when sharing a nonfiction book with children. The adult needs to understand how much knowledge the children have regarding a topic. Do they know everything about a fire engine, or have they never seen a fire engine up close? Depending on the need, the adult should spend from five to twenty minutes activating enough prior knowledge to build comprehension in a book about fire engines.

June at a Glance

*It's not what is poured into a child that
counts, but what is planted.*
—**Linda Conway**

June Reading Tip: Take time to talk about the illustrations after reading a book to children. They may have been so engaged in the story that they missed the exceptional pictures.

JUNE HIGHLIGHTS
National Dairy Month
Extra Cheese, Please! Mozzarella's Journey from Cow to Pizza (1995) by Cris Peterson, illustrated by Alvis Upitis, begins with the birth of a calf and ends with a pizza recipe. This is a good introduction to dairying.

National Safety Month
School Safety (1996) by Nancy Loewen, illustrated by Penny Dann, offers rules for behaving in a safe way in the classroom, during recess, and riding the school bus.

National Rivers Month
America's Top 10 Rivers (1997) by Jenny Tesar features ten unique rivers in the United States, including the Mississippi, Yukon, and Rio Grande.

National Rose Month
Roses (1998) by John Prevost describes the varieties of the most popular flowers in the world.

National Little League Baseball Week
We Love Baseball! (2003), written and illustrated by Peggy Harrison, introduces readers to a team of exuberant seven-year-olds who demonstrate that anyone who plays is a winner.

Helen Keller Deaf-Blind Awareness Week
Helen Keller: Courage in the Dark (1997) by Johanna Hurwitz, illustrated by Neverne Covington, is a biography of the blind and deaf girl who overcame both handicaps with the help of a very special teacher, Annie Sullivan.

June Reading Strategy: Into and Through

WEEKLY THEMES AND CURRICULUM CONNECTIONS
Week One: Wordplay/National Spelling Bee Finals (Language Arts)
Week Two: Cows (Science)
Week Three: Fathers (Social Studies)
Week Four: Native Americans (Social Studies)

Special Events in June

National Spelling Bee Finals	June 2
National Dairy Month	June 6
National Flag Week/Flag Day	June 14
Citizenship for Native Americans	June 15
Father's Day	June 19
Summer Solstice	June 20
Deaf-Blind Awareness Week	June 27

FEATURED JUNE BIRTHDAYS

Paul Galdone	June 2	Jacques Cousteau	June 11	Robert Kraus	June 21
Anita Lobel	June 3	Robert Munsch	June 11	Wilma Rudolph	June 23
Verna Aardema	June 6	Bruce Degen	June 14	Eric Carle	June 25
Paul Gauguin	June 7	Pat Hutchins	June 18	Charlotte Zolotow	June 26
Maurice Sendak	June 10	Chris Van Allsburg	June 18	Helen Keller	June 27

Week One: Wordplay/National Spelling Bee Finals

📖 Curriculum Connection: Language Arts

The National Spelling Bee finals are held Wednesday and Thursday of the week that includes Memorial Day. The following list includes resources on the various kinds of fun to be had with words and vocabulary development.

Young children love playing with words—rhyming them, substituting beginning or ending sounds, and especially making up new words to suit new meanings. They are curious and ask questions such as "How did spaghetti get its name?"

A—My Name Is Alice (1987) by Jane Bayer, illustrated by Steven Kellogg. This well-known jump rope ditty is built on the letters of the alphabet and is illustrated with animals.

Anna Banana: 101 Jump Rope Rhymes (1989) by Joanna Cole, illustrated by Alan Tiegreen. This illustrated collection of jump rope rhymes is arranged according to the type of jumping they are meant to accompany.

Can You Hear Me from Here? (2002) by Amanda Rondeau. The author introduces homophones through photographs and simple text.

A Chocolate Moose for Dinner (1988) written and illustrated by Fred Gwynne. The author keeps children of all ages laughing with hilarious wordplay and zany humor.

Dogs Don't Wear Sneakers (1996) by Laura Joffe Numeroff, illustrated by Joe Mathieu. Explore the many ways humans differ from our furry, feathered, and finny friends.

Eight Ate: A Feast of Homonym Riddles (1982) by Marvin Terban, illustrated by Giulio Maestro. This collection of original riddles from a bare bear to a foul fowl keeps children laughing as they learn.

Ellsworth's Extraordinary Electric Ears and Other Amazing Alphabet Anecdotes (2003) written and illustrated by Valorie Fisher. Explore twenty-six amazing and outlandish alphabet worlds where every picture tells a tale.

Fred Read the Red Book (2002) by Pam Scheunemann and **Fruit Trees Produce Produce** (2002) by Carey Molter. Both of these books use simple text and photographs to introduce homophones.

Green Eggs and Ham (1976) written and illustrated by Dr. Seuss. The author turns fifty simple words into magic in this classic.

A Hole Is to Dig (1972) by Ruth Krauss, illustrated by Maurice Sendak. This book is filled with funny definitions that explain things from faces to books.

Hop on Pop (1976) written and illustrated by Dr. Seuss. Pairs of rhyming words are used in simple sentences accompanied by humorous illustrations.

In a Pickle and Other Funny Idioms (1983) by Marvin Terban, illustrated by Giulio Maestro. This book explains and illustrates thirty popular expressions, such as "straight from the horse's mouth."

Jambo Means Hello: Swahili Alphabet Book (1981) by Muriel Feelings, illustrated by Tom Feelings. This is an introduction not only to the letters of the alphabet but also to a language and culture in Africa. A map of Africa is also included.

The King Who Rained (1975) written and illustrated by Fred Gwynne. A little girl pictures the things her parents talk about, such as a king who rained, bear feet, and the foot prince in the snow.

Kites Sail High (1998) written and illustrated by Ruth Heller. This is a celebration of verbs of all kinds in bold illustrations and playful rhymes.

Little Pigeon Toad (1990) written and illustrated by Fred Gwynne. The author uses homonyms and figures of speech to create this engaging, rib-tickling collection of word-and-picture jokes that is sure to delight readers.

Miss Alaineus: A Vocabulary Disaster (2000) written and illustrated by Debra Frasier. When Sage misunderstands one of the teacher's vocabulary words in her assignment, she is embarrassed in front of her classmates. Sage uses her mistake as inspiration for the vocabulary parade. The author provides information about staging a vocabulary parade in your school on her website (frasierbooks.com).

The Moon in the Man (2003) written and illustrated by Elizabeth Honey. This funny, warm-hearted picture book offers a fresh set of lively nonsense rhymes that allow children to discover the joy of language.

Mouse Makes Magic (2002) by Kathryn Heling and Deborah Hembrook, illustrated by Patrick Joseph. This story demonstrates how Mouse magically transforms words into totally new ones by changing their middle vowels.

One Whole Doughnut, One Doughnut Hole (1991) written and illustrated by Valjean McLenighan. This book introduces homophones, which are words that sound the same but have different meanings and usually different spellings.

Pete Presents the Presents (2002) by Carey Molter and **Sam Has a Sundae on Sunday** (2002) by Pam Scheunemann. Both books use simple text and photographs to introduce the concept of homophones.

Pocketful of Nonsense (2003) written and illustrated by James Marshall. This is a collection of humorous old favorites and original rhymes, limericks, and poems.

Richard Scarry's Best Little Word Book Ever! (1980). This introduction to new and familiar names for objects grouped by subject, theme, and setting is excellent for English as a second language learners as well as youngsters learning to read.

See the Yak Yak (1999) by Charles Ghigna, illustrated by Brian Lies. Humorous homonyms provide fun for young readers.

Take Me Out of the Bathtub and Other Silly Dilly Songs (2001) by Alan Katz, illustrated by David Catrow. Here are well-known songs, such as "Oh Susannah" and "Row, Row, Row Your Boat," with new words such as "I'm So Carsick" and "Go, Go, Go to Bed."

Taking a Walk: A Book in Two Languages (1994) written and illustrated by Rebecca Emberley. Simple phrases and bold, colorful images present basic words in both Spanish and English.

Ten Apples Up on Top (1976) written and illustrated by Dr. Seuss. This ingenious funny story in rhyme uses a vocabulary of only seventy-five different words.

There Was an Old Lady Who Swallowed a Fly (1997) written and illustrated by Simms Taback. Illustrated with die cut artwork, this is a rollicking, eye-popping version of the well-loved known poem.

There's a Wocket in My Pocket! (1974) written and illustrated by Dr. Seuss. A household of unusual creatures helps readers recognize common "household" words.

There's an Ant in Anthony (1992) written and illustrated by Bernard Most. After discovering an "ant" in his own name, Anthony searches for the word *ant* in other words.

June 2

PAUL GALDONE: BIRTHDAY
Paul Galdone, children's author and illustrator, was born in Budapest on June 2, 1914. He is best known for the books he both wrote and illustrated—*The Little Red Hen* (1991) and *Henny Penny* (1984). Children relate to the animal characters in both of these stories as they make mistakes and arrive at the wrong conclusions.

George Washington's Breakfast (1998) by Jean Fritz is a book that Paul Galdone illustrated. Older primary students might analyze how the illustrations in all three of Galdone's books are alike and how they differ.

NATIONAL SPELLING BEE FINALS
The National Spelling Bee finals are held in Washington, D.C., the Wednesday and Thursday after Memorial Day. Therefore, June is a great month to focus on spelling bees and other forms of wordplay. Jump rope rhymes, spelling bees, and silly stories about words and their meanings are three ways to "jazz up" the end of the school year. The book list for Week One contains several books of jump rope rhymes and other fun activities involving words.

June 3

ANITA LOBEL: BIRTHDAY
Anita Lobel was born in Poland on June 3, 1934, and is both an illustrator and an author. She received a Caldecott Honor in 1982 for her illustrations in *On Market Street* (1989), a very interesting alphabet book that tells a story (written by her husband, Arnold Lobel) and contains very intricate pictures. It is interesting to note that Anita Lobel was a fabric designer before she was a children's book illustrator.

Lobel also wrote and illustrated *One Lighthouse, One Moon* (2002). In this book a cat named Nini introduces the days of the week, the months of the year, and numbers one to ten.

June 6

NATIONAL DAIRY MONTH

June has been designated National Dairy Month since 1937. The month is set aside to pay tribute to the vital role that milk and other dairy products play in the American diet and economy. The Week Two book list on cows (both real and imaginary) will help students learn about these animals and explain the various processes involved in bringing milk to the table. *Extra Cheese, Please! Mozzarella's Journey from Cow to Pizza* (1995) by Cris Peterson includes many interesting facts as well as a recipe for pizza.

VERNA AARDEMA: BIRTHDAY

Verna Aardema was born on June 6, 1911, and died in 2000. She is best known for her retellings of African folktales. Her stories—such as *Bringing the Rain to Kapiti Plain* (1983), illustrated by Beatriz Vidal—combine humor, magic, and adventure to tell the truths of African tribal life. She won a Caldecott Medal in 1976 for *Why Mosquitoes Buzz in People's Ears: A West African Tale*, illustrated by Leo and Diane Dillon.

June 7

PAUL GAUGUIN: BIRTHDAY

It is never too early to introduce children to famous artists and their works. Usually children have strong opinions as to what they like and don't like about a piece of art. They enjoy giving their opinions and, with encouragement, will relate how a particular painting makes them feel.

Paul Gauguin, the French painter, was born in 1848 on June 7 and died in 1903 before his work had gained worldwide recognition. The following children's books give a look at Gauguin's life and his paintings. *Paul Gauguin: Art for Children* (1988) by Ernest Raboff gives a brief biography and has analyses of several of his works. *Paul Gauguin* (2002), written and illustrated by Paul Flux, presents a brief overview of the life of the artist and several examples of his more famous works.

Week Two: Cows

❊ Curriculum Connection: Science

June is National Dairy Month, which prompted this thematic collection of books on cows. Both fiction and nonfiction resources are provided. The process of getting dairy products from the farm to the dinner table is fascinating to children once they understand that milk is not made in a milk carton plant.

Curriculum connections can be made to nutritional health, allergies, Louis Pasteur, milk-processing technology, categorizing dairy products and groups of milk-producing animals, report writing on various aspects of the dairy industry, creative writing using a dairy cow as the main character, or graphing the class's favorite flavor of ice cream.

And the Cow Said Moo! (2000) by Mildred Phillips, illustrated by Sonja Lamut. A cow questions why the other animals don't say "moo." This rollicking barnyard tale makes for a great read-aloud.

Click, Clack, Moo: Cows That Type (2000) by Doreen Cronin, illustrated by Betsy Lewin. Come join the fun as Farmer Brown's cows type him notes demanding changes on the farm.

Cock-a-Doodle-Moo! (1996) written and illustrated by Bernard Most. What happens when the rooster loses its voice and asks the cow for help to wake everybody?

Cow (1998) by Jules Older, illustrated by Lyn Severance. This humorous book presents everything you want to know about cows.

Cow (2002) by Malachy Doyle, illustrated by Angelo Rinaldi. Follow a day in the life of a dairy cow in this leisurely paced picture book.

Cow Makes a Difference (2001) written and illustrated by Todd Aaron Smith. This humorously illustrated book is full of silly fun and simple truth.

The Cow That Went Oink (1990) by Bernard Most. This tale of tolerance and friendship teaches kids that it's OK to be different and sometimes it's even fun.

The Cow Who Wouldn't Come Down (2002) written and illustrated by Paul Brett Johnson. Gertrude the cow has a mind of her own and takes up a new hobby. Now her owner has a problem. How do you milk a flying cow?

Cows (1990) by Lynn M. Stone. The author presents in-depth information on the life of cows.

Cows (2000) by Rachel Bell. The author describes the life of cows on a dairy farm. She also discusses the various products obtained from cows.

A Cow's Alfalfa-Bet (2003) by Woody Jackson. This beautiful alphabet book transports readers to the dairy farms of Vermont.

The Cows Are Going to Paris (2002) by David Kirby and Allen Woodman, illustrated by Chris L. Demarest. When the cows grow tired of the fields, they take a trip to Paris.

Cows Have Calves (2000) by Lynn M. Stone. Presented in a simple question-and-answer format, this book is an introduction to the life cycle of cattle.

Daisy the Dancing Cow (2003) written and illustrated by Viki Woodworth. Daisy can stomp, hop, and step with the best and saves the show on opening night when one of the original dancers is injured.

Farmer McPeepers and His Missing Cows (2003) by Kathy Duffield, illustrated by Steve Gray. Farmer McPeepers' cows borrow his eyeglasses so they can have a little vacation.

From Calf to Cow (2002) by Jillian Powell. The author gives readers a well-rounded view of each cow species. Videos and websites listed for further information are appropriate for young students.

George Washington's Cows (1994) written and illustrated by David Small. These humorous rhymes about George Washington's farm where the cows wear dresses, the pigs wear wigs, and the sheep are scholars, suggests the reason he went into politics.

Grady's in the Silo (2003) by Una Belle Townsend, illustrated by Bob Artley. Based on an actual event that occurred in 1949, this is the story of a Hereford cow that got stuck in the silo of a farm in Yukon, Oklahoma. But how does she get out?

Herd of Cows! Flock of Sheep! (2002) by Rick Walton, illustrated by Julie Hansen Olson. Farmer Brown has just finished harvesting his crops and is so tired he sleeps through a heavy rain and rising water. The animals work together to save him. This is a good vocabulary lesson on groups.

How Now, Brown Cow? (1994) by Alice Schertle, illustrated by Amanda Schaffer. This is a delightful collection of poems about cows.

How to Speak Moo! (2002) written and illustrated by Deborah Fayerman. This silly book about cows is sure to make kids giggle. It explains how the cows do the high moo and the low moo, the bumpy moo and the jumpy moo.

Kiss the Cow! (2003) by Phyllis Root, illustrated by Will Hillenbrand. How does Mama May coax daily buckets of milk from the cow? It's time to pucker up!

Metropolitan Cow (1999) written and illustrated by Tim Egan. Bennett, a lonely calf, makes friends with his neighbor, a young pig named Webster. According to Bennett's parents, cows do not associate with pigs. This little tale of integration shows how Bennett and Webster change the status quo.

The Milk Makers (1986) written and illustrated by Gail Gibbons. This author explains where milk comes from and how it is processed.

Two Cool Cows (1997) by Toby Speed, illustrated by Barry Root. Millie and Maude are two cool cows who fly to the moon and back in search of fresh grass and a chance to do the bunny hop.

When Bluebell Sang (1992) written and illustrated by Lisa Campbell Ernst. A singing cow's talent brings her stardom, but she just wants to be back at the farm.

When Cows Come Home (1993) by David Lee Harrison, illustrated by Chris L. Demarest. It's when the farmer isn't looking that the fun begins. His herd of cows rides bicycles, square dance, swim, and more in this rhyming picture book.

June 10

MAURICE SENDAK: BIRTHDAY

Maurice Sendak, born on June 10, 1928, is best known for his book *Where the Wild Things Are* (1976). This book won the Caldecott Medal in 1964. Some critics thought the book was too frightening for young children, but it has remained a favorite. *In the Night Kitchen* (1995) was also a Caldecott Honor Book but has not retained the popularity of *Where the Wild Things Are.*

It is interesting to note that Sendak began his drawing career while he was still in school, with an after-school job drawing backgrounds for comic books. Later on he went to art school and illustrated his first book for author Marcel Ayme in 1951.

Chicken Soup with Rice (1990), a little book of poetry about the months of the year, is charming: "Each month is gay, each season is nice, when eating chicken soup with rice."

June 11

JACQUES COUSTEAU: BIRTHDAY

Jacques Cousteau was born on this day in 1910 and died in 1997. He purchased his ship, the *Calypso*, in 1950, making it into a floating sea laboratory and film studio. He wrote many books during his adventurous life and also produced films and television shows that opened up the wonders of the sea to a large audience.

Jacques Cousteau: Man of the Oceans (1990) by Carol Greene, illustrated by Steven Dobson, is a simple biography of this oceanographer who has focused the world's attention on ocean life.

ROBERT MUNSCH: BIRTHDAY

Robert Munsch, children's author, was born on this day in 1945. He writes contemporary children's books that humorously portray the trials of growing up today. In his book *Andrew's Loose Tooth* (2002), illustrated by Michael Martchenko, even the Tooth Fairy can't help Andrew remove his loose tooth. In his books *Stephanie's Ponytail* (1996), also illustrated by Michael Martchenko, and *Mud Puddle* (1996), illustrated by Sami Soumalainen, little girls have problems that seem unsolvable.

June 14

NATIONAL FLAG WEEK/FLAG DAY

The week that includes June 14 has been celebrated as National Flag Week since 1966. More information can be found on the Web at usflag.org.

June 14 was proclaimed Flag Day in 1916. The following books are great resources for teaching young students about Flag Day and Flag Week. *Flag Day* (2003) by Kelly Bennett introduces the traditions and festivities of Flag Day. This book also explains basic flag etiquette. *Flag Day* (2003) by Jason Cooper introduces the history behind Flag Day. *A Flag for All* (2001) by Larry Brimner, illustrated by Christine Tripp, presents different people's interpretations of what the flag means to them. Use this book as a springboard to a writing assignment on what the flag means to each student.

BRUCE DEGEN: BIRTHDAY

The illustrator, Bruce Degen, was born on this day in 1945. His illustrations enliven Joanna Cole's Magic Schoolbus series of science books. He also wrote and illustrated a wonderful book, *Jamberry* (1985), that younger primary children will love.

June 15

CITIZENSHIP FOR NATIVE AMERICANS

On June 15, 1924, the U.S. Congress passed a law granting citizenship to all Native Americans. The book *Children of Native America Today* (2003) by Yvonne Wakim Dennis, photography by Arlene Hirschfelder, offers photographs of traditions, activities, and lifestyles of various North American tribes. This book is written for older students, but the pictures are worth sharing with younger children.

Week Four's thematic listing on Native Americans provides many more resources. Often Native American traditions, crafts, and other contributions to our culture are overlooked in elementary social studies curricula. Space limits the number of resources that can be listed here, but the myths and legend section of your library should be fully explored when teaching about Native Americans.

Week Three: Fathers

🏛 Curriculum Connection: Social Studies

The first Father's Day was celebrated on June 19, 1910; currently, it is celebrated on the third Sunday in June. Sharing the books on the following list takes the same or even more sensitivity than that exercised with the May list on mothers. Unfortunately, many students do not get the time and attention they need from father figures.

Sharing as many of the books on this list as possible will give your students a broad picture of the joys that fathers can provide. Plan for lots of discussion about the role of a father and how it can differ in individual families and even in different situations within the same family.

A great art project for this theme is to have children draw what present they would give their dad (father figure) if money were not a factor. Or students could draw a picture of their dad and them spending a day together. What would they be doing, what would they be wearing, and what emotion would be on their faces?

The Best Father of All (2003) by Peter Horn, illustrated by Cristina Kadmon. This book tells about a turtle father and son celebrating the special bond they share.

The Biggest Bed in the World (2000) by Lindsay Camp, illustrated by Jonathan Langley. This is the story of a huge bed that Ben's dad built because there were too many children sleeping with him.

Can I Help? (1998) written and illustrated by Marilyn Janovitz. This light and bouncy story is fun to read aloud. A little wolf offers to help his father in the garden.

Cowboy Kid (2000) by Max Eilenberg, illustrated by Sue Heap. This is a delightful story about Cowboy Kid giving Sheriff Pa a hard time about going to bed.

The Daddy Book (2002) written and illustrated by Todd Parr. This book honors all the different types of fathers in the world.

The Father Who Had 10 Children (2001) by Benedicte Guettier, edited by Skip Skwarek. Family life is more fun when it's all for one— and one for ten!

Guess How Much I Love You (1995) by Sam McBratney, illustrated by Anita Jeram. This story featuring a young rabbit and his parent explains that a parent's love runs wide and deep.

How Many Stars in the Sky? (1996) by Lenny Hort, illustrated by James Ransome. One night, when a child can't sleep, he and his daddy look for a good place to count the stars.

In Daddy's Arms I Am Tall: African Americans Celebrating Fathers (2000), illustrated by Javaka Steptoe. This collection of poems from various authors celebrates African American fathers.

Just the Two of Us (2000) by Will Smith, illustrated by Kadir Nelson. Will Smith remade Bill Withers classic song of the same title and reworked it into this beautiful book featuring gorgeous pencil and oil illustrations that follow the relationship of a father and son.

Mail by the Pail (2000) by Colin Bergel, illustrated by Mark Koenig. This well-written book tells about a young girl who learns how a birthday card she makes for her father will get to him on a freighter on Lake Michigan.

Max, the Stubborn Little Wolf (2001) by Marie-Odile Judes and Joan Robins, illustrated by Martine Bourre. This engaging tale describes a battle of wills between a father wolf and his stubborn son.

My Dad Is Awesome (2003) by Nick Butterworth. This story is about dads—a most valuable resource.

My Dad (2001) written and illustrated by Anthony Browne. The author pays homage to dads everywhere as a boy describes many wonderful things about his dad.

Night Shift Daddy (2000) by Eileen Spinelli, illustrated by Melissa Iwai. A special bond between a little girl and her daddy is the theme of this touching story.

Owl Moon (1987) by Jane Yolen, illustrated by John Schoenherr. This 1988 Caldecott Medal winner shows that one of the charms of children is their ability to experience a walk in the woods at night as a magical adventure.

Papa Piccolo (1992) by Carol Talley, illustrated by Itoko Maeno. This is the story of a tomcat who leads a life of adventure until two homeless kittens adopt him.

Papa, Please Get the Moon for Me (1991) written and illustrated by Eric Carle. This is a heart-warming tale about love that also teaches children the cycles of the moon.

Ted (2001) written and illustrated by Tony DiTerlizzi. Here's the story of a lonely boy and a big raspberry-colored, fun-loving, trouble-making, imaginary best friend.

The Sick Day (2003) by Patricia MacLachlan, illustrated by Jane Dyer. Poor little Emily is having a sick day. Fortunately, Father is home to take care of her.

So Much (1997) by Trish Cooke, illustrated by Helen Oxenbury. This book illustrates the joy of belonging to a large family.

What Dads Can't Do (2000) by Douglas Wood, illustrated by Doug Cushman. The author describes, from a kid's point of view, how dads show love.

Whistling (2003) by Elizabeth Partridge, illustrated by Anna Grossnickle Hines. On a camping trip with his father, a boy whistles up the sun. Children will be entranced by the sweetness of this gentle book.

June 18

PAT HUTCHINS: BIRTHDAY

It is sometimes difficult to explain a mathematical concept, but Pat Hutchins has done a great job explaining division in her book *The Doorbell Rang* (1989). Hutchins was born on June 18 in 1942. She also wrote and illustrated the much-loved *Rosie's Walk* (1972). Children are thrilled as the chicken again and again leads the fox into accidents.

CHRIS VAN ALLSBURG: BIRTHDAY

Chris Van Allsburg was born on this day in 1949. As author and illustrator of *The Polar Express*, he won a Caldecott Medal in 1986. He also won the Caldecott for *Jumanji* in 1982. His stories are very intriguing, but the illustrations are dark. These two picture books are best shared with older primary- and elementary-age students. Both of these books are interesting to multiage audiences, including adults.

June 19

FATHER'S DAY

Father's Day was first celebrated on June 19, 1910, in the state of Washington. However, it was not made official nationally until 1966. At that time, it was proclaimed to be the third Sunday in June and remains that way today. Two resources that might be helpful when dealing sensitively with students from nontraditional families are *Rainy Day* (2004) by Emma Haughton, illustrated by Angelo Rinaldi, which is about a child spending a day with a father who doesn't live with him, and *Father's Day Blues: What Do You Do About Father's Day When All You Have Are Mothers?* (1995) by Irene Smalls, which is a sensitive message about the diversity that pervades the modern family. These two books can provide the springboards to much classroom discussion about families and how different they can be and still provide for the needs of children.

The thematic listing for this week provides more books about Father's Day and also some great fiction titles about fathers in general.

June 20

SUMMER SOLSTICE

The longest day of the year (summer solstice) marks the beginning of summer. This can occur anytime between June 20 and June 22. Summer solstice is celebrated as a time to be happy and spread joy. School children have traditionally been happy as summer marks the time for school vacations and other warm-weather activities such as baseball and swimming.

Lemonade Sun: and Other Summer Poems (2001) by Rebecca Dotlich, illustrated by Jan Gilchrist, is a collection of poems celebrating summer. It provides the starting point for students' summer poetry writing. Students will enjoy the chance to use their favorite summer activity as the subject of a poem.

This might be a good time to share *Casey at the Bat* (1997) by Ernest Thayer, illustrated by Patricia Polacco. Remember, poems don't have to rhyme, and they often tell a story.

How Do You Know It's Summer? (1992) by Allan Fowler provides the scientific explanations for heat, thunderstorms, and other summer phenomena.

June 21

ROBERT KRAUS: BIRTHDAY

Robert Kraus, who was both an author and illustrator of more than one hundred children's books, was born on June 21, 1925, and died in 2001. Kraus was also a famous cartoonist who drew twenty-one covers for the *New Yorker* magazine.

Leo the Late Bloomer (1994), illustrated by Jose Aruego, is his most beloved book. It gives hope to every child who has ever been compared to other children his age and found lacking. The book also explains the phrase *late bloomer* in a very sensitive, caring way.

Many of Kraus's books explain the perceived problems that young children have. Some of his best are *Mort the Sport* (2000), illustrated by John Himmelman; *Milton the Early Riser* (1987), illustrated by Ariane Dewey; and *Herman the Helper* (1991), illustrated by Ariane Dewey and Jose Aruego.

Fables Aesop Never Wrote (1994) is a great discussion starter for what a fable is and how these fables are different from those that Aesop created.

Week Four: Native Americans

🏛 Curriculum Connection: Social Studies

In 1924, U.S. citizenship was granted to all American Indians (now called Native Americans). This collection of resources focuses on the contributions that the different tribes have made to the fabric of our collective culture. There are too many wonderful books of folktales, myths, and legends from the various groups to include them all here. Be sure to check library sources in your area.

United States geography is a natural curriculum connection for this theme. Using a U.S. map, plot the different geographical areas that encompassed the tribal areas. Discuss with children why the various tribes developed different methods of handcrafts and providing food based on geography and environment.

Arrow to the Sun (1977) written and illustrated by Gerald McDermott. This boldly colorful Caldecott Medal winner is an adaptation of a legend from the Pueblo Indians that portrays the Indian reverence for the source of life: the Solar Fire.

The Blackfeet: People of the Dark Moccasins (2003) written and illustrated by Karen Bush Gibson. Here's an interesting overview of the Blackfeet people.

Brother Eagle, Sister Sky: A Message from Chief Seattle (1991) written and illustrated by Susan Jeffers. A Suquamish Indian chief sends a message to the government in Washington describing his respect and love for the earth.

Cherokee: Native Basket Weavers (2003) by Gina De Angelis, Therese De Angelis, and Rachel A. Koestler-Grack. This book focuses on the Cherokee tradition of weaving baskets. It includes a cookie recipe as well as instructions for playing a game and making a mat.

The Chief's Blanket (1998) by Michael Chanin, illustrated by Kim Howard. This colorful book presents the meaning of giving and receiving.

Dancing Teepees: Poems of American Indian Youth (1995) by Virginia Driving Hawk Sneve, illustrated by Stephen Gammell. This illustrated Native American collection blends poems from the past with those of contemporary poets.

The Forest Has Eyes (1998) written and illustrated by Bev Doolittle. Here is a collection of paintings that invite the reader to see the natural world through the eyes of Native Americans.

The Gift of the Sacred Dog (1984) written and illustrated by Paul Goble. The author tells the tale of how the first horses, the Sacred Dogs, were sent by the Great Spirit to the Native Americans of the Great Plains.

The Girl Who Loved Wild Horses (1986) written and illustrated by Paul Goble. In this legend from the Plains Indians, a Native American girl so loves horses that she becomes one. This book, which includes two Native American songs celebrating horses, has won numerous awards, including the Horn Book Award, the Caldecott Medal, and an American Library Association Notable Children's Book award.

The Goat in the Rug (1990) by Geraldine, as told to Charles L. Blood and Martin Link, illustrated by Nancy Winslow Parker. Each step is described as a goat and her Navajo friend make a rug.

Grandmother's Dreamcatcher (2001) by Becky Ray McCain, illustrated by Stacey Schett. A young Chippewa girl learns to make a dreamcatcher, which allows the sleeper to have only sweet dreams. Make your own dreamcatcher with the instructions that are included.

The Iroquois Indians (1997) written and illustrated by Bill Lund. The author describes how this tribe lived in the past and how their rich culture has endured the many changes of time.

Jingle Dancer (2000) by Cynthia Leitich Smith, illustrated by Cornelius Van Wright and Ying-Hwa Hu. This unusual, warm family story tells of Jenna, a young Muscogee Indian, who wants to honor a family tradition by jingle dancing at the next powwow. But where will she find enough jingles for her dress?

Knots on a Counting Rope (1997) by Bill Martin, John Archambault, and J. Clarke, illustrated by Ted Rand. In this poignant story, a grandfather and his blind grandson reminisce about an exciting horse race.

The Legend of the Indian Paintbrush (1991) written and illustrated by Tomie dePaola. This is another Plains Indian legend. Little Gopher becomes an artist for his people.

The Long March (2002) written and illustrated by Marie-Louise Fitzpatrick. The author presents a little-known historical episode from 1847, when the impoverished Choctaw Indians raised the modern equivalent of five thousand dollars to aid the Irish during the great potato famine. This is a deeply moving story.

Many Nations: An Alphabet of Native America (2004) written and illustrated by Joseph Bruchac. This alphabet book presents aspects of the lives of the many nations of native peoples across North America.

Native Americans (1998) by Raoul Sautai, Ute Fuhr, and Juenesse Gallimard. The authors present information about how the lifestyles and cultures held by Native Americans were changed when the Europeans arrived.

Powwow (1993) written and illustrated by George Ancona. This photo-essay shows a unique celebration of Native American pride. This particular powwow was held on the Crow Reservation in Montana.

Ten Little Rabbits (1995) by Virginia Grossman, illustrated by Sylvia Long. This counting book featuring ten little Native American rabbits introduces the numbers from one to ten. It is also a winner of an IRA Children's Book Award and *Parents* magazine's Best Book of the Year.

Thirteen Moons on Turtle's Back (1997) by Joseph Bruchac, illustrated by Thomas Locker. The seasons of the year are celebrated through poems derived from the legends of the Cherokee, Cree, and Sioux Indians.

The Very First Americans (1993) by Cara Ashrose, illustrated by Bryna Waldman. This is a brief discussion of some of the hundreds of Indian tribes that lived in America long before Columbus arrived.

We Are the Many: A Picture Book of American Indians (2002) by Doreen Rappaport, illustrated by Cornelius Van Wright and Ying-Hwa Hu. The biographies of sixteen influential Native Americans are included in this thoughtful collection.

June 23

WILMA RUDOLPH: BIRTHDAY
Wilma Rudolph, born on June 23, 1940, was the twentieth child of her father's twenty-two children from two marriages. She was in leg braces from polio until she was nine years old. She went on to overcome several other illnesses and win three gold medals at the 1960 Olympics. She was the fastest woman in the world at those Olympics. Wilma was inducted into the U.S. Olympic Hall of Fame in 1983.

Stick to It: The Story of Wilma Rudolph (2002) by David Conrad profiles Rudolph as the first woman to overcome such obstacles and become a gold medal–winning athlete. This book will spark discussions on persevering and overcoming great odds to develop individual potential.

June 25

ERIC CARLE: BIRTHDAY
Eric Carle, beloved children's book author and illustrator, was born June 25, 1929. His books, *The Very Hungry Caterpillar* (1994), *The Grouchy Ladybug* (1986), and *The Very Busy Spider* (1989) were instant favorites as soon as they hit the library shelves.

The books that Carle illustrates all use tissue-paper collages. There is a video (*Eric Carle: Picture Writer*) that shows children how he creates these collages and encourages them to try it. The video is available through the following website: eric-carle.com.

His books can be used in many different ways such as part of units on insects, health and nutrition, sequencing, predicting, and (of course) life cycles. Children may also be interested in going beyond the book and doing puppet plays and dramatizations.

Carle is a good choice for an author study and a comparison/contrast of different books he has written and illustrated.

June 26

CHARLOTTE ZOLOTOW: BIRTHDAY

Charlotte Zolotow, author of *Mr. Rabbit and the Lovely Present* (1977), illustrated by Maurice Sendak, and *William's Doll* (1985), illustrated by William Pene Dubois, was born on June 26, 1915. Both of these stories deal with children's predicaments and the sensitive ways adults help them solve their problems. While *William's Doll* has only people as the characters, *Mr. Rabbit* has a mix of animals and humans, and children relate equally well to both.

In *The Poodle Who Barked at the Wind* (2001), illustrated by Valerie Coursen, are again both animals and people, with the animal solving the problem for the human.

Zolotow has written more than seventy books. They are all comforting depictions of children's emotions and help children better understand the world around them.

June 27

DEAF-BLIND AWARENESS WEEK

The week that includes June 27 was proclaimed in 1984 as an observation of Deaf-Blind Awareness. Contact alhagemeyer@juno.com at the Library for Deaf Action for more information.

HELEN KELLER: BIRTHDAY

Helen Keller was born June 27, 1880, and died in 1968. She overcame the double challenge of being both blind and deaf. *The Picture Book of Helen Keller* (1998) by David A. Adler, illustrated by John and Alexandra Wallner, gives a brief biography for young readers.

The following books also provide general resources regarding the deaf and blind. *I Have a Sister—My Sister Is Deaf* (1984) by Jeanne Peterson, illustrated by Deborah Ray, is an excellent vehicle for explaining the world of the totally deaf to young children. *Some People Are Blind* (2000) by Lola Schaefer, illustrated by Gail Saunders-Smith, describes children who are blind, their challenges and adaptations, and their similarities to others.

June Reading Strategy

Into and Through

Into and Through is a two-pronged approach to helping readers understand and appreciate both fiction and nonfiction literary works. The Into phase is explained in the May Reading Strategy.

The Through phase of this approach is what the reader does while reading or listening to the literary work. Start by looking at the pictures throughout the story—not for detail but to raise curiosity about the story content and setting. During this walk-through of the book, ask children what they notice about the pictures in regard to setting, mood, story content, art forms used, and what questions the pictures raise in their minds. This process should take only a few minutes and helps engage students in the book.

Discussion to ensure comprehension is done during the reading. What do you think will happen next? Why did the main character do that? Could this really happen? Stops should be made while reading to address the predictions made during the Into phase: We wondered what sheep eat. Do we know now? As the reading continues, new predictions need to be made and verified if possible.

In nonfiction works, new knowledge questions will arise and should be answered as the reading progresses. It is amazing how many questions children can have during the reading of a thirty-two-page picture book.

In fiction works, comprehension of the sequence of events should be elicited during this Through stage. Stop occasionally and ask the children to summarize events that have happened so far. If this is done several times, the students will internalize the events and connect them to build a plot line. Too many stops, however, could break connections the students have to the flow of the story.

At the end of the work, ask questions to help clarify elements of the story. How did the characters change? How were the problems solved? What can we learn from this story? Ask enough questions to be sure the children have gotten the point of the particular work.

July at a Glance

We are what we repeatedly do. Excellence, then, is not an act, but a habit.
—Aristotle

July Reading Tip: As you read to children, be sure to let your emotions show. If you feel passionate about the subject, let it show in your voice and body language.

JULY HIGHLIGHTS
National Hot Dog Month
The Pigeon Finds a Hot Dog! by Mo Willems is a funny tale about sharing a hot dog. According to the National Hot Dog and Sausage Council, Americans are expected to enjoy 155 million hot dogs a year. Visit the council's website at hot-dog.org for interesting statistics and safe handling tips.

National Baked Bean Month
Silly Jack and the Bean Stack (1999) by Laurence Anholt, illustrated by Arthur Robins, provides a humorous version of the traditional tale. Jack climbs a stack of baked-bean tins and encounters a giant, an event that makes his and his mother's fortune in an unexpected way.

National Ice Cream Day (third Sunday in July)
Ice Cream (2002) by Jules Older, illustrated by Lyn Severance, is an entertaining history of everyone's favorite dessert. The fun and humorous facts will keep readers engaged.

Independence Day (July 4)
In *Hurray for the Fourth of July* (2000) by Wendy Watso, a small town celebrates America's birthday. Patriotic songs and traditional rhymes are interspersed throughout the pages.

July Reading Strategy: The Skill of Prediction

WEEKLY THEMES AND CURRICULUM CONNECTIONS
Week One: Patriotism (Social Studies)
Week Two: Hawaii (Social Studies)
Week Three: Moon (Science)
Week Four: Baseball (Social Studies)

Special Events in July

"Reading Rainbow" TV Premiere Anniversary	July 1
First Zoo Opens in America	July 1
"America the Beautiful" First Published	July 4
Independence Day	July 4
Annexation of Hawaii	July 7
Man Lands on the Moon	July 20

FEATURED JULY BIRTHDAYS

Emily Arnold McCully ......July 1	Ashley Bryan.................July 13	Eve Merriam ....July 19
Phineas T. Barnum ....July 5	Marcia Brown ....July 13	Amelia Earhart ....July 24
Harriet Ziefert..................July 7	Laura Numeroff ....July 14	Jan Berenstain................July 26
Raffi Cavoukian...............July 8	Peggy Parrish ....July 14	Beatrix Potter ....July 28
James Stevenson...........July 11	Rembrandt ....July 15	J. K. Rowling ....July 31
Patricia Polacco ....July 11	Karla Kuskin ....July 17	

Week One: Patriotism

🏛 Curriculum Connection: Social Studies

Patriotism is a value that should be instilled at a young age and reinforced throughout life. Primary-aged children are eager to learn about and love the world around them. Flags, parades, and the stories associated with these happy times provide the perfect opportunity to explain these symbols to young children. The music associated with patriotic times such as the Fourth of July appeals to them. Marching to John Philip Sousa's music is a great physical education activity. The making of flags to wave or display on the Fourth of July can be an art project that follows reading books about the holiday.

Many of the following resource books are about famous Americans. Children enjoy learning about the actual people behind the names and pictures they have seen and heard about.

America Is . . . (2002) by Louise Borden, illustrated by Stacey Schuett. In poetic text, the author presents our country and its rich heritage.

The Bald Eagle (2003) by Debbie Yanuck, illustrated by Melodie Andrews. This book presents information on bald eagles including how this bird became one of the symbols of the United States.

Betsy Ross (1998) written and illustrated by Alexandra Wallner. This book introduces the woman from Philadelphia who made the first American flag.

Capital! Washington D.C. from A to Z (2002) by Laura Krauss Melmed, illustrated by Frane Lessac. Using the alphabet in rhyming text, along with great illustrations, the author presents the sights of Washington, D.C.

Citizenship (2003) by Robin Doak. This book for older readers explains the rights and responsibilities that citizenship conveys to individuals.

F Is for Flag (2002) by Wendy Lewison, illustrated by Barbara Duke. This book introduces young readers to the flag and the meanings attached to it.

The Fourth of July Story (1995) by Alice Dalgliesh, illustrated by Marie Nonnast. The simple text of this book captures the excitement of when the thirteen colonies wanted their independence. It tells the historical story of the fourth of July.

God Bless America (2002) by Irving Berlin, illustrated by Lynn Munsinger. A family of bears experiences America in a version of the classic song.

Hats Off for the Fourth of July (2002) by Harriet Ziefert, illustrated by Gustaf Miller. All readers will enjoy this depiction of a small town parade.

Here's to You, America! (2002) by Charles Schulz, illustrated by Paige Braddock. Travel back in time with Charlie Brown, Snoopy, and friends for the story of the birth of the United States.

I Am a Good Citizen (2003) by Marie Bender, illustrated by Mary Elizabeth Salzmann. This book describes the ways a child can be a good citizen, including following rules and taking care of the environment.

I Am America (2003) by Charles Smith. The poetry of this book is enhanced by the photographs of children representing ethnic and racial diversity.

I Pledge Allegiance (2002) by Bill Martin and Michael Sampson, illustrated by Christopher Raschka. This book about the Pledge of Allegiance helps young readers understand the meaning of the pledge. It is intended for primary-aged children.

The Midnight Ride of Paul Revere (2001) by Henry Wadsworth Longfellow, illustrated by Christopher Bing. This famous poem recreates Paul Revere's midnight ride in 1775. He was warning the people of Boston that the British were coming. Many children memorize part of this poem. It makes a great read-aloud for patriotic assemblies.

A More Perfect Union: The Story of Our Constitution (1991) by Betsy Maestro, illustrated by Giulio Maestro. This book tells why and how the Constitution of the United States was created using text that is easy to understand for young readers.

Mr. Lincoln's Whiskers (1999) by Karen Winnick. This is the true story of Grace Bedell, who suggested to Abraham Lincoln that he should grow a beard.

Patriotism (2000) by Lucia Raatma, illustrated by Madonna Murphy. Young readers learn some ways to demonstrate patriotism in school, in their community, and with family and friends.

Patriotism (2002) by Pam Scheunemann. This book defines patriotism for young readers as being proud of your country. It describes patriotic activities and symbols such as the flying of the flag and saying the Pledge of Allegiance.

A Picture Book of Abraham Lincoln (1990) by David A. Adler, illustrated by Alexandra and John Wallner. This book follows the life of the popular president from childhood on the frontier to his assassination after the end of the Civil War.

A Picture Book of Benjamin Franklin (1991) by David A. Adler, illustrated by Alexandra and John Wallner. This book is a survey of the life of Benjamin Franklin; it highlights his work as an inventor and statesman.

A Picture Book of George Washington (1995) by David A. Adler, illustrated by Alexandra and John Wallner. The author gives an account of the life of the "Father of Our Country" for young readers.

A Picture Book of Thomas Jefferson (1996) by David A. Adler, illustrated by Alexandra and John Wallner. Trace the life and achievements of this president who was an author of the Declaration of Independence.

Red, White and Blue: The Story of the American Flag (1998) by John Herman, illustrated by Robin Roraback. This book gives factual information regarding the history of the American flag in an interesting manner for children.

Scrambled States of America (2002) written and illustrated by Laurie Keller. Packed with humorous illustrations, this book stars all fifty states ands makes learning geography fun.

The Star-Spangled Banner (2003) by Debbie Yanuck, illustrated by Linda Clavel and Melodie Andrews. This book discusses the authorship of this poem that was later set to music and became the national anthem.

We Live Here Too! Kids Talk About Good Citizenship (2003) by Nancy Loewen, illustrated by Omarr Wesley. This book defines citizenship and explains how it can be used in daily situations. It uses a unique advice-column format.

We the Kids: The Preamble to the Constitution of the United States (2002) written and illustrated by David Catrow. This look at the preamble to the Constitution brings students into its ideas and ideals. The book is a good discussion starter for older readers.

July 1

EMILY ARNOLD MCCULLY: BIRTHDAY
Emily Arnold McCully, who won the Caldecott Medal in 1993 for *Mirette on the High Wire*, was born on this day in 1939. She has written and illustrated more than one hundred books for children, including two more books with Mirette as the main character: *Mirette and Bellini Cross Niagara Falls* (2000) and *Starring Mirette and Bellini* (1997). McCully began writing at a very young age and feels very strongly that the books she writes should stir the imaginations of those who read them.

FIRST ZOO OPENS IN AMERICA
The first zoo in the United States opened on July 1, 1874, in Philadelphia. The price of admission was twenty-five cents for adults and ten cents for children. For more information visit phillyzoo.org.

"READING RAINBOW" TV PREMIERE: ANNIVERSARY
"Reading Rainbow" has its birthday on this day. This PBS show went on the air in 1983 and has won many prestigious awards. It can be used as a guide to finding high-quality books for children. See the website at gpn.unl.edu/rainbow.

July 4

INDEPENDENCE DAY
Happy Birthday, America! The Declaration of Independence was approved and signed by John Hancock on this day, but the "official" signing date is August 2.

On July 4, 1776, the Declaration of Independence was adopted. The Fourth of July is commemorated as Independence Day and is a legal holiday in the United States and its territories. The Week One thematic listing of patriotic books provides good resources for this day. *America: A Patriotic Primer* (2002) by Lynne Cheney, illustrated by Robin Preiss Glassner, contains important people, ideas, and events in the history of the United States and is useful as a review or introduction for students.

"AMERICA THE BEAUTIFUL" PUBLISHED
"America the Beautiful" first appeared in print on July 1, 1895. The original poem was revised twice by its author, Katherine Lee Bates, and the final version was published in 1913. The poem was later set to music and has become the unofficial second national anthem. *America the Beautiful* (2002) by Bates, illustrated by Chris Gall, is an illustrated edition of the poem that celebrates the beauty of America.

July 5

PHINEAS T. BARNUM: BIRTHDAY

Phineas T. Barnum, known as the creator of the Greatest Show on Earth, was born on July 5, 1810, in Bethel, Connecticut. In 1881, Barnum merged with his rival, J. A. Bailey, to form the famous Barnum and Bailey Circus. The book *P. T. Barnum* (1997) by David Wright introduces the life and accomplishments of this great showman.

Discussion of the life of this circus entrepreneur will spark the imaginations of all children. As a creative writing project, have each child imagine which circus performer they would like to be and write a diary entry as if they were that performer. If more resources are needed for this project, see the thematic list in August (Week One).

July 7

ANNEXATION OF HAWAII

On July 7, 1898, Hawaii was annexed to the United States by a resolution signed by President McKinley. The thematic list for Week Two provides resources for primary students to learn about the tropical paradise that became our fiftieth state. *Hawaii* (1998) by Bob Italia provides an introduction to the geography, history, natural resources, and people of these islands. *Hawaii: Facts and Symbols* (2003) by Emily McAuliffe presents further information about the state and its nickname, motto, and emblems.

HARRIET ZIEFERT: BIRTHDAY

Harriet Ziefert was born on July 7, 1941. Most of her books are based on challenges that children face, such as loose teeth and daily routines. *Clara Ann Cookie* (1999), illustrated by Emily Bolam, and *My Tooth Is Loose* (1991), illustrated by Amy Aitken, are two of her most famous books. She also wrote some stories with animals as the characters. *A Dozen Ducklings Lost and Found: A Counting Story* (2003), illustrated by Donald Dreifuss, is a children's favorite.

Week Two: Hawaii

🏛 Curriculum Connection: Social Studies

In 1959, Hawaii was the last state admitted to the union. The Hawaiian Islands had been annexed to the United States in 1898. This annexation made no change in Hawaii's government, but it opened the islands for tourism and cultural exchanges. Mainland Americans visited the islands and enjoyed what Hawaii offered in terms of culture, climate, music, and dance. Hawaiians learned from their visitors and began traveling to other parts of the world and sharing their culture. People from other Pan-Pacific countries also began to populate the islands. Today, Hawaii is a tourist destination for the rest of the United States and also for visitors from other countries, especially Japan.

The Hawaiian language is interesting to study in relation to English. It uses vowels much more than consonants. Children can be introduced to the differences by reading the alphabet books in the following list. These books provide an introduction to Hawaii—its people and its unique cultural aspects. The resources listed here will encourage children to learn more about our fiftieth state.

"A" Is for Aloha (1985) by Stephanie Feeney, photographs by Hella Hammid. This book introduces the alphabet with words that are unique to the Hawaiian culture.

Aloha! (2002) by Jacqueline Sweeney, illustrated by G. K. and Vikki Hart. Four animal friends travel to Hawaii where they are shown the sights by their gecko guide. Included are vocabulary lists, games, reading strategies, and suggestions for researching Hawaii, geckos, and volcanoes.

Aloha, Dolores (2000) written and illustrated by Barbara Samuels. Certain that she will win a trip to Hawaii, a young girl enters the contest and goes all out preparing for her trip to Hawaii. This is a good read-aloud book with detailed illustrations.

And the Birds Appeared (1989) by Julie Stewart Williams, illustrated by Robin Yoko Burningham. This is the legend of how Maui, a boy with magical powers, makes the birds appear in the islands of Hawaii.

A Beautiful Hawaiian Day (2000) by Henry Kapono, illustrated by Susan Szabo. This book tells the story of a little Hawaiian girl who finds a magical seashell while walking on the beach.

Dumpling Soup (1998) by Jama Kim Rattigan, illustrated by Lillian Hsu-Flanders. This is the story of a young Asian American girl living in Hawaii who tries to make dumplings for a family celebration.

Fables from the Sea (2000) by Leslie Ann Hayashi, illustrated by Kathleen Wong Bishop. This collection features a variety of sea creatures found in the waters around Hawaii.

Hawaii Is a Rainbow (1985) by Stephanie Feeney, photographs by Jeff Reese. This book provides an introduction to colors and to the diverse population of Hawaii.

The Island-Below-the-Star (1998) written and illustrated by James Rumford. Part legend and part history, this book tells of the belief that explorers from the other Polynesian Islands discovered the islands of Hawaii, which are below the star Arturus.

The Last Princess: The Story of Princess Ka'iulani of Hawai'i (2001) by Fay Stanley, illustrated by Diane Stanley. This book tells the story of Hawaii's last heir to the throne and why she never ruled.

Lava (2002) by Jacqueline Sweeney, illustrated by G. K. and Vikki Hart. A gecko takes his animal friends for a walk to see a volcano. Suggestions for reading and researching other famous volcanoes are included.

Let's Call Him Lau-Wiliwili-Humuhumu-Nukunuku-Nukunuku-Apua'A-Oi'Oi (1993) by Tim J. Myers, illustrated by Daryl Arakaki. This is a tale of finding the perfect name for a young fish. The author is a storyteller and lover of language.

Little Honu (2002) by Jacqueline Sweeney, illustrated by G. K. and Vikki Hart. A turtle on a trip to Hawaii learns to accept himself. This book contains an explanation of the Hawaiian alphabet and a pronunciation guide. It is also a good discussion starter about the differences between land and sea turtles.

Maui and the Secret of Fire (1994) by Suelyn Ching Tune, illustrated by Robin Yoko Burningham. In this Hawaiian legend, Maui forces from the mud hens the secret of how to make fire.

Maui Goes Fishing (1991) by Julie Stewart Williams, illustrated by Robin Yoko Burningham. In this story, Maui makes a fishing hook and, from the sea, he pulls land that becomes the big island of Hawaii.

Musubi Man: Hawaii's Gingerbread Man (1997) by Sandi Takayama, illustrated by Pat Hall. A freshly baked Musubi man escapes from an old woman's kitchen and runs away in this island version of the classic story.

Pat Hall's Hawaiian Animals (1994) written and illustrated by Pat Hall. This coloring book is often used in elementary schools to teach the Hawaiian language. Once colored, the pictures are suitable for display.

The Prince and the Li Hing Mui (1998) by Sandi Takayama, illustrated by Esther Szegedy. This Hawaiian version of *The Princess and the Pea* points out that a common man can be more princely that aristocrats.

Punia and the King of Sharks: A Hawaiian Folktale (1997) adapted by Lee Wardlaw, illustrated by Felipe Davalos. A young boy uses his wits to trick the King of Sharks in this Hawaiian folktale.

Ten Little Menehunes: A Hawaiian Counting Book (2000) by Demming Forsythe. This counting book includes a pronunciation guide for the Hawaiian numbers and features the "little people" of Hawaii.

The Three Little Hawaiian Pigs and the Magic Shark (1990) by Donivee M. Laird, illustrated by Carol Jossem. Three little pigs have built their houses of Hawaiian materials and are threatened by a shark in disguise.

Torch Fishing with the Sun (1999) by Laura E. Williams, illustrated by Fabricio Vanden Broeck. This fable about a boy and his grandfather relates how the sun sets each day.

July 8

RAFFI CAVOUKIAN: BIRTHDAY

Known simply as Raffi, this singer, songwriter, author, and activist for children was born in Egypt on July 8, 1948. He began performing for young children in 1974 and has sold more than twelve million records and CDs. Many of the songs he wrote have become children's books. *Wheels on the Bus, Baby Beluga,* and *Down by the Bay* were favorite songs before they became books. Raffi has become a beloved entertainer and author with uncommon integrity. His songs and books respect the child as a whole person and nurture the spirit of children no matter what their age.

Explore the rhythm of the language of the songs with children. Students can gain a new perspective on reading when songs are read as books and story text sung to music. Raffi and his music provide a different beat to read and sing to. Children will enjoy both his music and his stories.

July 11

PATRICIA POLACCO: BIRTHDAY

Patricia Polacco was born on July 11, 1944. She credits her grandparents for providing the inspiration for many of her stories.

Chicken Sunday (1998) and *Pink and Say* (2003) are two of her books that primary children love. In her book *Mr. Lincoln's Way* (2001), she helps children deal with prejudices and schoolyard bullies.

Polacco advises children to turn off the television and use their imaginations. Try reading a story that is new to your students without showing them any of the pictures. Read the first few pages and then talk about what the children see inside their heads or have them draw what the author is describing. This exercise helps children focus their listening and hone their imaginations.

JAMES STEVENSON: BIRTHDAY

James Stevenson was born on this day in 1929. He has written and illustrated more than one hundred books for children. *The Mud Flat Olympics* (1994) is a great book for math application problems. Use it for data gathering, estimation, classification, and computation activities.

July 13

MARCIA BROWN: BIRTHDAY

Marcia Brown was born on July 13, 1918. She received the Caldecott Medal three times: for *Cinderella* in 1955, *Once a Mouse...* in 1962, and *Shadow* in 1983. She is most famous for her illustrations in the classic 1946 book, *Stone Soup*. She believes strongly that each book she illustrates should be unique. Her favorite medium for illustration is the technique called woodcuts.

ASHLEY BRYAN: BIRTHDAY

Ashley Bryan was born on July 13, 1923. He began writing, illustrating, and making his own books when he was only five. His famous works include *Lion and the Ostrich Chicks* (1996), *All Night, All Day* (2003), and *Sing to the Sun* (1995). His illustrations are almost as glowing as the words of the poems themselves. Bryan believes that children should be "strongly rooted in who you are—your people and what they have to offer, then reach out and draw upon the gifts of other peoples of the world."

July 14

PEGGY PARRISH: BIRTHDAY

Peggy Parrish, author of the beloved Amelia Bedelia books, was born July 14, 1927, and died in 1988. She wrote more than forty books besides the twelve Amelia Bedelia books and began writing while she was a teacher. The favorite Amelia Bedelia book for most children is *Play Ball, Amelia Bedelia* (1995), illustrated by Wallace Trip. Is this the favorite of the children in your class?

The Amelia Bedelia books provide a wonderful resource for teaching multiple meanings of words in context. Children enjoy the humorous drawings that can be created from using the words that Amelia mixes up in her daily experiences.

LAURA JOFFE NUMEROFF: BIRTHDAY

Laura Numeroff, born on this date in 1953, has given children wonderful circular stories. She got the idea for *If You Give a Mouse a Cookie* (1985) while on a long, boring cross-country trip. *If You Give a Moose a Muffin* (1991) and *If You Give a Pig a Pancake* (1998) are equally as popular with children. All three of these books have great illustrations by Felicia Bond. See if you can brainstorm an equally silly story with your class.

Week Three: Moon

✳ Curriculum Connection: Science

People have always been fascinated with the moon, and young children are no exception. The facts and lore surrounding the moon are the subjects of the books on this list. The primary grades are an excellent time to introduce the science of space exploration and compare and contrast fact and fiction concerning the moon.

After reading several of the nonfiction books on this list, divide the class into pairs with one student acting as an interviewer and the other student as the interviewee. Ask them to make up three questions and answers about the moon and present the interview to the rest of the class in the form of an oral report.

Bringing Down the Moon (2001) by Jonathan Emmett, illustrated by Vanessa Cabban. A little mole thinks that the moon is so beautiful that he tries to get it from the sky but eventually learns to appreciate it in the sky.

Full Moon Rising (2002) by Joanne Taylor, illustrated by Susan Tooke. This book follows the rhythms of a farm family's life and introduces the names of each full moon.

Max Goes to the Moon: A Science Adventure with Max the Dog (2003) by Jeffrey Bennett, illustrated by Alan Okamoto. A science activity for children is included in this illustrated book that contains many science concepts in an engaging story.

The Moon Book (1998) written and illustrated by Gail Gibbons. The author discusses the movement and phases of the moon and how men have explored it over the years. This book is packed with facts and colorful illustrations.

The Moon Lady (1995) by Amy Tan, illustrated by Gretchen Schields. A young Chinese girl's adventures lead her to discover that the best wishes are those you make come true yourself.

The Moon Seems to Change (1990) by Franklyn M. Branley, illustrated by Barbara and Ed Emberley. The author explains the changes

that seem to happen to the moon as it goes around the earth.

Neil Armstrong (2002) by Shannon Zemlicka. This book for older primary students is a biography of the first man on the moon and includes highlights of his life.

New Moon (2000) by Pegi Deitz Shea, illustrated by Cathryn Falwell. This story brings to life the joy and wonder of a young child discovering the natural world.

Owl Moon (1987) by Jane Yolen, illustrated by John Schoenherr. A father and daughter trek into the woods to see the great horned owl in this 1988 Caldecott Medal winner.

Possum's Harvest Moon (1998) written and illustrated by Anne Hunter. Possum invites his friends to a party to celebrate the harvest moon one last time before the long winter.

Rocket to the Moon (1999) by Lisa M. Combs, illustrated by Robert F. Goetzl. The author describes *Apollo 11*'s journey to the moon, the landing of the *Eagle*, and the moonwalk of Neil Armstrong and Buzz Aldrin.

So That's How the Moon Changes Shape! (1997) by Allan Fowler. Follow this explanation of why the moon changes shape throughout the month.

Wait Till the Moon Is Full (1989) by Margaret Wise Brown, illustrated by Garth Williams. This is the story of a raccoon's adventure into the night on an evening when the moon is full.

What the Moon Is Like (2000) by Franklyn M. Branley, illustrated by True Kelley. This book helps children to imagine a moon visit now that we know what the moon is like.

When the Moon Is Full: A Lunar Year (2001) by Penny Pollock, illustrated by Mary Azarian. Short verses describe the names of twelve moons according to Native American tradition. This book showcases the defining characteristics of each moon.

Why the Sun and the Moon Live in the Sky (1990) by Elphinstone Dayrell, illustrated by Blair Lent. This is an African folktale about the Sun and the Moon, who lived on Earth until they were forced to move to the sky.

July 15

REMBRANDT: BIRTHDAY

The famous artist Rembrandt Harmensz van Rijn—known simply as Rembrandt—was born in Holland on July 15, 1606, and died in 1669. He is an undisputed genius in the world of Western art. He earned an excellent living before he fell out of favor with his patrons and died almost penniless. Rembrandt used light and shadows to show the character of the people he painted. *Rembrandt: See and Do Children's Book* (2001) by Ceciel de Bie and Martijn Leenen is a lively introduction to the painter's life and work. It has beautiful reproductions of many of his famous paintings. *Rembrandt* (1990) from the Getting to Know the World's Greatest Artists series by Mike Venezia brings to life the person behind the painting. This book combines cartoons with color photographs of Rembrandt's paintings.

Rembrandt did many self-portraits. After showing several of them to the students, encourage them to draw their own self-portraits.

July 17

KARLA KUSKIN: BIRTHDAY

Karla Kuskin was born on this day in 1932. She once said, "Trying to get a story or poem just the way you want it is hard work. I spend a great deal of time rewriting."

She wrote and illustrated *City Dog* (1998), which has become a favorite of many children. Her most famous book, *The Philharmonic Gets Dressed* (1986), contains wonderfully humorous illustrations by Marc Simont and is another children's favorite.

Many of the poems Kuskin wrote in *Soap Soup and Other Verses* (1993) are very descriptive. After sharing several of them with students, have them try writing a descriptive poem about a pet or favorite stuffed animal. Children should enjoy this writing experience, and remind them that poetry doesn't have to rhyme!

July 19

EVE MERRIAM: BIRTHDAY

Eve Merriam, one of the most prolific poets for children, was born July 19, 1916, and died in 1992. Even today, many of her poems are published in anthologies of children's poetry and turned into stand-alone picture books. She is best known for her book *You Be Good and I'll Be Night* (1996), illustrated by Karen Lee Schmidt, which is a classic for ages three to eight.

Her poem "Lullaby" about the color purple is a great model. As a class activity, ask the students to write poems about your school's colors. "Lullaby" is also a discussion starter for moods in poems. Why is this poem titled "Lullaby"? What does the color purple have to do with a lullaby? How does your favorite color make you feel?

Take time over the next few days to read several of Merriam's poems and talk about them with the children. She wrote many different kinds of poems and books and is an author worth spending time with.

July 20

MAN LANDS ON THE MOON

Man first landed on the moon on this day in 1969. Many people did not believe it was actually happening. Ask students to interview someone who remembers that day and report back to the class what people thought about this great event.

An excellent resource for this day is *One Giant Leap: The Story of Neil Armstrong* (2001) by Don Brown. Another useful resource is *First on the Moon* (2000) by Barbara Hehner, illustrated by Greg Ruhl. Upper primary students interested in the science of landing on the moon should be encouraged to visit NASA's website (nasa.gov) for more information.

This week's thematic listing of moon books has both scientific and poetic resources for young children. The moon is a fascinating topic for primary children and provides a great opportunity for them to discriminate between science and fiction on a topic.

Week Four: Baseball

🏛 Curriculum Connection: Social Studies

Baseball is called "America's pastime." There are wonderful books for children about all the different aspects of the game, from the history of baseball to the positive values to be learned from playing the game. Children will enjoy both the informational and fictional books listed here.

The Ball Game (1993) by David Packard, illustrated by R. W. Alley. A young player succeeds in making the play that wins the game.

The Baseball Bat (1989) by Ski Michaels, illustrated by George Guzzi. A bat wants to join the baseball team, even though he sleeps during the daylight hours when they play the games.

The Baseball Counting Book (1999) by Barbara McGrath and illustrated by Brian Shaw. In this book the numbers from one to twenty are used to introduce various aspects of the game of baseball.

Baseball for Fun (2003) written and illustrated by Sandra Will. Important people and events in the sport of baseball, as well as rules and skills, are described in this book.

The Baseball Star (1995) by Fred Arrigg, illustrated by Charles Micucci. This is the story of baseball magic that occurs when the Andover All-Stars face the Mudville Bad Guys in the championship game.

The Bat Boy and His Violin (1998) by Gavin Curtis, illustrated by E. B. Lewis. This book captures a special period in the history of the Negro Leagues as it tells a story of family ties and team spirit.

Beverly Billingsly Can't Catch (2004) written and illustrated by Alexander Stadler. Can a bear that has many other talents learn to play softball?

Casey at the Bat (1997) by Ernest Thayer, illustrated by Patricia Polacco. The author gives this poem a fresh look that is enhanced by the artwork.

Eight Animals Play Ball (2003) by Susan Middleton Elya, illustrated by Lee Chapman. Spanish vocabulary is intertwined with English in this book about animal friends playing baseball. Non-Spanish speakers as well as Spanish speakers who are learning English will enjoy this book.

George and the Pitching Machine (1994) by George McNamara, illustrated by Darrel Millsap. This story was written by a nine-year-old boy and is about facing something new and overcoming fear.

Get Ready to Play Tee Ball (1999) written and illustrated by Jan Cheripko. This book for young readers explains Tee ball basics and the rules of the game.

Here Comes the Strikeout (1978) written and illustrated by Leonard Kessler. A young boy becomes a better player with the help of a friend and a lot of hard work

The History of Baseball (2003) by Diana Star Helmer, illustrated by Thomas S. Owens. This book presents a timeline of important events in the history of baseball—America's favorite pastime.

Home Run: The Story of Babe Ruth (2003) by Robert Burleigh, illustrated by Mike Wimmer. This is a poetic account of the legendary Babe Ruth as he prepares for a home run.

Hooray for Snail! (1985) written and illustrated by John Stadler. In this fanciful tale, a snail hits the ball so hard that it flies to the moon and back.

Let's Go to a Baseball Game (2004) written and illustrated by Mary Hill. This book describes the experiences of a young boy when he goes to a stadium to watch a baseball game with his father.

Let's Play Ball (1996) by Kelli C. Foster and Gina Erickson, illustrated by Kerri Gifford and Kelli Foster. The only thing standing in the way of a perfect ball-playing day is the finding of a lost baseball.

Little Billy and Baseball Bob (2002) by Mitchell Axelrod, illustrated by Ron Campbell. A young boy wants a picture of his hero for his Wall of Favorite Pictures. This story has an ending all readers will enjoy.

Mama Played Baseball (2003) by David A. Adler, illustrated by Chris O'Leary. A young girl helps her mother get a job as a player in the All-American Girls Professional Baseball League while her father is serving in the army during World War II.

Max (1984) written and illustrated by Rachel Isadora. A young boy warms up for his Saturday baseball game in his sister's dancing class.

Mort the Sport (2000) by Robert Kraus, illustrated by John Himmelman. Mort's attempts to excel at both baseball and the violin confuse so much that he decides to take up chess. There's a lesson here for all readers.

My Baseball Book (2000) written and illustrated by Gail Gibbons. This introduction to baseball contains all the basics young readers will need.

My Lucky Hat (2002) written and illustrated by Kevin O'Malley. A young boy loans his lucky hat to his favorite player to help him get a home run.

Nick Plays Baseball (2003) written and illustrated by Rachel Isadora. This book combines information and fun for young readers.

Rhinos Who Play Baseball (2003) written and illustrated by Julie Mammano. Rhinos bring their sense of fun to the game of baseball.

Teammates (1992) by Peter Golenbock, illustrated by Paul Bacon. Young readers learn the details of the friendship that developed between Pee Wee Reese and Jackie Robinson who was the first black player in major league baseball.

We Love Baseball! (2003) written and illustrated by Peggy Harrison. In this story about good sportsmanship, young baseball players demonstrate that anyone who plays is a winner.

The World of Baseball (2003) by James Buckley. This is the story of major-league baseball's most exciting players who came to America to play ball.

Zachary's Ball (2002) written and illustrated by Matt Tavares. A young boy goes to his first major-league ball game where something magical happens.

July 24

AMELIA EARHART: BIRTHDAY

Amelia Earhart was born on July 24, 1897, at Atchison, Kansas. In 1932, she was the first woman to fly alone across the Atlantic Ocean (it took her fifteen hours) and the first woman to receive the Distinguished Flying Cross. Earhart disappeared in 1937 as she was trying to set a new record flying all the way around the world at the equator. Her pioneer spirit inspired many others to follow in her path.

Amelia Earhart: Pioneer of the Sky (1991) by John Parlin, illustrated by Anthony D'Adamo, and *Amelia and Eleanor Go for a Ride* (1999) by Pam Munoz Ryan, illustrated by Brian Selznick, are two excellent resources to use with primary students.

Children need to hear history in stories so they can comprehend what things were like in the past. Resources on real people focus children on the reality of history and the people who have become historical figures.

July 26

JAN BERENSTAIN: BIRTHDAY

Jan Berenstain, author and illustrator, was born July 26, 1923. Jan and Stan Berenstain are the husband-and-wife team who created the Berenstain Bears series of books. These books are loved by children everywhere and make great summertime reading. They are the childhood equivalent of adult beach books—enjoyable reading that is not too intellectually challenging or thought provoking.

The everyday situations the bears find themselves in and the semi-cartoonlike illustrations draw children to the books. Students can relate to the adventures and eagerly await the next book in the series. Many children have become more proficient readers by reading most of the books in this series. One of the best ways to become a better reader is by reading!

For fun activities, book lists, and other interesting information, visit the Berenstain Bears on the Web at berenstainbears.com.

July 28

BEATRIX POTTER: BIRTHDAY

(Helen) Beatrix Potter, author and illustrator of *Peter Rabbit*, was born in London on July 28, 1866, and died in 1943. She wrote more than forty books for children, most in a small format for little hands. She had great success with her books, which feature interesting animal characters and watercolor illustrations.

Many of her books are classics and have stood the test of time by remaining as popular today as they were when they were first written. Much discussion can be generated with students regarding what makes a book a classic and what role illustrations play in making a timeless favorite with children.

The book *Beatrix Potter* (1998) by Alexandra Wallner has much more information on this famous author and illustrator. *The Giant Treasury of Peter Rabbit* (1989) by Beatrix Potter, edited by Cary Wilkins, contains eight of her best-loved stories in full color. These stories will entertain both young and old. The website peterrabbit.co.uk is a wonderful resource as well.

July 31

J. K. ROWLING: BIRTHDAY

Happy Birthday to Harry Potter and the author of the Harry Potter books, J. K. Rowling! Each new installment that comes from this author is as successful as the previous ones. Although written for older students, many third and fourth graders will read and enjoy these books. Younger students will know Harry Potter from the movies and can be motivated to increase their reading skills in order to read the books themselves.

There have been several attempts to ban these books because of their emphasis on the supernatural. However, all attempts have failed so far due to the popularity of the series. Much discussion can be generated about why some people want these books banned and what banning a book means.

These highly popular books can be used to teach or reinforce several curriculum concepts such as vocabulary development, fantasy versus reality, plot development, character development, fantasy as a genre, the world of the supernatural, and good versus evil.

July Reading Strategy

The Skill of Prediction

In order to increase their comprehension of written text, children need to practice the skill of prediction. Children should be engaged in whatever text they are listening to or reading on their own. The best way to accomplish this is to ask them predictive type questions.

Questions such as the following can be asked before the book is read: From looking at the cover of this book, what do you think the book will be about? From the information on the back cover of the book, do you think you will like this book? Why or why not? Look at the pictures throughout this book and tell me what you think you might learn from this story. Do you think this book is fiction or nonfiction?

The following types of questions can be asked while the story is being read: What do you think will happen next? What caused _____ to happen? How do you think this story will end? So far, is the story fact or fiction? How can you tell?

When the story is completed, all predictions made before and during the reading can be checked for accuracy and engagement of critical thinking during the story.

Children need to have their thinking skills validated and practiced in order to enhance their comprehension. As children become more independent readers, remind them to ask themselves the same kinds of questions that you have modeled with them.

August at a Glance

Children seldom misquote you. In fact, they usually repeat
word for word what you shouldn't have said.
—Unknown

August Reading Tip: Children can look bored or restless and still be listening and engaged in the reading of a book. Ask children to be listening for something specific in the story as you read.

AUGUST HIGHLIGHTS
Children's Vision and Learning Month
Look . . . What Do You See? (1991), by Jennifer Rye, illustrated by Tony Kerins, discusses how animals and people use their eyes in different ways.

American Artist Appreciation Month
Norman Rockwell: The Life of an Artist (2002) by Jennifer Rozines Roy and Gregory Roy examines the life and work of the twentieth-century artist who portrayed Americans as they liked to see themselves.

National Inventors' Month
The Real McCoy: The Life of an African-American Inventor (1994) by Wendy Towle, illustrated by Wil Clay, is the biography of Elijah McCoy (1844–1929), who patented over fifty inventions despite the obstacles he faced because of his race.

Monarch Butterflies Fall Migration
Monarch Butterfly (1992), written and illustrated by Gail Gibbons, describes the life cycle of the monarch butterfly, including instructions for raising a monarch in a jar.

International Clown Week
Circus Clowns (2002), written and illustrated by Denise M. Jordan, introduces the entertaining world of circus clowns.

Smile Week
Smiling (1999), written and illustrated by Gwenyth Swain, explores the importance of smiling for people all over the world.

August Reading Strategy: Importance of Informational Texts

WEEKLY THEMES AND CURRICULUM CONNECTIONS
Week One: Circus (Social Studies)
Week Two: Siblings (Social Studies)
Week Three: Inventors (Science)
Week Four: Butterflies (Science)

Special Events in August

International Clown Week	Aug. 2
Sister's Day	Aug. 3
National Mustard Day	Aug. 3
UN International Youth Day	Aug. 12
National Inventors' Month	Aug. 16
National Aviation Day	Aug. 19
Hawaii Granted Statehood	Aug. 21
Fall Migration of Monarch Butterflies	Aug. 21
Civil Rights March on Washington	Aug. 28

FEATURED AUGUST BIRTHDAYS

Gail Gibbons.................Aug. 1	Seymour Simon ....Aug. 9	Orville Wright ....Aug. 19
Francis Scott Key............Aug. 1	Joanna Cole ....Aug. 11	Arthur Yorinks..............Aug. 21
Nancy White Carlstrom..Aug. 4	Don Freeman ....Aug. 11	Claude Debussy ....Aug. 22
Barbara Cooney ....Aug. 6	Mary Ann Hoberman ..Aug. 12	Roger Duvoisin ....Aug. 28
Frank Asch ....Aug. 6	Beatrice Schenk	Allen Say......................Aug. 28
Joy Cowley ....Aug. 7	de Regniers...............Aug. 16	Virginia Lee Burton ......Aug. 30
Patricia McKissack.........Aug. 9	"Davy" Crockett ....Aug. 17	Helen Craig..................Aug. 30
Hazel Hutchins ....Aug. 9	Myra Cohn Livingston..Aug. 17	Donald Crews..............Aug. 30

Week One: Circus

🏛 Curriculum Connection: Social Studies

The circus has fascinated people all over the world for centuries. There are so many aspects to learn about—the acts, the animals, the performers, and the history. Ringling Brothers, Barnum and Bailey is the name that most people associate with the circus of today. Unfortunately, not all children have the real experience of attending a circus, so the books listed here will introduce this world to them. It would be wonderful if these books could be the introduction to a field trip to a real circus. If not, perhaps the class could put on a circus of their own using ideas from the following resources.

Arthur's Chicken Pox (1994) written and illustrated by Marc Brown. Arthurs's case of the chicken pox threatens to keep him home from a trip to the circus. Nothing seems to console him.

At the Circus (2003) by Cathy Beylon. The author presents scenes of circus life that greet readers as they visit the big top.

Bandus the Bear (2002) by Jutta Gorschulter, illustrated by Michael Grejniec. This is the story of a bear who wants to be a circus bear until he discovers that his life in the forest is indeed special enough.

Bearymore (1979) written and illustrated by Don Freeman. A circus bear has trouble dreaming up a new act for the circus when he is supposed to be hibernating.

Chicken Chuck (2000) by Bill Martin, Bernard Martin, Michael Sampson, and illustrated by Steven Salerno. A rooster with a blue feather in his forehead meets a very special circus horse with two blue feathers.

Circus (1981) by Mabel Harmer. This is an account of life in the circus as everyone prepares for the next show in the next town.

Circus (1992) written and illustrated by Lois Ehlert. This unusual circus has marching snakes and leaping lizards. The cut-paper collages are wonderfully vivid.

Circus Animal Acts (2002) written and illustrated by Denise M. Jordan. This book tells how circus animals are trained to do tricks in the circus and details the types of tricks different animals can do.

Circus Caps for Sale (2002) written and illustrated by Esphyr Slobodkina. A famous peddler who sells caps by balancing them all on his head is invited to do an act in the circus.

Circus Clown ABC (2002) written and illustrated by Denise M. Jordan. Using an alphabet format, this book presents facts about circus clowns.

Circus Family Dog (2000) by Andrew Clements, illustrated by Sue Truesdell. This is the story of a circus dog, Grumps, and the one trick he does in the center ring.

Circus Play (2002) by Anne Laurel Carter, illustrated by Joanne Fitzgerald. A young boy whose mother is a trapeze artist in the circus wonders why he can't have an ordinary mom.

Clown Around (2001) by Dana Meachen Rau, illustrated by Nate Evans. A group of clowns prepare and present their entire act in this delightful picture book.

Dr. Anno's Magical Midnight Circus (1972) by Mitsumasa Anno. The midnight circus begins when the clock strikes twelve and vanishes at dawn.

Emeline at the Circus (2001) written and illustrated by Marjorie Priceman. A girl accidentally becomes part of the circus while on a field trip from school.

Harold's Circus (1981) written and illustrated by Crockett Johnson. With his purple crayon, Harold draws a circus and goes for a walk on the tightrope. This is a companion to the other adventure books about Harold and his purple crayon.

Last Night I Dreamed a Circus (2003) by Maya Gottfried, illustrated by Robert Rahway Zakanitch. With dramatic artwork and brief text for young readers, this is a story about a young girl who dreams she is part of the circus.

Little Black Goes to the Circus (2001) by Walter Farley, illustrated by James Schucker. This is the story of a pony who eventually becomes a success at the circus, following an initial failure.

Meg and Her Circus Tricks (1990) written and illustrated by Graham Percy. A young girl entertains the guests at her brother's birthday party by performing circus tricks.

Miss Bindergarten Plans a Circus with Kindergarten (2002) by Joseph Slate, illustrated by Ashley Wolff. This book shows what young children can do with creativity and a special teacher. The humorous illustrations in this joyous book will delight primary children.

Olivia Saves the Circus (2001) written and illustrated by Ian Falconer. A little pig relates her outrageous imaginary circus adventures as she tells classmates about her vacation.

P. T. Barnum (1997) by David Wright, illustrated by Mike White. This is an introduction to the life of the man who is known as the creator of "the Greatest Show on Earth."

Pamela Camel (1986) written and illustrated by Bill Peet. A sad camel runs away from the circus and has an adventure along a railroad track.

Patrick at the Circus (2002) written and illustrated by Geoffrey Hayes. In this adventure tale, the excitement of the circus comes to life for a young bear.

Peter Spier's Circus! (1995) written and illustrated by Peter Spier. A circus arrives, sets up its tents, performs, and then moves on again. Children will love the detail this artist puts in his illustrations. The brief text allows every reader to focus on the details.

Pippi Goes to the Circus (2000) by Astrid Lindgren, illustrated by Michael Chesworth. Pippi goes to the circus and walks on a tightrope and wrestles with the "World's Strongest Man."

Randy's Dandy Lions (1979) written and illustrated by Bill Peet. This is the story of lions who suffer from stage fright. Will they be able to perform in the circus?

Star of the Circus (1997) by Michael and Mary Beth Sampson, illustrated by Ariane Dewey and Jose Aruego. In this story, circus animals learn that they are indeed stars of the show.

August 1

GAIL GIBBONS: BIRTHDAY
Gail Gibbons was born on August 1, 1944. Having written and published more than one hundred books for children, she is considered a master of children's nonfiction. Her book *From Seed to Plant* (1993) is an introduction to how plants grow and includes a simple project for growing a bean plant. For more information, visit her website at gailgibbons .com. For a slightly older group, her book *Nature's Green Umbrella: Tropical Rain Forests* (1999) helps children understand the controversy centered on tropical rain forests.

FRANCIS SCOTT KEY: BIRTHDAY
The writer of the poem that became our national anthem was born on August 1, 1779. "The Star-Spangled Banner" was written in 1814 but did not become the national anthem until 1931. The flag that the poem was written about flew over Fort McHenry and is now in the Smithsonian in Washington, D.C. A good current version of the poem is *The Star-Spangled Banner* (2000) by Francis Scott Key, illustrated by Ingri D'Aulaire and Edgar Parin D'Aulaire.

August 2

INTERNATIONAL CLOWN WEEK
August 1–7 is celebrated as International Clown Week. This week's thematic listing contains many wonderful resources for introducing your students to all circus performers. After reading several of the circus books, children can make and decorate simple conical clown hats out of construction paper. Then have a circus parade around the classroom or schoolyard. A concluding activity for a clown unit could be making a class ABC book of circus words.

If I Ran the Circus (1956) by Dr. Seuss can spark the imaginations of your students to write their own creative ideas of what they would do if they really did get the chance to run a circus.

August 3

SISTER'S DAY

The special relationship that sisters have is celebrated nationally on the first Sunday in August. The Week Two listing of sibling books broadens to the idea that all siblings share special relationships, whether older, younger, brothers, or sisters. The book *Fathers, Mothers, Sisters, Brothers: A Collection of Family Poems* (2001) by Mary Ann Hoberman celebrates family members in both serious and humorous poems. Several of the books on the thematic list deal with the issue of the arrival of babies in families. Others detail the relationship issue from the blended family perspective. These resources can be especially useful for the teachable moment when a particular child has a special circumstance that needs discussion.

NATIONAL MUSTARD DAY

National Mustard Day is celebrated on the first Saturday in August. The Mustard Museum in Mount Horeb, Wisconsin, is the official sponsor of this annual celebration. As a simple science experiment, have children taste and describe the differences in several kinds of mustard.

August 4

NANCY WHITE CARLSTROM: BIRTHDAY

Nancy White Carlstrom was born on August 4, 1948, and is most famous for her series of books about Jesse Bear. The rhyming text in these books, such as *Jesse Bear, What Will You Wear?*, make perfect read-aloud books for younger children and read-alone books for older primary readers.

What Would You Do If You Lived at the Zoo? (1994) is a great springboard for a creative writing experience. Children can write their own answers to the question posed by the book title.

Blow Me a Kiss, Miss Lilly (1999) is a charming book about aging. Young children often have a difficult time understanding that aging is an aspect of life.

Week Two: Siblings

🏛 Curriculum Connection: Social Studies

It is inevitable that children will bicker and fight with their siblings. It is also inevitable that those same children will want to talk about their plight as youngest, oldest, middle, only boy, only girl, sister, or brother. The books listed here will help with discussions of these topics. There are also resource books listed for the special time when new siblings come into the family either through birth or blending of families.

The Baby Sister (1996) written and illustrated by Tomie dePaola. A young boy is excited about the arrival of a new baby to the family. He would like a baby sister.

Big Sister, Little Sister (2002) by Marci Curtis. Photo illustrations of real-life sisters are used to help describe sisterhood.

A Birthday for Frances (1976) by Russell Hoban, illustrated by Lillian Hoban. In this story, Frances is jealous of her sister having a birthday and getting presents.

Bridget and the Moose Brothers (2004) by Pija Lindenbaum. In this story full of humorous illustrations, an only child decides to try out some visiting moose for brothers.

The Chicken Sisters (1999) by Laura Numeroff, illustrated by Sharleen Collicott. Pictures highlight the silliness in this story of eccentric chicken sisters.

Do You Know What I'll Do? (2000) by Charlotte Zolotow, illustrated by Javaka Steptoe. A delightful story that presents a series of promises from a sister to her brother.

Fathers, Mothers, Sisters, Brothers: A Collection of Family Poems (2001) by Mary Ann Hoberman, illustrated by Marylin Hafner. This collection of poems celebrates all the members of a family and contains both serious and humorous poems.

Green Cat (2002) by Dayal Kaur Khalsa. In this humorous book, siblings are upset about

sharing their room. It gets even more crowded, and they get more upset when Green Cat shows up.

Harriet's Horrible Hair Day (2000) by Dawn Stewart, illustrated by Michael White. A young girl and her sisters try to turn a horrible hair day into a good day by taming a wayward curl.

Henry's First-Moon Birthday (2001) by Lenore Look, illustrated by Yumi Heo. A young girl helps with preparations for the traditional Chinese celebration welcoming a new baby.

Hey Willy, See the Pyramids (1988) by Maira Kalman. A young boy wants his older sister to tell him a million stories, but she will tell him just five very imaginative ones.

I Can't Talk Yet, but When I Do . . . (2003) by Julie Markes, illustrated by Laura Rader. If babies could talk, they would explain all the benefits of having an older sibling.

I'll Fix Anthony (1983) by Judith Viorst, illustrated by Arnold Lobel. A young boy thinks of all the ways he will someday get revenge on his brother. This is a book every child who has an older sibling can relate to.

Julius, the Baby of the World (1995) written and illustrated by Kevin Henkes. Lilly is not thrilled about a new baby coming, until Cousin Garland shows up and Lilly changes her mind.

Lots to Do (1991) by John Prater. This story details a series of adventures that two siblings have as they complete their household chores.

Max Cleans Up (2002) written and illustrated by Rosemary Wells. An older sister tries to take charge of cleaning her younger brother's room. He has ideas of his own, and it doesn't go as she planned.

Molly and the Magic Wishbone (2001) by Barbara McClintock. When a fairy godmother tells a young girl that she will find a wishbone and will be granted one wish, the rest of the family wants to know what the wish will be. Young readers will also want to know.

My Brother, Ant (1997) by Betsy Byars, illustrated by Marc Simont. In this story, a boy tells how his younger brother, Ant, keeps the family on its toes.

My Rotten Redheaded Older Brother (1998) written and illustrated by Patricia Polacco. After losing many contests (including a burping one) to her older brother, a young girl makes a wish on a falling star. This is an American Library Association Notable Children's Book and a *School Library Journal* Best Book of the Year.

Peter's Chair (1998) written and illustrated by Ezra Jack Keats. Peter runs away when he finds out his blue furniture is being painted pink for the arrival of a baby sister.

The Puddle Pail (1997) by Elisa Kleven. This story about two brothers, one who is practical and one who is fanciful, shows how using your imagination can be a good thing.

Sheila Rae, the Brave (1996) written and illustrated by Kevin Henkes. Sheila Rae, who is usually brave, becomes lost, and her sister Louise helps her to overcome her fear.

Sisters (2003) by David McPhail. A heartwarming story that details the differences and similarities among sisters.

Snipp, Snapp, Snurr and the Buttered Bread (1995) written and illustrated by Maj Lindman. In this Swedish story, three young boys want butter for their bread but find out that is not as easy as it sounds.

You'll Soon Grow into Them, Titch (1992) written and illustrated by Pat Hutchins. Younger siblings will relate to this story that discusses the practice of handing down outgrown clothes from one sibling to another.

Yucka Drucka Droni (1998) by Eugenia Radunsky, illustrated by Vladimir Radunsky. This version of the old tongue twister about Yucka, Drucka, and Droni contains illustrations that are as humorous as the characters.

Zack in the Middle (2001) by Dia Michels, illustrated by Fred Bell. This story with humorous illustrations tells of a young boy who is the middle child between two sisters.

August 6

BARBARA COONEY: BIRTHDAY

Barbara Cooney, children's author and illustrator, was born August 6, 1917, and died in 2000. From childhood, she intended to be an artist of some sort. She didn't begin to write books herself until after she had won her second Caldecott Medal for illustration in 1979.

Miss Rumphius (1985) is her most famous book. The illustrations are exquisite. They look like watercolors but are actually done with acrylics and colored pencils.

FRANK ASCH: BIRTHDAY

Frank Asch, born on August 6, 1946, has written in almost every category of children's literature: poetry, concept books, nonfiction, novels, and picture books. He wrote his first book in 1968. I Can Roar Like a Lion (1997) and I Can Blink Like an Owl (1997) can be acted out by children. As a little different twist on the popular tale of the Three Pigs, Asch wrote Ziggy Piggy and the Three Little Pigs (2001), in which a fourth brother is added to the mix, creating a hilarious story that's hard to put down.

August 7

JOY COWLEY: BIRTHDAY

Born in New Zealand on August 7, 1936, Joy Cowley is one of that country's most prolific and successful writers of children's books. She has traveled around the globe meeting children and teachers from Alaska to New York and from South Africa to the Middle East.

Love, humor, and a little twist at the end of the story are key components of Cowley's writing. She enjoys meeting children and hearing what they think about her stories and life in general.

The following books, written by Cowley, are excellent resources. Red-Eyed Tree Frog (1999), with photography by Nic Bishop, reveals the world of the tree frog in vibrant images. Mrs. Wishy-Washy's Farm (2003), illustrated by Elizabeth Fuller, is a delightful story. When Mrs. Wishy-Washy starts scrubbing all the animals on the farm, Duck, Cow, and Pig run away to the big city and get lost. Where is Mrs. Wishy-Washy when they need her? The Rusty, Trusty Tractor (2000), illustrated by Olivier Dunrea, tells of a grandfather's love for a worn-out old tractor.

August 9

PATRICIA MCKISSACK: BIRTHDAY

Patricia McKissack was born on August 9, 1944. She is the author of two especially notable picture books: *Mirandy and Brother Wind* (1997), illustrated by Jerry Pinkney, and *The Honest-to-Goodness Truth* (2002), illustrated by Giselle Potter. She has also written several books for older children.

HAZEL HUTCHINS: BIRTHDAY

Born on this day in 1952, Hazel Hutchins is a Canadian author who realized she wanted to be a writer when she was only ten years old. She has said that she usually rewrites a story at least twelve times before she is satisfied that it is the best it can be. *I'd Know You Anywhere* (2002) is a charming, rhyming book about the interactions between a father and his son.

SEYMOUR SIMON: BIRTHDAY

Seymour Simon was born on August 9, 1931, and has written more than two hundred highly acclaimed science books for children. His Let's Try It Out series has science activities on several different topics for grades K–2. Seymour Simon makes science fun. He is also known for his remarkable photography of the planets, moon, solar system, and wildlife. He has written books on the weather and on weather-related phenomena, such as earthquakes and tornadoes, as well.

August 11

JOANNA COLE: BIRTHDAY

Joanna Cole, best known for her nonfiction Magic School Bus series, was born on August 11, 1944. The Magic School Bus series has its own website: scholastic.com/magicschoolbus.

Cole is a parenting expert and has written two books—*I'm a Big Sister* (1997) and *I'm a Big Brother* (1997)—which blend into the sibling theme this week. Both books are illustrated by Maxie Chambliss.

She also wrote the book *Anna Banana: 101 Jump Rope Rhymes* (1989), illustrated by Alan Tiegreen, which has more than one hundred traditional jump rope rhymes. Jumping rope can be a great physical education activity. Remind the boys that many athletes use jumping rope in their training schedules.

DON FREEMAN: BIRTHDAY

The illustrator of the children's classic, *Corduroy*, Don Freeman was born on August 11 in 1908. This book can be used for many activities. As a creative-writing assignment, ask the students to imagine what a child's toys might do when no people are around. The sequel, *A Pocket for Corduroy*, is also well loved.

Week Three: Inventors

✣ Curriculum Connection: Science

Many of the questions that children ask are related to everyday items, how they came to be, and who thought them up. These questions can range from who invented airplanes to who came up with the idea of zippers.

The resources listed here detail the lives of several well-known inventors such as Ben Franklin and the Wright Brothers. They also tell the stories behind such common inventions as marbles, zippers, and potato chips. Students will be surprised at how many of these inventions were the result of thoughts that the inventors had as children. It is amazing what children can think up—maybe one of your students will invent something wonderfully useful from one of the ideas you share with them from this list of books!

Alexander Graham Bell: Inventor of the Telephone (2002) by Carin Ford. Children will be surprised to learn that Bell was a teacher and inventor. He was best known for his work with the deaf before he invented the telephone.

Ben Franklin and His First Kite (2002) by Stephen Krensky, illustrated by Bert Dodson. As a youngster Ben Franklin was quickly bored doing ordinary work. He was much more interested in doing experiments as this book tells.

Boing-Boing the Bionic Cat (2000) by Larry Hench, illustrated by Ruth Denise Lear. This story tells of a young boy with an allergy to cats. An engineering professor builds him a cat of his very own which delights the young boy.

The Day-Off Machine (1990) by John Himmelman. Young readers will delight in this talented beaver family who are inventors as well as fixer-uppers.

Clarence Birdseye (2003) by Tiffany Peterson. Children are introduced to the man who founded the Birdseye Frosted Foods Company in 1929 when he invented a quick-freeze method for food.

Eli Whitney: American Inventor (2003) by Katie Bagley and Ray Hurt. This book is the biography of Eli Whitney whose invention of the cotton gin changed agriculture.

Garrett Morgan, Inventor (1992) by Garnet Jackson, illustrated by Thomas Hudson. This biography of an African American inventor describes how his interest in machines led to the invention of the traffic signal.

George Eastman: The Kodak Camera Man (2004) by Carin Ford. This book for older primary readers describes the life of the man who developed a camera simple enough for anyone to use.

The Great Leaf Blast-Off (1990) by John Himmelman. The author tells the story of a family of inventors in a very entertaining way.

Herbert Binns and the Flying Tricycle (1987) by Caroline Castle, illustrated by Peter Weevers. Jealous friends plot to sabotage a new invention, a flying tricycle, invented by a very clever mouse.

How Ben Franklin Stole the Lightning (2002) by Rosalyn Schanzer. This is a good combination of information and illustrations that details the biography of Ben Franklin in a charming way.

I Wonder Why Zippers Have Teeth and Other Questions About Inventions (2003) written and illustrated by Barbara Taylor. Find answers to a variety of questions about the invention of common items.

Imaginative Inventions: The Who, What, Where, When and Why of Roller Skates, Potato Chips, Marbles, and Pie (and More!) (2001) written and illustrated by Charise Harper. This informative book explains how everyday things came to be in a very witty way.

Inventions: Great Ideas and Where They Came From (2002) by Sarah Houghton and Elaine Lally. This book for older primary readers features inventions throughout history.

Maria's Comet (1999) by Deborah Hopkinson, illustrated by Deborah Lanino. This book is based on the childhood of Maria Mitchell who was the first American woman to discover a comet.

One Thing Leads to Another (2003) by Debra Lucas. The author details how ideas can lead to inventions, such as Toll House cookies.

A Picture Book of Benjamin Franklin (1991) by David A. Adler, illustrated by John and Alexandra Wallner. This is a great resource for primary students who want to learn about the life of Benjamin Franklin.

A Picture Book of Thomas Alva Edison (1996) by David A. Adler, illustrated by Alexandra and John Wallner. This book, which appeals to both young and reluctant readers, is an introduction to Edison, who invented numerous items such as the movie camera, and the phonograph, as well as the lightbulb.

Popcorn at the Palace (1997) by Emily McCully. This book explains how American popcorn got to Europe in the 1800s

The Real McCoy: The Life of an African-American Inventor (1994) by Wendy Towle, illustrated by Wil Clay. This is the story of a black American who patented more than fifty inventions while overcoming the obstacles he faced because of his race.

Robert Fulton (2003) by Pam Rosenberg. Follow a discussion of the life and work of the inventor who developed the steamboat.

Samuel F. B. Morse: Inventor and Code Creator (2003) by Judy Alter. This book presents a biography of the inventor who devised the world's first practical telegraph system.

Samuel Todd's Book of Great Inventions (1999) by E. Konigsburg. Samuel Todd shows readers some of the inventions that make everyone's day easier and better, including the thermos bottle and backpacks.

The Wright Brothers (2003) by Pamela Edwards, illustrated by Henry Cole. In this picture book, young readers are introduced to the steps that led up to the Wright Brothers' flight.

August 12

UNITED NATIONS INTERNATIONAL YOUTH DAY

August 12 is International Youth Day at the United Nations. This is a good day to introduce your students to the United Nations website (un.org), which has information for all ages. Interesting facts and pictures of all members' flags are presented, as are many other teaching resources.

The book *Come Out and Play* (2001) by Maya Ajmera has gorgeous photographs of smiling children from more than thirty-five countries. John Ivanko provided the outstanding photographs.

MARY ANN HOBERMAN: BIRTHDAY

Mary Ann Hoberman was born on August 12, 1930. She wrote an expanded adaptation of the familiar hand-clapping rhyme, *Miss Mary Mack* (1998), illustrated by Nadine Wescott. This book contains the music and directions for the hand-clapping actions and would make a great physical education rhythm activity for August days that are too hot for more strenuous activities. Hoberman also wrote *One of Each* (2000), illustrated by Marjorie Priceman, that is a good read-aloud dealing with friendship.

August 16

BEATRICE SCHENK DE REGNIERS: BIRTHDAY

Beatrice Schenk de Regniers was born in 1914 and died in 2000. She was the author of *May I Bring a Friend?* (1974), illustrated by Beni Montresor, which won the Caldecott Medal in 1965.

Her book *So Many Cats* (2002), illustrated by Ellen Weiss, is a wonderful counting story in verse. It will have children chiming in as you read it to them.

What Can You Do with a Shoe? (2001), illustrated by Maurice Sendak, is a perfect model for a lesson in creative thinking. There's lots of fun to be had with this book as children produce more ways to use the everyday items mentioned.

NATIONAL INVENTORS' MONTH

August has been designated National Inventors' Month to heighten awareness of the value of creativity and the importance of inventions and inventors to the quality of our lives. The website invent.org has additional resources for teachers and students. The National Inventors Hall of Fame and Museum is located in Akron, Ohio. How about a field trip?

August 17

DAVID (DAVY) CROCKETT: BIRTHDAY

Davy Crockett, one of America's real-life heroes, was born on this day in 1786 and died at the Alamo in Texas in 1836. *Davy Crockett* (2004) by Larry Brimner, illustrated by Donna Berger, and *A Picture Book of Davy Crockett* (1998) by David A. Adler, illustrated by Alexandra and John Wallner, both describe the life and adventures of the famous congressman and legendary tall-tale hero. You can discuss tall tales with your class and make up a new one together starring Davy Crockett, King of the Wild Frontier. Remember that in a tall tale, everything becomes larger than life each time it is told.

MYRA COHN LIVINGSTON: BIRTHDAY

Children's poet Myra Cohn Livingston was born in 1926 and died in 1996. She compiled several anthologies of poetry, including *Christmas Poems* (1988), illustrated by Trina Hyman, and *If You Ever Meet a Whale* (1992), illustrated by Leonard Fisher. Her book *Lots of Limericks* (1991), illustrated by Rebecca Perry, is a great read-aloud for a day that needs some silliness and giggles.

August 19

ORVILLE WRIGHT: BIRTHDAY

August 19 is the birthday of aviation pioneer Orville Wright, who was born in 1871 and died in 1948. *The Wright Brothers* (2003) by Pamela Edwards, illustrated by Henry Cole, teaches children about the incredible advances that Orville (along with his brother, Wilbur) made in opening the sky for human travel. It is historically accurate and contains many pictures.

NATIONAL AVIATION DAY

National Aviation Day was first proclaimed in 1939 and has been celebrated on August 19 ever since. *The Wright Brothers for Kids: How They Invented the Airplane* (2003) by Mary Carson, illustrated by Laura D'Argo, is a fantastic resource for celebrating this day. The hands-on activities are great for helping children to understand the science involved in flight. This resource also includes websites for further investigation by interested students. The book has many illustrations and highlights the ingenuity and problem-solving abilities of the Wright brothers.

Week Four: Butterflies

✳ Curriculum Connection: Science

So much of the real world is too big for young children to grasp, and natural changes and growth take too long to happen. But this is not true of butterflies and other insect changes. By studying butterflies and their life cycle, children can learn many life lessons and scientific truths and also increase their vocabulary. Most of the resources listed here are both accurate and beautifully illustrated. However some fiction stories are included to provide a balance.

Angelina and the Butterfly (2002) by Sally-Ann Lever, illustrated by Helen Craig. When a mouse finds a butterfly with a twisted leg, she wants to look after it and keep it forever until a surprising turn of events sets the butterfly free.

Are You a Butterfly? (2003) by Judy Allen, illustrated by Tudor Humphries. This introduction to the life cycle of a butterfly has a special "Did you know . . ." section of interesting trivia.

Born to Be a Butterfly (2000) by Karen Wallace. Young readers will learn about the transformation of a caterpillar to a Red Admiral butterfly.

The Butterfly Alphabet Book (1995) by Brian Cassie and Jerry Pallotta, illustrated by Mark Astrella. This alphabet book presents fascinating information and beautiful illustrations of butterflies.

The Butterfly Alphabet (1999) written and photographed by Kjell Sandved. A nature photographer presents photographs of butterflies from around the world. His close-up views of wing designs look like letters of the alphabet.

The Butterfly's Dream (2003) retold by Ippo Keido and Marc Hendler, illustrated by Kazuko Stone. In ancient China, a man falls asleep beneath a willow tree and dreams he is a butterfly. This book teaches children to see the world from new and unique perspectives.

The Caterpillar and the Polliwog (1985) written and illustrated by Jack Kent. This book tells the story of the changes that a caterpillar goes through to become a butterfly. Readers will learn if the polliwog can also make those changes.

Charlie the Caterpillar (1993) by Dom Deluise, illustrated by Christopher Santoro. In this story about the meaning of friendship, a caterpillar is rejected by various animals until he achieves his wings.

Clara Caterpillar (2001) by Pamela Edwards, illustrated by Henry Cole. Using camouflage, a Caterpillar caterpillar becomes a cream-colored butterfly and courageously saves a crimson-colored butterfly from a crow.

Fabulous Fluttering Tropical Butterflies (2003) by Dorothy Patent, illustrated by Jan Jubb. This book describes the behavior of various kinds of butterflies and how they have adapted to survive in the rain forest environment.

Farfallina and Marcel (2002) by Holly Keller. As friends grow up they undergo changes that separate them.

From Egg to Butterfly (2002) by Shannon Zemlicka. This book follows the development of a butterfly from an egg to an insect that flies away.

Gotta Go! Gotta Go! (2000) by Sam Swope, illustrated by Sue Riddle. Follow the story of a small bug who is certain that she must go to Mexico even though she doesn't know why.

I Wish I Were a Butterfly (1994) by James Howe, illustrated by Ed Young. A dragonfly helps a sad cricket, who wants to be a butterfly, realize that he is special.

An Invitation to the Butterfly Ball: A Counting Rhyme (1997) by Jane Yolen, illustrated by Jane Zalben. All the invited animals busily prepare to attend the Butterfly Ball.

Isabel's House of Butterflies (2003) by Tony Johnston, illustrated by Susan Guevara. In autumn a miracle happens in Mexico as an area becomes a wintering place for thousands of monarch butterflies that migrate from the north. They transform the tree outside of a young girl's home into a house of butterflies. This special book is based on the fact that one three-hundred-square-mile area provides a sanctuary for monarch butterflies.

The Lamb and the Butterfly (1991) by Arnold Sundgaard, illustrated by Eric Carle. Two animals meet in a meadow and discuss the different ways they live in this story about accepting the differences of others and appreciating independence.

Painted Lady Butterflies (1999) by Donna Schaffer. The author describes the physical characteristics, habits, and stages of develop-

ment of painted lady butterflies. This book also includes additional reading suggestions and Internet websites about butterflies.

Peewee Pipes and the Wing Thing (2000) by Francine Poppo Rich, illustrated by Thomas Bone. This story provides some good, accurate information about the food chain while readers ponder what is more important, friendship or a meal.

Waiting for Wings (2001) written and illustrated by Lois Ehlert. This simple book provides answers to such questions as where butterflies come from, how they are born, and what they eat.

Where Did the Butterfly Get Its Name? (2003) by Gilda and Melvin Berger, illustrated by Barbara Bond. In this book children learn that butterflies taste with their feet and that the largest butterflies can grow to be almost a foot wide.

Where Does the Butterfly Go When It Rains? (1997) by May Garelick, illustrated by Nicholas Wilton. In simple text, this book describes what different animals do when it rains.

Wings of Change (2001) by Franklin Hill, illustrated by Aries Cheung. This book tells of a young caterpillar that is afraid of turning into a butterfly. It was written to help children adjust to the changes that occur in their lives.

August 21

HAWAII GRANTED STATEHOOD
Hawaii was admitted as the fiftieth state on August 21, 1959. Admission is celebrated as a state holiday in Hawaii on the third Friday in August. *Hawaii Facts and Symbols* (2003) by Emily McAuliffe presents information about the state for younger readers. The U.S. flag now in use was designed to include the fiftieth star for Hawaii. This flag was first flown on July 4, 1960.

FALL MIGRATION OF MONARCH BUTTERFLIES
The annual fall migration of monarch butterflies begins around August 21 and continues until early November. The butterflies fly south to avoid the cold northern winters. The thematic listing of books for Week Four has great resources.

ARTHUR YORINKS: BIRTHDAY
Arthur Yorinks was born on this day in 1953. He has written many books for children, including *Hey, Al*, which won the Caldecott Medal in 1987. His book *Maurice Sendak's Seven Little Monsters: What Time Is It?* (2004) is a great resource for learning to tell time.

August 22

CLAUDE DEBUSSY: BIRTHDAY
August 22 is the birthday of French composer Claude Debussy. He was born in 1862 and died in 1918. He is most remembered for his piano compositions *La Mer* (*The Sea*) and *Claire de Lune*. Both of these pieces are a good way to introduce children to this composer. A resource for more information is *Lives of the Musicians: Good Times, Bad Times (and What the Neighbors Thought)* (2002) by Kathleen Krull, illustrated by Kathryn Hewitt.

Children should be introduced to classical works and their composers at a young age and in small increments. Debussy believed that music is made up of colors and rhythms. This makes a perfect pairing of art and music. Have the children draw pictures of the sea as they listen to *La Mer*. Music, art, and literature can be melded effectively to help children develop cultural literacy.

August 28

CIVIL RIGHTS MARCH ON WASHINGTON

August 28, 1963, was the date of the March on Washington at which time Martin Luther King, Jr., made his "I Have a Dream" speech. *Martin Luther King, Jr., and the March on Washington* (2000) by Frances Ruffin captures the spirit of this demonstration by 250,000 people demanding equal rights and brings King's most famous speech to life.

ROGER DUVOISIN: BIRTHDAY

Roger Duvoisin, who was born on this day in 1904 and died in 1980, is best remembered for *Petunia*, the book he wrote and illustrated. The story of a silly goose, *Petunia* is still as fresh and entertaining as it was when it was written in 1950. Duvoisin won the Caldecott Medal in 1948 for the illustrations in *White Snow, Bright Snow* (1988) by Alvin Tresselt.

ALLEN SAY: BIRTHDAY

Allen Say, children's illustrator and author, was born in Japan on August 28, 1937. He wrote and illustrated *Grandfather's Journey*, which won the Caldecott Medal in 1994.

August 30

VIRGINIA LEE BURTON: BIRTHDAY

Virginia Burton, who was born in 1909 and died in 1968, is most remembered for her book *Mike Mulligan and His Steam Shovel*, written in 1939. It is still popular today, as is another favorite, *Katy and the Big Snow*. She always drew the illustrations for her books first then wrote the text, and her attention to detail paid off. In 1942, she won a Caldecott Medal for her illustrations in *The Little House*.

HELEN CRAIG: BIRTHDAY

Helen Craig was born in London in 1934. She illustrated the Angelina Ballerina books written by Katharine Holabird. Craig uses mice for her illustrations because they can mimic human postures and emotions. Her advice to aspiring illustrators is to never give up!

DONALD CREWS: BIRTHDAY

Donald Crews, author and illustrator, was born in 1938. He illustrated *Tomorrow's Alphabet* (1999) by George Shannon, which is a great book for practicing the skill of prediction. He also illustrated *Each Orange Had Eight Slices* (1999) by Paul Giganti, which is excellent for introducing the concept of multiplication. It has bold pictures and can be enjoyed by children of many ages.

August Reading Strategy

Importance of Informational Texts

In this book, a balance of fiction and informational (nonfiction) books is presented for use with young primary-aged children. It is believed that the various forms of informational books are not used as often as they should be with this age group. It is sometimes easier to fall back on fictional classics rather than expend the extra energy needed to introduce informational texts to students. There are several reasons for using nonfiction books with young primary-grade children.

The most compelling reason is that most of what children read outside of reading classes in school is informational text. The advances in technology and information put higher literacy demands on all readers starting with beginners. To fully comprehend informational text, children must have the necessary skills and motivation to challenge themselves. Another reason for helping children comprehend informational text is that most standardized tests include this form of text. However, the most important reason is that there are many children who truly enjoy reading when the material is factual rather than fully fictional, and there are more beautiful, engaging and interesting informational books being published today than ever before.

In choosing informational books for young children, it is important to choose those that have accurate content. It is also important that the format and design of the book support the content, and that the content is appropriate to the age of the reader. The writing style must use lively, engaging language with accurate terminology and with generalizations and concepts given in simple terms. Text should not be just a listing of facts. The book itself should be organized as an informational text so that readers become familiar with things such as the table of contents, the index, the glossary, headings, and subheadings.

The before and during reading strategies discussed in previous months are applicable to informational text as well as to fiction. Informational text provides many models for report writing for older primary students.

September at a Glance

One of the greatest gifts adults can give to their offspring—and to society—is to read to children.
—Carl Sagan

September Reading Tip: Make sure that children have enough time set aside during every day to practice reading skills. They need to have reading time specifically for both pleasure and information.

SEPTEMBER HIGHLIGHTS
National Honey Month
The Honey Makers (2000) by Gail Gibbons delves into the honeycomb to explore the life and habits of honeybees.

Library Card Sign-Up Month
Sam's First Library Card (2003) by Gail Herman, illustrated by Tamara Petrosino, is the story of a young boy who doesn't want to part with the library books he checked out with his new card.

National Hispanic Heritage Month (September 15–October 15)
Hispanic Holidays (1996) by Faith Winchester briefly introduces Hispanic Americans and discusses nine Hispanic holidays. Instructions for making a piñata are included.

National Dog Week (fourth week in September)
Get ready to howl over *The Dog from Arf! Arf! to Zzzzzz* (2004), written and illustrated by the Dog Artlist Collection staff. It's an ABC book of sweet and adorable puppies.

Deaf Awareness Week (fourth week in September)
This week is set aside by the World Federation of the Deaf to celebrate the culture, heritage, and language unique to deaf people of the world. For further information see the website nad.org.

September Reading Strategy: Time and Text

WEEKLY THEMES AND CURRICULUM CONNECTIONS
Week One: Grandparents (Social Studies)
Week Two: Insects (Science)
Week Three: Food (Science and Health)
Week Four: Hispanic Heritage (Social Studies)

Special Events in September

Labor Day	Sept. 1
National Honey Month	Sept. 3
National Grandparents Day	Sept. 4
National 911 Day	Sept. 11
Patriot Day	Sept. 11
Library Card Sign-Up Month	Sept. 13
Whooping Crane Fall Migration	Sept. 15
International Day of Peace	Sept. 16
Celebration USA	Sept. 17
Hispanic Heritage Month	Sept. 18
National Dog Week	Sept. 21
National Farm Animals Awareness Week	Sept. 21
Elephant Appreciation Day	Sept. 22

FEATURED SEPTEMBER BIRTHDAYS

Jim Arnosky ....Sept. 1	Alexandra Day ....Sept. 7	H. A. Rey ....Sept. 16
Jane Hissey ....Sept. 1	Eric Hill.........................Sept. 7	Paul Goble ....Sept. 17
Demi ....Sept. 2	Jack Prelutsky ....Sept. 8	Arthur Geisert ....Sept. 20
Bernard Most ....Sept. 2	Jon Scieszka ....Sept. 8	Tony Tallarico ....Sept. 20
Ellen Stoll Walsh ....Sept. 2	Else Minarik ....Sept. 13	Esphyr Slobodkina ......Sept. 22
Aliki ....Sept. 3	Tomie dePaola ....Sept. 15	Martin Handford ....Sept. 27
Syd Hoff.......................Sept. 4	Robert McClosky ....Sept. 15	Bernard Waber ....Sept. 27

Week One: Grandparents

🏛 Curriculum Connection: Social Studies

This thematic grouping of resources celebrates the older people in children's lives—not just their biological grandparents, but all older people with whom they may have contact on a daily basis.

The following books introduce children to an array of older people in various settings. Also found on this list are several books that deal sensitively with the death of an older person. Death is depicted as part of the natural cycle of life.

Abuela (1997) by Arthur Dorros, illustrated by Elisa Kleven. This fantasy is told by a Hispanic American child who imagines she is rising into the air and flying away with her grandmother. The story contains Spanish words integrated with the English text.

Abuela's Weave (1995) by Omar Castaneda, illustrated by Enrique Sanchez. A young Guatemalan girl and her grandmother grow closer as they weave some special creations about their country's rich past.

Annie and the Old One (1985) by Miska Miles, illustrated by Peter Parnall. A Navajo grandmother says that when a rug is completely woven, she will die; her granddaughter tries to hold back time by unweaving the rug.

The Bee Tree (1998) written and illustrated by Patricia Polacco. Explore the loving relationship between a grandfather and his granddaughter in this story that extols the value of books.

Grandma Summer (2001) written and illustrated by Harley Jessup. A young boy finds that family history and other treasures are at grandma's house.

Grandpa and Bo (2002) written and illustrated by Kevin Henkes. This story relates the feelings of a grandpa and his grandson who don't get to see each other very often.

Grandpa Never Lies (2000) by Ralph Fletcher, illustrated by Harvey Stevenson. This account of a man and his granddaughter who love and trust each other is written with humor and deep feeling.

Grandparent Poems (2004) compiled by John Micklos, illustrated by Layne Johnson. This book contains selections by various authors that celebrate intergenerational love.

Grandparents Are the Greatest Because . . . (2003) by Adele Greenspun and Joanie Schwarz, designed by Irene Vandevoort. Photographs accompany the lively text that highlights what's best about grandparents.

Grandparents: Around the World (1999) written and illustrated by Patricia Lakin. For the older primary reader, this book examines and compares the roles of older people in many countries of the world. It gives children in the United States a broader perspective concerning older people.

Grandpas Are for Finding Worms (2000) by Harriet Ziefert, illustrated by Jennifer Plecas. Grandpas seem to know where the worms are when children want to go fishing. Children and grandpas will enjoy this story.

Hurry! (2000) by Jessie Haas, illustrated by Joseph Smith. This 2001 Notable Children's Trade Book tells the story of how a young girl is able to help her grandparents.

Little Bear's Visit (1979) by Else Minarik, illustrated by Maurice Sendak. This 1962 Caldecott Honor Book depicts the wonderful time children have visiting with grandparents

The Moon Lady (1995) by Amy Tan, illustrated by Gretchen Schields. A grandmother relates to her granddaughters the story of her outing to see the Moon Lady and how she was granted a wish.

My Most Favorite Thing (2001) by Nicola Moon, illustrated by Carol Thompson. A young girl's relationship with her grandfather is explored in this warm story.

The Patchwork Quilt (1985) by Valerie Flournoy, illustrated by Jerry Pinkney. A young girl uses scraps to help her grandmother and mother make a quilt that tells the story of the family's life in this winner of the Coretta Scott King Illustrator Award.

The Squeaky, Creaky Bed (2003) by Pat Thomson, illustrated by Niki Daly. This tale is about a little boy who has trouble falling asleep at his grandparents' house.

Thank You, Grandpa (2003) by Lynn Plourde, illustrated by Jason Cockcroft. This story traces the lives of a girl and her grandfather through walks they take in the woods during their lifetimes.

Up, Up, Up! It's Apple-Picking Time (2003) by Jody Fickes Shapiro, illustrated by Kitty Harvill. This charming book tells the story of a boy's experience picking and selling apples at his grandparents' apple farm.

Walking with Maga (2002) by Maureen Boyd Biro, illustrated by Joyce Wheeler. This is a great read-aloud story about why it is slower to take walks with an older person.

The Wednesday Surprise (1990) by Eve Bunting, illustrated by Donald Carrick. This is a story about a granddaughter who is successful in teaching her grandmother to read.

What Grandmas Do Best (2001) by Laura Numeroff, illustrated by Lynn Munsinger. This book is a great discussion starter for what each child thinks their grandma does best.

What Grandpas Do Best (2001) by Laura Numeroff, illustrated by Lynn Munsinger. Animal grandpas share a variety of activities with their grandchildren much like humans do.

When I Am Old with You (1993) by Angela Johnson, illustrated by David Soman. In this Coretta Scott King Author Award Book, a child imagines being old with her granddaddy and joining him in his daily activities.

Zero Grandparents (2002) written and illustrated by Michelle Edwards. This book deals sensitively with the issue of unavailable grandparents and what one girl does about it.

September 1

LABOR DAY
Labor Day, celebrated on the first Monday in September, is set aside to honor the working people of America. First celebrated in 1882, Congress made it a legal holiday in 1894. Labor Day reminds us of the contributions workers have made to the strength, prosperity, and well-being of the United States.

JIM ARNOSKY: BIRTHDAY
Jim Arnosky—naturalist, author, and painter—was born September 1, 1946. He has written more than forty-five books—many of them sketching and drawing books. His character Crinkleroot adds a sense of adventure to books such as *Crinkleroot's Guide to Knowing Animal Habitats* (2000). Arnosky's website, jimarnosky.com, has coloring pages and information about this artist who originally wanted to be a cartoonist. He considers himself a wildlife watcher and lets his pictures determine the stories he writes.

JANE HISSEY: BIRTHDAY
Children's author and illustrator Jane Hissey has a website (janehissey.com) that provides a wealth of information on her book *Old Bear* (1986). She uses colored pencils for her illustrations and began drawing as a young child.

September 2

DEMI: BIRTHDAY
Demi, the children's author and illustrator who loves India, was born on this day in 1942. His book *One Grain of Rice* (1997) has stunning illustrations and makes for a great lesson in math concepts. *The Empty Pot* (1996) contains a wonderful message about honesty.

BERNARD MOST: BIRTHDAY
Bernard Most, born in 1937, is the author of *Cock-a-Doodle-Moo* (1996) and many books about dinosaurs. He always wanted to be an artist and started drawing at age four. Many of his books, like *There's an Ant in Anthony* (1992), are actually word games. He has a website for his fans at bernardmost.com.

ELLEN STOLL WALSH: BIRTHDAY
Ellen Stoll Walsh was born on September 2, 1942. She is the author and illustrator of *Mouse Count* (1995) and *Mouse Paint* (1995). Her illustrations are made of finely cut paper. *Mouse Paint* provides the motivation for an art lesson on mixing colors. *Mouse Count* has many avenues for teaching on planning ahead, cooperation, and problem solving.

September 3

ALIKI: BIRTHDAY

Aliki, a prolific author and illustrator, was born Aliki Brandenberg on September 3, 1929. She was recognized as having a talent for art when she was in kindergarten. Her Let's Read and Find Out series and her wonderful science book *Digging Up Dinosaurs* (1988) are well known. *The Listening Walk* (1993) by Paul Showers, which she illustrated, and *My Five Senses* (1991) and *How a Book Is Made* (1991) which she wrote and illustrated, are all wonderful nonfiction books for primary-aged students.

NATIONAL HONEY MONTH

September is National Honey Month. Honey immediately brings to mind bees and from bees it is just a small jump to all insects. Week Two's thematic listing has resources for children on the world of insects. To begin the celebration of National Honey Month, read *The Magic School Bus: Inside a Beehive* (1997) by Joanna Cole, illustrated by Bruce Degan. *Busy Buzzy Bee* (1999) by Karen Wallace is interesting for younger students.

September 4

SYD HOFF: BIRTHDAY

Syd Hoff was born on September 4, 1912. His *Danny and the Dinosaur* (1978) is a great book for boys who are transitioning to longer books. It is easy to read and has a boy as the main character. *Sammy the Seal* (1999), *Chester* (1991), and *Captain Cat* (1994) also appeal to beginning readers.

NATIONAL GRANDPARENTS DAY

National Grandparents Day is celebrated the first Sunday after Labor Day. It was first proclaimed in 1978 by former president Jimmy Carter. This week's thematic listing provides many resources on older people involved in the lives of primary children.

This is another area where adults need to be sensitive to the family structures of the children with whom they work. Many students are now being raised by grandparents or other caring older people. A creative writing exercise could be developed on the theme "What We Like About Older People."

Week Two: Insects

❋ Curriculum Connection: Science

The following list of books about insects can be used both now and again in the spring. Bugs of all kinds are fascinating to children.

Alpha Bugs (1994) written and illustrated by David Carter. This delightful alphabet book is truly interactive as it features scratch-and-sniff, touch-and-feel, and pop-ups. Younger children will enjoy the illustrations.

Bugs Are Insects (2001) by Anne Rockwell and Steve Jenkins. This is an introduction to common backyard insects. Discover a hidden world of tiny creatures building their homes, stalking their prey, and hiding from their enemies right in your own backyard.

Bugs! Bugs! Bugs! (1999) written and illustrated by Bob Barner. This nonsense rhyme introduces children to familiar bugs and includes a fun facts section, which gives bug-loving children more information.

Bugs: A Close-Up View of the Insect World (2001) by Chris Maynard. Answer questions about insects while encouraging readers to study more about them. This book also explains the difference between insects and bugs.

Bugs (1988) by Joan Wright, illustrated by Nancy Parker. This book has general information, jokes, and descriptions of the characteristics, habits, and natural environment of common insects.

Buzz! A Book About Insects (2000) by Melvin Berger. Explore the world of insects in this book that is full of information and good photographs, which accompanies the simple text.

Farfallina and Marcel (2002) written and illustrated by Holly Keller. This 2002 winner of the Best Children's Picture Book Award is the story of a caterpillar and a gosling who remain friends in the face of change.

The 512 Ants on Sullivan Street (1997) by Carol Losi, Laurence White, and Ray Broekel. In this cumulative story, the number of ants doubles each time they take a new treat from a picnic lunch. Children will enjoy the math lesson as well as the bug lesson in this book.

The Beetle Alphabet Book (2004) by Jerry Pallotta, illustrated by David Biedrzycki. Letters of the alphabet are used to introduce various kinds of beetles in this informative and humorous book. Children will be surprised to learn there are so many kinds of beetles.

The Best Book of Bugs (1998) by Claire Llewellyn, illustrated by David Wright, Christopher Forsey, and Andrea Ricciardi. The reader is presented with a worm's-eye view of a multitude of marching legs, scary-looking pincers, and fast-flying wings.

The Best Bug Parade (1996) by Stuart Murphy, illustrated by Holly Keller. A variety of different bugs compare their relative sizes. Comparing and contrasting sizes is an important early math skill.

Giggle Bugs: A Lift-and-Laugh Book (1999) written and illustrated by David Carter. Lift-the-flap riddles and a giggling sound chip will make children laugh out loud in this interactive bug book.

How Do Flies Walk Upside Down? (1999) by Melvin and Gilda Berger, illustrated by Jim Effler. A series of questions and answers provides information about the life cycles and behavior of different insects.

I Wish I Were a Butterfly (1994) by James Howe, illustrated by Ed Young. A wise dragonfly helps a sad cricket realize that he is special in his own way.

Insect Invaders (2002) by Anne Capeci, illustrated by John Speirs. When a girl brings ladybugs to school, the class ends up on an insect field trip.

Insect Soup: Bug Poems (1999) by Barry Polisar, illustrated by David Clark. This illustrated collection of funny poems about insects will delight readers.

It's a Good Thing There Are Insects (1991) by Allan Fowler. This book identifies the characteristics of insects and describes their useful activities and products.

The Magic School Bus Explores the World of Bugs (2002) by Nancy White. Board the Magic School Bus to learn about the world of insects with Ms. Frizzle's class.

Monster Bugs (1996) by Lucille Recht Penner. Some of the world's largest insects are described for slightly older primary readers.

Mystery in Bugtown (1997) by William Boniface, illustrated by Jim Harris. This book contains a pair of roaming eyeballs that wiggle and jiggle from page to page, adding to the children's enjoyment of this mystery of who flattened the roach.

On Beyond Bugs: All About Insects (1999) by Dr. Seuss and Tish Rabe, illustrated by Aristides Ruiz. The Cat in the Hat and company present an up-close view of life as a bug. Readers will find out more than they ever wanted to know about insects.

One Hundred Shoes (2002) by Charles Ghigna, illustrated by Bob Staake. This math book clearly demonstrates the math concepts of pairs and multiple sets using simple text and bright illustrations.

Over in the Garden (2002) by Jennifer Ward, illustrated by Kenneth Spengler. This counting book uses the familiar tune of "Over in the Meadow" to present many ugly bugs.

Snug as a Big Red Bug (1999) by Frank Edwards, illustrated by John Bianchi. The colorful illustrations add greatly to this book as readers follow the trail of a little red bug searching for a warm place to spend the winter.

Two Bad Ants (1988) written and illustrated by Chris Van Allsburg. When two bad ants desert their colony, they experience a dangerous adventure.

Under One Rock: Bugs, Slugs, and Other Ughs (2001) by Anthony Fredericks, illustrated by Jennifer DiRubbio. Prior to reading this book, ask the children if they have ever looked underneath a rock. This book details the creatures living there.

September 7

ALEXANDRA DAY: BIRTHDAY

Alexandra Day is the pen name of Sandra Darling, who was born on this date in 1941. A discussion could be held on the meaning of pen names and why some authors use them. Alexandra Day calls herself a realistic illustrator. She believes that genuineness is the one essential ingredient in a children's book.

Good Dog, Carl (1985) and the many other Carl books were written by Day. Carl even has his own website at gooddogcarl.com.

The concept of making a scrapbook could be introduced using the book *Carl Makes a Scrapbook* (1994). You could have a class scrapbook or each child could make his or her own for the school year. Add pages as a monthly art activity.

ERIC HILL: BIRTHDAY

Eric Hill, the author of *Where's Spot?* (2003) and the many other Spot books, was born on September 7, 1927. *Where's Spot?* has been published in sixty-five languages in more than a hundred countries since it was written in 1980.

September 8

JACK PRELUTSKY: BIRTHDAY

Jack Prelutsky, children's poet, was born on September 8, 1940. With more than thirty-six books published for children, his advice to young writers is to *read, read, read* and *write, write, write.*

His most famous collection of poems is *New Kid on the Block* (1990), illustrated by James Stevenson. He also wrote *It's Raining Pigs and Noodles* (2000), illustrated by James Stevenson, and *Monday's Troll* (2000), illustrated by Peter Sis. He has a website for teachers to help children write poetry—teacher.scholastic.com.

JON SCIESZKA: BIRTHDAY

Jon Scieszka's birthday is also September 8; he was born in 1954. He first became a teacher and then an author. He was influenced by *Green Eggs and Ham* to write *The Stinky Cheese Man* (2000), a 1993 Caldecott Honor Book, and *The True Story of Three Little Pigs* (1996). He enjoys writing fractured fairy tales that offer a different point of view. His motto in writing is "never underestimate the intelligence of a young audience." Kids can be silly and smart.

September 11

NATIONAL 911 DAY

Prior to September 11, 2001, this day was known as National 911 Day to increase awareness of the telephone 911 system for help in emergencies. It was so designated in 1987 by then-president Ronald Reagan. This is the perfect time to review the use of 911, discuss what an emergency is, and ask if any of the students have used the 911 system.

PATRIOT DAY

This day was designated Patriot Day by President George W. Bush in memory of those who died in the terrorist attacks on September 11, 2001. The flag is to be flown at half-staff from sunup to sundown. The president asked citizens to always remember their collective obligation to ensure that justice is done, that freedom prevails, and that the principles upon which our nation was founded endure. There are several good Internet sites where you can obtain further information.

September 13

ELSE MINARIK: BIRTHDAY

Else Minarik, author of the beloved Little Bear books, was born in Denmark on September 13, 1920. Minarik was a primary teacher who wanted to write books that children could read on their own during the summer following first grade. Maurice Sendak illustrated the first five Little Bear books in the 1950s, but in recent years, the series has expanded to include picture books and more titles for early readers. There are now more than thirty-five titles available about this beloved character.

Currently there is a website for Little Bear fans at elseminarik.com. Minarik's personal favorite of her Little Bear books is *A Kiss for Little Bear* (1984), the story of a kiss that gets passed around and how happy it makes the recipients. All of her books are about animals that have human traits.

LIBRARY CARD SIGN-UP MONTH

September is Library Card Sign-Up Month, sponsored by the American Library Association. The website ala.org can provide resources for helping students obtain library cards. Studies show that children who are read to at home and who use the library do better in school. Some great books about the library include Sarah Stewart's *The Library* (1995) and Mary Ann Fraser's *IQ Goes to the Library* (2003). Your school librarian probably has a personal favorite too.

Week Three: Food

❋ ◔ Curriculum Connection: Science and Health

This list of resources is designed to complement National 5 A Day Month, which encourages the eating of at least five servings of fruit and vegetables per day. Several great alphabet books that feature fruits and vegetables are included, as are some cookbooks to help encourage students to eat healthy snacks.

American Grub: Eats for Kids (2003) by Lynn Kuntz and Jan Fleming, illustrated by Mark Hicks. Find recipes from each of the fifty states as well as background information relating to the cuisine.

Beef Stew (1990) by Barbara Brenner, illustrated by Catherine Siracusa. Follow this story of a young boy's search for friends to share his favorite dinner, beef stew.

Chewy Chuckles: Deliciously Funny Jokes About Food (2003) by Michael Dahl, illustrated by Jeff Yesh. This is an easy-to-read collection of riddles about foods, including strawberries and alphabet soup.

Chocolatina (2004) by Erik Kraft, illustrated by Denise Brunkus. The humor in this story of a girl who turns into chocolate will delight young readers.

Cooking Art (1997) by Mary Ann Kohl, illustrated by Ronni Roseman-Hall. Children can explore over a hundred art projects to make and eat, including cantaloupe canoes.

Corn Is Maize: The Gift of the Indians (1996) written and illustrated by Aliki. Read about the discovery of corn and how it was used by the Indians. The book also details how corn became an important food throughout the world.

A Day in the Life of a Chef (2001) written and illustrated by Liza Burby. Follow the chef of a restaurant as she goes about the tasks necessary to prepare and serve good food.

Dinner at the Panda Palace (1995) by Stephanie Calmenson, illustrated by Nadine Westcott. Dozens of animals journey to the Panda Palace for a meal.

Eat Your Peas, Louise! (1991) by Pegeen Snow, illustrated by Mike Venezia. Louise's brother thinks of all sorts of reasons for eating peas and other vegetables in this funny book.

Eating the Alphabet: Fruits and Vegetables from A to Z (1993) written and illustrated by Lois Ehlert. Using the alphabet, the author introduces fruits and vegetables from around the world. The book also has a glossary which provides more facts about each food.

Energy: Heat, Light and Food (2004) by Darlene Stille, illustrated by Sheree Boyd. Learn about the different forms of energy, such as how the human body uses the energy from food for movement.

Fast Food! Gulp! Gulp! (2001) written and illustrated by Bernard Waber. What happens when the cook quits because she has had enough of serving food faster and faster?

Fun Food (1997) by Judy Bastyra, illustrated by Stephen Shott, Mei Lim, and Michael Michaels. This creative book includes instructions for making eatable treats, including an ice cream clown, an egg man, and a melon crab.

Gregory, the Terrible Eater (1983) by Mitchell Sharmat, illustrated by Ariane Dewey and Jose Aruego. A very picky eater, a goat refuses the usual goat diet in favor of healthy human food.

The High Rise Glorious Skittle Skat Roarious Sky Pie Angel Food Cake (1996) by Nancy Willard, illustrated by Richard Watson. A young girl has an adventure while making a special cake for her mother's birthday

I Scream, You Scream: A Feast of Food Rhymes (1997) by Lillian Morrison, illustrated by Nancy Dunaway. This collection includes rhymes, chants, street cries, and jingles about food.

I Will Never Not Ever Eat a Tomato (2003) written and illustrated by Lauren Child. A brother gets his sister to eat foods that she says she will never eat.

Munch! Crunch! What's for Lunch? Experiments in the Kitchen (2002) by Janice Lobb, illustrated by Ann Savage and Peter Utton. Discover scientific explanations and learn some amazing facts about food in this book.

Ogres! Ogres! Ogres! A Feasting Frenzy from A to Z (1999) by Nicholas Heller, illustrated by Joseph Smith. Letters of the alphabet are represented by an assortment of ogres eating all sorts of foods. The clever text makes this a great read-aloud story.

Picky Nicky (1996) by Cathy and Mark Dubowski. Learn how a picky eater handles eating dinner at a friend's house.

The Popcorn Book (1984) written and illustrated by Tomie dePaola. This book presents interesting popcorn stories and legends. Two recipes are included.

The Seven Silly Eaters (1997) by Mary Ann Hoberman, illustrated by Maria Frazee. Seven picky eaters find a way to surprise their mother.

Walter the Baker (1998) written and illustrated by Eric Carle. This is the tale of a baker who invented the pretzel.

Who Took the Cookies from the Cookie Jar? (2000) written and illustrated by Bonnie Lass. The familiar chant, "Who Stole the Cookies from the Cookie Jar," is made into a mystery in this book that also includes a circle game and a song to sing.

The Wolf's Chicken Stew (1996) written and illustrated by Keiko Kasza. The results are unexpected when a wolf decides to fill his stewpot with a chicken.

September 15

TOMIE DEPAOLA: BIRTHDAY
Tomie dePaola, a favorite children's author and illustrator, was born September 15, 1934. His website (tomie.com) has many activities for children. He has written and illustrated more than two hundred books for children and won a Caldecott Honor in 1976 for *Strega Nona*. His favorite food is popcorn, which is why he wrote *The Popcorn Book* (1984). Of all the books he has written, his favorite is *Nana Upstairs, Nana Downstairs* (2000).

ROBERT MCCLOSKY: BIRTHDAY
Robert McClosky, who won the Caldecott Medal in 1942 for *Make Way for Ducklings* and again in 1958 for *Time of Wonder*, was born on this day in 1914. *Make Way for Ducklings* has sold more than two million copies since it was first published.

WHOOPING CRANE FALL MIGRATION
The whooping crane fall migration from Canada to Texas begins around September 15. The website savingcranes.org will provide information to discuss this migration with your students. The book *Whooping Crane* (1997) by Bonnie Graves provides a further resource and an introduction to this endangered species.

September 16

H. A. REY: BIRTHDAY
H. A. Rey, the illustrator of the original Curious George books, was born in 1898 and died in 1977. *Curious George* was first published in 1941 and remains popular today. Rey worked with his wife, Margaret Rey; she usually did the stories and he did the illustrations. The books written prior to H. A. Rey's death seem to show more of the irresistible qualities of ingenuity, opportunity, determination, and curiosity in the lovable character of Curious George.

INTERNATIONAL DAY OF PEACE
In 2001, the General Assembly of the United Nations declared September 16 the International Day of Peace. A good resource is *Peace Begins with You* (1994) by Katherine Scholes, illustrated by Robert Ingpen.

September 17

PAUL GOBLE: BIRTHDAY

Paul Goble, author and illustrator of books about Native Americans, was born September 17, 1933. He won the Caldecott Medal in 1978 for *The Girl Who Loved Wild Horses*, which is based on a Cheyenne myth. Although born in England, he has always been interested in everything concerning Native Americans. He now lives in South Dakota. His book *Beyond the Ridge* (1993) is a heartfelt story of death as part of the process of living. He also wrote *The Legend of the White Buffalo Woman* (1998), *The Gift of the Sacred Dog* (1984), and *Dream Wolf* (1997). Any curriculum incorporating the study of Native Americans is greatly enhanced by Goble's books.

CELEBRATION USA

Every school in the United States is invited to participate in Celebration USA on September 17. A coast-to-coast, synchronized recitation of the Pledge of Allegiance is planned. For more information on how to participate, visit celebrationusa.org.

September 18

HISPANIC HERITAGE MONTH

September 15 to October 15 was designated Hispanic Heritage Month in 1989 to focus attention on the contributions made by people of Hispanic heritage to the United States. It is designed to foster appreciation and respect for the uniqueness of all the peoples who have contributed to the current culture of the United States.

Many activities can be combined with the book resources listed in Week Four's thematic unit. Younger students can learn to count in Spanish and produce a class book. Cultural items such as a piñata can be drawn to represent the number counted. Older students can locate geographical place names that have Hispanic origins. After researching famous Latinos, students can report back to the class on what they have learned. This would be a great time to invite any Latino parents or community members to visit the class and tell students about their cultures. A class cooking project could involve learning how to make tortillas.

Week Four: Hispanic Heritage

🏛 Curriculum Connection: Social Studies

Hispanic Heritage Month is celebrated across the United States from September 15 to October 15. It is a time when we can learn about the great contributions people of Hispanic origins have made to the cultural fabric of America. Sources listed here are just a few of the many picture books providing a look into the traditions, languages, and peoples of Latin America and Mexico.

Amelia's Road (1995) by Linda Altman, illustrated by Enrique Sanchez. The daughter of migrant farm workers dreams of a home of her own.

Barrio: El Barrio de José (1998) by George Ancona. Through an eight-year-old boy, we see life in a San Francisco barrio, describing school, recreation, holidays, and family life in this book for older primary students.

A Birthday Basket for Tia (1997) written and illustrated by Pat Mora. A young girl prepares a surprise gift for her great-aunt's ninetieth birthday with the help of her cat.

Calling the Doves (2001) by Juan Herrera, illustrated by Elly Simmons. This bilingual text tells about the childhood of the author as a migrant farm worker.

Chato's Kitchen (1997) by Gary Soto, illustrated by Susan Quevara. In this tale the cat prepares all kinds of good food to get the mice to move into his house.

A Day's Work (1997) by Eve Bunting, illustrated by Ronald Himler. A boy goes with his grandfather as he seeks work. The grandfather's integrity teaches the boy a lesson about honor.

De Colores and Other Latin-American Folk Songs for Children (1994), assembled by José-Luis Orozco and illustrated by Elisa Kleven. This collection of Latin American songs

is a tribute to Latino culture and includes traditional tunes and hand games.

Drum, Chavi, Drum!/¡Toca, Chavi, Toca! (2003) by Mayra Dole, illustrated by Tonel. This story tells of a young girl who knows she is a good drummer and wants the chance to prove it—even though the music teacher believes that only boys make good drummers.

Ellen Ochoa (2001) by Pam Walker. This easy-to-read book features the first Hispanic female astronaut.

Estela's Swap (2002) by Alexis O'Neill, illustrated by Enrique Sanchez. This is the story of a young Mexican American girl who hopes to sell her music box at the swap meet so she can pay for dance lessons.

The Face at the Window (1997) by Regina Hanson, illustrated by Linda Saport. In this gentle and compassionate story set in Jamaica, a young girl learns to overcome her fear of strangers.

Going Home (1998) by Eve Bunting, illustrated by David Diaz. Follow the story of Mexican farm laborers in the United States who consider Mexico their homeland.

The Gold Coin (1994) by Alma Flor Ada, illustrated by Neil Waldman. Read what happens when a young thief becomes involved in a series of unexpected activities because he is determined to steal from an old woman.

Harvesting Hope: The Story of Cesar Chavez (2003) by Kathleen Krull, illustrated by Yuyi Morales. This winner of the 2004 Christopher Award for Children's Books is a biography about the important Hispanic civil rights leader, Cesar Chavez.

I Love Saturdays y Domingos (2001) by Alma Flor Ada, illustrated by Elivia Savadier. A young girl enjoys the similarities and differences between her English-speaking and Spanish-speaking grandparents.

In My Family (2000) written and illustrated by Carmen Garza. The bilingual text describes the author's experiences growing up in a Hispanic community in Texas.

The Magic Bean Tree: A Legend from Argentina (1998) by Nancy Van Laan, illustrated by Beatriz Vidal. Read about a young boy who sets out to bring the rains back to his homeland and is rewarded by a gift of carob beans that become prized across Argentina.

Mice and Beans (2001) by Pam Ryan, illustrated by Joe Cepeda. In this rhythmic tale, birthday party preparations are going on both in the house and in the walls of the house.

A Movie in My Pillow (2001) by Jorge Argueta, illustrated by Elizabeth Gómez. In this collection of poems, a young boy gathers images of his neighborhood and connects them with memories of his former life in El Salvador.

A New Barker in the House (2004) written and illustrated by Tomie dePaola. The children are excited when they learn that their family is adopting a three-year-old Hispanic boy.

The Old Man and His Door (1998) by Gary Soto, illustrated by Joe Cepeda. An old man sets out for a party with a door (*la puerta*) instead of a pig (*el puerco*).

The Pot That Juan Built (2002) by Nancy Andrews-Goebel, illustrated by David Diaz. This book written in cumulative rhyme tells about the work of Mexican potter, Juan Quezada.

Tortillitas Para Mama and Other Nursery Rhymes: Spanish and English (1990) by Margot Griego, illustrated by Barbara Cooney. This collection of nursery rhymes, many with instructions for accompanying finger plays and other activities, will be treasured by younger children.

September 20

ARTHUR GEISERT: BIRTHDAY
This is the birthday of Arthur Geisert, the author and illustrator of *Pigs from A to Z* (1996). He was born in Dallas, Texas, in 1941. His book *Roman Numerals from I to MM* (1996) provides a great introduction to Roman numerals. There really are one thousand pigs on the page for *M*.

He wrote several books, such as *Pigs from 1 to 10* (1992) and *Haystack* (1995), with pigs as the main characters. Geisert uses etchings to illustrate many of his books because he believes that etching is the most beautiful way of putting ink on paper.

TONY TALLARICO: BIRTHDAY
Tony Tallarico was born on September 20, 1933. He is most famous for his I Can Draw books such as *I Can Draw Animals* (1980) and *I Can Draw Monsters* (1996). His books can help the struggling artist draw all sorts of things, from trucks to cartoons to animals.

September 21

NATIONAL DOG WEEK
The last full week in September is National Dog Week. It began in 1928 to share the fun of dog ownership and promote better care for all dogs. How many of your students have dogs? Even those who don't are sure to enjoy stories about them.

There are many good books about dogs for primary students. *Harry the Dirty Dog* (1976) by Gene Zion, illustrated by Margaret Graham, and *The Adventures of Taxi Dog* (2000) by Debra Barracca, illustrated by Mark Buehner, are just two examples. *The Complete Dog Book for Kids* by the American Kennel Club is a useful nonfiction resource. *It's About Dogs* (2000) by Tony Johnston, illustrated by Ted Rand, is a book of poems about all kinds of dogs.

NATIONAL FARM ANIMALS AWARENESS WEEK
The third week in September is set aside to promote awareness of farm animals and to appreciate their many interesting and unique qualities. Animal Information Centers has an Internet site sponsored by the Humane Society of the United States (hsus.org) that provides fascinating facts about farm animals and contains suggestions for celebrating this week.

September 22

ELEPHANT APPRECIATION DAY

September 22 is Elephant Appreciation Day. It was started in 1996 by Wayne Hepburn to celebrate elephants because they are the largest land animal, have the unique feature of a trunk, and are threatened by extinction. Students might creatively plan a celebration by reporting on the various kinds of elephants and where they live. The website himandus.net is a wonderful resource. *Elephants* (2000) by Kevin Holmes and *Elephants* (2003) by John Wexo are also useful. The Babar books by Jean and Laurent de Brunhoff provide great stories about the world's most beloved elephant.

ESPHYR SLOBODKINA: BIRTHDAY

Esphyr Slobodkina was born September 22, 1908, and died in 2002. She wrote *Caps for Sale* (1987), which is a true classic, remaining popular ever since it was written in 1940. She also wrote *Circus Caps for Sale* (2002), starring an elephant instead of the naughty monkey that appeared in the original. Since today is her birthday and Elephant Appreciation Day, it seems most appropriate to read *Circus Caps for Sale*.

September 27

MARTIN HANDFORD: BIRTHDAY

Martin Handford, the author and illustrator of *Where's Waldo* and the many related books, was born September 27, 1956. For older primary students, the books where Waldo travels through time periods are especially useful resources. The Waldo books provide practice for students who are having difficulty focusing on details. These popular books have sold a phenomenal forty million copies.

BERNARD WABER: BIRTHDAY

Bernard Waber, the author of *Lyle, Lyle Crocodile* (1972), was born on September 27, 1924. Waber says he thinks best when in motion. Trains, subways, and even elevators seem to shake ideas loose, and he finds himself thinking of children's books most of the time.

His book *Ira Sleeps Over* (1975) presents the risks of new experiences and the personal courage it takes to confront childhood fears. *Lyle and the Birthday Party* (1966) is a good read-aloud for today since it is the author's birthday.

September Reading Strategy

Time and Text

Research has shown that there are common elements to effective literacy instruction. The time to practice the skills learned in formal instruction and a plentitude of text to practice reading are two of those elements.

It is imperative for teachers of primary-aged students to set aside a high percentage of the instructional day for reading by the students. It is common practice in classrooms for a very small percentage of time to actually be spent on reading and writing. In many classrooms, only 12 to 20 percent of the day is actually spent in reading text and writing about that text; up to 90 percent of the day is spent doing other "stuff." Even useful stuff such as building background knowledge for a story often takes twenty minutes when, according to research studies, three or four minutes would be sufficient. The student would benefit more by spending the extra fifteen minutes actually reading the text.

The text provided to students must include a multitude of books and other reading materials that they can read on an independent level. Time spent practicing reading skills on material that is too difficult will not lead to higher student comprehension or overall reading achievement. To determine whether children can successfully read the material, each child should be taught a self-selection strategy such as the "rule of five."

The rule of five is easy for children from the middle of first grade on to learn and use.

A book or other reading material is opened to the middle. The child then tries to read a page. If the child can read the page and encounters fewer than five words (other than names) that are unknown or can't be decoded, the child will probably comprehend the text. If more than five words cause problems to the reader, the printed text is too difficult. High motivation for the content sometimes causes children to persevere with text that is technically too difficult. As the reading abilities of students spread out in primary grades, it becomes necessary to provide more and more reading material and more and more levels of difficulty. Thank goodness for libraries—classroom, school, and public!

Many of the picture books listed in this guide are written at a very difficult reading level. They have few pages, but the vocabulary has not been controlled for beginning reading levels. On the other hand, many of the books written for beginning readers are not as interesting to primary students. Reading to children is still vitally important in order for them to hear beautiful writing and the sounds and vocabulary that they will grow into as their skills increase. It is also imperative that children continue to develop the love of listening to great literature and gain information through listening as well as independent reading.

October at a Glance

Each day and the living of it has to be a conscious creation in which discipline and order are relieved with some play and pure foolishness.
—May Sarton

October Reading Tip: Take time to talk about the style of the book as well as the content prior to reading. Help children notice the cover, author, and genre before exploring other prereading areas.

OCTOBER HIGHLIGHTS
National Dinosaur Month
Dinosaurs, Dinosaurs (1993), written and illustrated by Byron Barton, is an introduction to dinosaurs for younger readers. Direct the children to look for the eyebrows on each dinosaur.

Kids Love a Mystery Month
Many of the mystery series books are very useful to help beginning readers transition to longer, chapter-type books. *Nate the Great* and the Young Cam Jensen series are favorites with second through fourth grade readers.

Child Magazine Month
Ask your librarian to recommend the best children's magazines for you to share with your students during this month.

Fire Prevention Month
Most city fire departments will schedule school visits if asked. *Fire! Fire!* (1987) by Gail Gibbons shows firefighters fighting fires in a variety of locations.

National Pasta Month
Strega Nona (1979), written and illustrated by Tomie dePaola, is the perfect book to read for National Pasta Month. The story is a blend of fantasy, magic, and humor that revolves around a pasta pot and its contents.

October Reading Strategy: Vocabulary Development

WEEKLY THEMES AND CURRICULUM CONNECTIONS
Week One: International Children (Social Studies and Geography)
Week Two: Teeth (Science and Health)
Week Three: Mysteries (Language Arts)
Week Four: Dinosaurs (Science)

Special Events in October

Universal Children's Week	Oct. 1
National Dental Hygiene Month	Oct. 5
National Orthodontics Month	Oct. 5
Columbus Day	Oct. 12
Kids Love a Mystery Month	Oct. 12
World Food Day	Oct. 16
United Nations Day	Oct. 24
National Roller-Skating Month	Oct. 24
International Dinosaur Month	Oct. 27
Statue of Liberty Dedicated	Oct. 28
Halloween	Oct. 31
National Magic Day	Oct. 31
National UNICEF Day	Oct. 31

FEATURED OCTOBER BIRTHDAYS

Ann Morris ....Oct. 1	Wynton Marsalis ....Oct. 18	Eric Rohmann ....Oct. 26
Susan Meddaugh ....Oct. 4	Shel Silverstein ....Oct. 18	Theodore Roosevelt......Oct. 27
Gene Zion ....Oct. 5	Ed Emberley ....Oct. 19	Jonas Salk ....Oct. 28
Eleanor Roosevelt ....Oct. 11	Bernard Lodge.............Oct. 19	Emily Post ....Oct. 30
Mary Hays (Molly	Pablo Picasso ....Oct. 25	Eric Kimmel.................Oct. 30
Pitcher) ....Oct. 13	Fred Marcellino ....Oct. 25	
Noah Webster ....Oct. 16	Steven Kellogg ....Oct. 26	

Week One: International Children

🏛 ⚖ Curriculum Connection: Social Studies and Geography

Primary-aged children are just beginning to realize that there is a world beyond their own family, so they are naturally curious about children from other places. The following list is a sampling of the picture books published on this topic. Each of these books lends itself to comparing the circumstances of here and now with the circumstances of there and now. Older primary-aged children will probably be amazed that all children don't live in the same conditions they do. They are also at the age where they can be empathetic and aware of the need to help others. This thematic list ties in with Universal Children's Week and National UNICEF Day.

All Kinds of Children (1999) by Norma Simon, illustrated by Diane Paterson. Children have much in common with each other, including people to love them and the opportunity to play.

All the Colors of the Earth: Poems from Around the World (2004) selected by Wendy Cooling. This collection of poetry celebrates the diverse experiences of children all over the world.

All the Way to Morning (1999) by Marc Harshman, illustrated by Felipe Dávalos. This is an interesting look at what children might hear at night before they go to sleep.

Angel Child, Dragon Child (1990) by Michele Maria Surat, illustrated by Vo-Dinh Mai. A child from Vietnam has trouble adjusting to life in America.

Back to School (2001) by Maya Ajmera, photographed by John Ivanko. Photographs from thirty-seven countries are included in this book that is about returning to school after summer vacation.

Beatrice's Goat (2001) by Page McBrier, illustrated by Lori Lohstoeter. The gift of a goat enables a young girl to attend school in Uganda.

Celebrating Birthdays in Brazil (1998), **Celebrating Birthdays in Russia** (1998), **Celebrating Birthdays in China** (1998), and **Celebrating Birthdays in Australia** (1998), all by Cheryl Enderlein. These books discuss parties and presents found at birthday parties in each country.

Children Around the World (2001) by Donata Montanari. This book features children from different countries telling about their lifestyles. The text is enhanced by using the children's own words.

A Child's Day in an Egyptian City (2002) by Khaled Eldash and Dalia Khattab. This story follows one child throughout the course of the day to learn about his way of life in a city in modern Egypt.

A Child's Day in an Indian Village (2001) by Prodeepta Das. This book introduces the country of India with readable text and beautiful photos.

Come Out and Play (2001) by May Ajmera, photographed by John Ivanko. Color photographs from around the world show the smiling faces of children.

Dear Children of the Earth: A Letter from Home (1994) by Schim Schimmel. An imaginary letter from Mother Earth tells children about the earth and asks readers to take care of her for their generation and generations yet to come.

Grandfather's Dream (1994) written and illustrated by Holly Keller. When the Vietnam War is over, Grandfather and his young grandson dream that the wetlands will be restored and the cranes will come back.

Hopscotch Around the World (1996) by Mary Lankford, illustrated by Karen Milone. Hopscotch is played in nearly every country in the world. This book details the many different forms of the game.

I Live In Tokyo (2001) written and illustrated by Mari Takabayashi. Follow a young girl month by month through a year of her life in Tokyo.

Madlenka (2000) by Peter Sis. As a young girl goes around the block to show her friend her loose tooth, she finds that her neighborhood is very multicultural.

Mei-Mei Loves the Morning (1999) by Margaret Tsubakiyama, illustrated by Cornelius Van Wright and Ying-Hwa Hu. This book is a blend of illustrations and text that turns the morning routine of a young girl into an adventure.

My Father's Boat (1998) by Sherry Garland, illustrated by Ted Rand. A Vietnamese American boy spends the day on his father's shrimp boat listening to the story of fishing on the South China Sea.

A Ride on Mother's Back (1996) by Emery Bernhard, illustrated by Durga Bernhard. Explore the ways in which people from different cultures carry their young and what children see and learn as they are carried.

Schools (2002) by Margaret Hall. This book provides views of the world's schools, including various customs, activities, and subjects studied.

Skip Across the Ocean: Nursery Rhymes from Around the World (1995) by Floella Benjamin, illustrated by Sheila Moxley. This collection of rhymes and lullabies from many different countries is for younger children.

The Stars in My Geddoh's Sky (2002) by Claire Sidhom Matze, illustrated by Bill Farnsworth. Grandfather comes to visit, and his young grandson learns about his Middle Eastern homeland.

To Be a Kid (2000) by Maya Ajmera, photographed by John Ivanko. This multicultural book features photographs that illustrate the activities shared by children in many countries around the world.

The World Turns Round and Round (2000) by Nicki Weiss. This book describes the gifts that children have received from around the world. The book helps readers to see how small the world really is.

October 1

ANN MORRIS: BIRTHDAY

Children's author Ann Morris was born on October 1, 1930. Her photo-essay books on topics such as hats, shoes, bread, and families are wonderful additions to multicultural studies. Her books give children practice in finding visual similarities and differences and opportunities for increasing their vocabulary.

UNIVERSAL CHILDREN'S WEEK

October 1 through 7 is Universal Children's Week, which was started by the United Nations in 1954 to celebrate the basic rights of children. Those rights include free education, adequate nutrition, medical care, special care if handicapped, and the right to be brought up in a spirit of peace and universal brotherhood. Great strides have been made since 1954, but many children in the world still don't enjoy all these rights. *Children Just Like Me* (1995) by Barnabas and Anabel Kindersley is a very useful resource for promoting children's understanding of the differences in conditions experienced by children in other countries.

October 4

SUSAN MEDDAUGH: BIRTHDAY

Susan Meddaugh, writer and illustrator of Martha the Dog books, was born on October 4, 1944. *Martha Speaks* (1995) describes the problems that arise when Martha, the family dog, learns to speak after eating alphabet soup. Alphabet macaroni is available at most supermarkets, and using it to motivate children in learning the alphabet or spelling their names makes a great activity to accompany this book.

Another favorite is *Cinderella's Rat* (2002), a delightful retelling of the Cinderella story from the coachman rat's point of view. The plot is short, the playfulness of the story is tall, and it is sure to delight and entertain young readers. Meddaugh enjoys rewriting fairy tales to give a different slant to the story. In *Hog-Eye* (1998), she presents a hilarious story about a young pig who outwits a wolf that intends to eat her. After she convinces him that her "Hog-Eye" magic will make him itch everywhere, he finally agrees to let her go.

October 5

GENE ZION: BIRTHDAY

Gene Zion, author of *Harry the Dog* and several related books, was born in 1913 and died in 1975. He envisioned his stories through the eyes of a child, and Harry, the family dog, has adventures as if he were a human member of the family.

Most of Zion's books were illustrated by Margaret Graham. In *Harry the Dirty Dog* (1976), he describes what happens when Harry runs away from home and gets so dirty his family doesn't recognize him. *No Roses for Harry!* (1976) is a hilarious story about Harry getting an unwelcome present from Grandma—a sweater covered with roses.

NATIONAL DENTAL HYGIENE MONTH

October is National Dental Hygiene Month and National Orthodontics Month. This is a good time to take a field trip to a dental office to see these professionals at work. *Make Way for Tooth Decay* (2002) by Bobbi Katz, illustrated by Steve Bjorkman, explains in rhyming verse how bacteria live in the mouth and cause plaque, cavities, and other problems.

October 11

ELEANOR ROOSEVELT: BIRTHDAY

Eleanor Roosevelt was born October 11, 1884, and died in 1962. Her life is an inspiration to children. *A Picture Book of Eleanor Roosevelt* (1995) by David A. Adler, illustrated by Robert Casilla, portrays the outstanding character of Mrs. Roosevelt and calls her the First Lady of the World. She urged all people to rise above that which is expected to the greatest heights personally possible and was a champion of the poor.

The books *Eleanor* (1999) by Barbara Cooney, illustrated by Dena Neusner; *Learning About Integrity from the Life of Eleanor Roosevelt* (2001), written and illustrated by Nancy Ellwood; *Amelia and Eleanor Go for a Ride* (1999) by Pam Ryan, illustrated by Brian Seiznick; and *The Story of Eleanor Roosevelt* (2004) by Rachel Koestler-Grack all help children to know this remarkable woman as more than a first lady to her husband, President Franklin D. Roosevelt.

As a class project, make a historical time line of what was happening in the world when Eleanor was alive.

Week Two: Teeth

❄ 🍎 Curriculum Connection: Science and Health

October is National Dental Hygiene Month and National Orthodontics Month, prompting this week's thematic listing of books about teeth. Primary-aged children are very curious about teeth, especially when they lose their baby teeth and the permanent ones start to appear. The books on this list should help answer the questions children have about teeth.

Agapanthus Hum and Angel Hoot (2003) by Joy Cowley, illustrated by Jennifer Plecas. Agapanthus Hum has lost her first tooth, but her trademark humming has turned into a special sound.

Airmail to the Moon (1989) by Tom Birdseye, illustrated by Stephen Gammell. This book tells the story of a girl's missing tooth and her search for the culprit.

Andrew's Loose Tooth (1999) by Robert Munsch, illustrated by Michael Martchenko. Read about Andrew's problem with a loose tooth and the remedy that saved the day.

Brushing Well (1998) by Helen Frost, illustrated by Gail Saunders-Smith. This book simply describes how to brush teeth, from putting the toothpaste on the brush to swishing water in your mouth.

Dear Tooth Fairy (2003) by Pamela Edwards, illustrated by Marie-Louise Fitzpatrick. In a series of letters, a six-year-old and the Tooth Fairy discuss the important matter of the first loose tooth and when it is going to fall out.

Fluffy Meets the Tooth Fairy (2002) by Kate McMullan, illustrated by Mavis Smith. Read about a guinea pig's adventure with the tooth fairy.

Food for Healthy Teeth (2003) by Helen Frost. The author provides a list of foods that will help make teeth strong.

George Washington's Teeth (2003) by Deborah Chandra and Madeleine Comora, illustrated by Brock Cole. George Washington's lifelong struggle with bad teeth is depicted in a humorous rhyme.

Healthy Teeth (2003) by Angela Royston. The author answers questions about teeth and why children should see a dentist.

How Many Teeth? (1991) by Paul Showers, illustrated by True Kelley. This book describes how many teeth we have at different stages of life, why they fall out, and what their various functions are.

A Look at Teeth (1999) by Allan Fowler discusses baby teeth, permanent teeth, and the importance of each for various animals.

Loose Tooth (2003) by Anastasia Suen, illustrated by Allan Eitzen. Problems that come with loosing teeth are detailed in this story, including the gap that appears in a smile.

Loose Tooth (2004) by Lola Schaefer, illustrated by Sylvie Wickstrom. The rhyming text contains very short sentences with a catchy refrain that describes the condition of a loose tooth.

The Lost Tooth Club (2000) by Arden Johnson. A young girl's loose tooth isn't ready to come out, keeping her from joining The Lost Tooth Club.

Mabel the Tooth Fairy and How She Got Her Job (2003) by Katie David. Learn how an ordinary fairy named Mabel became the tooth fairy.

Make Way for Tooth Decay (2002) by Bobbie Katz, illustrated by Steve Bjorkman. In this witting text with rhyming verse, learn how bacteria live in the mouth and cause problems with the teeth and gums.

My Tooth Is About to Fall Out (1995) by Grace Maccarone, illustrated by Betsy Lewin. This is a tale about a young girl who's about to lose her first tooth. What do your readers do when their teeth fall out?

Nice Try, Tooth Fairy (2003) by Mary Olson, illustrated by Kathleen Tillotson. A child writes a series of letters to the tooth fairy in hopes of getting back a lost tooth.

The Night Before the Tooth Fairy (2003) by Natasha Wing, illustrated by Barbara Newman. This tale of a boy's lost tooth, based on the classic poem "'Twas the Night Before Christmas," is a great read-aloud book.

One Morning in Maine (1976) written and illustrated by Robert McCloskey. This 1953 Caldecott Honor book will make you fall in love with Maine as you read about a girl who looses her tooth while digging for clams.

Open Wide: Tooth School Inside (2003) by Laurie Keller. In a humorous way, this book presents information about the structure and care of teeth and the ways dentists help. The setting is a classroom where the students are teeth.

Rotten Teeth (2002) by Laura Simms, illustrated by David Catrow. A first grade girl becomes a celebrity when she brings a jar of teeth for show and tell.

Staying Healthy: Dental Care (1999) by Alice McGinty. This book for younger children provides an overview of teeth, including the kinds we have, what they are made of, and how children should take care of them.

Tabitha's Terrifically Tough Tooth (2001) by Charlotte Middleton. Read about the story of a young girl and her plans to get her loose tooth to fall out.

Throw Your Tooth on the Roof: Tooth Traditions from Around the World (2001) by Selby Beeler, illustrated by Brian Karas. This interesting book relates what children from around the world do with a tooth that has fallen out. A great class discussion can follow.

The Tooth Book (2000) by Theo Lesieg, illustrated by Joseph Mathieu. Using rhyming text and illustrations, this book points out who has teeth, their uses, and how to care for them.

What Do the Fairies Do with All Those Teeth? (1996) by Michel Luppens, illustrated by Phillipe Béha. This is a nonsense tale about how the Tooth Fairy uses all the teeth that are collected.

October 12

COLUMBUS DAY

Columbus Day is celebrated in the United States on the second Monday in October. The first official celebration of Christopher Columbus's discovery of the Americas was in 1892, but it did not become a federal holiday until 1971. The following books provide background material for this day: *A Picture Book of Christopher Columbus* (1994) by David A. Adler, illustrated by John and Alexandra Wallner; *Columbus* (1996) by Ingri D'Aulaire; and *Encounter* (1996) by Jane Yolen, illustrated by David Shannon.

KIDS LOVE A MYSTERY MONTH

October is also Kids Love a Mystery Month. Resources are available at kidsloveamystery .com. Most mysteries are chapter books, but the thematic list for Week Three has some excellent picture book mysteries. When reading a picture book mystery aloud, be sure that you talk about the genre of mystery books, what makes a story a mystery, and how the mystery is solved. This type of book helps children develop problem-solving skills as well as the skills needed for critical thinking and organization of facts and details.

October 13

MARY HAYS: BIRTHDAY

Mary Hays (later known as Molly Pitcher) was born on October 13, 1754, and died in 1833. The book *They Called Her Molly Pitcher* (2002) by Anne Rockwell, illustrated by Cynthia von Buhler, details how she became an American legend during the Revolutionary War.

Katie's Trunk (1997) by Ann Turner, illustrated by Ron Himler, and *Paul Revere's Ride* (1996) by Henry Wadsworth Longfellow, illustrated by Ted Rand, are both good picture books to introduce this time period to primary students. *Buttons for General Washington* (1986) by Peter and Connie Roop, illustrated by Peter Hanson, reconstructs the possible mission of a fourteen-year-old spy who carried messages to Washington's camp in the buttons of his coat during the Revolutionary War.

American history introduced through stories of the times helps children relate to the events and remember important people and what they did.

October 16

NOAH WEBSTER: BIRTHDAY

Noah Webster, the father of the American dictionary, was born on October 16 in 1758. Beginning when he was forty-three, it took him more than twenty-seven years to finish what became the first American dictionary. Many resources about dictionaries can be found at dictionary.com, which also has games using the dictionary and thesaurus.

Your library media person can show several different dictionaries to your class and also introduce other resources that can only be used in the library.

Webster also wrote a book titled *The Blue-Backed Speller*, which was used to teach reading for more than one hundred years.

WORLD FOOD DAY

October 16 is also World Food Day. This designation started in 1981 to heighten awareness of world hunger. The website education-world.com is a resource to links on nutrition. Students need to be aware that many children of the world go to bed hungry or even die each day from hunger and malnutrition. The various United Nations websites can provide more information on world hunger.

October 18

WYNTON MARSALIS: BIRTHDAY

Wynton Marsalis, one of the world's most acclaimed jazz artists, was born on this day in 1961. He is accomplished on the trumpet in both jazz and classical styles of music. The book *Wynton Marsalis: Gifted Trumpet Player* (1996) by Craig Awmiller provides background for young children on this famous musician. His website wyntonmarsalis.net can provide more information.

SHEL SILVERSTEIN: BIRTHDAY

Shel Silverstein was born on October 18, 1932, and died in 1999. His website shelsilverstein.com provides wonderful background on this beloved children's poet. His books of poetry, *Where the Sidewalk Ends* (1973) and *Falling Up* (1996), are necessary resources in any classroom library. He did his own illustrations and didn't allow any of his books to be published in paperback. Children love his poems dealing with common topics such as taking out the garbage and will memorize many of his poems on their own.

His book *The Giving Tree* (1986) is a thought-provoking book for older primary children dealing with the giving of oneself for others.

Week Three: Mysteries

📖 Curriculum Connection: Language Arts

Kids love a mystery! Mystery stories are a favorite genre for emerging readers to explore. Children will often struggle to read a mystery that is written above their independent reading level because they want to solve the puzzle. Most of the classic mystery series, such as Nancy Drew, are written for older elementary readers and are not picture books. However, the ones on this list are shorter and more accessible to younger readers.

The picture book mysteries listed here will introduce younger readers to the mystery genre and to the joys of a good mystery.

Alphabet Mystery (2003) by Audrey Wood, illustrated by Bruce Wood. What happened to Little x? The other letters of the alphabet set out to find him.

Cowgirl Rosie and Her Five Baby Bison (2001) written and illustrated by Stephen Gulbis. Cowpoke humor takes the stage in this mystery of five missing baby bison. As the mystery is solved, the bison are returned to their rightful owner—Cowgirl Rosie.

Dot and Jabber and the Big Bug Mystery (2003) written and illustrated by Ellen Walsh. In this story the two mice detectives try to solve the mystery of the disappearing bugs.

Dot and Jabber and the Great Acorn Mystery (2001) written and illustrated by Ellen Walsh. Two mice detectives try to solve the mystery of how a small acorn turns into an oak tree.

Dot and Jabber and the Mystery of the Missing Stream (2002) written and illustrated by Ellen Walsh. Can two mouse detectives solve the mystery of the empty stream? Where did the water go?

Farmer McPeepers and His Missing Cows (2003) by Katy Duffield, illustrated by Steve Gray. Readers solve the mystery of how the farmer's eyeglasses allow the cows to have a day on the town.

Grandpa's Teeth (1999) written and illustrated by Rod Clement. This mystery story is about the disappearance of grandpa's teeth. Everyone in town becomes a suspect according to Inspector Rat.

The Great Valentine Mystery (2003) by Megan Bryant, illustrated by Mindy Pierce. Uncover the mystery of the missing valentine treats. Will the students be able to find them in time for the party?

I Spy Mystery: A Book of Picture Riddles (1993) by Jean Marzollo, photographed by Walter Wick. Here is a challenge for detectives, with riddles and photos featuring several mysteries to solve.

I Spy Spooky Night: A Book of Picture Riddles (1996) by Jean Marzollo, photographed by Walter Wick. This riddle book contains thirteen different riddle rooms for readers to solve. Each one of the environments is spookier that the one before.

Mystery Mansion (2001) written and illustrated by Michael Garland. This book offers hidden pictures and clues that lead to a surprise ending in this treasure hunt plot.

Mystery on the Docks (1984) written and illustrated by Thacher Hurd. The cook at the diner on Pier 46 saves his favorite singer from Big Al and his gang of nasty rats.

Nate the Great and the Halloween Hunt (1990) by Marjorie Sharmat, illustrated by Marc Simont. This series of books are favorites with beginning readers. This particular one involves the mystery of the missing cat. There are many more books in this series that more able primary readers will love.

Olivia . . . and the Missing Toy (2003) written and illustrated by Ian Falconer. A pig is determined to find out who is responsible for the disappearance of her favorite toy.

Piggins (1992) by Jane Yolan, illustrated by Jane Dyer. Piggins the butler quickly discovers the real thief of the beautiful diamond necklace.

Santa's Snow Cat (2001) by Sue Stainton, illustrated by Anne Mortimer. Read about a Christmas mystery involving Santa and his pet cat who falls out of Santa's sleigh over New York City.

Snow Music (2003) written and illustrated by Lynne Perkins. This unique picture book begins and ends with a whisper of snow.

Where Do Balloons Go? An Uplifting Mystery (2000) by Jamie Lee Curtis, illustrated by Laura Cornell. A child imagines what happens to a balloon that is let go and what it might encounter.

Young Cam Jansen and the Ice Skate Mystery (1999) by David A. Adler, illustrated by Susanna Natti. Cam uses her amazing memory to find the lost key to the locker at the ice skating rink.

Young Cam Jansen and the Lost Tooth (1999) by David A. Adler, illustrated by Susanna Natti. Cam Jansen's photographic memory is put to the test when a classmate's tooth falls out and disappears.

Young Cam Jansen and the Missing Cookie (1998) by David A. Adler, illustrated by Susanna Natti. This is one in a series of mysteries that are children's favorites. The young detective has a photographic memory that helps solve mysteries.

Young Cam Jansen and the Pizza Shop Mystery (2001) by David A. Adler, illustrated by Susanna Natti. Cam's jacket disappears at the mall. Can she find her lost jacket and solve the mystery at the pizza shop?

October 19

ED EMBERLEY: BIRTHDAY

Ed Emberley, the author and illustrator of more than forty-eight drawing books, was born in 1931. He won a Caldecott Medal in 1968 for the book he illustrated titled *Drummer Hoff* (1990), which his wife, Barbara Emberley, wrote.

His drawing books can stir the creativity of any child. *Ed Emberley's Great Thumbprint Drawing Book* (1994) can be used to introduce the uniqueness of individual thumbprints and what those prints can be made into. *Ed Emberley's Drawing Book of Faces* (1992) enables children to add expressions and emotions to their drawings of people by modeling simple ways to embellish their drawings.

BERNARD LODGE: BIRTHDAY

Illustrator Bernard Lodge was born on this day in 1933. He began his career as a graphic designer and used woodcuts with soft pastels to illustrate stories. *Grandma Went to Market* (1996) by Stella Blackstone is an around-the-world counting rhyme. This book is a great motivator for creating word problems using addition and subtraction. Although out of print, you may find it at your local library.

October 24

UNITED NATIONS DAY

Since 1948, October 24 has been designated United Nations Day to commemorate its founding in 1945. The name "United Nations" was coined by President Franklin D. Roosevelt to bind the fifty nations that signed the charter. The United Nations (UN) now has 191 member nations, and each nation has one vote. The basic purpose of the UN is to bring all nations of the world together to work for peace and development, basing decisions on the principles of justice, human dignity, and well-being for all people.

Many resources are available online at un.org. *Children Just Like Me* (1995) by Barnabas and Anabel Kindersley is also a good resource, providing background material on life in many of the UN's member nations.

NATIONAL ROLLER-SKATING MONTH

This celebration recognizes the health benefits and recreational enjoyment of skating with an emphasis on safety. For further information, see the website rollerskating.com. A good reading resource is *Roller Skates!* (1992) by Stephanie Calmenson, illustrated by True Kelley—a fun story about a whole town that ends up on wheels.

October 25

PABLO PICASSO: BIRTHDAY

Pablo Picasso, one of the most influential and prolific artists of the twentieth century, was born on October 25, 1881, and died in 1973. *Pablo Picasso: Breaking All the Rules* (2002) by True Kelley contains bits of information that will appeal to primary children. Another good resource is Shelley Sateren's *Picasso* (2002), from the Masterpieces: Artists and Their Works series.

FRED MARCELLINO: BIRTHDAY

Fred Marcellino was born on this day in 1936 and died in 2001. He won a Caldecott Honor for his illustration of the classic tale *Puss in Boots* (1990) by Charles Perrault. He was a graphic designer, then an illustrator, and finally an author. He illustrated classics such as *The Steadfast Tin Soldier* (1997) by Hans Christian Andersen before he authored his own books, including *I, Crocodile* (2002) for which he won the 2000 American Library Association Notable Children's Book Award, the 1999 New York Times Book Review Best Illustrated Children's Book Award, and the 2000–2001 Georgia's Picture Storybook Award.

October 26

STEVEN KELLOGG: BIRTHDAY

Steven Kellogg, who was born on this day in 1941, always wanted to be an author. So far he has written more than ninety books for children. One of his most famous books is *Pinkerton, Behave!* (2002), and there really was a dog named Pinkerton. Many of his books have jovial, detailed illustrations that greatly enhance the stories. This is especially true in his tall tale book *Paul Bunyan* (1985). *How Much Is a Million?* (1993) by David Schwartz also contains Kellogg's illustrations.

ERIC ROHMANN: BIRTHDAY

Eric Rohmann, born on this date in 1957, won the Caldecott Medal in 2003 for his book *My Friend Rabbit*, which is a celebration of friendship. He was also awarded a Caldecott Honor in 1995 for *Time Flies* (1994), which is a wordless picture book about a bird and a dinosaur trapped in a natural history museum. He believes that children are the best audience and that all illustrations should work to make the story stronger.

Week Four: Dinosaurs

✳ Curriculum Connection: Science

October is designated National Dinosaur Month, but dinosaurs fascinate some children all year long for several years. Boys are especially attracted to the study and names of dinosaurs. Books must be chosen carefully to ensure that students receive the most accurate information and the best fiction available, both of which should be age appropriate.

The following thematic list is by no means exhaustive of the good books that are published on this topic. Since there are so many books written about dinosaurs, you might want to discuss with children what makes a good nonfiction book. Children can be taught to be careful consumers of nonfiction as well as fiction.

An Alphabet of Dinosaurs (1995) by Peter Dodson, illustrated by Wayne Barlowe. This ABC book with lush artwork and simple text brings the exciting world of dinosaurs roaring to life for younger readers.

Digging Up Dinosaurs (1988) written and illustrated by Aliki. This book explains how those huge dinosaur skeletons get inside museums.

Dinosaur Babies (1999) by Kathleen Zoehfeld, illustrated by Lucia Washburn. This book reveals discoveries about the littlest dinosaurs.

Dinosaur Dinners (1998) by Lee Davis, illustrated by Barbara Taylor. Readers find out what things dinosaurs consumed—including other dinosaurs.

Dinosaur Dream (1994) written and illustrated by Dennis Nolan. In his dream a young boy travels back to the Jurassic time period.

The Dinosaur Who Lived in My Backyard (1990) by B. G. Hennessy, illustrated by Susan Davis. A young boy imagines what it was like long ago when a dinosaur lived in his backyard.

Dinosaurs Are Different (1986) written and illustrated by Aliki. The author explains how the various dinosaurs were similar and different in structure and appearance.

Dinosaurs! The Biggest, Baddest, Strangest, Fastest (2000) by Howard Zimmerman, illustrated by George Olshevsky. In this collection, you will find dinosaurs larger than houses and dinosaurs as small as cats. Pronunciation guides will help readers with the long names.

Dinosaurumpus! (2003) by Tony Milton, illustrated by Guy Rees. Here's a rhyming tale of assorted dinosaurs gathering at the swamp to dance.

The Discovering Dinosaurs Series (2003) by Daniel Cohen and Don Lessem, illustrated by Brent Breithaupt, Larry Martin, and Donna Braginetz. Books in this series provide an in-depth examination of what is known about the physical characteristics, behavior, and habitat of these interesting dinosaurs: ankylosaurus (armor-plated dinosaur), diplodocus (long-necked, long-tailed dinosaur), maiasaura (plant-eating dinosaur), pachycephalosaurus (big headed, plant-eating dinosaur), seismosaurus (the longest dinosaur), and triceratops (the last dinosaur).

Field Mouse and the Dinosaur Named Sue (2000) by Jan Wahl, illustrated by Bob

Doucet. A field mouse finds himself in the museum when the roof of his home is transported there with the bones of a dinosaur.

Harry and the Bucketful of Dinosaurs (2003) by Ian Whybrow, illustrated by Adrian Reynolds. A young boy discovers toy dinosaurs that will come to life as he names each one.

How Big Were the Dinosaurs? (1995) written and illustrated by Bernard Most. Children can grasp the relative size of dinosaurs as they are compared to more familiar objects.

How Do Dinosaurs Say Good Night? (2000) by Jane Yolen, illustrated by Mark Teague. This beautifully illustrated tale shows that young dinosaurs go to sleep at night just like children do.

I Wonder Why Triceratops Had Horns and Other Questions About Dinosaurs (2003) by Rod Theodoro. This book is a good introduction to the world of dinosaurs, answering many questions children may have about them.

My Visit to the Dinosaurs (1985) written and illustrated by Aliki. A visit to a museum of natural history provides a young boy with an introduction to the habits, characteristics, and habitats of fourteen kinds of dinosaurs.

Oh, Say Can You Say Di-no-saur? (1999) by Bonnie Worth, illustrated by Steve Haefele. The Cat in the Hat shows how fossils are excavated, assembled, and displayed in a museum.

Ten Little Dinosaurs (1996) by Pattie Schnetzler, illustrated by Jim Harris. Rhyming verses describe the antics of ten different dinosaurs in this appealing counting book that won many awards.

Triceratops: The Last Dinosaur (1991) by Elizabeth Sandell. The author gives information on the plant-eating dinosaur that looked like a rhinoceros.

Troodon (2003) by Daniel Cohen, illustrated by Larry Martin. Learn about what the Troodon looked like, what it ate, where it lived, and how scientists learned about it.

What Happened to the Dinosaurs? (1991) by Franklyn Branley, illustrated by Marc Simont. This book explores the various theories about the extinction of the dinosaurs.

What the Dinosaurs Saw: Animals Living Then and Now (1998) by Miriam Schlein, illustrated by Carol Schwartz. Illustrations and text come together in this story that details what the world was like when dinosaurs were on the earth.

Where to Look for a Dinosaur (1997) written and illustrated by Bernard Most. The author describes various dinosaurs, tells where fossils have been found, and gives a list of museums with dinosaur collections.

October 27

THEODORE ROOSEVELT: BIRTHDAY
Teddy Roosevelt was born on October 27, 1858, and died in 1919. *Young Teddy Roosevelt* (1998) by Cheryl Harness tells of the future president overcoming asthma. *So You Want to Be President?* (2000) by Judith St. George, illustrated by David Small, makes the presidency more interesting by providing tidbits such as Roosevelt was the youngest man to become president (he was forty-two).

INTERNATIONAL DINOSAUR MONTH
October started as International Dinosaur Month in 1997 to promote a permanent yearly event celebrating dinosaurs. The websites dinofun.com and dinosaur.org provide resources for everything having to do with dinosaurs.

As a topic, the dinosaur is popular with many primary-aged students, especially boys. The thematic unit listing for this week provides additional resources, but space limitations dictate how many books can be listed. *The Big Book of Dinosaurs* (1994) by Angela Wilkes is a great introduction to the topic for the youngest primary students. *Dinosaurs! The Biggest, Baddest, Strangest, Fastest* (2000) by Howard Zimmerman, illustrated by George Olshevsky, is good for older primary students.

October 28

JONAS SALK: BIRTHDAY
Jonas Salk, one of the heroes in the world of science, was born on this day in 1914 and died in 1995. He created the vaccine for polio while overcoming the pressure of time and pursuing seemingly impossible dreams. *Jonas Salk* (2002) by Deanne Durrett provides resource information for this true science hero.

STATUE OF LIBERTY DEDICATED
The Statue of Liberty was dedicated on October 28, 1886. It is made of copper, steel, and concrete and was a gift from France. The website sccorp.com/cam is a live camera shot of the Statue of Liberty. The twenty-five windows in the crown represent the twenty-five gemstones found in the earth. The seven rays of the crown represent the seven seas and continents of the world.

The story of the creation of the Statue of Liberty is told in the book *Liberty* (2002) by Lynn Curlee. *A Picnic in October* (1999) by Eve Bunting, illustrated by Nancy Carpenter, is a good read-aloud story about the statue.

October 30

EMILY POST: BIRTHDAY

Emily Post, the household name in matters of etiquette, was born on this day in 1872 and died in 1960. She wrote her famous book on manners in 1922, which is now in its sixteenth edition and is updated by her great-granddaughter-in-law. Children can honor this wonderful woman by learning good manners. Some of the best resources on manners are *What Do You Say, Dear?* (1986) by Sesyle Joslin, illustrated by Maurice Sendak; *Perfect Pigs* (1983) by Marc Brown, illustrated by Stephen Krensky; and *What Do You Know about Manners?* (2000) by Cynthia MacGregor, illustrated by Lev Oertel.

ERIC KIMMEL: BIRTHDAY

Eric Kimmel, born October 30, 1946, wanted to be an author from the time he was in kindergarten. His first book was published in 1971, and he has now authored more than fifty books for children. He loves to share stories from different countries and cultures, such as *Baba Yaga: A Russian Folktale* (1991), illustrated by Megan Lloyd. His biography and lists of books he has authored are on his website ericakimmel.com.

October 31

HALLOWEEN

It's trick-or-treat time! A good website for Halloween is halloween.com. The following books are excellent resources. *Scary, Scary Halloween* (1988) by Eve Bunting, illustrated by Jan Brett, features a holiday poem that possesses all the atmosphere of the spookiest Halloween. *Halloween Is . . .* (2003) by Gail Gibbons describes the origins and history of Halloween traditions and festivities from ancient times to the present.

NATIONAL MAGIC DAY

October 31 is also National Magic Day and was started in 1938 to honor Harry Houdini. You might want to focus on National Magic Week, which is the last week in October and is sponsored by the Society of American Magicians. *My First Magic Book* (1993) by Lawrence Leyton and *Magic Tricks* (2002) by Jon Tremaine are good resources for magic information.

NATIONAL UNICEF DAY

In 1967, October 31 was declared National UNICEF Day by a Presidential Proclamation. Since that time, U.S. children have collected more than $100 million by going door-to-door on Halloween. More information can be obtained at unicef.org.

October Reading Strategy

Vocabulary Development

Children come to school with a working verbal vocabulary. The number and kind of words the child knows can vary widely depending on the number and kind of experiences the child has had with words and their meanings. A child with a rich experiential background will have a much larger verbal vocabulary than one with limited experiences.

One of the main goals of the primary years in vocabulary development is to increase the child's verbal vocabulary and then to teach the skills necessary to enable the child to increase his or her reading vocabulary.

Hearing a book read is the best way for increasing vocabulary. To help children's vocabulary expand, it is necessary to explain the new words or connect them to a familiar context. As the teacher chooses books to share with children, one of the variables to carefully consider is the vocabulary used in that particular book versus other available books. When choosing books for specific children, their individual vocabularies should be considered. For example, if a child only reads controlled-vocabulary books, there will be limited exposure to real-world vocabulary. This child would greatly benefit from the challenge of a nonfiction book on a subject of interest to him or her. If the vocabulary words are pointed out as the book is read, the child learns the words as well as their meanings and can make them part of his or her own vocabulary.

Classic literary works read to primary-aged children are conduits to increased vocabulary, both verbal and written. Once children have heard and discussed new words in the context of a story, they are more apt to internalize the words and use them in their own speech and writing. More complex patterns of language can also be introduced via read-alouds.

Choose poetry and rhymes carefully to help children develop a sense of play with words that stimulate vocabulary growth. The more words children hear, the more their personal vocabulary will increase. It is also true that the more times children hear a new word in context, the more likely they will incorporate the word into their own vocabulary.

New Word of the Day is a strategy to focus directly on vocabulary development. As part of the morning calendar routine, a word can be introduced and discussed. The teacher can use the word throughout the day as appropriate. Children can be encouraged to share the new word with parents as a homework assignment. The word can come from current events, classroom activities, cultural studies, science, or any area the teacher feels is appropriate.

Choosing a word with multiple meanings is a variation that is often used in older primary classes. For example, if the word for the day is *play*, children can discuss the many meanings the word can have and be encouraged to use as many meanings as they can throughout the day.

Word walls (placing words in categories on walls of the classroom) are an effective vocabulary development strategy. If *see* is the core word on the wall, children are encouraged to put up alternate words that could be used instead of *see* (*understand, spy, imagine, gaze.*)

Beginning readers need encouragement to ask what words mean as they come across them in their reading. Children often get so engrossed in decoding a new word that they forget to attach meaning to it. One of the critical questions to ask after a child has read a passage is "Were there any new words in that story?" Discussing the vocabulary contained in a story prior to reading it is always a good idea.

Modeling an interest in learning new words and their meanings helps children realize that vocabulary building is another of those lifelong skills that reading a wide variety of materials enhances.

November at a Glance

*A person who won't read has no advantage
over one who can't read.*
—**Mark Twain**

November Reading Tip: Introduce children to books that discuss their hobbies, interests, or new experiences.

NOVEMBER HIGHLIGHTS
National Adoption Month
Aunt Minnie McGranahan (1999) by Mary Prigger, illustrated by Betsy Lewin, tells the story of what happens in a small town when a spinster adopts her nine orphaned nieces and nephews.

Peanut Butter Lover's Month
Peanut Butter and Jelly: A Play Rhyme (1991), illustrated by Nadine Westcott, is a popular rhyme that explains how to make a peanut butter and jelly sandwich. Hand and foot motions for accompanying the rhyme appear at the end of the book.

National Geography Awareness Week (third week in November)
Blast Off to Earth! A Look at Geography (1992), written and illustrated by Loreen Leedy, tells about the unique features of the continents from the perspective of a group of aliens on a field trip to Earth.

National Farm/City Week (last week in November)
Country Kid, City Kid (2002) by Julie Cummins, illustrated by Ted Rand, is the story of two children; one who lives in the country and one who lives in the city. They discover they have a lot in common when they meet at camp.

Thanksgiving Day
This First Thanksgiving Day: A Counting Story (2003) by Laura Krauss Melmed, illustrated by Mark Buehner, presents short poems that tell the story of the first Thanksgiving.

November Reading Strategy: The Use of References

WEEKLY THEMES AND CURRICULUM CONNECTIONS
Week One: History of Aviation (Science)
Week Two: Geography (Geography)
Week Three: Farm/City Life (Social Studies and Geography)
Week Four: Pilgrims and Immigrants (Social Studies, Geography, and Holidays)

Special Events in November

National Author Day	Nov. 1
National Family Literacy Day	Nov. 1
National Sandwich Day	Nov. 3
National Aviation History Month	Nov. 6
Veterans Day	Nov. 11
Geography Week	Nov. 18
National Farm/City Week	Nov. 21
National Adoption Week	Nov. 24
First American Automobile Race	Nov. 28
Celebrate November	Nov. 30

FEATURED NOVEMBER BIRTHDAYS

Hilary Knight..................Nov. 1	Robert Louis Stevenson Nov. 13	Ruth Sanderson............Nov. 24
Daniel Boone ....Nov. 2	Claude Monet..............Nov. 14	Marc Brown ....Nov. 25
Jeannie Baker ....Nov. 2	William Steig...............Nov. 14	Shirley Climo ....Nov. 25
Natalie Kinsey-Warnock..Nov. 2	Victoria Chess ....Nov. 16	P. D. Eastman ....Nov. 25
Janell Cannon ....Nov. 3	Jean Fritz......................Nov. 16	Kevin Henkes ....Nov. 27
John Philip Sousa............Nov. 6	Angela Shelf Medearis..Nov. 16	Stephanie Calmenson ..Nov. 28
Benjamin Banneker ....Nov. 9	Nancy Van Laan ....Nov. 18	Ed Young ....Nov. 28
Lois Ehlert......................Nov. 9	Mary Jane Auch............Nov. 21	Margot Zemach ....Nov. 30

Week One: History of Aviation

✳ Curriculum Connection: Science

This week's unit will be intriguing as well as entertaining to primary students. Both fiction and nonfiction books are included, as are some offbeat subjects like stunt flying and airplane noises.

Air Show (2001) by Anastasia Suen, illustrated by Cecco Mariniello. The moves and historical aspects of airplanes that were named after different animals are introduced for young readers.

Airplanes (1997) by Darlene Stille, illustrated by Linda Cornwell. This book for young readers discusses the different parts that comprise an airplane, what each part does, and how planes fly.

Amelia Earhart: More than a Flier (2003) by Patricia Lakin, illustrated by Lea and Alan Daniel. Amelia Earhart loved adventure. Many of the "firsts" she accomplished in her short life as well as her approach to life in general are explored in this biography.

Dream Planes (1993) by Thomas Gunning. Here's a look at the planes of tomorrow and the future of flight. Machines from super jets that can go around the world in two hours to cars that will fly are featured in this book.

Extreme Machines . . . in the Air (1999) by Patricia and David Armentrout. This book contains brief descriptions of the Wrights brothers' flying machine, ultralights, dirigibles, hurricane-hunting planes, supersonic airplanes, and other lesser-known types of flying machines.

Fantastic Flights: One Hundred Years of Flying on the Edge (2003) by Patrick O'Brien. This is a short history of several twentieth-century flights and their pilots from the Wright brothers to those of the more recent space shuttles.

First Flight: The Story of Tom Tate and the Wright Brothers (1997) by George Shea, illustrated by Don Bolognese. Tom Tate was known around Kitty Hawk as a teller of tall tales, and the Wright Brothers dream of flying topped his tales.

Fly, Bessie, Fly (1998) by Lynn Joseph, illustrated by Yvonne Buchanan. This is a biography of the woman who, in 1921, became the first African American to earn a pilot's license.

Flying: Just Plane Fun (2003) by Julie Grist. The photos and illustrations bring airplanes and flying to life while preserving the magical aspects of flight in this humorous nonfiction book for older readers.

The Glorious Flight Across the Channel with Louis Bleriot (1987) by Alice Provensen, illustrated by Martin Provensen. This 1984 Caldecott Medal winning biography explores the life of Louis Bleriot, who produced the *Bleriot XI*, which was the first machine to fly the English Channel.

Helicopters (2001), **Jet Airliners** (2001), and **Military Planes** (2001) by Kelly Baysura. These three books provide great information on each type of aircraft in these categories.

High in the Sky: Flying Machines (1997) by Steve Parker. Text and illustrations explore the various types of aircraft, including hot-air balloons, airships, gliders, helicopters, cargo planes, and airliners.

The Hindenburg (2000) by Patrick O'Brien. This beautifully illustrated book chronicles the story of the vessel whose crash ended the age of the dirigible.

The Jet Alphabet Book (1999) by Jerry Pallotta, illustrated by Rob Bolster. This richly illustrated alphabet book presents facts about a variety of jet planes from the Airocomet to the Zephr.

Lettice, the Flying Rabbit (2004) written and illustrated by Mandy Stanley. A rabbit is wishing that she could fly when a battery-powered airplane lands at her feet. Is it possible that her dreams of flight will come true?

The Magic School Bus Taking Flight: A Book About Flight (1997) by Joanna Cole, illustrated by Bruce Degan. The colorful illustrations show Ms. Frizzle and her class shrunk inside a model airplane where they discover how wings and moving air affect flight.

My Brothers' Flying Machine: Wilbur, Orville and Me (2003) by Jane Yolen, illustrated by Jim Burke. Take a look at the lives of the Wright Brothers as seen through the eyes of their sister, Katharine, who provided support and encouragement as they worked on their inventions.

Night Flight: Charles Lindbergh's Incredible Adventure (2002) by Sydelle Kramer, illustrated by Kan Andreasen. This biography captures and explains the excite-

ment surrounding Charles Lindbergh's amazing long flight across the Atlantic.

The Noisy Airplane Ride (2003) by Mike Downs, illustrated by David Gordon. Using rhyming text, this fun book describes the sounds of an airplane and what those sounds mean. Facts about airplanes are included in a special section of the book.

Plane Song (1995) by Diane Siebert, illustrated by Vincent Nasta. This 1994 Outstanding Science Trade Book for Children uses rhymed text and illustrations to describe different kinds of planes and their features.

Stunt Planes (2003) by Jeff Savage. This book describes stunt flying, including the history, basic stunts, and contests for stunt flyers.

Things That Fly (1990) by Kate Little, illustrated by A. Thomas. This book for older primary students explores twelve aspects of flight including power, airlines, and airports.

Wright vs. Wrong: The True and Not-So-True Story of the Airplane (1998) written and illustrated by Gigi Tegge. The wacky illustrations and silly verse used to tell the origins of the airplane are a delight for children. This is a clever book relating how the Wright brothers made their historic flight.

November 1

NATIONAL AUTHOR DAY
November 1 is National Author Day. Ask the students to present a report about their favorite author and three reasons why they chose that author. Children usually want to say they like the illustrations, so refocus their attention on the story—or the content if they choose a nonfiction author. Eileen Christlow's book *What Do Authors Do?* (1997) walks readers through the writing process step-by-step.

NATIONAL FAMILY LITERACY DAY
As a homework assignment on National Family Literacy Day, ask students to share a book or story with the rest of the family. *The Wednesday Surprise* (1990) by Eve Bunting, illustrated by Donald Carrick, is a wonderful book about sharing the gift of reading ability with those who don't know how to read.

HILARY KNIGHT: BIRTHDAY
This is the birthday of Hilary Knight (born in 1926) who wrote and illustrated new versions of *Cinderella* (2001) and *The 12 Days of Christmas* (2001). *Where's Wallace?* (2000), which is similar to the Where's Waldo stories, is also one of her books and is great for focusing children on the details in illustrations.

November 2

DANIEL BOONE: BIRTHDAY
Daniel Boone was born on this day in 1734. A famous early American pioneer, he explored much of what later became Kentucky and Tennessee. *Daniel Boone* (2003) by Rick Burke is a good read-aloud for today. Boone said, "I have never been lost, but I will admit to being confused for several weeks." Discuss with your students what this might mean to an explorer in the early 1800s and how today's technology would have helped Daniel Boone.

JEANNIE BAKER: BIRTHDAY
The website for artist and author Jeannie Baker, born in 1950, is jeanniebaker.com. Her book *Where the Forest Meets the Sea* (1990) is visually stunning and contains a simple, profound message on saving the rain forest.

NATALIE KINSEY-WARNOCK: BIRTHDAY
Natalie Kinsey-Warnock was born on this day in 1956. She lives in Vermont and has written more than thirty books based on family experiences. *The Bear That Heard Crying* (1996), illustrated by Ted Rand, is the true story of a little girl lost in the woods in 1783.

November 3

JANELL CANNON: BIRTHDAY
Children's author Janell Cannon, who was born on this date in 1957, loves bats, spiders, komodo dragons, and snakes. *Stellaluna* (1993) and *Verdi* (1996), her most famous books, reflect those loves. *Trupp: A Fuzzhead Tale* (1995) is about an encounter with a homeless woman. Her newest book, *Pinduli* (2004), is about a little hyena on the African savannah.

NATIONAL SANDWICH DAY
Sam's Sandwich (1991) by David Pelham is a good book to share today. November 3 was chosen for National Sandwich Day because it is the birthday of the fourth Earl of Sandwich, who died in 1792. He is credited with making the first "sandwich." Did you know the hamburger is the most popular sandwich in America? Americans consume an average of one hundred burgers per year. However, the average child will consume fifteen hundred peanut butter and jelly sandwiches before graduating from high school. Which sandwich is the favorite of your class? More sandwich trivia can be found at jackinthebox.com.

November 6

JOHN PHILIP SOUSA: BIRTHDAY
John Philip Sousa, the March King, was born on this day in 1854 and died in 1932. His most famous musical composition is "Stars and Stripes Forever," which was written in 1896. This is a wonderful march to use for physical movement. It is also great music with which to take a break from testing or other hard work—what a tension reliever! *John Philip Sousa* (1999) by Mike Venezia is a good book to share with primary-aged children. The marches by John Philip Sousa are often included in patriotic celebrations.

NATIONAL AVIATION HISTORY MONTH
November is National Aviation History Month. The most informational website for this topic is aviation-history.com, and the thematic resources provided for this week should help primary students understand the concepts and history of flight, which is one of the most fascinating wonders to children. Encourage students to observe birds and airplanes to better understand the science of flight, and use the listed resources to help answer their questions.

Week Two: Geography

Curriculum Connection: Geography

Primary children are fascinated by the world but usually have very limited exposure to areas or countries outside of their immediate neighborhood. Introducing them to the big, wide world is fun! Much geography can be learned incidentally by pointing out settings in stories and locales mentioned in nonfiction classroom resources. Using maps and globes as daily resources also helps with geography, and children need to have time to explore these resources on their own. Many lifelong skills center on geography concepts and tools.

The Amazing Pop-Up Geography Book (1998) by Kate Petty, illustrated by Jennie Maizels. Flaps, tabs, word balloons, and pop-ups help to interactively illustrate the geography of the earth and solar system.

America's Landscape (2002) by Lynn Stone. This book offers an excellent description of the range of geographical features throughout the United States in a way children can easily understand.

Antarctica (2001) by Allan Fowler, photographed by Caroline Anderson. Even though there aren't any people native to Antarctica, many people go there to study the weather and native plants and animals. This book introduces readers to this one-of-a-kind continent.

Australia (2001) by Allan Fowler. Explore the unique land forms and other fascinating aspects of Australia, the smallest continent, in this book for young readers.

Beginning Geography: How to Use a Map (1992) by Ellen Jo Moore, illustrated by Joy Evans. This resources book helps children enhance their skills in using maps and globes. It also helps children become more familiar in locating things on a map.

Countries (1998) by David Stienecker. This introduction to major cities of various countries of the world includes maps, riddles, puzzles, and other activities for older elementary readers.

Earth's Changing Continents (2004) by Neil Morris, illustrated by Ann Morris. Discover how the earth has changed throughout time, and learn about the geography and how it impacts the people living on the different continents.

Geography from A to Z: A Picture Glossary (1997) by Jack Knowlton, illustrated by Harriett Barton. This vivid pictorial geography glossary defines and illustrates over 60 terms in a way that even the youngest student can understand them.

Hottest, Coldest, Highest, Deepest (1998) written and illustrated by Steve Jenkins. Some of the Earth's most remarkable places, including the hottest, windiest, highest, and deepest are described for children in this collage-illustrated book.

How to Dig a Hole to the Other Side of the World (1990) by Faith McNulty, illustrated by Marc Simont. Take an imaginary journey through the earth to discover what is inside of it by reading this colorful story.

Latitude and Longitude (2003) by Rebecca Aberg. Readers are introduced to how lines of latitude and longitude are used on maps and globes and terms such as the equator and the prime meridian.

Living in the Forest (2003) by Donna Loughran, illustrated by Nanci Vargus. Living near or in a forest can be a different way of life.

How would living there affect your life? What resources are found there?

Living in the Tundra (2003) by Donna Loughran, illustrated by Nanci Vargus. Journey into the tundra environment and learn about the animals and people who live there in this wonderfully illustrated book.

Map Keys (2003) by Rebecca Aberg, illustrated by Jeanne Clidas. This easy-to-understand guide offers both introductory text on how to read and use a map key as well as instructions on how to create a map.

North America: Geography (2001) written and illustrated by Allan Fowler. Full-color photos and illustrations offer an introduction to the geographic features, people, and animals of North America.

P Is for Passport: A World Alphabet (2003) written and illustrated by Devin Scillian. This beautifully illustrated alphabet book uses a rhyming text and a passport format to present similarities and differences throughout the world.

Thomas's Sheep and the Great Geography Test (1998) by Steven Layne, illustrated by Perry Board. Thomas is worried about a geography test and is unable to sleep. He conjures up some sheep and sends them on a journey around the globe. As they explore the world, the sheep get into all kinds of mischief, and Thomas learns geography at the same time.

Where Do I Live? (1995) by Neil Chesanow, illustrated by Ann Iosa. This book uses words and amazingly detailed illustrations to explain to children exactly where they live. It starts with a child's room, then moves out to her home, neighborhood, town, state, and country, and finally expands to Earth. It makes a very visual presentation.

Where People Live (1998) by Angela Royston. Why do people live in difficult geographical locations? Learn how people survive in towns that are in the mountains or cities right on or next to water.

November 9

BENJAMIN BANNEKER: BIRTHDAY

Benjamin Banneker—African American scientist, clockmaker, and surveyor—was born on November 9, 1731, and died in 1806. He took a clock apart piece by piece. He then used the pieces as patterns to make a wooden clock that worked perfectly and ran for more than forty years. *Dear Benjamin Banneker* (1998) by Andrea Pinkney, illustrated by Brian Pinkney, provides more information on this man of science.

LOIS EHLERT: BIRTHDAY

Children's author and illustrator Lois Ehlert, who was born in 1934, celebrates her birthday on this day. She uses mostly collage in her books because she likes cutting and pasting better than drawing. She loves plants and animals and gets ideas from those areas. The website readingrockets.org has a recorded interview with Lois Ehlert that older primary students will enjoy. Her most famous books are *Growing Vegetable Soup* (1990), *Planting a Rainbow* (1992), and *Eating the Alphabet* (1993).

November 11

VETERANS DAY

Congress initiated Veterans Day in 1926 to commemorate the end of World War I on November 11, 1918. In 1954, the intention was changed to honor American veterans of all wars. More information on Veterans Day is available at proteacher.com. *Veterans Day* (1998) by Mir Tamim Ansary introduces the holiday, explaining the historical events behind it, how it became a holiday, and how it is observed. *Veterans Day* (2001) by Jacqueline Cotton also explains its history and suggests ways of honoring veterans on this special day such as flying the flag, attending parades, buying poppies, and visiting hospitals.

Our unofficial national anthem, "God Bless America," was first performed on Veterans Day in 1938. Written by Irving Berlin, all the royalties from the song are given to the Girl Scouts and Boy Scouts of America. *God Bless America* (2002), illustrated by Lynn Munsinger, comes with a CD. The words of the song are used to tell the story of a bear family on a road trip.

November 13

ROBERT LOUIS STEVENSON: BIRTHDAY
Robert Louis Stevenson, author and poet, was born November 13, 1850, and died in 1894. His most famous work for primary-aged children is *A Child's Garden of Verses*, which is a classic in children's literature. This book, revised and published in 1999 and illustrated by Tasha Tudor's watercolors, is a visual delight as well as a treasure trove of wonderful poetry for children. Many of the poems will bring back memories of your own childhood.

JEZ ALBOROUGH: BIRTHDAY
Jez Alborough, born on this day in 1959, had his first book published in 1984. He is a jazz recording artist as well a painter and an author. He likes writing stories as much as he enjoys painting the pictures. *Some Dogs Do* (2003) and *Duck in a Truck* (2002) are two of his best-known books. His writing shows the power of positive thinking, and his tips for young writers and illustrators are to do what you love and don't compare yourself to others.

November 14

NANCY TAFURI: BIRTHDAY
Nancy Tafuri won a Caldecott Honor in 1985 for her book *Have You Seen My Duckling?* She has written and illustrated more than thirty-five books for children. *Where Did Bunny Go?* (2001) is a sweet, old-fashioned story about a bunny and a bird.

CLAUDE MONET: BIRTHDAY
Claude Monet was born on November 14, 1840, and died in 1926. Good resources on this French artist include *Once Upon a Lily Pad: Froggy Love in Monet's Garden* (1995) by Joan Sweeney, illustrated by Kathleen Fain; *Monet* (1990) by Mike Venezia; and *The Magical Garden of Claude Monet* (2003) by Laurence Anholt.

WILLIAM STEIG: BIRTHDAY
William Steig was born in 1907 and died in 2003. He won the Caldecott Medal in 1970 for *The Amazing Bone*. He also wrote *Sylvester and the Magic Pebble* (1973). He was a cartoonist as well as a children's author, and his characters are animals that act like humans. The website williamsteig.com offers more information on this author.

Week Three: Farm/City Life

🏛 🌐 Curriculum Connection: Social Studies and Geography

The following list can be used as an introduction to various lifestyles. Those who live on farms can compare their lives with those who live in urban apartments and vice versa. Primary children are amazed to learn that people who appear very different are, in reality, very much like themselves.

Albert, the Dog Who Liked to Ride in Taxies (2004) by Cynthia Zarin, illustrated by Pierre Pratt. Albert loves taxi rides. One day Albert gets to ride alone in a taxi. Can you guess where he is going?

All the Places to Love (1994) by Patricia MacLachlan, illustrated by Michael Wimmer. This book won the 1995 Children's Trade Book awards for social studies and language arts. It describes a young boy's favorite places on his grandparent's farm.

Alphabet City (1999) by Stephen Johnson, illustrated by Kristin Gilson. The beautiful paintings of New York City in this 1996 Caldecott Medal Honor Book reveal the alphabet in an unusual way.

Beep! Beep! Oink! Oink! Animals in the City (1997) written and illustrated by Patricia Casey. Discover the remarkable ways in which animals live side-by-side, as wells as above and below people in the city.

C Is for City (2002) by Nikki Grimes, illustrated by Pat Cummings. Enchanting illustrations and rhyming verses featuring each letter of the alphabet describe life in the city.

City Cats, Country Cats (1999) by Barbara Hazen, illustrated by Pam Paparone. Beginning readers will discover the different ways city cats and country cats like to play in this vividly illustrated story.

Curious George in the Big City (2001) by Margret Rey, illustrated by Martha Weston.

George is swept away on a tour of the city while he is out holiday shopping with the man in the yellow hat.

Down on the Funny Farm (1986) by Patrick King, illustrated by Alastair Graham. This is a humorous tale about farm animals that are confused about their jobs on the farm.

Farmer Duck (1996) by Martin Waddell, illustrated by Helen Oxenbury. Barnyard justice is dealt out to a lazy farmer by the animals that feel sorry for the hardworking duck that really runs this farm.

The Gardener (2000) by Sarah Stewart, illustrated by David Small. This 1998 Caldecott Honor Book explores what happens during the Great Depression when a young girl goes to live with her uncle in the city.

Harvey Potter's Balloon Farm (1998) by Jerdine Nolen, illustrated by Mark Buehner. Harvey Potter and his balloon farm were the strangest known in his area. Children will delight in discovering what was particularly strange on this genuine government-inspected farm.

I Stink (2002) by Kate McMullan, illustrated by Jim McMullan. *The New York Times Book Review* Best Illustrated Children's Book of 2002 tells the story of a big city garbage truck and the things it picks up as it makes its rounds.

Kiss the Cow (2003) by Phyllis Root, illustrated by Will Hillenbrand. A little girl delightfully observes her mother milking the cow and she wants to try it for herself. What happens when it comes time to kiss the cow?

Life on a Chicken Farm (2001), **Life on a Dairy Farm** (2001), **Life on a Sheep Farm** (2001), **Life on a Cattle Farm** (2001), and **Life on a Crop Farm** (2001) by Judy Wolfman, photographed by David Winston. Color photographs and descriptive text bring to life what it's like to live on different kinds of farms. Children who have not experienced farm life first hand particularly enjoy these books.

Night on Neighborhood Street (1996) by Eloise Greenfield, illustrated by Jan Spivey Gilchrist. This collection of poems explores a black neighborhood in a city during one evening. All of the sounds, sights, and emotions are described in the poems.

Nuts to You! (1993) written and illustrated by Lois Ehlert. A squirrel has an adventure in a city apartment instead of out of doors in this stunningly illustrated book.

Our Animal Friends at Maple Hill Farm (2001) by Alice Provensen, illustrated by Martin Provensen. Read stories about the various animals living at Maple Hill Farm, including goats, sheep, cats, and dogs.

Raising Yoder's Barn (2002) by Jane Yolen, illustrated by Bernie Fuchs. An eight-year-old Amish boy tells the amazing story of how a barn was raised in just one day when the community helped his family replace the one that recently burned down.

Round Trip (1991) written and illustrated by Ann Jonas. This book is an interactive adventure for readers. Children can read it forward and backward to make a round trip from the country to the city and back again.

Scarecrow (2001) by Cynthia Rylant, illustrated by Lauren Stringer. What does the world look like through a scarecrow's eyes?

Serious Farm (2003) written and illustrated by Tim Egan. Farmer Fred takes life on the farm very seriously and the animals on his farm do, too. One day they decide it is time to make the farm more fun and to make Farmer Fred laugh.

Wake Up, City (2004) written and illustrated by Susan Verlander. The sounds, sights, and rhythms of a city are brought to life in this artfully illustrated story.

A Weekend in the City (1991) by Lee Lorenz. This tall tale describes what happens when Pig and Duck lure Moose to the city for a surprise party.

The Year at Maple Hill Farm (2001) by Alice Provensen, illustrated by Martin Provensen. This book is an enchanting story of life on a farm for children who live in the country as well as those who live in the city.

November 16

VICTORIA CHESS: BIRTHDAY

Victoria Chess, born November 16, 1939, has illustrated more than one hundred books for children, including *Slugs* (1983) by David Greenberg and *The Scaredy Cats* (2003) by Barbara Bottner. Her illustrations are clever and have a mischievous sense of humor.

JEAN FRITZ: BIRTHDAY

Jean Fritz, born on November 16, 1915, mostly writes biographies and books based on history for older elementary students. Her picture book *George Washington's Breakfast* (1998), illustrated by Paul Galdone, is suitable for children who are able readers. Encompassing only nonfiction, her books make interesting reading for children who are beginning to write reports.

ANGELA SHELF MEDEARIS: BIRTHDAY

Angela Shelf Medearis is a children's author, born on this day in 1956, who also writes cookbooks for adults. She gets her ideas from the research she does on African American history. *Seven Spools of Thread* (2000), illustrated by Daniel Minter, and *Annie's Gifts* (1997), illustrated by Anna Rich, are two of her books that show African American life, history, and culture in a positive way. Her website is found at medearis.com.

November 18

NANCY VAN LAAN: BIRTHDAY

Nancy Van Laan, born in 1939, is a children's author who also writes plays. She was an English teacher before she became a professional writer. *When Winter Comes* (2000), illustrated by Susan Gaber, tells the story of what happens to living things when a pond freezes. *Possum Come a-Knockin'* (1992), illustrated by George Booth, is a funny trickster tale told in dialect. It was written in one day to retell the story of an actual visit to the author's house by an opossum. *A Tree for Me* (2002), illustrated by Sheila Samton, tells of a child's search for the perfect tree in which to hide.

GEOGRAPHY WEEK

The third week in November is Geography Week, which has been sponsored by the National Geographic Society since 1987. It is so designated to promote geographic literacy with a focus on the education of children. The resources listed for Week Two's thematic unit will help children prepare for a world that is increasingly interconnected and interdependent. Additional resources are located at nationalgeographic.com.

November 21

MARY JANE AUCH: BIRTHDAY
The Easter Egg Farm (1996) was the first book written and illustrated by Mary Jane Auch, who was born on this day in 1938. Her childhood visits to her grandparents' farm led to her fascination with chickens. Her books, such as *The Nutquacker* (1999), *Bantam of the Opera* (1997), and *Souperchicken* (2003), each star poultry as the main characters. The website mjauch.com offers more information on this author.

NATIONAL FARM/CITY WEEK
National Farm/City Week is customarily designated as the week containing Thanksgiving and is meant to honor the hard work of those who earn a living from the land and to recognize the importance of partnerships among cities, towns, and farms. A field trip to a food processing plant, meat processor, or bakery would be a good tie-in. The thematic resources for this week are very useful. Children are curious about animals and have been learning about farm animals versus zoo animals since they were in preschool.

November 24

NATIONAL ADOPTION WEEK
National Adoption Week is the fourth week in November. Resources for sharing this subject with primary students are *Little Miss Spider* (1999) by David Kirk, which is a lively and endearing adoption tale, and *Our Twitchy* (2003) by Kes Gray, illustrated by Mary McQuillan, which is the delightful story of a bunny that is adopted by a cow and a horse. Adoption is another of those areas where teachers must use a lot of sensitivity in presenting books and discussing the topic.

RUTH SANDERSON: BIRTHDAY
Ruth Sanderson, illustrator and author, was born on November 24, 1951. *Beauty and the Beast* (1992), written by Samantha Easton and illustrated by Sanderson, has truly amazing fine art–like illustrations. *The Twelve Dancing Princesses* (1993), retold and illustrated by Sanderson, has richly colored oil paintings. *The Golden Mare, the Firebird and the Magic Ring* (2001), which Sanderson wrote and illustrated, is based on a classic Russian folktale. Her books are for lovers of both fine art and fairy tales.

Week Four: Pilgrims and Immigrants

🏛 ⚖ 📅 Curriculum Connection: Social Studies, Geography, and Holidays

This week's thematic unit extends the usual Thanksgiving Pilgrim idea to include other people who have historically or recently immigrated to the United States.

Chinese Immigrants, 1850–1900 (2001) by Kay Olson. This book gives voice to the experiences and stories of the first Chinese immigrant workers during the California Gold Rush and the thousands of Chinese men who came to work on the railroads of the west.

Coming to America: The Story of Immigration (1996) by Betsy Maestro, illustrated by Susannah Ryan. This picture book is an introduction to the story of immigration to the Unites States. It contains prose and illustrations that are enticing to young children.

Don't Know Much About the Pilgrims (2002) by Kenneth Davis, illustrated by S. D. Schindler. This book uncovers a wealth of facts about the Pilgrims and answers questions about life on the *Mayflower* and the first Thanksgiving.

The First Thanksgiving (1990) by Linda Hayward, illustrated by James Watling. This is a retelling of the story of the Pilgrims and the first Thanksgiving is good for beginning readers.

French Immigrants, 1840–1940 (2002) by Kay Olson. The author details the historic immigration of over two million French to the Unites States between 1840 and 1940, who mainly settled in New England and New Orleans.

German Immigrants, 1820–1920 (2001) by Helen Frost. See historical photos and discover why there was a concentrated influx of Germans into the United States between 1820 and 1920.

Immigrant Children, Late 1800s to Early 1900s (2000) by Sylvia Whitman. This book focuses on immigrant children's experiences of immigration. What was it like for them?

Irish Immigrants, 1840–1920 (2001) by Megan O'Hara. Learn why so many people left Ireland for life in the United States. How did they fit in? Photos, maps, recipes, and sidebars are some of the special features in this book.

Italian Immigrants, 1820–1920 (2001) by Anne Todd. Compelling black-and-white photos and detailed text explain why over four million immigrants came from Italy to the United States between 1820 and 1920 as well as what they did once they arrived.

Japanese Immigrants, 1850–1950 (2001) by Rosemary Wallner. Why did thousands of Japanese immigrate to the United States? How was their experience different from that of other immigrant groups? This book addresses the unfair detention of Japanese and Japanese Americans in internment camps during World War II.

Milly and the Macy's Parade (2002) by Shana Corey, illustrated by Brett Helquist. Based on a true story of why the Macy's parade was started, this book tells about a young girl's concern for New York's immigrant people being away from their native lands at holiday time.

Norwegian, Swedish, and Danish Immigrants, 1820–1920 (2001) by Kay Olson. Explore the experience of Scandinavian people who came to the United States: why did they leave their native lands and what have they done to keep their cultures alive in their new country?

One Little, Two Little, Three Little Pilgrims (2001) by B. G. Hennessy, illustrated by Lynne Crave. Find out what each group brought to the harvest feast of the Pilgrims and the Wampanoag children.

P Is for Pilgrim: A Thanksgiving Alphabet (2003) by Carol Crane, illustrated by Helle Urban. Using the alphabet, this book examines the history and lore of Thanksgiving from the perspectives of the settlers.

Plymouth Partnership: Pilgrims and Native Americans (2002) by Susan Whitehurst. The history of the partnership between Native Americans and Pilgrims is relayed with respect for both groups in this beautifully illustrated book.

Samuel Eaton's Day: A Day in the Life of a Pilgrim Boy (1996) by Kate Waters, photographed by Russ Kendall. A six-year-old Pilgrim boy takes readers through his day. Photographs show him doing his chores and spending time with his family.

Sarah Morton's Day: A Day in the Life of a Pilgrim Girl (1993) by Kate Waters, photographed by Russ Kendall. Color photos from the Plimouth Plantation show readers what a typical day for a Pilgrim girl looked like.

Tapenum's Day: A Wampanoag Indian Boy in Pilgrim Times (1996) by Kate Waters, photographed by Russ Kendall. What was life like for the Wampanoags, the Indians who had early interactions with the Pilgrims?

Thanksgiving Day (1983) written and illustrated by Gail Gibbons. The origins and traditions of Thanksgiving as well as how this holiday is celebrated today are explored in this introductory text for children.

A Very Important Day (1995) by Maggie Rugg Herold, illustrated by Catherine Stock. On this historic day, people from thirty-two different countries make their way to a swearing in ceremony to become United States citizens.

When This World Was New (2003) by D. H. Figueredo, illustrated by Enrique Sanchez. This is the story of a young immigrant who overcomes his fear of living in New York.

Why Mexican Immigrants Came to America (2003) by Lewis Parker. Mexican immigration to what is now the United States has special historic significance. This book also looks at the contributions of these immigrants to the culture of this country.

Why Vietnamese Immigrants Came to America (2003) by Lewis Parker. Explore the contributions of Vietnamese immigrants who came to the United States from the 1960s to the present.

November 25

MARC BROWN: BIRTHDAY
Arthur, the famous creation of Marc Brown (born on November 25, 1946), has his own website for kids at pbskids.org. Brown has written more than thirty Arthur and D.W. books since the first one in 1976. It takes him about a year to go from a story idea to a published book.

SHIRLEY CLIMO: BIRTHDAY
Shirley Climo, born in 1928, has written eighteen books for children, including several versions of the Cinderella story; best known is *Egyptian Cinderella* (1991), illustrated by Ruth Heller. Her Mexican fable *The Little Red Ant and the Great Big Crumb* (1999), illustrated by Francisco Mora, and *Cobweb Christmas* (2001), illustrated by Jane Manning, are two of her other well-known books.

P. D. EASTMAN: BIRTHDAY
P. D. Eastman was also born on this day in 1909 and is often confused with Dr. Seuss. In fact, he did work on *The Cat in the Hat Dictionary* with Dr. Seuss. *Are You My Mother?* (1960) and *Go, Dog, Go* (1976) are two of his most beloved books. He died in 1986.

November 27

KEVIN HENKES: BIRTHDAY
Kevin Henkes was born on November 27, 1960. His first book, *All Alone* (2003), was published in 1981 when he was just twenty-one. *Lilly's Purple Plastic Purse* (1996), *Sheila Rae the Brave* (1996), and *Chrysanthemum* (1996) are his best-known books. His characters are usually mice who deal with childhood problems. Henkes has a light touch, and his stories have hopeful endings. Help your students notice the mice's ears, fur, and tails; they often convey more emotion than do the facial expressions. According to his website, kevinhenkes.com, Henkes used to think of himself as an artist but now is beginning to like writing more. He wouldn't trade being an author and illustrator for anything. Behind each of Henke's books is a wide-open heart to which children eagerly respond, making his characters some of the most beloved in all children's literature.

After reading *Chester's Way* (1997) and *Julius, Baby of the World* (1995), have students write about how they would spend a day with one of these characters.

November 28

FIRST AMERICAN AUTOMOBILE RACE
On November 28, 1895, six "horseless carriages" raced from Chicago to Evanston, Illinois, and back. In just over ten hours, with an average speed of 7.3 miles per hour, J. Frank Duryea won the two-thousand-dollar prize sponsored by the *Chicago Times Herald* newspaper. A good resource to mark this day is *The Racecar Alphabet* (2003) by Brian Floca.

STEPHANIE CALMENSON: BIRTHDAY
Born on this day in 1952, Stephanie Calmenson has written more than one hundred books. Some of her most popular stories include *Dinner at the Panda Palace* (1995), illustrated by Nadine Westcott; *Teeny Tiny Teacher* (2002), illustrated by Denis Roche; and *Frog Principal* (2001), illustrated by Denise Brunkus.

ED YOUNG: BIRTHDAY
Ed Young, born in China in 1931, has illustrated more than forty books for children, many of which he has also written. *Lon Po Po* (1996), his version of the Red Riding Hood story set in China, won the 1990 Caldecott Medal as well as the Boston Globe Horn Book Award. In 1993, his book *Seven Blind Mice* (2002) was selected as a Caldecott Honor Book.

November 30

MARGOT ZEMACH: BIRTHDAY
Margot Zemach was born on November 30, 1931, and died in 1989. As a young child she drew to keep herself company and to make herself and others laugh. She won the Caldecott Medal in 1974 for *Duffy and the Devil*, which was written by her husband Harve Zemach. She and her husband have worked on thirteen books together. She also illustrated other authors' works.

Her book *Some from the Moon, Some from the Sun* (2001) is a wonderful collection of timeless verses. *It Could Always Be Worse* (1990) and *The Little Red Hen* (1993) are children's favorites. Many of her books have also been published in Spanish.

CELEBRATE NOVEMBER
In November (2000) by Cynthia Rylant, illustrated by Jill Kastner, captures the cherished moments of this autumn month when the air grows cold and the earth and all of its creatures prepare for winter. It's a time of harvest and thanksgiving, when people gather together to celebrate their blessings with family and friends.

November Reading Strategy

The Use of References

Primary students need to be taught directly how to use references that are available and age appropriate. These resources can include dictionaries, atlases, maps, globes, and charts. Students also should be taught how to use resources and references that are embedded in books, such as tables of contents, glossaries, and indexes. The best way to teach the use of these resources is by modeling your use of them and "thinking aloud" when the need to use these references comes up in your daily teaching. The teachable moment is excellent for practicing the use of references.

Direct teaching of the uses of a dictionary should be taught and reviewed every year in elementary school. Kindergarten students can use a picture dictionary, while older primary children are ready for a children's dictionary. Upper-level elementary students can use a simplified adult dictionary. The big dictionary in the library is fun to use once so children will know that it works the same way as other simpler dictionaries do. How many meanings does that dictionary have for the word *go*? Children often view the dictionary with disdain because they haven't been taught effective and efficient ways to use it as a tool for learning about words. Modeling the use of a dictionary for word meaning instead of spelling helps children change their perceptions.

There are several games to play using elementary dictionaries. One that requires little advance preparation is a relay race game for finding a given set of words. Each team is given one dictionary and a list of words. As each word is found, the page number is written down and the dictionary is passed to the next child. The team that locates all the words first is the winner.

Dictionaries are essential tools for emerging readers so that they may become more independent as their reading skills increase and the text they want to read becomes more complex. Dictionaries help children answer many of their own questions without the help of an adult. Children often have an idea about a word's meaning but are not quite sure; a dictionary can clarify the meaning.

Both picture and word dictionaries are essential for children learning the English language. Teach the use of the dictionary clearly so that it is a tool rather than a source of frustration. Just telling a child to look up a word in the dictionary is not helpful if the child doesn't understand the words used in the definition.

The use of guide words in the dictionary is an exciting lesson for older primary students. They love learning shortcuts. You can also help students transfer the knowledge of guide words in the dictionary to the use of guide words in the telephone book.

December at a Glance

You're braver than you believe, and stronger than you seem, and smarter than you think. (Christopher Robin to Pooh)
—A. A. Milne

December Reading Tip: Choose books to read aloud that are a stretch for students to read on their own but will hold their interest as they listen.

DECEMBER HIGHLIGHTS
Write to a Friend Month
Dear Calla Roo . . . Love, Savannah Blue: A Letter to a Pen Pal (2000) by Sudie Rakusin introduces the reader to Savannah Blue, a Great Dane who has made a new friend, a little girl named Calla Ruth. Since they live far apart, they become pen pals.

Universal Human Rights Month
Eleanor Roosevelt (1998) by Lucile Davis presents the life story of the First Lady who worked for human rights and became known as the First Lady of the World.

Read a New Book Month
Boom Chicka Rock (2004) by John Archambault, illustrated by Suzanne Chitwood, is a new counting adventure for children of all ages.

Love Your Neighbor Month
Raising Yoder's Barn (2002) by Jane Yolen, illustrated by Bernie Fuchs, is a story about what happens when fire destroys a barn and all the Amish neighbors come to rebuild it in one day.

Deaf Heritage Week (first full week in December)
I Have a Sister—My Sister Is Deaf (1984) by Jeanne Peterson, illustrated by Deborah Ray, is a great resource for explaining the world of the totally deaf to younger children. This is a 1979 Coretta Scott King Award Honor Book.

December Reading Strategy: Word Classes

WEEKLY THEMES AND CURRICULUM CONNECTIONS
Week One: Hats (Social Studies)
Week Two: Mice (Science and Language Arts)
Week Three: Trees (Science)
Week Four: Pioneers (Social Studies and Language Arts)

Special Events in December

Rosa Parks Day	Dec. 1
Game of Basketball Created	Dec. 1
Saint Nicholas Day	Dec. 6
National Poinsettia Day	Dec. 12
Bill of Rights Day	Dec. 15
Death of Sitting Bull	Dec. 15
Boston Tea Party	Dec. 16
Hanukkah (approx.)	Dec. 20
Death of Sacagawea	Dec. 20
Winter Solstice	Dec. 22
Christmas	Dec. 25
Kwanzaa	Dec. 26
National Whiners Day	Dec. 26
Creation of Endangered Species Act	Dec. 28
First Bank Opened in United States	Dec. 31
New Year's Eve	Dec. 31

FEATURED DECEMBER BIRTHDAYS

Jan Brett ....Dec. 1	Bonnie Pryor ....Dec. 22	Jean Van Leeuwen ....Dec. 26
Walt Disney...............Dec. 5	Jerry Pinkney ....Dec. 22	Elizabeth Howard ....Dec. 28
Bill Pickett ....Dec. 5	Kit Carson ....Dec. 24	Nancy Luenn...............Dec. 28
Jean de Brunhoff ....Dec. 9	Johnny Gruelle ....Dec. 24	Rudyard Kipling ....Dec. 30
Ludwig van Beethoven Dec. 16	Lynn Munsinger ....Dec. 24	Mercer Mayer ....Dec. 30
Eve Bunting................Dec. 19	Debra Barracca ....Dec. 24	Henri Matisse ....Dec. 31
Lulu Delacre ....Dec. 20	Clara Barton ....Dec. 25	

Week One: Hats

🏛 Curriculum Connections: Social Studies

In most cultures of the world, certain things are common and universal. Bread is one of the foods found in most cultures. Though its form changes, its use stays the same. Hats are almost as universal and can be used to keep the head dry, warm, or cool, or used for adornment or protection depending on the climate and culture of the wearer.

This resource list presents stories about some fictional hats as well as some functional ones to share with young readers. Many creative-writing lessons can be developed from the stories provided here.

Abe Lincoln's Hat (1994) by Martha Brenner, illustrated by Donald Cook. Why did Abe Lincoln always wear a tall black hat? To keep his important papers safe! This and other stories about Lincoln as a young lawyer show just how fair and funny he was.

Aunt Flossie's Hats (1995) written and illustrated by James Ransome. Why do the children love to visit Aunt Flossie? Could if be to hear the funny stories about each hat she owns?

Aunt Lucy Went to Buy a Hat (2004) by Alice Low, illustrated by Laura Huliska-Beith. This rhyme has repetition, wordplay, and memorable characters who chase down a missing hat.

Boss of the Plains: The Hat That Won the West (2000) by Laurie Carlson, illustrated by Holly Meade. This story about John Stetson tells how he created the most popular hat in the West, which is still worn by many people today.

Ella, the Elegant Elephant (2004) by Carmela D'Amico, illustrated by Steve D'Amico. Ella is nervous about the first day of school in her new town and wearing her grandmother's bright red hat helps—until the other students tease her.

Halloween Hats (2003) by Elizabeth Winthrop, illustrated by Sue Truesdell. The silly and varied hats in this cute story help the characters create costumes for the Halloween parade.

The Hat (1997) written and illustrated by Jan Brett. This wonderfully illustrated story about a hedgehog, who ends up wearing a woolen stocking as a hat, is delightful for young children.

A Hat for Minerva Louise (1996) written and illustrated by Janet Stoeke. A snow-loving chicken decides that a pair of mittens is really two hats to keep both ends of her body warm.

A Hat So Simple (1994) written and illustrated by Jerry Smath. A lady alligator needs a hat to wear when she goes fishing with her husband in this cute and rhyming watercolor-illustrated tale.

Hats! (2001) by Dana Rau, illustrated by Paul Harvey. Cartoonish illustrations help tell the story about this boy who gets to try on different hats while he decides which one to wear.

Hats, Hats, Hats (1993) by Ann Morris, illustrated by Ken Heyman. A hat can tell a lot about the person who wears it. Full-color photographs show people in hat from different places in the world.

Hello Cat, You Need a Hat (1999) by Rita Geiman, illustrated by Dana Regan. A girl tries to convince her grumpy cat to try on a variety of hats in this easy-to-read story.

Jennie's Hat (2003) written and illustrated by Ezra Jack Keats. Jennie's hat is drab and uninspiring until the birds help out and decorate it.

Lasso Lou and Cowboy McCoy (2003) by Barbara Failing, illustrated by Tedd Arnold. McCoy buys himself a cowboy hat, which is the beginning of many silly adventures in this engaging story.

The Magic Hat (2002) by Mem Fox, illustrated by Tricia Tusa. A magical wizard's hat can change people into animals in this colorful story.

Miss Fannie's Hat (2001) by Jan Karon, illustrated by Toni Goffe. When Miss Fannie gives up her hat to help raise money for her church, something unexpected happens.

Miss Hunnicutt's Hat (2003) by Jeff Brumbeau, illustrated by Gail de Marcken. Miss Hunnicutt wants to wear her new hat with a live chicken on it for the queen's visit.

Mr. Frumble's Biggest Hat Flap Book Ever! (2002) written and illustrated by Richard Scarry. This is the story of what happens to a hat as it is run over by various cars and trucks.

Mrs. Honey's Hat (1989) written and illustrated by Pam Adams. Mrs. Honey's hat changes without her noticing as a variety of animals take items from it and leave other objects in their place.

A Three Hat Day (1987) by Laura Geringer, illustrated by Arnold Lobel. This is a charming story about finding true love in a department store.

What a Hat! (2003) written and illustrated by Holly Keller. Newton is teased for always wearing his hat, but the hat comes in handy for helping others.

Who Took the Farmer's Hat? (1988) by Joan Nodset, illustrated by Fritz Siebel. This is a wonderful story about a farmer who lost his hat, finds it, and why he still decides to buy a new one.

Whose Hat? (1992) by Margaret Miller. Color photographs of hats represent various occupations in this fun book for young children.

Zara's Hats (2003) written and illustrated by Paul Meisel. This tale, based on the author's great-grandfather and grandmother, depicts the loving relationship between a daughter and her father who is a hat maker.

December 1

JAN BRETT: BIRTHDAY
Jan Brett, born December 1, 1949, has more than twenty-six million books in print and is one of America's most beloved authors and illustrators for children. Her first book, *Fritz and the Beautiful Horses*, was published in 1981. *Trouble with Trolls* (1999) and *The Mitten* (1989) are two of her best-known works. *The Wild Christmas Reindeer* (1991) is a good book to read on her birthday.

ROSA PARKS DAY: ANNIVERSARY OF ARREST
On December 1, 1955, African American Rosa Parks was arrested for not letting a white bus rider take her seat. This act led to the start of the civil rights movement. *If a Bus Could Talk: The Story of Rosa Parks* (2002) by Faith Ringgold provides background information for primary students.

GAME OF BASKETBALL CREATED
James Naismith invented basketball in 1891. He nailed peach baskets at opposite ends of the gym and gave students soccer balls to toss into them. By 1905, basketball was recognized as a permanent winter sport. *My Basketball Book* (2000) by Gail Gibbons is an excellent resource.

December 5

WALT DISNEY: BIRTHDAY
Walt Disney was born on December 5, 1901, and died in 1966. He created Mickey Mouse and made the concept of theme parks a reality. He also produced the first full-length animated movie.

One of the most recognized hats in the world, the Mickey Mouse ears hat, is the number one souvenir from Disney parks around the world. More resources on hats can be found in this week's thematic unit. A good resource on Walt Disney is *Walt Disney: A Photo-Illustrated Biography* (2003) by June Preszler, illustrated by Enoch Peterson.

BILL PICKETT: BIRTHDAY
Bill Pickett, born on this date in 1870, was the first African American cowboy to be inducted into the Rodeo Hall of Fame. In 1903, he invented bulldogging, which is now called steer wrestling. His picture is on a U.S. postage stamp in the Legends of the West series. *Bill Pickett: Rodeo-Riding Cowboy* (1999) by Andrea Pinkney, illustrated by Brian Pinkney, is a good resource for more information on this famous cowboy who died in 1932.

December 6

SAINT NICHOLAS DAY

In many European countries, this is the day on which Saint Nicholas (our Santa Claus) visits children and leaves gifts. In some cultures, he visits in secret during the night. The poem *A Visit from St. Nicholas* (1998) by Clement Moore has been reprinted and adapted in many ways since it was first published in 1848. The famous line "Not a creature was stirring, not even a mouse" leads us to mice as one of the themes for this month.

A tradition attached to this day is to leave shoes outside the door. The shoes are filled with hay and carrots for Saint Nicholas's beautiful white horse. If the owner of the shoes has been good, the saint will fill the shoe with gifts. If not—oh, well.

WASHINGTON MONUMENT COMPLETED: ANNIVERSARY

The Washington Monument in Washington, D.C., was completed on this day in 1884. *The Washington Monument* (2003) by Kristin Nelson gives a good introduction to the purpose, structure, and history of this important monument to our first president.

December 9

JEAN DE BRUNHOFF: BIRTHDAY

Jean de Brunhoff, world-famous children's book author and illustrator, was born in Paris on December 9, 1899. His most famous book, *The Story of Babar*, was published in 1933 in the United States. He wrote six more Babar books, including *The Travels of Babar* (1976), *Babar the King* (1976), and *Babar and Father Christmas* (2001), which was the last book to be published before his death.

De Brunhoff's son Laurent continued writing more stories about Babar after his father died in 1937. Laurent's books include *Babar's Museum of Art* (2003), *Meet Babar and His Family* (2002), *Babar's ABC* (2001), and *Back to School for Babar* (2003).

The Babar stories continue to entertain children today as they did when they were written more than three generations ago. Perhaps this is because Babar has a unique gift for discovering a silver lining in the clouds of life.

Week Two: Mice

✳ 📖 Curriculum Connections: Science and Language Arts

Children's literature, both fiction and nonfiction, abounds with books about mice. Mice are sometimes used as substitutes for people in stories that teach values, such as *Town Mouse and Country Mouse* (2002) written and illustrated by Jan Brett. The following list provides a mixture of resources to engage students in the world of mice and can be used as an introduction to having a mouse as a classroom pet.

Angelina and the Butterfly (2002) by Sally Ann Lever, illustrated by Helen Craig. Angelina found a butterfly with an injured leg. After a surprising turn of events she decides to set it free.

Blabber Mouse (2001) written and illustrated by True Kelley. In this colorfully illustrated story, young readers will discover that even the smallest animals have the same personality traits as humans.

The Bravest Mouse (2002) by Maria Barbero, illustrated by Sibylle Kazeroid. The illustrations for this story about Sasha, who doesn't like the black mark around his eye, are gorgeous. What does Sasha do when the younger mice want to look just like him?

Busy, Busy Mouse (2003) by Virginia Kroll, illustrated by Fumi Kosaka. When the family goes to sleep after a busy day, the cute little mouse gets the run of the house, and his adventures keep him so busy.

Come Out and Play, Little Mouse (1995) by Robert Kraus, illustrated by Ariane Dewey and Jose Aruego. In this brightly illustrated tale, the cat invites Little Mouse to play but, luckily, his big brother protects him.

Country Mouse Cottage (2000) by Nigel Brooks, illustrated by Abigail Horner. In the year 1900, cottage life is very hard work: mouse is busy doing chores, working the garden, and going to school.

Do You See a Mouse? (1995) written and illustrated by Bernard Waber. There is a mouse in every busy illustration in this book about a mouse in a fancy hotel.

Doctor De Soto (1982) written and illustrated by William Steig. A mouse dentist treats the toothaches of animals, but he doesn't treat animals who might turn on him.

Grey Mouse (2002) by Anke de Vries, illustrated by Willemien Min. Grey Mouse changes her appearance to see if that will help with her loneliness. She is also tired of always being grey.

House Mouse, Senate Mouse (1996) by Peter Barnes, illustrated by Cheryl Barnes. It is not always easy to reach agreement on important issues as the Squeaker of the House and the Senate Mousejority leader discover.

It's a Mouse! (1997) by Dorothy Souza. Full-color photographs and detailed text describes the life cycles of various species of mice.

Little Mouse's Painting (2002) by Diane Wolkstein, illustrated by Maryjane Begin. This beautifully illustrated, enduring story, tells about Little Mouse's friends who do not all see the same thing when they look at her painting.

A Look Through the Mouse Hole (1988) by Heiderose Fischer-Nagel, illustrated by Andreas Fischer-Nagel. Photographs and text help the reader observe the behavior of a family of mice living in a basement. Behavior comparisons between indoor and outdoor mice are examined, and information on the care of pet mice is included.

Mice Twice (1986) by Joseph Low. This 1981 Caldecott Honor Book tells of the hospitality between a mouse, a dog, and a cat.

Mice (1998) by Kevin Holmes. A great introduction to nonfiction, this book explores the world of mice, including their physical characteristics and interactions with humans.

Mouse (2004) by Barrie Watts. Photographs and text show the development of a mouse from birth to eight weeks old.

Mouse Mess (1997) written and illustrated by Linnea Riley. A huge mess is made by a hungry mouse when he decides he wants a snack in this vividly illustrated story.

Mouse Paint (1995) written and illustrated by Ellen Walsh. Three mice explore the world of color when they discover jars of paint. The cute illustrations and fun story help teach colors to little ones.

Mouse Tail Moon (2002) by Joanne Ryder, illustrated by Maggie Kneen. These poems in this richly illustrated book depict the environment of a field mouse from the time the sun goes down to the time the sun comes up again.

The Mouse That Snored (2004) written and illustrated by Bernard Waber. The snoring of the mouse living in the house disturbs the human residents.

A Mouse's Life (2001) written and illustrated by John Himmelman. This impressively illustrated tale describes the daily activities and life cycle of a white-footed mouse in a very entertaining way.

Mrs. Mortifee's Mouse (1995) written and illustrated by Linda Henry. This is the delightful story of the adventures a mouse, a woman with a strange name, and a cat.

Norman, the Doorman (1981) written and illustrated by Don Freeman. Norman, a mouse, is a doorman in an art museum. He finds a way to see the treasures in the rest of the museum.

Once a Mouse (1982) written and illustrated by Marcia Brown. In this 1962 Caldecott Medal winner, a hermit's pet changes to different animals and becomes more vain throughout the story.

Shy Charles (2001) written and illustrated by Rosemary Wells. A young mouse rescues his babysitter even though he is timid and shy.

The Story of Jumping Mouse (1989) written and illustrated by John Steptoe. This is the tale of a courageous mouse who goes to a far-off land and becomes an eagle. Based on a Native American legend, it was a 1985 Caldecott Honor Book.

Wemberly Worried (2000) written and illustrated by Kevin Henkes. A mouse named Wemberly worries about everything, especially the first day of preschool in this vividly illustrated tale.

December 12

NATIONAL POINSETTIA DAY

National Poinsettia Day, a holiday designated by an act of Congress, is celebrated on the death anniversary of Joel Robert Poinsett, ambassador to Mexico, who introduced the native Mexican plant to the United States. *The Legend of the Poinsettia* (1997), written and illustrated by Tomie dePaola, tells the story of the girl who picked some plants on her way to church for Christmas. As she entered the church, the ends of the leaves turned into bright red flowers.

CHRISTMAS TREES

Christmas trees and evergreen wreaths are two more plants that are symbolic of the month of December. Several resources for a study of trees are on the thematic list of books for Week Three. *The Trees of the Dancing Goats* (2000), written and illustrated by Patricia Polacco, combines the traditions of Jewish families with those of their Christian neighbors. *The Year of the Perfect Christmas Tree* (1996) by Gloria Houston, illustrated by Barbara Cooney, is an Appalachian story about providing a tree for the local church.

December 15

BILL OF RIGHTS DAY

Although the Bill of Rights was incorporated into the U.S. Constitution in 1789, it wasn't until 1941 that President Franklin D. Roosevelt designated a Bill of Rights Day. The website billofrights.com provides rich resources for this day. *The Bill of Rights* (2003) by Karen Hossell tells older primary students about the ten amendments and the rights they are intended to protect.

SITTING BULL: DEATH ANNIVERSARY

Sitting Bull, a famous Native American, died on this day in 1890. As a young boy he was given the name "Slow" because he was very deliberate in all he did. He was a highly revered warrior and excellent horseman with a reputation for upholding strict moral principles and obeying tribal rules. In 1885, he toured the East Coast with Buffalo Bill Cody's Wild West Show. Resources include *Sitting Bull* (1995) by Lucille Penner, illustrated by Will Williams, and *A Boy Called Slow* (1998), written by Joseph Bruchac and illustrated by Rocco Baviera.

December 16

BOSTON TEA PARTY ANNIVERSARY

On this day in 1773, Boston patriots boarded a British vessel anchored in Boston Harbor and dumped nearly 350 chests of tea into the water. This was one of several events leading to the American Revolution.

Boston Tea Party (2001) by Pamela Duncan Edwards, with rich illustrations by Henry Cole, provides an introduction to the colonial period in our history. *Joining the Boston Tea Party* (2001) by Diane Stanley, illustrated by Holly Berry, tells the story of twins who journey back in time to the Boston Tea Party.

LUDWIG VAN BEETHOVEN: BIRTHDAY

Ludwig van Beethoven was born on December 16, 1770, and died in 1827. He performed in public for the first time at the age of eight and studied with Mozart in Vienna during his teenage years. In 1798, he noticed he was having trouble hearing, and by 1820, he was completely deaf.

Beethoven (1994) by Ann Rachlin, illustrated by Susan Hellard, details the composer's childhood and will inspire children to be creative, work hard, and follow their dreams. Barbara Nichol's *Beethoven Lives Upstairs* (1994), illustrated by Scott Cameron, is a creative biography of the musician's young downstairs neighbor. It is also available in audio and video versions; check your resource center or public library.

December 19

EVE BUNTING: BIRTHDAY

Eve Bunting was born in Northern Ireland on December 19, 1928, and came to the United States in 1958. She is the author and illustrator of more than 150 books for every age group and has written on a wide range of topics. *Smoky Night* (1999), a book that Bunting wrote and David Diaz illustrated, won the Caldecott Medal in 1995.

A few of her works include the following. *December* (2000), also illustrated by David Diaz, is about a homeless boy and his mother who share what little they have with a stranger. *Ducky* (1997), illustrated by David Wisniewski, is based on an actual event. *The Wednesday Surprise* (1991), illustrated by Donald Carrick, is a loving story of a girl who teaches her grandmother to read. *A Day's Work* (1997), illustrated by Ronald Himler, is an honest story about a young Mexican American boy and his grandfather.

Bunting is a prolific writer whose stories are timely, interesting, and thought provoking for children of all ages. Many of her books are great class discussion starters.

Week Three: Trees

❄ Curriculum Connection: Science

December is a great month to study trees. The tree brought into the house for Christmas, the lots where people buy those trees, and the different kinds used in various locations are all interesting starting points for this theme. The science behind which trees stay green and which ones lose their leaves is a concept to explore with primary students.

The following resources contain science concept books, poetry, and literary references to trees.

Be a Friend to Trees (1993) by Patricia Lauber, illustrated by Holly Keller. This colorful picture book discusses the importance of trees for their beauty as well as their resources.

The Dream Tree (2002) by Stephen Cosgrove, illustrated by Robin James. A caterpillar wonders what life as a butterfly will be like in this vividly illustrated story.

Evergreen Trees (1998) by John Prevost. Young readers learn basic information about evergreens, including how they are structured and what value they have economically.

Fir Trees (1989) by Heiderose and Andreas Fischer-Nagel. Learn the development and ecosystem of the endangered fir tree.

Flower Fairies of the Trees (2001) by Cicely Barker. These illustrated poems describe the beauty of various trees that flower.

Forest Plants (1999) by Ernestine Giesecke, illustrated by Eileen Neill. This book teaches young readers how different plants adapt to living in a forest.

Franklin Plants a Tree (2001) by Paulette Bourgeois, illustrated by Brenda Clark. Franklin plants a sapling he was given for Earth Day. He hopes it will grow big enough for a tree house.

It Could Still Be a Tree (1991) by Allan Fowler. This clearly written book explains how to identify trees as well as the structure and environment that different trees thrive in.

A Log's Life (1997) by Wendy Pfeffer, illustrated by Robin Brickman. This well-done science picture book is a good introduction to the life cycle of a tree.

The Magic School Bus in the Rain Forest (2000) by Eva Moore, illustrated by John Spiers. What happens when Mrs. Frizzle's cocoa tree stops growing cocoa beans?

Mighty Tree (1996) written and illustrated by Dick Gackenbach. This colorfully illustrated story traces the growth of three seeds into trees that have different uses.

Miss Twiggley's Tree (2002) written and illustrated by Dorothea Fox. This classic story is about Miss Twiggley, a character with strange habits, who also happens to live in a tree.

Mr. Willowby's Christmas Tree (2000) written and illustrated by Robert Barry. The humorous illustrations and fun text tell about a Christmas tree that is so tall that the top has to be cut off, and how that top brings the joy of smaller trees for various people and animals.

Nature's Green Umbrella (1997) by Gail Gibbons. This beautifully illustrated book describes the characteristics of a rain forest and the different layers of plants and animals that make up the ecosystem.

Night Tree (1994) by Eve Bunting, illustrated by Ted Rand. Follow this richly illustrated story about an annual pilgrimage a family makes to decorate a tree with food for the animals in winter.

Old Elm Speaks: Tree Poems (1998) by Kristine O'Connell George, illustrated by Kate Kiesler. These poems present the images of trees in various environments throughout the seasons while the vibrant paintings bring the book to life.

Once There Was a Tree (1989) by Natalia Romanova, illustrated by Gennady Spirin. This enchanting story reveals how a stump attracts many creatures and how the new tree that grows out of the old stump attracts the same creatures.

One Small Place in a Tree (2004) by Barbara Brenner, illustrated by Tom Leonard. One tiny scratch in a tree can turn into a home for a variety of animals over many years.

Red Leaf, Yellow Leaf (1991) by Lois Ehlert. Using very simple language and detailed photographs the growth of a maple tree from seed to sapling is described.

Sky Tree: Seeing Science Through Art (2001) by Thomas Locker, illustrated by Candace Christiansen. The lovely illustrations enhance this story of how a tree changes as the environment around it changes.

Tell Me, Tree: All About Trees for Kids (2002) written and illustrated by Gail Gibbons. This is a fine introduction to trees for young readers.

The Tree (2002) by Dana Lyons, illustrated by David Danioth. An ancient Douglas fir wonders about the things it has seen during the years it has been growing in this thoughtful story with stunning illustrations.

A Tree for All Seasons (2001) by Robin Bernard. Beautiful photos and easy-to-read text lets young readers follow the seasonal changes that occur in the life of a sugar maple tree.

A Tree Is a Plant (2001) by Clyde Bulla, illustrated by Stacey Schett. This book includes activities to help readers investigate how trees absorb water as well as how to determine the age of a tree.

A Tree Is Nice (1987) by Janice Udry, illustrated by Marc Simont. This 1957 Caldecott Medal winner contains both colored and black and white photographs depicting the importance of trees to humans.

The Tremendous Tree Book (1998) by Barbara Brenner, illustrated by Fred Brenner. This informative book takes complex information about trees and makes it understandable for children.

What Good Is a Tree? (1999) by Larry Brimner, illustrated by Leo Landry. Together, a brother and sister find how much fun a tree can be if they use their imaginations.

Why Do Leaves Change Color? (1994) by Betsy Maestro, illustrated by Loretta Krupinski. The process that leaves go through when they change colors is detailed in this book.

December 20

HANUKKAH
Hanukkah, the Jewish Festival of Lights, starts sometime in December and lasts for eight days. The exact day fluctuates with the Jewish calendar. Using simple text and photographs, *Hanukkah* (2001) by Lola Schaefer presents the history of Hanukkah and how it is celebrated.

SACAGAWEA: DEATH ANNIVERSARY
December 20 marks the death anniversary (in 1812) of Sacagawea, the Shoshone Indian woman who was with the Lewis and Clark expedition. She exemplified all of the traits of the early pioneers. Week Four's thematic books about pioneers illustrate the challenges these brave people endured to explore and populate the far reaches of the United States. More information specifically about Sacajawea can be found in *A Picture Book of Sacagawea* (2001) by David A. Adler, illustrated by Dan Brown.

LULU DELACRE: BIRTHDAY
Lulu Delacre was born December 20, 1957. Her book *Arroz Con Leche* (1992) is a wonderful collection of beloved Latin American songs, games, and rhymes. She also illustrated *Señor Cat's Romance and Other Favorite Stories from Latin America* (2001) by Lucía González.

December 22

JERRY PINKNEY: BIRTHDAY
Jerry Pinkney was born on this day in 1939. He has won Caldecott Honors in illustration for *John Henry* (1999), *The Talking Eggs* (1990), and *Mirandy and Brother Wind* (1997). An example of one of his latest works is *Sam and the Tigers* (2000) by Julius Lester.

WINTER SOLSTICE
The winter solstice occurs between December 21 and December 23. *The Shortest Day: Celebrating the Winter Solstice* (2003) by Wendy Pfeffer, illustrated by Jesse Reisch, is an excellent resource book.

BONNIE PRYOR: BIRTHDAY
Bonnie Pryor, author of more than thirty books for children, was born on December 22, 1922. *The Porcupine Mouse* (2002), illustrated by Mary Begin, and *The House on Maple Street* (1992), illustrated by Beth Peck, are two of her more famous books.

FIRST GORILLA BORN IN CAPTIVITY: BIRTHDAY
The first gorilla born in captivity was born on December 22, 1956. The book *Gorillas: Gentle Giants of the Forest* (1997) by Joyce Milton and Robert Hynes, illustrated by Bryn Barnard, presents a good overview of gorillas.

December 24

CHRISTOPHER (KIT) CARSON: BIRTHDAY
Kit Carson, authentic legend of the Old West, was born on December 24, 1809, and died in 1868. *Kit Carson* (2003) by Rick Burke profiles the life of this great frontiersman.

JOHNNY GRUELLE: BIRTHDAY
Johnny Gruelle, who created the world of Raggedy Ann and Andy, was born on December 24, 1888, and died in 1938. *Raggedy Ann and Andy and the Camel with the Wrinkled Knees* (2003), illustrated by Kees Moerbeek and published more than fifty years ago, is still enjoyed today.

LYNN MUNSINGER: BIRTHDAY
Illustrator Lynn Munsinger was born on December 24, 1951. She illustrated the Tacky the Penguin series by Helen Lester, as well as Lester's *Princess Penelope's Parrot* (2001), *Me First* (1995), and *Hooway for Wodney Wat* (2002).

DEBRA BARRACCA: BIRTHDAY
Debra Barracca (who writes with her husband, Sal) was born on December 24, 1953. Their book *The Adventures of Taxi Dog* (1990), illustrated by Mark Buehner, follows a day in the life of a dog befriended by a cab driver.

December 25

CHRISTMAS
Christmas, the most popular of Christian holidays, is observed on December 25. It commemorates the birth of Jesus of Nazareth. Resources for this day, its legends, traditions, music, and stories are readily available in libraries and stores. The website noblenet.org has a list of recommended books for children about this holiday. An Internet search will produce more websites from which a selection can be made. Robert Sabuda's version of *The Night Before Christmas* (2002) by Clement Clarke Moore is an art book as well as a rendition of the poem. It makes a wonderful read-aloud for this season.

CLARA BARTON: BIRTHDAY
Clara Barton, a courageous female pioneer, was born on December 25, 1821, and died in 1912. She volunteered to help wounded soldiers in the Civil War and became known as the Angel of the Battlefield. She founded the American Red Cross almost single-handedly. *Clara Barton* (2001) by Wil Mara and *Clara Barton* (2003) by Kathleen W. Deady are good resources about this pioneering lady.

Week Four: Pioneers

🏛 📖 Curriculum Connection: Social Studies and
     Language Arts

Pioneers in the exploration of land as well as ideas provide a way to make the study of history more of a story that draws students in and lets them experience what people did long ago. The list provided here is limited to early American pioneers. These resources could easily be a springboard to further adventures with different kinds of pioneers.

Bronco Charlie and the Pony Express (2004) by Marlene Brill, illustrated by Craig Orback. This biography of Charlie Miller describes how he became the youngest rider in the Pony Express in 1861.

California Gold Rush (2002) by Peter Roop, illustrated by Connie Roop. This reader describes how gold was discovered, how miners got to the gold fields, and the impact of these events on history.

Covered Wagons, Bumpy Trails (2000) by Verla Kay, illustrated by S. D. Schindler. Illustrations and simple text follow a family as they make the difficult journey by wagon to a new home.

Dakota Dugout (1989) by Ann Turner, illustrated by Ronald Himler. Through text and expansive illustrations, readers learn of life on the prairie as the pioneers experienced it.

Dandelions (2001) by Eve Bunting, illustrated by Greg Shed. A young girl and her family find strength in each other in the Nebraska Territory.

Homes of the West (1999) by Bobbie Kalman. What type of houses existed in the West during the 1800s? How were they built? What were the lives of the occupants like?

Johnny Kaw: The Pioneer Spirit of Kansas (1997) by Jerri Garretson, illustrated by Diane Dollar. In this colorfully illustrated tall tale, Kansas is created by cutting off the tops

of hills, digging riverbeds, and making pioneer trails.

Kids in Pioneer Times (1997) written and illustrated by Lisa Wroble. This insightful book describes various aspects of early pioneer family life in South Dakota.

Long Johns for a Small Chicken (2003) by Godeane Eagle and Esther Silverstein Blanc, illustrated by Tennessee Dixon. A pioneer woman makes clothing to protect a chick from the cold. This allows the chick to grow into a fine rooster.

The Mormon Pioneer Trail: From Nauvoo, Illinois, to the Great Salt Lake, Utah (2003) by Arlan Dean. The easy-to-read story is about the Mormons and their migration to Salt Lake City.

New Land: A First Year on the Prairie (1999) by Marilynn Reynolds, illustrated by Stephen McCallum. The first year of a pioneer family's adventure is beautifully depicted in this primary reader.

A Picture Book of Lewis and Clark (2003) by David A. Adler, illustrated by Ronald Himler. This is a beautifully illustrated biography of Lewis and Clark and the expedition they led from St. Louis to the Pacific Ocean in the early nineteenth century.

A Picture Book of Sacagawea (2001) by David A. Adler, illustrated by Dan Brown. The brave and adventurous Native American woman who joined the Lewis and Clark expedition as they traveled west is the subject of this biography for young readers.

Pioneer Farm: Living on a Farm in the 1880s (1998) by Megan O'Hara, illustrated by Tim Rummelhoff. Life on a Minnesota farm in the nineteenth century is simply told for young readers.

Pioneer Life from A to Z (1997) by Bobbie Kalman. Striking pictures and easy-to-read text introduce the pioneer lifestyle in North America.

Wagons West! (2000) by Roy Gerrard. This is the story of a family's move by wagon train from Missouri to Oregon in the 1850s. A young girl outwits cattle thieves during the journey.

Who Settled the West? (1999) by Bobbie Kalman. What was it like to be one of the first people to inhabit the West? Who moved there and why? Early routes used by these adventurers are explored and some of the difficulties they faced are revealed in this story.

You Wouldn't Want to Be an American Pioneer! (2002) by Jacqueline Morley, illustrated by David Antram. This book looks at the difficulties faced by the pioneers who traveled by wagon train to settle in the West.

Pioneer Girl: The Story of Laura Ingalls Wilder (2000) by William Anderson and Dan Andreasen. This chronicle of the life of the "Little House on the Prairie" author will be enticing for some older readers. The following are picture book versions of the Little House chapter book series adapted from the work of Laura Ingalls Wilder and illustrated by Renee Graef.

Dance at Grandpa's (1995) tells of a pioneer girl's family as they attend a wintertime party at the grandparent's house in Wisconsin.

The Deer in the Woods (1999) is the story of a father relating to his daughters why he was unable to shoot a deer.

Going to Town (1996) is the story of a pioneer girl and her family living in the Big Woods of Wisconsin and their first trip into town to visit the general store.

Going West (1997) chronicles a young pioneer girl and her family as they prepare to leave Wisconsin and travel west in a covered wagon.

Sugar Snow (1999) tells how Christmas was celebrated in pioneer days.

December 26

KWANZAA

Kwanzaa is becoming a more widely celebrated holiday. It begins December 26 and continues until January 1. Kwanzaa is an African American cultural holiday with no ties to any particular religion; it celebrates the principles of an upright life. In *Celebrating Kwanzaa* (1994) by Diane Hoyt-Goldsmith, photographed by Lawrence Migdale, the rituals of this holiday are clearly presented.

NATIONAL WHINERS DAY

December 26 is National Whiners Day. This day is set aside for those people who complain about everything—especially gifts they did or didn't receive for Christmas and Hanukkah. A good resource book for complaining children is *Alexander and the Horrible, Terrible, No Good, Very Bad Day* (1976) by Judith Viorst, illustrated by Ray Cruz.

JEAN VAN LEEUWEN: BIRTHDAY

Jean Van Leeuwen, born on December 26, 1937, has written more than forty books. The most famous are *Tales of Oliver Pig* (1979) and the rest of the Oliver and Amanda pig books. *Nothing Here but Trees* (1998), illustrated by Phil Boatwright, is an example of her work in historical fiction in picture book format.

December 28

ELIZABETH HOWARD: BIRTHDAY

Elizabeth Howard was born on December 28, 1927. Many of her books are based on historical fact and creative fiction, including *Chita's Christmas Tree* (1993), illustrated by Floyd Cooper, and *Lulu's Birthday* (2000), illustrated by Pat Cummings. *Aunt Flossie's Hats* (1995), illustrated by James Ransome, and *What's in Aunt Mary's Room?* (2002), illustrated by Cedric Lucas, are two of her stories based on favorite family experiences.

ENDANGERED SPECIES ACT OF 1973: ANNIVERSARY

The Endangered Species Act was passed on December 28, 1973. *Will We Miss Them?* (1993), illustrated by Marshall Peck, is a resource written by eleven-year-old Alexandra Wright. *Endangered Animals* (1996) by Faith McNutty, illustrated by Carol Schwartz, discusses the changes in animal habitats and the importance of helping to protect endangered species.

NANCY LUENN: BIRTHDAY

Nancy Luenn, born December 28, 1954, has written many books, ranging from picture books to young adult novels. *Mother Earth* (1995), illustrated by Neil Waldman and *A Celebration of Light* (1998), illustrated by Mark Bender, are two of her best.

December 30

RUDYARD KIPLING: BIRTHDAY

Rudyard Kipling was born on December 30, 1865, and died in 1936. He is most famous in children's literature for *The Jungle Book*, written in 1894 and suitable for older elementary students. His version of *Rikki Tikki Tavi*, illustrated by Jerry Pinkney, was published in 2004 and became as popular as the original. *How the Camel Got His Hump* (2003), written by Kipling and illustrated by Lisbeth Zwerger, is another timeless classic that was recently published.

MERCER MAYER: BIRTHDAY

Mercer Mayer, born on this date in 1943, has a great website for children at littlecritter .com. He began illustrating children's books in 1966. His wife, Gina, helps write the Little Critter books, which teach lessons about life. He also illustrates books for other authors.

His first book was *A Boy, a Dog, and a Frog*, a wordless picture book published in 1967. His other well-loved books include *There's a Nightmare in My Closet* (1976), *There's an Alligator under My Bed* (1987), and *What Do You Do with a Kangaroo?* (1976).

December 31

FIRST BANK OPENED IN UNITED STATES: ANNIVERSARY

The Bank of North America received its charter from the Confederation Congress on this date in 1781. Simple banking information can be found in *If You Made a Million* (1994) by David Schwartz, illustrated by Steven Kellogg, which describes the various forms money can take, including coins, paper money, and personal checks, and how it can be used to make purchases, pay off loans, or build interest.

HENRI MATISSE: BIRTHDAY

Born on this day in 1869, Henri Matisse was a painter who broke away from tradition to paint works filled with bold, bright colors. Two good resources on Matisse, who died in 1954, are *A Bird or Two* (1999) by Bijou Le Tord and *The Life and Work of Henri Matisse* (2002) by Paul Flux.

NEW YEAR'S EVE

December 31 is traditionally a time to welcome the coming year. *Just in Time for New Year's!* (2004) by Karen Ruelle and *Angelina Ice Skates* (2002) by Katharine Holabird, illustrated by Helen Craig, are excellent resources.

December Reading Strategy

Word Classes

To increase reading comprehension and writing skills, it is important that children become familiar with different classes of words and how to use those words properly in the context of their own writing. Direct teaching of the different classes of words should be done in context as students come across them in their own reading or in reading shared by the teacher or parent.

As the teacher is preparing a reading lesson, different word classes such as well-known synonyms, antonyms, homonyms, and homophones should be noted. Minilessons can be built around each word class individually or as a word study lesson on them all. Many books are available as backup lessons if current reading doesn't yield the right words for a teachable moment.

To help with the understanding and correct use of homophones, the following books are useful: *Can You Hear Me from Here?* (2002) by Amanda Rondeau, *Fred Read the Red Book* (2002) by Pam Scheunemann, and *One Whole Doughnut . . . One Doughnut Hole* (1991) by Valjean McLenighan.

To help with the understanding and use of antonyms, the following three books provide good resources: *The Greatest Gymnast of All* (1998) by Stuart Murphy, *Opposites* (1996) by George Coulter, and *Black Cat, White Cat* (1998) by Chuck Murphy.

Word study is essential to help students grow in their writing skills and to comprehend more complex texts as they become more independent readers. Wall charts listing common word pairs such as *hear-here*, *knew-new*, and *for-four* help students focus on correct usage as well as increase sight comprehension when these words are encountered in context.

Antonyms are best learned in context. Have children write sentence pairs for the words being studied. Then delete the antonyms from the sentences, mix them up, and have the students put the correct word in each sentence. This exercise (Choose the Right Word) can also be done with the other classes of words.

Pointing out synonyms for common words such as *like* and *said* will help children develop their vocabulary for writing, speaking, and reading. A technique for enlarging vocabulary is to have students create their own writing notebooks in which they enter words they find in their reading or words they hear that are of interest to them personally. This notebook could have one page for synonyms, one for antonyms, and one for homonyms. Students can then refer to these pages when they are writing.

Parents can use commute time to engage children in word games. One such game could be to see how many synonyms for a given word can be recalled. For instance, how many words can you think of that mean the same or nearly the same as *big*?

Index of Books by Author

Aardema, Verna, 40, 95
Aberg, Rebecca, 186, 187
Ackerman, Karen, 51
Ada, Alma Flor, 4, 158, 159
Adams, Pat, 11, 201
Adler, David A., 5, 9, 21, 26, 27, 31, 34, 107, 111, 123, 137, 139, 167, 170, 173, 210, 212–13
Adoff, Arnold, 66
Ajmera, Maya, 164, 165
Alderman, Peter, 33
Aliki, 5, 25, 55, 149, 154, 176, 177
Allard, Harry, 16
Allen, Judy, 140
Alter, Judy, 137
Altman, Linda, 158
Ancona, George, 105, 158
Andersen, Hans Christian, 7
Anderson, William, 213
Andreae, Giles, 68, 69
Andreasen, Dan, 213
Andrews-Goebel, Nancy, 159
Anglund, Joan Walsh, 4, 24
Anholt, Laurence, 53, 109, 189
Anno, Mitsumasa, 48, 60, 128
Ansary, Mir Tamim, 2, 31
Appelt, Kathi, 60
Archambault, John, 105, 199
Argueta, Jorge, 159
Armentrout, David, 86, 182
Armentrout, Patricia, 86, 182
Arnold, Caroline, 28, 65
Arnold, Tedd, 57
Arnosky, Jim, 148
Arrigg, Fred, 122
Artley, Bob, 97
Asch, Frank, 134
Ashrose, Cara, 105
Auch, Mary Jane, 193
Awmiller, Craig, 171
Axelrod, Amy, 39, 61
Axelrod, Mitchell, 123
Aylesworth, Jim, 6, 57, 68

Bagley, Katie, 136
Baker, Jeannie, 184
Balkwill, Richard, 86
Bania, Michael, 3
Banks, Kate, 83
Banneker, Benjamin, 188
Barber, Barbara E., 32
Barbero, Maria, 204
Barker, Cicely, 208
Barner, Bob, 150
Barnes, Peter, 204
Barracca, Debra, 211
Barrett, Judi, 42, 56
Barry, Robert, 208
Barton, Byron, 163
Barton, Clara, 211
Base, Graeme, 62

Bastyra, Judy, 154
Bates, Katherine Lee, 112
Bauld, Jane Scoggins, 75
Baysura, Kelly, 182
Bead, Darleen Bailey, 43
Becker, Bonny, 78
Becker, Michelle, 22
Beeler, Selby, 169
Behrens, June, 77
Belarde-Lewis, Miranda, 3
Bell, Rachel, 96
Bemelmans, Ludwig, 50, 71
Bender, Marie, 110
Benjamin, Floella, 165
Bennett, Frank, 32
Bennett, Jeffrey, 118
Bennett, Kelly, 99
Bergel, Colin, 100
Berger, Gilda, 42, 141, 150
Berger, Melvin, 42, 141, 150
Berlin, Irving, 110
Bernard, Robin, 209
Bernhard, Emery, 165
Bertram, Debbie, 78
Beskow, Elsa, 47
Beylon, Cathy, 128
Bingham, Caroline, 86
Birdseye, Tom, 57, 168
Biro, Maureen Boyd, 147
Bizley, Kirk, 33
Blackstone, Stella, 175
Blake, Robert, 2, 3
Blanc, Esther Silverstein, 212
Blood, Charles L., 104–5
Bloom, Susan, 78
Blue, Rose, 37
Bober, Suzanne, 53
Bolden, Tonya, 19
Bond, Michael, 8
Boniface, William, 151
Borden, Louise, 23, 110
Boring, Mel, 28
Bottner, Barbara, 192
Bourgeois, Paulette, 33, 82, 208
Bowdish, Lynea, 43
Bowman-Kruhm, Mary, 82
Bradby, Marie, 21
Branley, Franklyn M., 42, 118, 119, 177
Brenner, Barbara, 71, 154, 209
Brenner, Martha, 200
Brett, Jan, 6, 200, 202
Bridwell, Norman, 31
Brill, Marlene, 213
Brimner, Larry, 99, 139, 209
Broekel, Ray, 150
Brooks, Nigel, 204
Brown, Dan, 121
Brown, Jo, 11
Brown, Kathryn, 11
Brown, Laurie Krasny, 24
Brown, Marc, 24, 128, 179

Brown, Marcia, 117, 205
Brown, Margaret Wise, 88, 119
Brown, Tricia, 2
Browne, Anthony, 101
Bruchac, Joseph, 105, 206
Brumbeau, Jeff, 201
Brunkus, Denise, 154
Bryan, Ashley, 117
Bryant, Megan, 172
Buckley, James, 123
Bulla, Clyde, 19, 209
Bunting, Eve, 10, 147, 158, 179, 184, 207, 209, 212
Burby, Liza, 154
Burke, Rick, 184, 211
Burleigh, Robert, 23, 122–23
Burnham, Saranne, 3
Burningham, John, 71
Burns, Marilyn, 60
Burton, Virginia Lee, 87, 143
Butterworth, Nick, 101
Byrd, Robert, 76

Calmenson, Stephanie, 154, 175, 197
Camp, Lindsay, 100
Cannon, Janell, 185
Capeci, Anne, 151
Capucilli, Alyssa Satin, 65
Carle, Eric, 29, 101, 106, 141, 155
Carlson, Laurie, 200
Carlson, Nancy, 24
Carlstrom, Nancy White, 131
Carpenter, Eric, 21
Carpenter, Nancy, 178
Carr, Jan, 39
Carson, Mary, 139
Carter, Anne Laurel, 128
Carter, David, 150
Casey, Patricia, 190
Cassie, Brian, 140
Castaneda, Omar, 146
Castle, Caroline, 136
Catrow, David, 111, 169
Cavoukian, Raffi, 116
Chamberlin-Calamar, Pat, 2
Champion, Joyce, 24
Chandra, Deborah, 168
Chanin, Michael, 104
Chapman, Gillian, 76
Charlip, Remy, 79
Cheney, Lynne, 112
Cheripko, Jan, 122
Cherry, Lynne, 5
Chesanow, Neil, 187
Child, Lauren, 155
Christelow, Eileen, 38, 49, 184
Clarke, J., 105
Clement, Rod, 57, 172
Clements, Andrew, 25, 128
Climo, Shirley, 196
Cohen, Daniel, 176, 177

Cohen, Miriam, 25
Cole, Joanna, 42, 62, 92, 135, 149, 183
Collicutt, Paul, 87
Combs, Lisa M., 118
Comora, Madeleine, 168
Compestine, Ying Chang, 75
Connolly, Jim, 61
Connolly, Sean, 76
Conrad, David, 81, 106
Cooke, Trish, 101
Cooling, Wendy, 164
Cooney, Barbara, 134, 167
Cooper, Jason, 2, 99
Corey, Shana, 194
Cort, Ben, 39
Cos, Judy, 11
Cosgrove, Stephen, 208
Cotton, Jacqueline, 89
Coughlan, John, 87
Coulter, George, 216
Couvillon, Alice, 26
Cowley, Joy, 134, 168
Craig, Paula, 19
Crane, Carol, 195
Crews, Donald, 50
Crispin, Barbara, 64
Cristaldi, Kathryn, 61
Cronin, Doreen, 96
Cummins, Julie, 181
Curlee, Lynn, 178
Curtis, Gavin, 122
Curtis, Jamie Lee, 55, 173
Curtis, Marci, 132

Dahl, Michael, 154
Dahl, Roald, 68
Dalgliesh, Alice, 110
D'Amico, Carmela, 200
Das, Prodeepta, 164
D'Aulaire, Ingri, 170
David, Katie, 168–69
Davis, Kenneth, 194
Davis, Lee, 176
Davis, Lucille, 199
Davol, Marguerite W., 41
Day, Alexandra, 152
Day, Jan, 11
Dayrell, Elphinstone, 13, 119
De Angelis, Gina, 104
De Bie, Ceciel, 120
De Brunhoff, Jean, 203
De Brunhoff, Laurent, 203
De Regniers, Beatrice Schenk, 25, 138
De Vries, Anke, 204
Deady, Kathleen W., 211
Dean, Arlan, 34, 212
Debussy, Claude, 50
DeFelice, Cynthia, 57
Degen, Bruce, 62, 99
Delacre, Lulu, 210
Deluise, Dom, 140
Demarest, Chris L., 69
Demi, 74, 148
Dennis, Yvonne Wakim, 99
dePaola, Tomie, 7, 42, 45, 46, 47, 56,
   105, 132, 155, 156, 159, 163, 206
Dillon, Leo, 40
DiTerlizzi, Tony, 101
Doak, Robin, 110
Dodson, Peter, 176
Dolan, Penny, 14
Dole, Mayra, 158

Doolittle, Bev, 104
Dorros, Arthur, 42, 146
Dotlich, Rebecca, 103
Douglas, Richardo Keens, 7
Downs, Mike, 183
Doyle, Malachy, 96
Drummond, Allan, 44
Duble, Kathleen Benner, 84
Dubois, Muriel L., 2
Dubowski, Cathy, 155
Dubowski, Mark, 155
Duffield, Kathy, 97, 172
Duggleby, John, 30
Dunlap, Julie, 31
Durrett, Deanne, 178
Duvoisin, Roger, 143
Dwyer, Mindy, 3

Eagle, Godeane, 212
Eastman, P. D., 196
Easton, Samantha, 193
Edwards, Frank, 151
Edwards, Michelle, 147
Edwards, Pamela, 137, 139, 140, 168,
   207
Edwardson, Debby Dahl, 3
Egan, Tim, 97, 191
Egielski, Richard, 50
Ehlert, Lois, 128, 141, 154, 188, 191,
   209
Ehrlich, Amy, 47
Eilenberg, Max, 100
Eldash, Khaled, 164
Ellwood, Nancy, 167
Elya, Susan Middleton, 122
Emberly, Ed, 175
Emberly, Rebecca, 93
Emmett, Jonathan, 118
Enderlein, Cheryl, 164
Erickson, Gina, 123
Ernst, Lisa Campbell, 97
Everitt, Betsy, 78
Evert, Laura, 28

Failing, Barbara, 201
Falconer, Ian, 38, 129, 173
Farley, Walter, 129
Farris, Christine King, 9
Fayerman, Deborah, 97
Feelings, Muriel, 21, 92
Feeney, Stephanie, 115
Feldman, Heather, 25
Fiarotta, Noel, 37
Fiarotta, Phyllis, 37
Figueredo, D. H., 195
Fisher, Valorie, 92
Fitterer, C. Ann, 73
Fitzpatrick, Marie-Louise, 105
Flack, Marjorie, 75
Flanagan, Alice K., 82
Fleming, Denise, 17
Fletcher, Ralph, 146
Floca, Brian, 197
Florian, Douglas, 45, 68
Flournoy, Valerie, 147
Flux, Paul, 95, 215
Ford, Carin, 4, 136
Foreman, Michael, 28
Forsythe, Demming, 115
Foster, Kelli C., 123

Fowler, Allan, 64, 103, 118, 151, 168,
   186, 208
Fowler, Susi, 2
Fox, Dorothea, 208
Fox, Merrion Frances (Mem), 40, 201
Fraser, Mary Ann, 153
Frasier, Debra, 93
Fredericks, Anthony, 151
Freeman, Don, 128, 135, 205
Friedman, Ina, 8
Fritz, Jean, 13, 78
Frost, Helen, 89, 168, 194
Fuhr, Ute, 105

Gabbert, Lisa, 26
Gackenbach, Dick, 71, 208
Gag, Wanda, 44
Gál, Lászlóand Raffaella, 7
Galdone, Paul, 94, 192
Gallimard, Juenesse, 105
Gans, Roma, 28
Garcia, Aurora, 77
Garelick, May, 29, 71, 141
Garland, Michael, 172
Garland, Sherry, 165
Garretson, Jerri, 212
Garza, Carmen, 159
Geiman, Rita, 200
Geisel, Theodor "Dr. Seuss," 15, 40, 55,
   57, 92, 93, 130, 151
Geisert, Arthur, 39, 160
George, Kristine O'Connell, 66, 209
Geringer, Laura, 201
Gerrard, Roy, 213
Ghigna, Charles, 93, 151
Gibbons, Gail, 11, 24, 30, 32, 33, 39, 43,
   45, 55, 62, 65, 71, 82, 83, 86, 97,
   118, 123, 127, 130, 145, 179, 181,
   195, 202, 208, 209
Giblin, James Cross, 66
Gibson, Karen Bush, 104
Giesecke, Ernestine, 208
Giganti, Paul, 60, 143
Gill, Shelley, 3
Glass, Andrew, 35
Glassman, Peter, 83
Goble, Paul, 104, 157
Goin, Kenn, 32, 33
Golding, Theresa, 89
Golenbock, Peter, 123
González, Lucí, 210
Gorschulter, Jutta, 128
Gorton, Julia, 42
Gottfried, May, 129
Gowan, Barbara, 35
Graham, Joan Bransfield, 68
Graves, Bonnie, 156
Gray, Kes, 193
Green, John, 28
Greenberg, David, 192
Greene, Carol, 53
Greenfield, Eloise, 191
Greenspun, Adele, 146
Griego, Margot, 159
Grimes, Nikki, 190
Grist, Julie, 182
Grossman, Bill, 61, 69
Grossman, Virginia, 105
Gruelle, Johnny, 211
Guettier, Benedicte, 100
Gulbis, Stephen, 172
Gunderson, Mary, 81

Gunning, Thomas, 182
Gwynne, Fred, 92, 93

Haas, Jessie, 146
Hague, Kathleen, 46
Hall, Donald, 51
Hall, Margaret, 165
Hall, Pat, 115
Hallinan, P. K., 25
Handford, Martin, 161
Hanson, Anne E., 86
Hanson, Regina, 158
Harmer, Mabel, 128
Harness, Cheryl, 178
Harper, Charise, 137
Harrison, David Lee, 97
Harrison, Peggy, 91, 123
Harshman, Marc, 164
Hartman, Gail, 59
Harvey, Miles, 75
Harvey, Paul, 200
Haskins, Jim, 74
Haughton, Emma, 102
Hayashi, Leslie Ann, 114
Hayes, Geoffrey, 129
Hayward, Linda, 82, 84, 194
Hazen, Barbara, 190
Hehner, Barbara, 121
Heling, Kathryn, 93
Hellard, Susan, 80
Heller, Nicholas, 155
Heller, Ruth, 58, 93
Helmer, Diana, 32–33, 122
Hembrook, Deborah, 93
Hench, Larry, 136
Henkes, Kevin, 132, 133, 146, 196, 205
Hennessy, B. G., 176, 195
Henry, Linda, 205
Herbert, Janis, 81
Herkert, Barbara, 19, 28
Herman, Gail, 145
Herman, John, 111
Herold, Maggie Rugg, 195
Herrera, Juan, 158
Herzog, Brad, 33
Hesse, Karen, 78
Hill, Eric, 152
Hill, Franklin, 141
Hill, Mary, 123
Himmelman, John, 123, 136, 205
Hirano, Cathy, 37
Hissey, Jane, 148
Hoban, Lillian, 85, 132
Hoban, Russell, 23, 24, 85
Hoban, Tana, 61
Hoberman, Mary Ann, 24, 131, 132, 138, 155
Hoff, Syd, 15, 149
Holabird, Katharine, 215
Holland, Gini, 52
Holmes, Kevin, 160, 205
Holub, Joan, 53
Honey, Elizabeth, 93
Hong, Lily Toy, 75
Hopkins, Lee Bennett, 66
Hopkinson, Deborah, 137
Horn, Peter, 100
Hort, Lenny, 100
Hossell, Karen, 206
Houghton, Sarah, 137
Houston, Gloria, 206
Howard, Elizabeth Fitzgerald, 21, 214

Howe, James, 141, 151
Hoyt-Goldsmith, Diane, 214
Hubbell, Patricia, 14
Hughes, Langston, 22
Hunter, Anne, 118
Huntington, Amy, 43
Hurd, Thacher, 41, 172
Hurt, Ray, 136
Hurwitz, Johanna, 91
Hutchins, Hazel, 135
Hutchins, Pat, 60, 102, 133
Hyman, Trina Schart, 63
Hynes, Robert, 210

Irving, Washington, 59
Isaacs, Anne, 30
Isadora, Rachel, 123
Italia, Bob, 113
Iwamura, Kazuo, 25

Jackson, Garnet, 136
Jackson, Byron, 15
Jackson, Kathryn, 15
Jackson, Woody, 96
Jaggi, J., 11
James, Ellen Foley, 15
James, J. Allison, 11
Janovitz, Marilyn, 100
Jeffers, Susan, 104
Jenkins, Martin, 15
Jenkins, Priscilla Belz, 29
Jenkins, Steve, 150, 186
Jessup, Harley, 146
Johnson, Angela, 147
Johnson, Arden, 168
Johnson, Paul Brett, 96
Johnson, Stephen, 190
Johnston, Tony, 141, 160
Jonas, Ann, 191
Jordan, Deloris, 32
Jordan, Denise M., 127, 128
Joseph, Lynn, 182
Joseph, Paul, 33
Joslin, Sesyle, 179
Judes, Marie-Odile, 101

Kalman, Bobbie, 29, 82, 86, 212, 213
Kalman, Maira, 87, 132
Kane, Katharine, 19, 89
Kane, Marie, 35
Kapono, Henry, 114
Karon, Jan, 201
Kasza, Keiko, 79, 155
Katz, Alan, 93
Katz, Bobbi, 167, 169
Kavanagh, Peter, 15
Kay, Verla, 212
Keats, Ezra Jack, 44, 133, 201
Keenan, Sheila, 61
Keido, Ippo, 140
Keillor, Garrison, 57
Keller, Holly, 140, 150, 165, 201, 208
Keller, Laurie, 56, 111, 169
Kelley, True, 175, 204
Kellog, Steven, 24, 92, 175
Kelly, Irene, 29
Kendler, Marc, 140
Kennedy, Kim, 11
Kennedy, X. J., 14
Kenney, Cindy, 10
Kent, Jack, 140
Kerr, Judith, 1

Kessler, Leonard, 122
Key, Francis Scott, 130
Khalsa, Dayal Kaur, 132
Khattab, Dalia, 164
Kimmel, Eric, 179
Kindersley, Anabel, 52, 166, 175
Kindersley, Barnabas, 52, 166, 175
King, Martin Luther, Jr., 9
King, Patrick, 190
Kinsey-Warnock, Natalie, 184
Kipling, Rudyard, 215
Kirby, David, 96
Kirk, David, 193
Kirkpatrick, Rob, 32
Kleven, Elisa, 29, 133
Kleven, Sandy, 55
Klingel, Cynthia, 32, 73
Knight, Hilary, 184
Knowlton, Jack, 186
Knutson, Barbara, 6
Koestler-Grack, Rachel, 167
Kohl, Mary Ann, 154
Konigsburg, E., 137
Korman, Justine, 46, 83
Koscielniak, Bruce, 24
Kottke, Jan, 70
Kramer, Sydelle, 183
Kraus, Robert, 103, 204
Krauss, Ruth, 92
Krebs, Laurie, 82
Kreeger, Charlene, 2
Krensky, Stephen, 136
Krishnaswami, Uma, 43
Kroll, Steven, 22
Kroll, Virginia L., 74, 204
Krosoczka, Jarrett J., 10
Krull, Kathleen, 142, 159
Kuklin, Susan, 86
Kuntz, Lynn, 154
Kuskin, Karla, 120
Kvasnosky, Laura, 16, 24

Labuer, Patricia, 23
Laden, Nina, 37
Laird, Donivee M., 115
Lakin, Patricia, 49, 146, 182
Lally, Elaine, 137
LaMarche, Jim, 46
Lambert, Martha, 61
Lankford, Mary, 164
Lasky, Kathryn, 21
Lass, Bonnie, 155
Lauber, Patricia, 23, 30, 65
Lavallee, Barbara, 3
Layne, Steven, 187
Le Tord, Bijou, 215
Lear, Edward, 81
Leedy, Loreen, 61, 181
Leigh, Susannah, 11
Leighton, Maxinne, 4
Lesieg, Theo, 169
Lessem, Don, 176
Lesser, Rika, 6
Lesynski, Loris, 69
Lever, Sally-Ann, 140, 204
Levin, Freddie, 87
Levine, Abby, 22
Levinson, Riki, 4
Lewin, Ted, 82
Lewis, J. Patrick, 60, 69
Lewison, Wendy, 110
Leyton, Lawrence, 179

Lichtenheld, Tom, 57
Liebman, Dan, 83
Lillegard, Dee, 69
Lindenbaum, Pija, 132
Lindgren, Astrid, 47, 129
Lindman, Maj, 133
Link, Martin, 104–5
Lionni, Leo, 80
Little, Kate, 183
Littlefield, Holly, 74
Litzinger, Rosanne, 38
Livingstone, Myra Cohn, 139
Llewellyn, Claire, 150
Lobb, Janice, 155
Lobel, Anita, 94
Lobel, Arnold, 88, 132
Locker, Thomas, 209
Loewen, Nancy, 73, 91, 111
Long, Melinda, 10
Longfellow, Henry Wadsworth, 4, 69, 111
Look, Lenore, 132
Lorbiecki, Marybeth, 74
Lord, John Vernon, 56
Lorenz, Lee, 191
Losi, Carol, 150
Low, Alice, 200
Low, Joseph, 205
Lowell, Susan, 39
Lucas, Debra, 137
Luenn, Nancy, 214
Lund, Bill, 105
Luppens, Michel, 169
Lyon, George Ella, 65
Lyons, Dana, 209

Maass, Robert, 48
Maccarone, Grace, 31, 169
MacDonald, Suse, 14
MacGregor, Cynthia, 179
MacLachlan, Patricia, 101, 190
MacLean, Christine Kole, 78
MacMillan, Dianne M., 80
Maestro, Betsy, 111, 194, 209
Mahy, Margaret, 15, 75, 90
Mammano, Julie, 33, 123
Mara, Wil, 211
Marcellino, Fred, 175
Marcus, Leonard S., 49
Markes, Julie, 132
Marshall, James, 39, 93
Martin, Bernard, 128
Martin, Bill, Jr., 32, 65, 76, 105, 111, 128
Martin, Jacqueline Briggs, 51
Martin, Patricia Stone, 20
Marx, David, 19
Marzollo, Jean, 172
Massie, Diane Redfield, 28, 64
Mastin, Colleayn, 3
Mathers, Petra, 24–25
Mathieu, Joe, 86
Matsuno, Masako, 75
Matze, Claire Sidhom, 165
Mayer, Mercer, 215
Mayers, Florence Cassen, 32
Maynard, Chris, 150
Maze, Stephanie, 83
McAuliffe, Emily, 113, 142
McBratney, Sam, 78, 100
McBrier, Page, 164
McCain, Becky Ray, 105
McClintock, Barbara, 133

McCloskey, Robert, 50, 156, 169
McCourt, Lisa, 78
McCully, Emily Arnold, 112, 137
McDaniel, Melissa, 73
McDermott, Gerald R., 17, 47, 104
McDonald, Megan, 35
McGinty, Alice, 169
McGrath, Barbara Barbieri, 33, 61, 122
McKee, David, 14
McKissack, Fredrick, 20, 31
McKissack, Patricia, 20, 31, 50, 135
McLenighan, Valjean, 93, 216
McMillan, Bruce, 64
McMullan, Kate, 46, 87, 168, 190
McNamara, George, 122
McNaughton, Colin, 10, 39
McNeill, Shannon, 56
McNulty, Faith, 186, 214
McPhail, David, 10, 133
Meddaugh, Susan, 38, 166
Medearis, Angela Shelf, 192
Meeker, Clare Hodgson, 15
Meisel, Paul, 201
Melmed, Laura Krauss, 110, 181
Merberg, Julie, 53
Merriam, Eve, 61, 121
Metaxas, Erick, 10
Michaels, Ski, 122
Michels, Dia, 133
Micklos, John, 146
Middleton, Charlotte, 169
Miles, Miska, 146
Miller, Debbi S., 3
Miller, Margaret, 201
Millman, Isaac, 37
Milne, A. A., 9
Milton, Joyce, 210
Milton, Tony, 176
Minarik, Else, 24, 147, 153
Molter, Carey, 92, 93
Montanari, Donata, 164
Montes, Marisa, 6–7
Moon, Nicola, 147
Moore, Clement, 203, 211
Moore, Ellen Jo, 186
Moore, Eva, 208
Mora, Pat, 12, 158
Morgan, Allen, 10, 46
Morley, Jacqueline, 213
Morris, Jan, 200
Morris, Neil, 186
Morrison, Lillian, 155
Mosel, Arlene, 13, 74, 75
Moss, Lloyd, 69
Most, Bernard, 93, 96, 148, 177
Munsch, Robert, 57, 98, 168
Munsinger, Lynn, 188
Murphy, Chuck, 216
Murphy, Jill, 14, 78
Murphy, Stuart J., 33, 61, 150, 216
Musgrove, Margaret, 20, 40
Myers, Tim J., 115
Myers, Walter Dean, 69
Myller, Rolf, 61

Naden, Corinne J., 37
Napoli, Donna Jo, 35
Neitzel, Shirley, 65
Nelson, Kristin, 34, 203
Nettleton, Pamela Hill, 89
Neuschwander, Cindy, 60
Nichols, Barbara, 207

Nielsen, Shelley, 73
Niven, Penelope, 8
Nodset, Joan, 201
Nolan, Dennis, 176
Nolan, Janet, 37
Nolen, Jerdine, 190
Noyed, Robert B., 32
Numeroff, Laura Joffe, 92, 117, 132, 147

O'Brien, Patrick, 182–83
O'Conner, Karen, 73
O'Hara, Megan, 194, 213
Older, Jules, 96, 109
Olson, Kay, 194–95
Olson, Mary, 169
O'Malley, Kevin, 123
O'Neill, Alexis, 158
O'Neill, Mary, 69
Oppenheim, Joanne, 28
Orgill, Roxane, 20
Orozco, José-Luis, 67, 158

Packard, David, 122
Palatini, Margie, 38
Pallotta, Jerry, 86, 140, 150, 183
Park, Frances, 74
Park, Ginger, 74
Parker, Lewis, 195
Parker, Steve, 182
Parlin, John, 124
Parr, Todd, 78, 100
Parrish, Peggy, 117
Partridge, Elizabeth, 101
Patent, Dorothy, 140
Paterson, Diane, 164
Patey, R. L. "Buddy," 33
Patrick, Jean L. S., 26
Peake, Mervyn, 10
Peck, Marshall, 214
Peet, Bill, 14, 38, 46, 86, 129
Pegeen, Snow, 154
Pelham, David, 185
Penner, Lucille Recht, 151, 206
Percy, Graham, 129
Perkins, Lynne, 173
Perrault, Charles, 175
Petersen, David, 2
Peterson, Cris, 91
Peterson, Jeanne, 107, 199
Peterson, Tiffany, 136
Petrie, Glen, 10
Petty, Kate, 186
Pfeffer, Wendy, 208, 210
Phillips, Mildred, 96
Pinczes, Elinor J., 61
Pinkney, Andrea, 202
Pinkney, Jerry, 210
Piper, Watty, 87
Plourde, Lynn, 147
Polacco, Patricia, 29, 116, 133, 146, 206
Polisar, Barry, 151
Pollock, Penny, 119
Potter, Beatrix, 125
Powell, Jillian, 97
Prager, Ellen, 52
Prater, John, 133
Prediletto, Jewel, 65
Prelutsky, Jack, 30, 68, 69, 152
Preszler, June, 202
Prevost, John, 91, 208
Priceman, Marjorie, 128
Prigger, Mary, 181

Pringle, Laurence, 28
Provensen, Alice, 44, 182, 191
Provensen, Martin, 44
Pryor, Bonnie, 210

Raatma, Lucia, 27, 73, 111
Rabe, Tish, 28, 151
Raboff, Ernest, 95
Rachlin, Ann, 16, 80, 207
Radunsky, Vladimir, 133
Raffi, 116
Rakusin, Sudie, 199
Randolph, Ryan, 20
Ransom, Candice, 7
Ransome, Arthur, 12
Rappaport, Doreen, 20, 105
Raschka, Chris, 41, 51
Rathmann, Peggy, 64
Rattigan, Jama Kim, 114
Rau, Dana, 2, 128
Rex, Michael, 65
Rey, H. A., 156
Rey, Margaret, 84, 190
Reynolds, Marilynn, 212
Rice, David L., 78
Rich, Francine Poppo, 141
Ride, Sally, 89
Riley, Linnea, 205
Ringgold, Faith, 202
Rink, Cynthia, 43
Robbins, Ken, 87
Roberts, Bethany, 14
Robertson, Ivan, 46
Robins, Joan, 101
Rockwell, Anne, 26, 86, 150, 170
Rogers, Fred, 25
Rohmann, Eric, 50, 175
Romanova, Natalia, 209
Rondeau, Amanda, 92, 216
Roome, Diana Reynolds, 14
Roop, Connie, 170, 212
Roop, Peter, 170, 212
Root, Barry, 97
Root, Phyllis, 97, 190–91
Rosenberg, Pam, 137
Roth, Susan L., 75
Roy, Gregory, 127
Roy, Jennifer Rozines, 127
Royston, Angela, 168, 187
Ruelle, Karen Gray, 79, 215
Ruffin, Frances, 143
Rumford, James, 114–15
Ryan, Pam Munoz, 124, 159, 167
Ryder, Joanne, 5, 65, 205
Rye, Jennifer, 127
Rylant, Cynthia, 51, 191

Sabuda, Robert, 41
Saltzberg, Barney, 33, 55
Sampson, Mary Beth, 129
Sampson, Michael, 32, 111, 128, 129
Samuels, Barbara, 114
Sandburg, Carl, 8
Sandell, Elizabeth, 177
Sanderson, Ruth, 193
Sandved, Kjell, 140
Sateren, Shelley, 175
Sautai, Raoul, 105
Savage, Jeff, 183
Say, Allen, 75, 143
Scarry, Richard, 29, 83, 93, 201
Schaefer, Lola M., 27, 77, 107, 168, 210

Schaffer, Donna, 141
Schanzer, Rosalyn, 136–37
Schertle, Alice, 97
Scheunemann, Pam, 92, 93, 111, 216
Schiller, Melissa, 58
Schimmel, Schim, 164–65
Schlein, Miriam, 177
Schnetzler, Pattie, 177
Schoenherr, John, 50
Scholes, Katherine, 156
Schulz, Charles, 110
Schwabacher, Martin, 14
Schwartz, Amy, 15
Schwartz, David M., 61, 215
Schwarz, Joanie, 146
Scieszka, Jon, 39, 152
Scillian, Devin, 187
Scoones, Simon, 74
Scott, Ann Herbert, 79
Seeger, Pete, 49
Sendak, Maurice, 51, 98
Seuss, Dr. (Theodor Geisel), 15, 40, 55,
    57, 92, 93, 130, 151
Shannon, David, 56
Shannon, George, 143
Shapiro, Jody Fickes, 147
Sharmat, Mitchell, 154–55, 173
Shaw, Charles G., 42
Shea, George, 182
Shea, Pegi Deitz, 118
Sheppard, Jeff, 15
Shields, Charles J., 35
Showers, Paul, 168
Siebel, Fritz, 56
Siebert, Diane, 69, 183
Sierra, Judy, 6, 68
Sill, Cathryn, 28
Silverstein, Shel, 171
Simms, Laura, 57
Simon, Seymour, 42, 52
Simont, Marc, 133
Singer, Marilyn, 43
Sis, Peter, 31, 165
Slate, Joseph, 70, 129
Sloat, Teri, 61
Slobodkina, Esphyr, 128, 161
Small, David, 57, 97
Smalls, Irene, 102
Smath, Jerry, 200
Smith, Charles R., Jr., 24, 32, 110–11
Smith, Cynthia Leitich, 105
Smith, Todd Aaron, 96
Smith, Will, 100
Sneve, Virginia Driving Hawk, 104
Soto, Gary, 158, 159
Souza, Dorothy, 204
Spier, Peter, 129
Spinelli, Eileen, 101
St. George, Judith, 27, 178
Stadler, Alexander, 122
Stadler, John, 123
Stainton, Sue, 173
Stanley, Diane, 76, 207
Stanley, Fay, 115
Stanley, Mandy, 183
Steig, William, 24, 51, 189, 204
Steptoe, Javaka, 7, 100
Steptoe, John, 205
Stevens, Janet, 47
Stevenson, James, 42, 58, 68, 116
Stevenson, Robert Louis, 189
Stewart, Dawn, 132, 190

Stewart, Sarah, 27, 153
Stienecker, David, 186
Stier, Catherine, 83
Stihler, Chérie B., 2
Stille, Darlene, 154, 182
Stillwell, Fred, 86
Stoeke, Janet, 200
Stone, Lynn, 29, 96, 186
Suen, Anastasia, 55, 168, 182
Sundgaard, Arnold, 141
Suomalainen, Sami, 57
Supree, Burton, 79
Surat, Michele Maria, 164
Suyenaga, Ruth, 80
Swain, Gwenyth, 127
Sweeney, Jacqueline, 114, 115
Sweeney, Joan, 189
Swope, Sam, 140–41

Taback, Simms, 30, 50, 51, 93
Tafuri, Nancy, 189
Takabayashi, Mari, 164
Takayama, Sandi, 115
Tallarico, Tony, 160
Talley, Carol, 101
Tan, Amy, 118, 147
Tavares, Matt, 123
Taylor, Barbara, 137
Taylor, Joanne, 118
Tegge, Gigi, 183
Teramura, Terua, 14
Terban, Marvin, 92
Tesar, Jenny, 91
Thayer, Ernest, 103, 122
Theodoro, Rod, 177
Thompson, Carol, 19
Thomson, Pat, 147
Tillotson, Katherine, 46
Todd, Anne, 194
Tompert, Ann, 15, 45
Torres, Leyla, 29
Towle, Wendy, 127, 137
Trapani, Iza, 37
Tremaine, Jon, 179
Tresselt, Alvin, 143
Trivizas, Eugene, 39
Tsubakiyama, Margaret, 165
Tucker, Kathy, 10
Tune, Suelyn Ching, 115
Turner, Ann, 170, 212
Turner, Sandy, 15

Udry, Janice, 209
Uegaki, Chieri, 75
Usel, T. M., 66

Van Allsburg, Chris, 102, 151
Van Kampen, Vlasta, 6
Van Laan, Nancy, 57, 159, 192
Van Leeuwen, Jean, 214
Vargus, Nanci, 19, 89, 186–87
Venezia, Mike, 12, 30, 120, 185, 189
Verlander, Susan, 191
Vieira, Linda, 35
Viorst, Judith, 22, 56, 214

Waber, Bernard, 154, 161, 204, 205
Waddell, Martin, 63, 190
Wahl, Jan, 46, 176–77
Walker, Pam, 158
Wallace, Ian, 3
Wallace, Karen, 58, 62, 140, 149

Wallner, Alexandra, 4, 43, 110, 125
Wallner, Rosemary, 194
Walsh, Ellen Stoll, 148, 172, 205
Walton, Rick, 97
Ward, Jennifer, 151
Wardlaw, Lee, 115
Waters, Kate, 195
Watso, Wendy, 109
Watts, Barrie, 205
Weiss, Ellen, 14
Weiss, Nicki, 165
Welch, Catherine A., 20
Wells, Rosemary, 17, 25, 60, 133, 205
Welsh-Smith, Susan, 2
Westcott, Nadine, 181
Wettasinghe, Sybil, 37
Wexo, John, 160
White, Laurence, 150
White, Mike, 129
White, Nancy, 42, 151
Whitehurst, Susan, 195
Whitman, Candace, 65

Whitman, Sylvia, 194
Whybrow, Ian, 177
Wiesner, David, 23, 39
Wilkes, Angela, 178
Will, Sandra, 122
Willard, Nancy, 155
Willems, Mo, 109
Williams, Julie Stewart, 114, 115
Williams, Laura E., 115
Williams, Maria, 2
Williams, Sherley Anne, 21
Williams, Vera B., 16, 50, 78
Winchester, Faith, 20, 145
Wing, Natasha, 169
Winnick, Karen B., 27, 111
Winter, Jeanette, 48
Winters, Kay, 78
Winthrop, Elizabeth, 38, 200
Wisniewski, David, 48, 57
Wolff, Patricia Rae, 47
Wolfman, Judy, 44, 191
Wolkstein, Diane, 204

Wong, Su Tien, 2
Wood, Audrey, 47, 77, 172
Wood, Don, 77
Wood, Douglas, 79, 101
Woodman, Allen, 96
Woods, Samuel, 26
Woodson, Jacqueline, 27
Woodworth, Viki, 97
Worth, Bonnie, 15, 177
Wright, David, 113
Wright, Joan, 150
Wroble, Lisa, 212

Yanuck, Debbie, 110, 111
Yashima, Taro, 74
Yates, Philip, 61
Yolen, Jane, 27, 38–39, 50, 101, 118,
 141, 170, 173, 177, 183, 191, 199
Yorinks, Arthur, 50, 142
Young, Ed, 197

Ziefert, Harriet, 79

Index of Books by Title

"A" Is for Aloha (Feeney), 114
Abe Lincoln's Hat (Brenner), 200
Abiyoyo (Seeger), 49
About Birds: A Guide for Children (Sill),
 28
Abuela (Dorros), 146
Abuela's Weave (Castaneda), 146
Adventures of Taxi Dog, The (Barracca),
 160, 211
African Elephant, The (Weiss), 14
African-American Holidays (Winchester),
 20
Agapanthus Hum and Angel Hoot
 (Cowley), 168
Air Show (Suen), 182
Airmail to the Moon (Birdseye), 168
Airplane Alphabet Book, The (Pallotta and
 Stillwell), 86
Airplanes (Stille), 182
Akiak: A Tale from the Iditarod (Blake), 2
Alaska (Wong), 2
Alaska ABC Book (Kreeger), 2
Alaska Brown Bear (Cooper), 2
Alaska Facts and Symbols (Dubois), 2
Alaska's 12 Days of Summer (Chamberlin-
 Calamar), 2
*Albert, the Dog Who Liked to Ride in
 Taxies* (Zarin), 190
*Alexander and the Terrible, Horrible, No
 Good, Very Bad Day* (Viorst), 22,
 56, 214
*Alexander Graham Bell: Inventor of the
 Telephone* (Ford), 136
All Alone (Henkes), 196
All Kinds of Children (Simon), 164
All Night, All Day (Bryan), 117

*All the Colors of the Earth: Poems from
 Around the World* (Cooling), 164
All the Places to Love (MacLachlan), 190
All the Way to Morning (Harshman), 164
Allie's Basketball Dream (Barber), 32
Aloha, Dolores (Samuels), 114
Alpha Bugs (Carter), 150
Alphabet City (Johnson), 190
Alphabet Mystery (Wood), 172
Alphabet of Dinosaurs, An (Dodson), 176
Alphabet Under Construction (Fleming),
 17
Amanda Bean's Amazing Dream
 (Neuschwander and Burns), 60
Amazing Bone, The (Steig), 189
Amazing Pop-Up Geography Book, The
 (Petty), 186
Ambulances (Hanson), 86
Amelia and Eleanor Go for a Ride (Ryan),
 124, 167
Amelia Bedelia (Parish), 56
Amelia Earhart: More than a Flier
 (Lakin), 182
Amelia Earhart: Pioneer of the Sky
 (Parlin), 124
Amelia's Road (Altman), 158
America: A Patriotic Primer (Cheney),
 112
America Is . . . (Borden), 110
American Grub: Eats for Kids (Kuntz and
 Fleming), 154
America the Beautiful (Bates), 112
America's Landscape (Stone), 186
America's Top Rivers (Tesar), 91
Amos and Boris (Steig), 24
A—My Name Is Alice (Bayer), 92

Anansi the Spider (McDermott), 17
And the Birds Appeared (Williams), 114
And the Cow Said Moo! (Phillips), 96
*And to Think That We Thought That We'd
 Never Be Friends* (Hoberman), 24
Andrew's Loose Tooth (Munsch), 98, 168
Andy: Alaskan Tale (Welsh-Smith), 2
Angel Child, Dragon Child (Surat), 164
Angelina and the Butterfly (Lever), 140,
 204
Angelina Ice Skates (Holabird), 215
Animalia (Base), 62
Animals in the Zoo (Fowler), 64
*Animals Should Definitely Not Wear
 Clothes* (Barrett), 56
Anna Banana: 101 Jump Rope Rhymes
 (Cole), 92, 135
Annie and the Old One (Miles), 146
Annie's Gifts (Medearis), 192
Anno's Counting Book (Anno), 48, 60
Anno's Journey (Anno), 48
Ant and the Elephant, The (Peet), 14
Antarctic Antics: A Book of Penguin Poems
 (Sierra), 186
Antarctica (Fowler), 186
April Fool's Day (Schiller), 58
Arctic Adventure: Inuit Life in the 1800s
 (Rau), 2
Arctic Peoples (Ansary), 2
Are We There Yet? (Mackall), 56
Are You a Butterfly? (Allen), 140
Are You My Mother? (Eastman), 196
Arithme-Tickle (Lewis), 60
Arnie the Doughnut (Keller), 56
Arrow to the Sun (McDermott), 17, 104
Arroz Con Leche (Delacre), 210

Art Dog (Hurd), 41
Arthur and the Sword (Sabuda), 41
Arthur's Chicken Pox (Brown), 128
Artist in Overalls: The Life of Grant Wood (Duggleby), 30
As the Crow Flies: A First Book of Maps (Hartman), 59
Ashanti to Zulu: African Traditions (Musgrove), 20, 40
Ask Nurse Pfaff, She'll Help You! (Flanagan), 82
ASPCA: The American Society for the Prevention of Cruelty to Animals (Suen), 55
At the Circus (Beylon), 128
Aunt Flossie's Hats (Howard), 200, 214
Aunt Lucy Went to Buy a Hat (Low), 200
Aunt Minnie McGranahan (Prigger), 181
Australia (Fowler), 186
Awful Ogre's Awful Day (Prelutsky), 30

Baba Yaga: A Russian Folktale (Kimmel), 179
Babar and Father Christmas (de Brunhoff), 203
Babar the King (de Brunhoff), 203
Babar's ABC (de Brunhoff), 203
Babar's Museum of Art (de Brunhoff), 203
Babe and I, The (Adler), 26
Baby Beebee Bird, The (Massie), 28, 64
Baby Beluga (Raffi), 116
Baby Sitter, The (dePaola), 132
Baby Zoo, The (McMillan), 64
Back to School (Ajmera), 164
Back to School for Babar (de Brunhoff), 203
Bad Case of Stripes, A (Shannon), 56
Bald Eagle, The (Yanuck), 110
Ball Game, The (Packard), 122
Bandus the Bear (Gorschulter), 128
Bantam of the Opera (Auch), 193
Barrio: El Barrio de José (Ancona), 158
Baseball Bat, The (Michaels), 122
Baseball Counting Book, The (McGrath), 122
Baseball for Fun (Will), 122
Baseball Star, The (Arrigg), 122
Basketball ABC: The NBA Alphabet (Mayers), 32
Bat Boy and His Violin, The (Curtis), 122
Bat Jamboree (Appelt), 60
Be a Friend to Trees (Lauber), 208
Bear Called Paddington, A (Bond), 8
Bear That Heard Crying, The (Kinsey-Warnock), 184
Bearymore (Freeman), 128
Beast Feast (Florian), 45
Beatrice's Goat (McBrier), 164
Beatrix Potter (Wallner), 125
Beautiful Hawaiian Day, A (Kapono), 114
Beauty and the Beast (Brett), 6
Beauty and the Beast (Easton), 193
Because Brian Hugged His Mother (Rice), 78
Bee Tree, The (Polacco), 146
Beef Stew (Brenner), 154
Beeman, The (Krebs), 82
Beep! Beep! Oink! Oink! Animals in the City (Casey), 190
Beethoven (Rachlin), 207
Beethoven Lives Upstairs (Nichols), 207
Beetle Alphabet Book, The (Pallotta), 150

Beginning Geography: How to Use a Map (Moore), 186
Ben Franklin and His First Kite (Krensky), 136
Ben Franklin Book of Easy and Incredible Experiments, The (Franklin Institute Science Museum), 9
Beneath a Blue Umbrella (Prelutsky), 68
Best Book of Bugs, The (Llewellyn), 150
Best Book of Trains, The (Balkwill), 86
Best Bug Parade, The (Murphy), 150
Best Father of All, The (Horn), 100
Best Friends: Stories and Pictures (Kellog), 24
Best Friends Book, The (Parr), 24
Best Friends for Frances (Hoban), 23, 24
Best Place to Read, The (Bertram and Bloom), 78
Betsy Ross (Wallner), 4
Beverly Billingsly Can't Catch (Stadler), 122
Beyond the Ridge (Goble), 104
Bicycle Book (Gibbons), 86
Bicycle Safety (Loewen), 73
Big Anthony: His Story (dePaola), 56
Big Book of Airplanes (Bingham), 86
Big Book of Dinosaurs, The (Wilkes), 178
Big Book of Monster Machines (Bingham), 86
Big Book of Rescue Vehicles (Bingham), 86
Big Jimmy's Kum Kau Chinese Take Out (Lewin), 82
Big Joe's Trailer Truck (Mathieu), 86
Big Sister, Little Sister (Curtis), 132
Big Wheel's (Rockwell), 86
Biggest Animal on Land, The (Fowler), 64
Biggest Bed in the World, The (Camp), 100
Bill of Rights, The (Hossell), 206
Bill Pickett: Rodeo-Riding Cowboy (Pinkney), 202
Bird (Burnie), 28
Bird or Two, A (Le Tord), 215
Birds, Nests, and Eggs (Boring), 28
Birds in Your Backyard (Herkert), 19, 28
Birthday Basket for Tia, A (Mora), 12, 158
Birthday for Frances, A (Hoban), 132
Blabber Mouse (Kelley), 204
Black Cat, White Cat (Murphy), 216
Black Cowboys (Randolph), 20
Blackfeet: People of the Dark Moccasins (Gibson), 104
Blast Off: Poems About Space (Hopkins), 66
Blast Off to Earth! A Look at Geography (Leedy), 181
Blow Me a Kiss, Miss Lilly (Carlstrom), 131
Blue Sky Bluebird (Chrustowski), 28
Boing-Boing the Bionic Cat (Hench), 136
Boom Chica Rock (Archambault), 199
Born to Be a Butterfly (Wallace), 140
Boss of the Plains: The Hat That Won the West (Carlson), 200
Boston Tea Party (Edwards), 207
Bow Wow Meow Meow: It's Rhyming Cats and Dogs (Florian), 68
Boy, a Dog, and a Frog, A (Mayer), 215
Boy Called Slow, A (Bruchac), 206
Brahms (Rachlin), 80
Bravest Mouse, The (Barbero), 204
Bread and Jam for Frances (Hoban), 23, 85
Bridget and the Moose Brothers (Lindenbaum), 132

Bringing Down the Moon (Emmett), 118
Bringing the Rain to Kapiti Plain (Aardema), 95
Bronco Charlie and the Pony Express (Brill), 212
Brother Eagle, Sister Sky: A Message from Chief Seattle (Jeffers), 104
Brushing Well (Frost), 168
Bubble Bath Pirates (Krosoczka), 10
Buffalo Bill Cody (Shields), 35
Bugs (Wright), 150
Bugs: A Close-Up View of the Insect World (Maynard), 150
Bugs Are Insects (Rockwell and Jenkins), 26, 150
Bugs! Bugs! Bugs! (Barner), 150
Bunnies on the Go: Getting from Place to Place (Walton), 85
Bunny Money (Wells), 60
Burger and the Hot Dog, The (Aylesworth), 68
Buster (Fleming), 17
Busy, Busy Mouse (Kroll), 204
Busy Buzzy Bee (Wallace), 149
But Mom, Everyone Else Does (Winters), 78
Butterfly Alphabet, The (Sandved), 140
Butterfly Alphabet Book, The (Cassie and Pallotta), 140
Butterfly's Dream, The (Keido and Hendler), 140
Buttons for General Washington (Roop), 170
Buzz! A Book About Insects (Berger), 150

C Is for City (Grimes), 190
Caboose Who Got Loose, The (Peet), 86
Caldecott Celebration, A (Marcus), 49
California Gold Rush (Roop), 212
Calling the Doves (Herrera), 158
Camille and the Sunflowers (Anholt), 53
Campbell Kids' Alphabet Soup (Campbell Soup), 1
Can I Help? (Janovitz), 100
Can It Rain Cats and Dogs? (Berger), 42
Can You Hear Me from Here? (Rondeau), 92, 216
Can't You Sleep, Little Bear? (Waddell), 63
Capital! Washington D.C. from A to Z (Melmed), 110
Caps for Sale (Slobodkina), 161
Captain Abdul's Pirates School (McNaughton), 10
Captain Cat (Hoff), 149
Captain Slaughterboard Drops Anchor (Peake), 10
Carl Makes a Scrapbook (Day), 152
Carl Sandburg: Adventures of a Poet (Niven), 8
Carol of the Brown King: Nativity Poems (Hughes), 22
Carp for Kimiko, A (Kroll), 74
Carson, Kit (Burke), 211
Carter G. Woodson: The Father of Black History (McKissack), 20
Casey at the Bat (Thayer), 103, 122
Casey Jones (Drummond), 44
Cat and Canary (Foreman), 28
Cat in the Hat Dictionary, The (Eastman), 196
Caterpillar and the Polliwog, The (Kent), 140

Celebrating Birthdays in Australia
(Enderlein), 164
Celebrating Birthdays in Brazil (Enderlein),
164
Celebrating Birthdays in China (Enderlein),
164
Celebrating Birthdays in Russia (Enderlein),
164
Celebrating Kwanzaa (Hoyt-Goldsmith),
214
Celebrating Mother's Day (Nielsen), 73
Celebration of Light, A (Luenn), 214
Chair for My Mother, A (Williams), 16,
50, 78
Charlie the Caterpillar (Deluise), 140
Chato's Kitchen (Soto), 158
Check It Out! (Gibbons), 55
Cherokee: Native Basket Weavers (De
Angelis), 104
Cherries and Cherry Pits (Williams), 16
Chester (Hoff), 149
Chester, the Worldy Pig (Peet), 38
Chester's Way (Henkes), 196
*Chew Chuckles: Deliciously Funny Jokes
About Food* (Dahl), 154
Chicken Chuck (Martin, Martin, and
Sampson), 128
Chicken Sisters, The (Numeroff), 132
Chicken Soup with Rice (Sendak), 98
Chicken Sunday (Polacco), 116
Chickens Aren't the Only Ones (Heller), 58
Chief's Blanket, The (Chanin), 104
Children Around the World (Montanari),
164
Children Just Like Me: Celebrations!
(Kindersley), 52, 166, 175
Children of Native America Today
(Dennis), 99
Children of Vietnam (Lorbiecki), 74
Child's Day in an Egyptian City, A (Eldash
and Khattab), 164
Child's Day in an Indian Village, A (Das),
164
Child's Garden of Verses, A (Stevenston),
189
Chinese Americans (Raatma), 73
Chinese Immigrants (Olson), 194
Chita's Christmas Tree (Howard), 214
Chocolate Moose for Dinner, A (Gwynne),
92
Chocolatina (Kraft), 154
Christmas Alphabet, The (Sabuda), 41
Christmas Poems (Livingstone), 139
Chrysanthemum (Henkes), 196
Cinco de Mayo (Garcia), 77
Cinco de Mayo (Schaefer), 77
Cinderella (Brown), 117
Cinderella (Knight), 184
Cinderella's Rat (Meddaugh), 166
Circle of Thanks (Fowler), 2
Circus (Ehlert), 128
Circus (Harmer), 128
Circus Animal Acts (Jordan), 128
Circus Caps for Sale (Slobodkina), 128,
161
Circus Clown ABC (Jordan), 128
Circus Clowns (Jordan), 127
Circus Family Dog (Clements), 128
Circus Play (Carter), 128
Citizenship (Doak), 110
City Cats, Country Cats (Hazen), 190
City Dog (Kuskin), 120

City Zoo Blizzard Revue (Crispin), 64
Claire de Lune (Debussy), 50
Clara Ann Cookie (Ziefert), 113
Clara Barton (Deady), 211
Clara Barton (Mara), 211
Clare Caterpillar (Edwards), 140
Clarence Birdseye (Peterson), 136
Clic, Clac, Moo: Cows That Type (Cronin),
96
Clifford the Big Red Dog (Bridwell), 31
Cloud Book, The (dePaola), 42
Cloudy With a Chance of Meatballs
(Barrett), 42
Clown Around (Rau), 128
Cobweb Christmas (Climo), 196
Cock-a-Doodle-Moo! (Most), 96, 148
*Color Me a Rhyme: Nature Poems for Young
People* (Yolen), 27
Colors of Japan (Littlefield), 74
*Colossal Book of Crafts for Kids and Their
Families, The* (Fiarotta), 37
Columbus (D'Aulaire), 170
Come on, Rain!, 78
Come Out and Play (Ajmera), 138, 164
Come Out and Play, Little Mouse (Kraus),
204
*Coming to America: The Story of
Immigration* (Maestro), 194
Commotion in the Ocean (Andreae), 68
Community Helpers from A to Z (Kalman),
82
Complete Dog Book for Kids, The
(American Kennel Club), 160
Cooking Art (Kohl), 154
Cooking on the Lewis and Clark Expedition
(Gunderson), 81
Corduroy (Freeman), 135
Corn Chowder (Stevenson), 68
Corn Is Maize: The Gift of the Indians
(Aliki), 154
Count! (Fleming), 17
Count to 100 with the NBA! (Scholastic,
Inc.), 32
Count Your Way Through China (Haskins),
74
Count Your Way Through Japan (Haskins),
74
Count Your Way Through Korea (Haskins),
74
Countries (Stienecker), 186
Country Kid, City Kid (Cummins), 181
Country Mouse Cottage (Brooks), 204
Covered Wagons, Bumpy Trails (Kay), 212
Cow (Doyle), 96
Cow (Older), 96
Cow Makes a Difference (Smith), 96
Cow That Went Oink, The (Most), 96
Cow Who Wouldn't Come Down, The
(Johnson), 96
Cowboy Kid (Eilenberg), 100
Cowgirl Rose and Her Five Baby Bison
(Gulbis), 172
Cows (Bell), 96
Cows (Stone), 96
Cow's Alfalfa-Bet, A (Jackson), 96
Cows Are Going to Paris, The (Kirby and
Woodman), 96
Crayons: From Start to Finish (Woods),
26
Crazy Hair Day (Saltzberg), 55
*Crinkleroot's Guide to Knowing Animal
Habitats* (Arnosky), 148

*Crossing the Delaware: George Washington
and the Battle of Trenton* (Dean),
34
Crow Boy (Yashima), 74
Crows! Strange and Wonderful (Pringle), 28
Curious George (Rey), 156
Curious George in the Big City (Rey), 190

Daddy Book, The (Parr), 100
Daisy Comes Home (Brett), 6
Daisy the Dancing Cow (Woodworth), 97
Dakota Dugout (Turner), 212
Dance at Grandpa's, 213
Dancing Pig, The (Sierra), 6
*Dancing Teepees: Poems of American Indian
Youth* (Sneve), 104
Dandelions (Bunting), 212
Daniel Boon (Burke), 184
Danny and the Dinosaur (Hoff), 149
David Goes to School (Shannon), 56
Davy Crockett (Brimner), 139
Day in the Life of a Builder, A (Hayward),
82
Day in the Life of a Chef, A (Burby), 154
Day in the Life of a Coach, A (Bowman-
Kruhm), 82
Day in the Life of a Doctor, A (Hayward),
82
Day in the Life of a Firefighter, A
(Hayward), 82
Day in the Life of a Musician, A
(Hayward), 82
Day in the Life of a Police Officer, A
(Hayward), 84
Day in the Life of a Teacher, A (Hayward),
82
Day in the Life of a TV Reporter, A
(Hayward), 82
Day the Teacher Went Bananas, The
(Hoban), 85
Day with a Librarian, A (Kottke), 70
Day-Off Machine, The (Himmelman),
136
Day's Work, A (Bunting), 158, 207
*De Colores and Other Latin-American Folk
Songs for Children* (Orozco), 67,
158
Dear Benjamin Banneker (Banneker), 188
*Dear Calla Roo. . .Love, Savannah Blue: A
Letter to a Pen Pal* (Rakusin), 199
*Dear Children of the Earth: A Letter from
Home* (Schimmel), 164–65
Dear Peter Rabbit (Ada), 4
Dear Tooth Fairy (Edwards), 168
December (Bunting), 207
Deer in the Woods, The, 213
Denali National Park and Preserve
(Petersen), 2
Digging Up Dinosaurs (Aliki), 149, 176
Dinner at the Panda Palace (Calmenson),
154, 197
Dinosaur Babies (Zoehfeld), 176
Dinosaur Dinners (Davis), 176
Dinosaur Dream (Nolan), 176
Dinosaur Who Lived in My Backyard, The
(Hennessy), 176
Dinosaurs, Dinosaurs (Barton), 163
*Dinosaurs! The Biggest, Baddest, Strangest,
Fastest* (Zimmerman), 176, 178
Dinosaurs Are Different (Aliki), 176
Dinosaurumpus! (Milton), 176
Dirt Movers (Kalman), 86

Dirty Beasts (Dahl), 68

Discovering Dinosaurs Series, The (Cohen and Lessem), 176

Do Pirates Take Baths? (Tucker), 10

Do You Know What I'll Do? (Zolotow), 132

Do You See a Mouse? (Waber), 204

Doctor De Soto (Steig), 204

Dog from Arf! Arf! to Zzzzzz, The, 145

Dogs Don't Wear Sneakers (Numeroff), 92

Don't Know Much About the Pilgrims (Davis), 194

Doorbell Rang, The (Hutchins), 60, 102

Dot and Jabber and the Big Bug Mystery (Walsh), 172

Dot and Jabber and the Great Acorn Mystery (Walsh), 173

Doug Flutie: International Football Star (Kirkpatrick), 32

Down by the Bay (Raffi), 116

Down Comes the Rain (Branley), 42

Down on the Funny Farm (King), 190

Dozen Ducklings Lost and Found: A Counting Story (Ziefert), 113

Dr. Anno's Magical Midnight Circus (Anno), 128

Dragons Are Singing Tonight, The (Prelutsky), 68

Dream Planes (Gunning), 182

Dream Tree, The (Cosgrove), 208

Dream Wolf (Goble), 157

Drum, Chavi, Drum!/Toca, Chavi, Toca! (Dole), 158

Duck in a Truck (Alborough), 189

Ducky (Bunting), 207

Duffy and the Devil (Zemach), 197

Dumpling Soup (Rattigan), 114

Dumpy La Rue (Winthrop), 38

Each Orange Had 8 Slices (Giganti), 60, 143

Eagles (Evert), 28

Earthquake! (Haduch), 52

Earthquakes (Prager), 52

Earthquakes (Simon), 52

Earth's Changing Continents (Morris), 186

Easter Egg Farm, The (Auch), 193

Eat Your Peas, Louise! (Snow), 154

Eating the Alphabet: Fruits and Vegetables from A to Z (Ehlert), 154, 188

Ed Emberly's Drawing Book of Faces (Emberley), 175

Ed Emberly's Great Thumbprint Drawing Book (Emberley), 175

Edward and the Pirates (McPhail), 10

Egyptian Cinderella (Climo), 196

Eight Animals Play Ball (Elya), 122

Eight Ate: A Feat of Homonym Riddles (Terban), 92

Eight Enormous Elephants (Dolan), 14

Eleanor (Cooney), 167

Eleanor Roosevelt (Davis), 199

Elephant Rescue (Teramura), 14

Elephants (Holmes), 160

Elephants (Schwabacher), 14

Elephants (Wexo), 160

Elephants: Life in the Wild (Kulling), 14

Elephants on Board (MacDonald), 14

Elephant's Pillow, The (Roome), 14

Eleven Elephants Going Up! (Roberts and Hubbell), 14

Elf Night (Wahl), 46

Eli Whitney: American Inventory (Bagley and Hurt), 136

Ella (Peet), 14

Ella, the Elegant Elephant (D'Amico), 200

Ellen Ochoa (Walker), 158

Elliott, Laura Malone, 24

Ellis Island Christmas (Leighton), 4

Ellsworth's Extraordinary Electic Ears and Other Amazing Alphabet Anecdotes (Fisher), 92

Elmer (McKee), 14

Elves and the Shoemaker, The (LaMarche), 46

Elympics (Kennedy), 14

Emeline at the Circus (Priceman), 129

Emily and Alice, Best Friends (Champion), 24

Emily's First 100 Days of School (Wells), 60

Emperor and the Kite, The (Yolen), 27

Empty Pot, The (Demi), 74, 148

Encounter (Yolen), 170

Endangered Animals (McNulty), 214

Energy: Heat, Light, and Food (Stille), 154

Erie Canal Pirates, The (Kimmel), 10

Estella's Swap (O'Neill), 158

Even Firefighters Hug Their Moms (MacLean), 78

Even Steven and Odd Todd (Cristaldi), 61

Evergreen Trees (Prevost), 208

Everything I Know About Pirates (Lichtenheld), 10

Exploring Our Solar System (Ride), 89

Exploring Parks with Ranger Dockett (Flanagan), 82

Exploring the Deep, Dark Sea (Gibbons), 62

Extra Cheese, Please! Mozzarella's Journey from Cow to Pizza (Peterson), 91

Extreme Machines. . .in the Air (Armentrout and Armentrout), 182

Extreme Machines on Land (Armentrout and Armentrout), 86

Eye on the Wild: A Story About Ansel Adams (Dunlap), 31

F Is for Flag (Lewison), 110

Fables (Lobel), 88

Fables Aesop Never Wrote (Kraus), 103

Fables from the Sea (Hayashi), 114

Fabulous Fluttering Tropical Butterflies (Patent), 140

Face at the Window, The (Hanson), 158

Falling Up (Silverstein), 171

Family from Vietnam, A (Scoones), 74

Fantastic Flights: One Hundred Years of Flying on the Edge (O'Brien), 182

Farfallina and Marcel (Keller), 140, 150

Farmer Duck (Waddell), 190

Farmer McPeepers and His Missing Cows (Duffield), 97, 172

Farming (Gibbons), 82

Fast Food! Gulp! Gulp! (Waber), 154

Father Who Had 10 Children, The (Guettier), 100

Fathers, Mothers, Sisters, Brothers: A Collection of Family Poems (Hoberman), 131, 132

Father's Day Blues: What Do You Do About Father's Day When All You Have Are Mothers? (Smalls), 102

Feel the Wind (Dorros), 42

Field Mouse and The Dinosaur Named Sue (Wahl), 176–77

Fiesta! (Behrens), 77

Fighting Fires (Kuklin), 86

Fine Feathered Friends: All About Birds (Rabe), 28

Fir Trees (Fischer-Nagel), 208

Fire! Fire! (Gibbons), 163

Fire! Fire! Hurry! Hurry! (Zimmerman), 82

Fireboat: The Heroic Adventures of the John J. Harvey (Kalman), 87

First Flight: The Story of Tom Tate and the Wright Brothers (Shea), 182

First on the Moon (Hehner), 121

First Thanksgiving, The (Watling), 194

First Thanksgiving Day, The: A Counting Story (Melmed), 194

512 Ants on Sullivan Street, The (Losi, White, and Broekel), 150

Five Minutes' Peace (Murphy), 14, 78

Flag Day (Bennett), 99

Flag Day (Cooper), 99

Flag for All, A (Brimner), 99

Flash, Crash, Rumble, and Roll (Branley), 42

Flicker Flash (Graham, Joan Bransfield), 68

Flight: The Journey of Charles Lindbergh (Burleigh), 23

Flower Fairies of the Trees (Barker), 208

Fluffy Meets the Tooth Fairy (McMullan), 46, 168

Fly, Bessie, Fly (Joseph), 182

Flying: Just Plane Fun (Grist), 182

Food for Healthy Teeth (Frost), 168

Fool of the World and the Flying Ship, The: A Russian Tale (Ransome), 12

Football for Fun (Goin), 32

Football That Won, The (Sampson), 32

Forest Has Eyes, The (Doolittle), 104

Forest Plants (Giesecke), 208

Fourth of July Story (Dalgliesh), 110

Frank and Izzy Set Sail (Kvasnosky), 24

Franklin and the Tooth Fairy (Bourgeois), 46

Franklin Plants a Tree (Bourgeois), 208

Franklin Plays the Game (Bourgeois), 33

Franz Joseph Hayden: Great Man of Music (Greene), 53

Fred Read the Red Book (Scheunemann), 92, 216

Frederick (Lionni), 80

Frederick Douglass: Leader Against Slavery (McKissack), 31

Frederick Douglass (Welch), 20

Freedom River (Rappaport), 20

Freight Train (Crews), 50

French Immigrants (Olson), 194

Friend Is Someone Who Likes You, A (Anglund), 4, 24

Friends (Heine), 24

Fritz and the Beautiful Horse (Brett), 6, 202

Froggie Went A-Courtin (Trapani), 37

Frogs Wore Red Suspenders, The (Prelutsky), 69

From Calf to Cow (Powell), 97

From Daybreak to Good Night: Poems for Children (Sandburg), 8

From Egg to Butterfly (Zemlicka), 140

From One to One Hundred (Sloat), 61
From Seed to Plant (Gibbons), 130
Fruit Trees Produce Produce (Molter), 92
Full Moon Rising (Taylor), 118
Fun Food (Bastyra), 154
Funny Little Woman, The (Mosel), 13, 74

*G Is for Grand Canyon: An Arizona
    Alphabet* (Gowan), 35
Game Time! (Murphy), 33
Garbage Collectors (Bourgeois), 82
Gardener, The (Stewart), 190
Garrett Morgan, Inventor (Jackson), 136
Gentle Giant Octopus (Wallace), 62
Geoffrey Groundhog Predicts the Weather
    (Koscielniak), 24
Geography from A to Z: A Picture Glossary
    (Knowlton), 186
George Eastman: The Kodak Camera Man
    (Ford), 136
George the Pitching Machine (McNamara),
    122
George Washington's Breakfast (Galdone),
    94, 192
George Washington's Cows (Small), 97
George Washington's Mother (Fritz), 78
George Washington's Teeth (Chandra and
    Comora), 168
German Immigrants (Frost), 194
Get Ready to Play Tee Ball (Cheripko), 122
Get Up and Go (Murphy), 61
Giant Cabbage, The: An Alaska Folktale
    (Stihler), 2
Giant Jam Sandwich, The (Lord), 56
Giant Treasury of Peter Rabbit, The
    (Potter), 125
*Gift of the Poinsettia, The: El Regalo de la
    Flor de Nochebuena* (Mora), 12
Gift of the Sacred Dog, The (Goble), 104
Giggle Bugs: A Lift-and-Laugh Book
    (Carter), 150
Gingerbread Baby (Brett), 6
Girl Who Loved Wild Horses, The (Goble),
    104, 157
Girl Who Struck Out Babe Ruth, The
    (Patrick), 26
Giving Tree, The (Silverstein), 171
*Glorious Flight Across the Channel with
    Louis Bleriot, The* (Provensen), 182
Go, Dog, Go (Eastman), 196
Goat in the Rug, The (Blood and Link),
    104–5
God Bless America (Berlin), 110
God Bless America (Munsinger), 188
Goin' Someplace Special (McKissack), 20
Going Home (Bunting), 158
Going to Town, 213
Going West 213
Gold Coin, The (Ada), 4, 158
*Golden Mare, the Firebird, and the Magic
    Ring, The* (Sanderson), 193
Goldilocks and the Three Bears
    (Aylesworth), 6
Golem (Wisniewski), 48
Good Dog, Carl (Day), 152
Good Mousekeeping (Lewis), 69
Good Night, Fairies (Hague), 46
Good Night, Gorilla (Rathmann), 64
Good-bye, 382 Shin Dang Dong (Park), 74
*Good-bye, Charles Lindbergh: Based on a
    True Story* (Borden), 23
Goodnight Moon (Brown), 88

Gorillas: Gentle Giants of the Forest
    (Milton and Hynes), 210
Gotta Go! Gotta Go! (Swope), 140–41
Grady's in the Silo (Townsend), 97
Grand Canyon: A Trail Through Time
    (Vieira), 35
Grandfather's Dream (Keller), 165
Grandfather's Journey (Say), 75, 143
Grandma Elephant's in Charge (Jenkins),
    15
Grandma Summer (Jessup), 146
Grandma Went to Market (Blackstone),
    175
Grandmother's Dreamcatcher (McCain),
    105
Grandpa and Bo (Henkes), 146
Grandpa Never Lies (Fletcher), 146
Grandparent Poems (Micklos), 146
Grandparents: Around the World (Lakin),
    146
Grandparents Are the Greatest Because. . .
    (Greenspun and Schwarz), 146
Grandpas Are for Finding Worms (Ziefert),
    146
Grandpa's Teeth (Clement), 57, 172
Grant Wood (Venezia), 30
Greatest Gymnast of All, The (Murphy),
    216
Great Leaf Blast-Off, The (Himmelman),
    136
Great Pig Escape, The (Christelow), 38
Great Valentine Mystery, The (Bryant), 172
Green Cars: Earth-Friendly Electric Vehicles
    (Coughlan), 87
Green Cat (Khalsa), 132
Green Eggs and Ham (Seuss), 40, 92
Green Wilma (Arnold), 57
Gregory, the Terrible Eater (Sharmat),
    154–55
Gretchen Groundhog, It's Your Day!
    (Levine), 22
Grey Mouse (de Vries), 204
Groucho's Eyebrows (Brown), 2
Grouchy Ladybug, The (Carle), 106
Groundhog Day (Becker), 22
*Growing Up in Africa's Elephant Kingdom:
    The Story of Little Bull* (James), 15
Growing Vegetable Soup (Ehlert), 188
Guess How Much I Love You (McBratney),
    100

Hailstones and Halibut Bones (O'Neil), 69
Halloween Hats (Winthrop), 200
Halloween Is. . . (Gibbons), 179
*Hansa, the True Story of an Asian Elephant
    Baby* (Meeker), 15
Hansel and Gretel (Isaacs), 30
Hansel and Gretel (Lesser), 6
Hanukkah (Schaefer), 210
Happy Birthday, Mr. Kang (Roth), 75
Happy Hippopotami, The (Martin), 76
Harlem (Myers), 69
Harold's Circus (Johnson), 129
Harriet's Horrible Hair Day (Stewart), 132
Harry and the Bucketful of Dinosaurs
    (Whybrow), 177
Harry Houdini: Escape Artist (Lakin), 49
Harry the Dirty Dog (Zion), 160, 167
Harry the Dog (Zion), 167
*Harvesting Hope: The Story of Cesar
    Chavez* (Krull), 158
Harvey Potter's Balloon Farm (Nolen), 190

Hat, The (Brett), 200
Hat for Minerva Louise, A (Stoeke), 200
Hat So Simple, A (Smath), 200
Hats, Hats, Hats (Morris), 200
Hats Off for the Fourth of July (Ziefert),
    110
Hats! (Rau), 200
Hattie and the Fox (Mullins), 40
Have You Seen Birds? (Oppenheim), 28
Have You Seen My Duckling? (Tafuri), 189
Hawaii (Italia), 113
Hawaii: Facts and Symbols (McAuliffe),
    113, 142
Hawaii Is a Rainbow (Feeney), 114
Healthy Teeth (Royston), 168
Heartland (Siebert), 69
Heat Wave at Mud Flat (Stevenson), 42
Helen Keller: Courage in the Dark
    (Hurwitz), 91
Helicopters (Baysura), 182
Hello Cat, You Need a Hat (Geiman), 200
Henny Penny (Galdone), 94
Henry's First-Moon Birthday (Look), 132
Herbert Binns and the Flying Tricycle
    (Castle), 136
Herd of Cows! Flock of Sheep! (Walton), 97
Here Comes the Strikeout (Kessler), 122
Here's to You, America! (Schulz), 110
Herman the Helper (Kraus), 103
Hey, Al (Yorinks), 50, 142
Hey! Get Off Our Train (Burningham), 71
Hey Willy, See the Pyramids (Kalman), 132
High in the Sky: Flying Machines (Parker),
    182
*High Rise Glorious Skittle Skat Roarious
    Sky Pie Angel Food Cake, The*
    (Willard), 155
Hindenberg, The (O'Brien), 182–83
Hispanic Holidays (Winchester), 145
History of Baseball, The (Helmer), 122
History of Football, The (Helmer), 32–33
History of Soccer, The (Helmer), 33
Hog-Eye (Meddaugh), 38, 166
Hole Is to Dig, A (Krauss), 92
Home Run: The Story of Babe Ruth
    (Burleigh), 122–23
Homes of the West (Kalman), 212
Honest-to-Goodness Truth, The
    (McKissack), 135
Honey Makers, The (Gibbons), 145
Hooray for Snail! (Stadler), 123
Hop on Pop (Seuss), 92
Hopscotch Around the World (Lankford),
    165
Horton Hatches the Egg (Seuss), 15
Hottest, Coldest, Highest, Deepest (Jenkins),
    186
House Mouse, Senate Mouse (Barnes), 204
House on Maple Street, The (Pryor), 210
House Sparrows Everywhere (Arnold), 28
How a Book Is Made (Aliki), 149
How Ben Franklin Stole the Lighting
    (Schanzer), 136–37
How Big Is a Foot? (Myller), 61
How Big Were the Dinosaurs? (Most), 177
How Do Birds Find Their Way? (Gans), 28
How Do Dinosaurs Say Good Night?
    (Yolen), 177
How Do Flies Walk Upside Down? (Berger),
    150
How Do You Know It's Summer? (Fowler),
    103

How Groundhog's Garden Grew (Cherry), 5

How Hungry Are You? (Napoli), 35

How I Became a Pirate (Long), 10

How Many Stars in the Sky? (Hort), 100

How Many Teeth? (Showers), 168

How Much Is a Million? (Schwartz), 61, 175

How My Parents Learned to Eat (Friedman), 8

How Now, Brown Cow? (Schertle), 97

How Raven Stole the Sun (Williams), 2

How the Camel Got His Hump (Kipling), 215

How the Guinea Fowl Got Her Spots: A Swahili Tale of Friendship (Knutson), 6

How to Be a Friend: A Guide to Making Friends and Keeping Them (Brown and Brown), 24

How to Catch an Elephant (Schwartz), 15

How to Dig a Hole to the Other Side of the World (McNulty), 186

How to Draw Birds (Green), 28

How to Lose All Your Friends (Carlson), 24

How to Speak Moo! (Fayerman), 97

Hunter's Best Friend at School (Elliott), 24

Hurray for the Fourth of July (Watso), 109

Hurry! (Haas), 146

I, Crocodile (Marcellino), 175

I Am a Good Citizen (Bender), 110

I Am America (Smith), 110–11

I Am Not Going to Get Up Today! (Seuss), 57

I Can Blink Like an Owl (Asch), 134

I Can Draw Animals (Tallrico), 160

I Can Draw Monsters (Tallrico), 160

I Can Roar Like a Lion (Asch), 134

I Can't Talk Yet, but When I Do. . . (Markes), 132

I Face the Wind (Cobb), 42

I Have a Dream (King, Jr.), 9

I Have a Sister—My Sister Is Deaf (Peterson), 107, 199

I Invited a Dragon to Dinner (Demarest), 69

I Like You (Warburg), 24

I Live in Tokyo (Takabayashi), 165

I Love My Mama (Kavanagh), 15

I Love Saturdays y Domingos (Ada), 159

I Love You, Stinky Face (McCourt), 78

I Pledge Allegiance (Martin and Sampson), 111

I Scream, You Scream: A Feast of Food Rhymes (Morrison), 154

I Spy Mystery: A Book of Picture Riddles (Marzollo), 172

I Spy Spooky Night: A Book of Picture Riddles (Marzollo), 172

I Stink! (McMullan and McMullan), 87, 190

I Want to Be a Chef (Maze), 83

I Want to Be a Doctor (Liebman), 83

I Want to Be a Police Officer (Liebman), 83

I Want to Be a Teacher (Liebman), 83

I Want to Be a Truck Driver (Liebman), 83

I Want to Be a Zookeeper (Liebman), 83

I Want to Be an Astronaut (Maze), 83

I Will Never Not Ever Eat a Tomato (Child), 155

I Wish I Were a Butterfly (Howe), 141, 151

I Wonder Why Triceratops Had Horns and Other Questions About Dinosaurs (Theodoro), 177

I Wonder Why Zippers Have Teeth and Other Questions About Inventions (Taylor), 137

I Won't Get Lost (Lambert), 61

Ice Cream (Older), 109

I'd Know You Anywhere (Hutchins), 135

Ida B. Wells-Barnett: A Voice Against Violence (McKissack), 20

If a Bus Could Talk: The Story of Rosa Parks (Ringgold), 202

If I Only Had a Horn: Young Louis Armstrong (Orgill), 20

If I Ran the Circus (Seuss), 130

If I Were President (Stier), 83

If You Ever Meet a Whale (Livingstone), 139

If You Give a Mouse a Cookie (Numeroff), 117

If You Give a Pig a Pancake (Numeroff), 117

If You Hopped Like a Frog (Schwartz), 61

If You Made a Million (Schwartz), 215

If You Want to See a Caribou (Root), 30

I'll Always Be Your Friend (McBratney), 78

I'll Fix Anthony (Viorst), 132

Illustrated Rules of Basketball, The (Bennett), 32

Illustrated Rules of Football, The (Patey), 33

I'm a Big Brother (Cole), 135

I'm a Big Sister (Cole), 135

I'm Mighty! (McMullan), 87

Imaginative Inventions: The Who, What, Where, When, and Why of Roller Skates, Potato Chips Marbles, and Pie (and More!) (Harper), 137

Imagine You Are a Crocodile (Wallace), 58

Immigrant Children, Late 1800s to Early 1900s (Whitman), 194

Imogene's Antlers (Small), 57

In a Pickle and Other Funny Idioms (Terban), 92

In a Pumpkin Shell: A Mother Goose ABC (Anglund), 4

In Daddy's Arms I Am Tall: African Americans Celebrating Fathers (Steptoe), 100

In My Family (Garza), 159

In November (Rylant), 197

In the Garden with Van Gogh (Merberg and Bober), 53

In the Night Kitchen (Sendak), 98

Inch by Inch (Lionni), 80

Insect Invaders (Capeci), 151

Insect Soup: Bug Poems (Polisar), 151

Insectlopedia (Florian), 45

Insects Are My Life (McDonald), 35

Inside a Zoo in the City (Capucilli), 65

Inventions: Great Ideas and Where They Came From (Houghtin and Lally), 137

Invitation to the Butterfly Ball, An: A Counting Rhyme (Yolen), 141

IQ Goes to the Library (Fraser), 153

Ira Sleeps Over (Waber), 161

Irish Immigrants, 1840–1920 (O'Hara), 194

Iroquois Indians, The (Lund), 105

Isabel's House of Butterflies (Johnston), 141

Island-Below-the-Star, The (Rumford), 114–15

It Could Always Be Worse (Zemach), 197

It Could Still Be a Tree (Fowler), 208

It Couldn't Be Worse (van Kampen), 6

It Looked Like Spilt Milk (Shaw), 42

Italian Immigrants, 1850–1950 (Wallner), 194

It's a Good Thing There Are Insects (Fowler), 151

It's a Hummingbird's Life (Kelly), 29

It's a Mouse! (Souza), 204

It's About Dogs (Johnston), 160

It's Groundhog Day (Kroll), 22

It's Raining Pigs and Noodles (Prelutsky), 152

It's Valentines Day (Prelutsky), 30

Jack and the Leprechaun (Robertson), 46

Jacques Cousteau: Man of the Oceans (Green), 98

Jamberry (Degen), 99

Jambo Means Hello: Swahili Alphabet Book (Feelings), 92

Jamie O'Rourke and the Big Potato (dePaola), 46

Japanese Americans (McDaniel), 73

Japanese Children's Day and the Obon Festival (MacMillan), 80

Japanese Immigrants, 1850–1950 (Wallner), 194

Jennie's Hat (Keats), 201

Jesse Bear, What Will You Wear? (Carlstrom), 131

Jesse Jackson: A Rainbow Leader (Martin), 20

Jet Airliners (Baysura), 182

Jet Alphabet Book, The (Pallotta), 183

Jethro and Joel Were a Troll (Peet), 46

Jingle Dancer (Smith), 105

Joe and Betsy the Dinasaur (Hoban), 85

John Philip Sousa (Venezia), 185

Johnny Kaw: The Pioneer Spirit of Kansas (Garretson), 212

Joining the Boston Tea Party (Stanley), 207

Jonah and the Pirates Who (Usually) Don't Do Anything (Metaxas and Kenney), 10

Jonas Salk (Durrett), 178

Joseph Had a Little Overcoat (Taback), 6, 30, 50

Journey, The (Stewart), 27

Journey of the Third Seed (Bauld), 75

Juan Bobo Goes to Work: A Puerto Rican Folk Tale (Montes), 6–7

Julius, the Baby of the World (Henkes), 132, 196

Jumanji (Van Allsburg), 102

Jumbo: The Most Famous Elephant in the World! (Worth), 15

Jungle Book, The (Kipling), 215

Just a Little Bit (Tompert), 15

Just a Minute (Becker), 78

Just in Time for New Year's! (Ruelle), 215

Just Plain Fancy (Polacco), 29

Just the Two of Us (Smith), 100

K Is for Kick: A Soccer Alphabet (Herzog), 33

K Is for Kissing a Cool Kangaroo (Andreae), 68
Katie's Trunk (Turner), 170
Katy and the Big Snow (Burton), 143
Kids in Pioneer Times (Wroble), 212
King Who Rained, The (Gwynne), 93
King Bidgood's in the Bathtub (Wood), 77
Kiss for Little Bear, A (Minarik), 153
Kiss the Cow! (Root), 30, 97, 190–91
Kites Sail High (Heller), 93
Knots on a Counting Rope (Martin, Archambault, and Clarke), 105
Koala Lou (Fox), 40
Korean Children's Day (Suyenaga), 80
Kumak's Fish, 3

La Mer (Debussy), 50
Lamb and the Butterfly, The (Carle), 141
Lasso Lou and Cowboy McCoy (Failing), 201
Last Night I Dreamed a Circus (Farley), 129
Last Princess, The: The Story of Princess Ia'iulani of Hawai'i (Stanley), 115
Latitude and Longitude (Aberg), 186
Lava (Sweeney), 115
Learning About Integrity from the Life of Eleanor Roosevelt (Ellwood), 167
Legend of the Bluebonnet, The: An Old Tale of Texas (dePaola), 7
Legend of the Indian Paintbrush, The (dePaola), 105
Legend of the Poinsettia, The (dePaola), 206
Legend of the White Buffalo Woman, The (Goble), 104
Lemonade Sun: and Other Summer Poems (Dotlich), 103
Leo the Late Bloomer (Kraus), 103
Leonardo, Beautiful Dreamer (Byrd), 76
Leonardo da Vinci (Lepscky), 76
Leonardo da Vinci (Stanley), 76
Let's Call Him Lau-Wiliwili-Humuhumu-Nukunuku-Nukunuku-Apua'A-Oi-Oi (Myers), 115
Let's Count (Hoban), 61
Let's Go to a Baseball Game (Hill), 123
Let's Play Ball (Foster and Erickson), 123
Let's Play Basketball (Smith), 32
Lettice, the Flying Rabbit (Stanley), 183
Lewis and Clark for Kids: Their Journey of Discovery with 21 Activities (Herbert), 81
Liberty (Curlee), 178
Library, The (Stewart), 27, 153
Life and Work of Henri Matisse, The (Flux), 215
Life and Work of Leonardo da Vinci, The (Connolly), 76
Life on a Cattle Farm (Wolfman), 191
Life on a Chicken Farm (Wolfman), 191
Life on a Crop Farm (Wolfman), 44, 191
Life on a Dairy Farm (Wolfman), 191
Life on a Sheep Farm (Wolfman), 191
Lightning (Simon), 42
Lilly's Purple Plastic Purse (Henkes), 196
Lion and the Little Red Bird, The (Kleven), 29
Lion and the Ostrich Chicks (Bryan), 117
Listening Walk, The (Showers), 149
Little Badger, Terror of the Seven Seas (Bunting), 10

Little Bear's New Friend (Minarik), 24
Little Bear's Visit (Minarik), 147
Little Billy and Baseball Bob (Axelrod), 123
Little Blue and Little Yellow (Lionni), 80
Little Engine That Could, The (Piper), 87
Little Honu (Sweeney), 115
Little House, The (Burton), 143
Little Miss Spider (Kirk), 193
Little Mouse's Painting (Wolkstein), 204
Little Panda: The World Welcomes Hua Mei at the San Diego Zoo (Ryder), 65
Little Pigeon Toad (Gwynne), 93
Little Red Ant and the Great Big Crumb, The (Climo), 196
Little Red Hen, The (Galdone), 94
Little Red Hen, The (Zemach), 197
Little Red Riding Hood (Hyman), 63
Little Red Riding Hood (Ransom), 7
Little Story About a Big Turnip, A (Zunshine), 7
Lives of the Musicians: Good Times, Bad Times (and What the Neighbors Thought) (Krull), 142
Living in the Forest (Loughran), 186–87
Living in the Tundra (Loughran), 187
Log's Life, A (Pfeffer), 208
Loki and Alex: The Adventures of a Dog and His Best Friend (Smith), 24
Lon Po Po (Young), 197
Long Johns for a Small Chicken (Eagle and Silverstein), 212
Long March, The (Fitzpatrick), 105
Look. . . What Do You See? (Rye), 127
Look at Teeth, A (Fowler), 168
Look Through the Mouse Hole, A (Fischer-Nagel), 204–5
Look What Came from China (Harvey), 75
Look What Came from Japan (Harvey), 75
Loose Teeth (Schaefer), 168
Loose Teeth (Suen), 168
Lorax, The (Seuss), 55
Lost Tooth Club, The (Johnson), 168
Lots of Limericks (Livingstone), 139
Lots to Do (Prater), 133
Lottie's New Friend (Mathers), 24–25
Louella Mae, She's Run Away! (Litzinger), 38
Luckiest Leprechaun, The (Korman), 46
Lucy and the Pirates (Petrie), 10
Lulu's Birthday (Howard), 214
Lyle, Lyle Crocodile (Waber), 161
Lyle and the Birthday Party (Waber), 161

Mable the Tooth Fairy and How She Got Her Job (David), 168–69
Macaroni Math (Ohanesian), 61
Madeline (Bemelmans), 50, 71
Madlenka (Sis), 165
Mae Jemison: Out of This World (Naden and Blue), 37
Magic Bean Tree, The: A Legend from Argentina (Van Laan), 159
Magic Hat, The (Fox), 40, 201
Magic Matt and the Skunk in the Tub (Maccarone), 31
Magic Porridge Pot, The (Ziefert), 1
Magic School Bus Explores the World of Bugs, The (White), 151
Magic School Bus in the Rain Forest, The (Moore), 208

Magic School Bus Inside a Hurricane, The (Cole), 42
Magic School Bus Kicks Up a Storm, The (White), 42
Magic School Bus on the Ocean Floor, The (Cole and Degen), 62
Magic School Bus Taking Flight, The: A Book About Flight (Cole), 183
Magic School Bus, The: Inside a Beehive (Cole), 149
Magic Tricks (Tremaine), 179
Magical Garden of Claude Monet, The (Anholt), 189
Mail by the Pail (Bergel), 100
Make Friends (Rogers), 25
Make New Friends (Wells), 25
Make Way for Ducklings (McCloskey), 50, 156
Make Way for Tooth Decay (Katz), 167, 169
Mama Played Baseball (Adler), 123
Mammalabilia (Florian), 45
Many Nations: An Alphabet of Native America (Bruchac), 105
Map Keys (Aberg), 187
Mardi Gras: A City's Masked Parade (Gabbert), 26
Maria's Comet (Hopkinson), 137
Martha Speaks (Meddaugh), 166
Martin Luther King, Jr., and the March on Washington (Ruffin), 143
Mary McLeod Bethune: A Great American Educator (McKissack), 20–21
Matthew and the Midnight Pirates (Morgan), 10
Maui and the Secret of Fire (Tune), 115
Maui Goes Fishing (Williams), 115
Max Cleans Up (Wells), 133
Max Goes to the Moon: A Science Adventure with Max the Dog (Bennett), 118
Max (Isadora), 123
Max, the Stubborn Little Wolf (Judes and Robins), 101
May I Bring a Friend? (de Regniers), 25, 138
Maybelle, the Cable Car (Burton), 87
Mealtime for Zoo Animals (Arnold), 65
Mean Soup (Everitt), 78
Measuring Penny (Leedy), 61
Meet Babar and His Family (de Brunhoff), 203
Meet Lydia: A Native Girl from Southeast Alaska (Belarde-Lewis), 3
Meg and Her Circus Tricks (Percy), 129
Mei-Mei Loves the Morning (Tsubakiyama), 165
Memorial Day (Cotton, Kane, and Vargus), 89
Memorial Day (Frost), 89
Memorial Day Surprise (Golding), 89
Metropolitan Cow (Egan), 97
Mice (Holmes), 205
Mice and Beans (Ryan), 159
Mice Twice (Low), 205
Michelangelo (Venezia), 41
Midnight Ride of Paul Revere, The (Longfellow), 4, 111
Mighty Tree (Gackenbach), 71, 208
Mike Mulligan and His Steam Shovel (Burton), 87, 143
Military Planes (Baysura), 182
Milk Makers, The (Gibbons), 97

Millions of Cats (Gag), 44

Milly and the Macy's Parade (Corey), 194

Milton the Early Riser (Kraus), 103

Mimi's First Mardi Gras (Couvillon), 26

Mirandy and Brother Wind (McKissack), 50, 135

Mirette and Bellini Cross Niagara Falls (McCully), 112

Miss Alaineus: A Vocabulary Disaster (Frasier), 93

Miss Bindergarten Celebrates the 100th Day of Kindergarten (Slate), 70

Miss Bindergarten Gets Ready for Kindergarten (Slate), 70

Miss Bindergarten Plans a Circus with Kindergarten (Slate), 129

Miss Fannie's Hat (Karon), 201

Miss Hunnicutt's Hat (Brumbeau), 201

Miss Mary Mack (Hoberman), 138

Miss Nelson Has a Field Day (Allard), 16

Miss Nelson Is Back (Allard), 16

Miss Nelson Is Missing (Allard), 16

Miss Rumphius (Cooney), 134

Miss Twiggley's Tree (Fox), 208

Moja Means One: Swahili Counting Book (Feelings), 21

Molly and the Magic Wishbone (McClintock), 133

Momma, Where Are You From? (Bradby), 21

Mommy Book, The (Parr), 78

Monarch Butterflies (Gibbons), 127

Monday's Troll (Prelutsky), 152

Monet (Venezia), 189

Monsoon (Krishnaswami), 43

Monster Bugs (Penner), 151

Moon Book, The (Gibbons), 118

Moon in the Man, The (Honey), 93

Moon Lady, The (Tan), 118, 147

Moon Seems to Change, The (Branley), 118

More Perfect Union, A: The Story of Our Constitution (Maestro), 111

Morgan Plays Soccer (Rockwell), 26

Mormon Pioneer Trail, The: From Nauvoo, Illinois, to the Great Salt Lake, Utah (Dean), 212

Morris's Disappearing Bag (Wells), 17

Mort the Sport (Kraus), 103, 123

Moses Goes to a Concert (Millman), 37

Mother, Mother, I Feel Sick; Send for the Doctor Quick, Quick, Quick (Charlip and Supree), 79

Mother Earth (Luenn), 214

Mother for Choco, A (Kasza), 79

Mother to Tigers (Lyon), 65

Mother's Day Mess (Ruelle), 79

Mountain That Loved a Bird, The (McLerran), 29

Mouse (Watts), 205

Mouse Count (Walsh), 148

Mouse Makes Magic (Heling and Hembrook), 93

Mouse Mess (Riley), 205

Mouse Paint (Walsh), 148, 205

Mouse Tail Moon (Ryder), 205

Mouse That Snored, The (Waber), 205

Mouse's Life, A (Himmelman), 205

Movie in My Pillow, A (Argueta), 159

Mozart (Rachlin), 16

Mr. Frumble's Biggest Hat Flap Book Ever! (Scarry), 201

Mr. Lincoln's Way (Polacco), 116

Mr. Lincoln's Whiskers (Winnick), 27, 111

Mr. Rabbit and the Lovely Present (Zolotow), 79, 107

Mr. Wiggle's Library (Thompson and Craig), 19

Mr. Willowby's Christmas Tree (Barry), 208

Mrs. Honey's Dream (Adams), 11

Mrs. Honey's Hat (Adams), 201

Mrs. Mortifee's Mouse (Henry), 205

Mrs. Wishy-Washy's Farm (Cowley), 134

Mud Flat April Fool (Stevenson), 58

Mud Flat Olympics, The (Stevenson), 116

Mud Puddle (Munsch), 57, 98

Mufaro's Beautiful Daughters: An African Tale (Steptoe), 7

Munch! Crunch! What's for Lunch? Experiments in the Kitchen (Lobb), 155

Musubi Man: Hawaii's Gingerbread Man (Takayama), 115

My Baseball Book (Gibbons), 123

My Basketball Book (Gibbons), 32, 202

My Beastie Book of ABC (Frampton), 68

My Best Friend: A Book About Friendship (Feldman), 25

My Brother, Ant (Simont), 133

My Brother Martin: A Sister Remembers Growing Up with the Rev. Dr. Martin Luther King, Jr. (Farris), 9

My Brothers' Flying Machine: Wilbur, Orville, and Me (Yolen), 183

My Dad (Browne), 101

My Dad Is Awesome (Butterworth), 101

My Dad's Job (Glassman), 83

My Father's Boat (Garland), 165

My First Magic Book (Leyton), 179

My Five Senses (Aliki), 149

My Football Book (Gibbons), 33

My Friend John (Zolotow), 25

My Friend Rabbit (Rohmann), 50, 175

My Little Sister Ate One Hare (Grossman), 61

My Lucky Hat (O'Malley), 123

My Most Favorite Thing (Moon), 147

My Rotten Redheaded Older Brother (Polacco), 133

My Soccer Book (Gibbons), 33

My Tooth Is About to Fall Out (Maccarone), 169

My Tooth Is Loose (Ziefert), 113

My Visit to the Aquarium (Aliki), 55

My Visit to the Dinosaurs (Aliki), 177

Mystery in Bugtown (Boniface), 151

Mystery Mansion (Garland), 172

Mystery on the Docks (Hurd), 172

Nana Upstairs, Nana Downstairs (dePaola), 156

Napping House, The (Wood), 77

Nate the Great and the Halloween Hunt (Sharmat), 173

Native Americans (Sautai, Fuhr, and Gallimard), 105

Nature's Green Umbrella: Tropical Rain Forests (Gibbons), 130, 208

Neil Armstrong (Zemlicka), 118

Nest Full of Eggs, A (Jenkins), 29

New Barker in the House, A (dePaola), 159

New Kid on the Block (Prelutsky), 152

New Land: A First Year on the Prairie (Reynolds), 212

New Moon (Shea), 118

Nice Try, Tooth Fairy (Olson), 46, 169

Nick Plays Baseball (Isadora), 123

Night Before Christmas, The (Moore), 211

Night Before the Tooth Fairy, The (Wing), 169

Night Flight: Charles Lindberg's Incredible Adventure (Kramer), 183

Night on Neighborhood Street (Greenfield), 191

Night Shift Daddy (Spinelli), 101

Night Tree (Bunting), 209

Night Worker, The (Banks), 83

No Roses for Harry! (Zion), 167

No! Where Are My Pants? (Hopkins), 66

Noisy Airplane Ride, The (Downs), 183

Noisy Nora (Wells), 17

Norman, the Doorman (Freeman), 205

Norman Rockwell: The Life of an Artist (Roy and Roy), 127

North America: Geography (Fowler), 187

North American Animals of the Arctic (Mastin), 3

Norwegian, Swedish, and Danish Immigrants, 1820–1920 (Olson), 194–95

Nothing Beats a Pizza (Lesynski), 69

Nothing Here but Trees (Van Leeuwen), 214

Nurses (Klingel), 73

Nutquacker, The (Auch), 193

Nuts to You! (Ehlert), 191

Octopus Is Amazing, An (Lauber), 23

Ogres! Ogres! Ogres! A Feasting Frenzy from A to Z (Heller), 155

Oh, Say Can You Say Di-no-saur? (Worth), 177

Oink (Geisert), 38

Old Bear (Hissey), 148

Old Black Fly (Aylesworth), 57

Old Elm Speaks: Tree Poems (George), 66, 209

Old Granny and the Bean Thief (DeFelice), 57

Old Man and His Door, The (Soto), 159

Old Man Who Loved Cheese, The (Keillor), 57

Oliver (Hoff), 15

Olivia (Falconer), 38

Olivia. . .and the Missing Toy (Falconer), 173

Olivia Saves the Circus (Falconer), 129

On Beyond Bugs: All About Insects (Seuss and Rabe), 151

On Market Street (Lobel), 94

On Mother's Lap (Scott), 79

On the Same Day in March: A Tour of the World's Weather (Singer), 43

Once a Mouse . . . (Brown), 117, 205

Once There Was a Tree (Romanova), 209

Once Upon a Lily Pad: Froggy Love in Monet's Garden (Sweeney), 189

One Giant Leap: The Story of Neil Armstrong (Brown), 121

One Grain of Rice (Demi), 148

One Hundred Hungry Ants (Pinczes), 61

One Hundred Shoes (Ghigna), 151

One Lighthouse, One Moon (Lobel), 94

One Little, Two Little, Three Little Pilgrims (Hennessy), 195

One Monday (Huntington), 43

One Morning in Maine (McCloskey), 169

One of Each (Hoberman), 138
One Small Place in a Tree (Brenner), 209
One Thing Leads to Another (Lucas), 137
One Whole Doughnut, One Doughnut Hole (McLenighan), 93, 216
1-2-3 Draw Cars, Trucks, and Other Vehicles (Levin), 87
Open Wide: Tooth School Inside (Keller), 169
Opposites (Coulter), 216
Otto's Trunk (Turner), 15
Our Animal Friends at Maple Hill Farm (Provensen), 191
Our Class Took a Trip to the Zoo (Neitzel), 65
Our Twitchy (Gray), 193
Over in the Garden (Ward), 151
Owl and the Pussycat, The (Lear), 81
Owl Babies (Waddell), 63
Owl Moon (Yolen), 27, 50, 101, 118
Ox-Cart Man (Hall), 51

P. T. Barnum (Wright), 113, 129
P Is for Passport: A World Alphabet (Scillian), 187
P Is for Pilgrim: A Thanksgiving Alphabet (Crane), 195
Pablo Picasso: Breaking All the Rules (Kelley), 175
Painted Lady of Butterflies (Schaffer), 141
Painting Gorilla, The (Rex), 65
Pair of Red Clogs, A (Matsuno), 75
Pamela Camel (Peet), 129
Papa, Please Get the Moon for Me (Carle), 101
Papa Piccolo (Talley), 101
Paper Dragon, The (Davol), 41
Parrott: An Italian Folktale (Gál), 7
Pat Hall's Hawaiian Animals (Hall), 115
Patchwork Quilt, The (Flournoy), 147
Patrick: Patron Saint of Ireland (dePaola), 45
Patrick at the Circus (Hayes), 129
Patriotism (Raatma), 111
Patriotism (Scheunemann), 111
Paul Bunyan (Kellogg), 175
Paul Cézanne (Venezia), 12
Paul Gauguin (Flux), 95
Paul Gauguin: Art for Children (Raboff), 95
Paul Revere: Patriot (Ford), 4
Paul Revere's Ride (Longfellow), 69
Peace Begins with You (Scholes), 156
Peanut Butter and Jelly: A Play Rhyme (Westcott), 181
Peewee Pipes and the Wing Thing (Rich), 141
Penguin and Little Blue (McDonald), 35
Perfect Pigs (Brown), 179
Pete the Presents (Molter), 93
Peter Spier's Circus! (Spier), 129
Peter's Chair (Keats), 133
Petunia (Duvoisin), 143
Philharmonic Gets Dressed, The (Kuskin), 120
Picasso (Sateren), 175
Picky Nicky (Dubowski), 155
Picnic in October, A (Bunting), 178
Picture Book of Abraham Lincoln, A (Adler), 27, 111
Picture Book of Benjamin Franklin, A (Adler), 9, 111, 137

Picture Book of Christopher Columbus, A (Adler), 170
Picture Book of Davy Crockett, A (Adler), 139
Picture Book of Eleanor Roosevelt, A (Adler), 167
Picture Book of Frederick Douglass, A (Adler), 31
Picture Book of George Washington, A (Adler), 34, 111
Picture Book of Harriet Tubman, A (Adler), 21
Picture Book of Helen Keller, A (Adler), 107
Picture Book of Jackie Robinson, A (Adler), 17
Picture Book of Lewis and Clark, A (Adler), 212
Picture Book of Louis Braille, A (Adler), 5
Picture Book of Martin Luther King, Jr., A (Adler), 9, 21
Picture Book of Rosa Parks, A (Adler), 21
Picture Book of Sacagawea, A (Adler), 210, 212–13
Picture Book of Thomas Alva Edison, A (Adler), 137
Picture Book of Thomas Jefferson, A (Adler), 111
Pigeon Finds a Hot Dog!, The (Willems), 109
Piggie Pie (Palatini), 38
Piggins (Yolen), 38–39, 173
Pigs (Gibbons), 39
Pigs Can't Fly (Cort), 39
Pigs from 1 to 10 (Geisert), 39, 160
Pigs from A to Z (Geisert), 39, 160
Pigs on a Blanket: Fun with Math and Time (Axelrod), 39
Pigs Will Be Pigs: Fun with Math and Money (Axelrod), 61
Pilot Mom (Duble), 84
Pinduli (Cannon), 185
Pink and Say (Polacco), 116
Pink Pirate, The (Day), 11
Pinkerton, Behave! (Kellogg), 175
Pioneer Farm: Living on a Farm in the 1880s (O'Hara), 213
Pioneer Girl: The Story of Laura Ingalls Wilder (Anderson and Andreasen), 213
Pioneer Life from A to Z (Kalman), 213
Pippi Goes to the Circus (Lindgren), 129
Pirate Jam (Brown), 11
Pirate Pee Sets Sail (James and Jaggi), 11
Pirate Pete (Kennedy), 11
Pirates (Anastasio), 11
Pirates: Robbers of the High Seas (Gibbons), 11
Plane Song (Siebert), 183
Planting a Rainbow (Ehlert), 188
Play Ball, Amelia Bedelia (Parrish), 117
Plymouth Partnership: Pilgrims and Native Americans (Whitehurst), 195
Pocket for Corduroy, A (Freeman), 135
Pocketful of Nonsense (Marshall), 93
Polar Bear, Polar Bear, What Do You Hear? (Martin), 65
Polar Express, The (Van Allsburg), 102
Poodle Who Barked at the Wind, The (Coursen), 107
Popcorn at the Palace (McCully), 137
Popcorn Book, The (dePaola), 155, 156

Porcupine Mouse, The (Pryor), 210
Portraits of African-American Heroes (Bolden), 19
Possom Magic (Fox), 40
Possom Comes a-Knockin (Van Laan), 57, 192
Possum's Harvest Moon (Hunter), 118
Pot That Juan Built, The (Andrews-Gobel), 159
Powwow (Ancona), 105
Presidents' Day (Ansary), 31
Presidents' Day (Marx, Kane, and Vargus), 19
Prince and the Li Hing Mui, The (Takayama), 115
Princess and the Pea, The (Andersen), 7, 58
Princess Mouse, The: A Tale of Finland (Shepard), 7
Principal Frog (Calmenson), 197
Puddle Pail, The (Kleven), 133
Punia and the King of Sharks: A Hawaiian Folktale (Wardlaw), 115
Puss In Boots (Perrault), 175

Quackadack Duck (Morgan), 46

Rabbit Pirates: A Tale of the Spinach Main (Cos), 11
Racecar Alphabet, The (Floca), 197
Raggedy Ann and Andy and the Camel with the Wrinkled Knees (Gruelle), 211
Ragtime Tumpie (Schroeder), 21
Rainbow of Friends, A (Hallinan), 25
Rainforest Birds (Kalman), 29
Rainy Day (Haughton), 102
Raising Yoder's Barn (Yolen), 191, 199
Randy's Dandy Lions (Peet), 129
Rapunzel (Zelinsky), 7, 30
Rattletrap Car (Root), 30
Raven (McDermott), 17
Real McCoy, The: The Life of an African-American Inventor (Towle), 127, 137
Reasons for the Seasons, The (Gibbons), 43
Red, White, and Blue: The Story of the American Flag (Herman), 111
Red Leaf, Yellow Leaf (Ehlert), 209
Red-Eyed Tree Frog (Cowley), 134
Relatives Came, The (Rylant), 51
Rembrandt (Venezia), 120
Rembrandt: See and Do Children's Book (de Bie), 120
Rhinos Who Play Baseball (Mammano), 123
Rhinos Who Play Soccer (Mammano), 33
Richard Scarry's Best Little Word Book Ever! (Scarry), 83
Richard Scarry's Busy, Busy, Town (Scarry), 83
Richard Scarry's The Early Bird (Scarry), 29
Ride on Mother's Back, A (Bernhard), 165
Right Number of Elephants, The (Sheppard), 15
Right Touch, The (Kleven), 55
Rikki Tikki Tavi (Kipling), 214
Rip Van Winkle (Irving), 59
River of Life (Miller), 3
Robert Fulton (Rosenberg), 137
Rocket to the Moon (Combs), 118
Rocky, the Cat Who Barks (Napoli and Kane), 35
Roller Skates! (Calmenson), 175

Roman Numerals from I to MM (Geisert), 160
Roses (Prevost), 91
Rosie's Walk (Hutchins), 102
Rotten Teeth (Simms), 57, 169
Round Trip (Jonas), 191
Rumble in the Jungle (Andreae), 69
Rumpelstiltskin (Isaacs), 30
Rumpelstiltskin (Zelinsky), 7, 46
Runaway Bunny (Brown), 88
Rusty, Trusty Tractor, The (Cowley), 134

Saggy Baggy Elephant, The (Jackson), 15
Saint Patrick (Tompert), 45
Saint Valentine (Sabuda), 41
Sally Ride (Nettleton), 89
Salmon Princess, The: An Alaska Cinderella Story (Dwyer), 3
Salt in His Shoes: Michael Jordan in Pursuit of a Dream (Jordan), 32
Sam Has a Sundae on Sunday (Scheunemann), 93
Sammy the Seal (Hoff), 149
Sam's First Library Card (Herman), 145
Sam's Sandwich (Pelham), 185
Samuel Eaton's Day: A Day in the Life of a Pilgrim Boy (Waters), 195
Samuel F. B. Morse: Inventor and Code Creator (Alter), 137
Samuel Todd's Book of Great Inventions (Konigsburg), 137
Sandra Day O'Connor (Holland), 52
Santa's Snow Cat (Stainton), 173
Sarah Morton's Day: A Day in the Life of a Pilgrim Girl (Waters), 195
Scarecrow (Rylant), 191
Scaredy Cats, The (Bottner), 192
Scary, Scary Halloween (Bunting), 179
School Safety (Loewen), 91
Schools (Hall), 165
Scrambled States of America (Keller), 111
Sebastian: A Book About Bach (Winter), 48
Secret Knowledge of Grown-Ups, The (Wisniewski), 57
See the Yak Yak (Chigna), 93
Señor Cat's Romance and Other Favorite Stories from Latin America (González), 210
Sergio and the Hurricane (Wallner), 43
Serious Farm (Egan), 15
Service with a Smile (O'Conner), 73
Seven Blind Mice (Young), 51, 197
Seven Chinese Brothers, The (Mahy), 75, 90
Seven Silly Eaters, The (Hoberman), 155
Seven Spools of Thread (Medearis), 192
17 Kings and 42 Elephants (Mahy), 15
Shadow (Brown), 117
Sheila Rae, the Brave (Henkes), 133, 196
Shortest Day, The: Celebrating the Winter Solstice (Pfeffer), 210
Shy Charles (Wells), 205
Sick Day, The (MacLachlan), 101
Silly Jack and the Bean Stalk (Anholt), 109
Sisters (McPhail), 133
Sitting Bull (Penner), 206
Skip Across the Ocean: Nursery Rhymes from Around the World (Matze), 165
Skittles Math Riddles (McGrath), 61
Sky Tree: Seeing Science Through Art (Locker), 209
Sleepytime for Zoo Animals (Arnold), 65

Slugs (Greenberg), 192
Smiling (Swain), 127
Smoky Night (Bunting), 207
Snipp, Snapp, Snurr and the Buttered Bread (Lindman), 133
Snow Music (Perkins), 173
Snow Queen, The (Andersen), 58
Snowflake Bentley (Martin), 51
Snowy Day, The (Keats), 44
Snug as a Big Red Bug (Edwards), 151
So Many Cats (De Regniers), 138
So Much (Cooke), 101
So That's How the Moon Changes Shape! (Fowler), 118
So You Want to Be President? (St. George), 27, 178
Soap! Soap! Don't Forget the Soap! (Glass), 57
Soap Soup and Other Verses (Kuskin), 120
Soccer (Bizley), 33
Soccer (Joseph), 33
Soccer Counts! (McGrath and Alderman), 33
Soccer for Fun (Goin), 33
Soccer Mom from Outer Space (Saltzberg), 33
Some Dogs Do (Alborough), 189
Some from the Moon, Some from the Sun (Zemach), 197
Some People Are Blind (Schaefer), 107
Something Special for Me (Williams), 16
Song and Dance Man (Ackerman), 51
Souperchicken (Auch), 193
Squeaky, Creaky Bed, The (Thomson), 147
St. Patrick's Day (Gibbons), 45
St. Patrick's Day Shillelagh, The (Nolan), 37
"Stand Back," Said the Elephant, "I'm Going to Sneeze!" (Thomas), 15
Star of the Circus (Sampson), 129
Starring Mirette and Bellini (McCully), 112
Starry Messenger (Sis), 31
Star-Spangled Banner, The (Key), 130
Star-Spangled Banner, The (Yanuck), 111
Staying Healthy: Dental Care (McGinty), 169
Stellaluna (Cannon), 185
Stephanie's Ponytail (Munsch), 57, 98
Stick to It: The Story of Wilma Rudolph (Conrad), 106
Stinky Cheese Man, The (Scieszka), 152
Stone Soup (Brown), 117
Storm Book, The (Zolotow), 43
Story About Ping, The (Flack), 75
Story of Babar, The (de Brunhoff), 203
Story of Chopsticks, The (Compestine), 75
Story of Eleanor Roosevelt, The (Koestler-Grack), 167
Story of Jumping Mouse, The (Steptoe), 205
Story of Valentine's Day, The (Bulla), 19
Strega Nona (dePaola), 47, 156, 163
Strega Nona Takes a Vacation (dePaola), 47
Strega Nona's Magic Lesson (dePaola), 47
Stunt Planes (Savage), 183
Subway Sparrow (Torres), 29
Suddenly! A Preston Pig Story (McNaughton), 39
Sugar Snow, 213
Suki's Kimono (Uegaki), 75
Summer (Chapman), 76

Sun Egg, The (Beskow), 47
Swamp Angel (Isaacs), 30
Sweet and Sour Animal Book, The (Hughes), 22
Sweetwater Run, The: The Story of Buffalo Bill Cody and the Pony Express (Glass), 35
Swine Divine (Carr), 39
Swine Lake (Marshall), 39
Swish! (Marting and Sampson), 32
Sylvester and the Magic Pebble (Steig), 51, 189

Tabitha's Terrifically Tough Teeth (Middleton), 169
Take Me Out of the Bathtub and Other Silly Dilly Songs (Katz), 93
Taking a Walk: A Book in Two Languages (Emberley), 93
Tales of Oliver Pig (Van Leeuwen), 214
Tapenum's Day: A Wampanoag Indian Boy in Pilgrim Times (Waters), 195
Tara and Tiree, Fearless Friends: A True Story (Clements), 25
Tchaikovsky (Rachlin and Hellard), 80
Teammates (Golenbock), 123
Ted (DiTerlizzi), 101
Teeny Tiny Teacher (Calmenson), 197
Tell Me, Tree: All About Trees for Kids (Gibbons), 71, 209
Ten Apples Up on Top (Seuss), 93
Ten Little Dinosaurs (Schnetzler), 177
Ten Little Menehunes: A Hawaiian Counting Book (Forsythe), 115
Ten Little Mummies: An Egyptian Counting Book (Yates), 61
Ten Little Rabbits (Grossman), 105
Tenth Good Thing About Barney, The (Viorst), 22
Thank You, Grandpa (Plourde), 147
Thanksgiving Day (Gibbons), 181, 195
That's What a Friend Is (Hallinan), 25
There Was an Old Lady Who Swallowed a Fly (Taback), 30, 51, 93
There's a Nightmare in My Closet (Mayer), 215
There's a Wocket in My Pocket! (Seuss), 93
There's an Alligator Under My Bed (Mayer), 215
There's an Ant in Anthony (Most), 93, 148
They Call Her Molly Pitcher (Rockwell), 170
Things That Fly (Little), 183
Thirteen Moons on Turtle's Back (Bruchac), 105
31 Uses for a Mom (Ziefert), 79
This Boat (Collicutt), 87
This Is the Way We Go to School (Baer), 87
This Place Is Cold (Lavallee), 3
This Plane (Collicutt), 87
Thomas Edison (Raatma), 27
Thomas Edison (Schaefer), 27
Thomas Jefferson: A Photo-Illustrated Biography (Usel), 66
Thomas Jefferson: A Picture (Giblin), 66
Thomas's Sheep and the Great Geography Test (Layne), 187
Three Billy Goats Gruff, The (Stevens), 47
Three Days on a River in A Red Canoe (Williams), 16
Three Hat Day, A (Geringer), 201

Three Little Hawaiian Pigs and the Magic Shark, The (Laird), 115
Three Little Javelinas, The (Lowell), 39
Three Little Pigs, The (Marshall), 39
Three Little Pigs, The (Wiesner), 39
Three Little Wolves and the Big Bad Pig, The (Trivizas), 39
Three Pigs, The (Wiesner), 23
Three River Junction: A Story of an Alaskan Bald Eagle Preserve (Burnham), 3
Throw Your Tooth on the Roof: Tooth Traditions from Around the World (Beeler), 169
Thumbelina (Ehrlich), 47
Thunder Doesn't Scare Me! (Bowdish), 43
Tiger Has a Toothache, The: Helping Animals at the Zoo (Lauber), 65
Tiger Who Came to Tea, The (Kerr), 1
Tikki Tikki Tembo (Mosel), 13, 75
Tim O'Toole and the Wee Folk (McDermott), 47
Time Flies (Rohmann), 175
Time of Wonder (McClosky), 156
Timothy Tunny Swallowed a Bunny (Grossman), 69
To Be a Kid (Ajmera), 165
To Space and Back (Ride), 89
Today I Feel Silly and Other Moods That Make My Day (Curtis), 55
Togo (Blake), 3
Tomorrow's Alphabet (Shannon), 143
Tomten, The (Lindgren), 47
Tonka: Working Hard with the Mighty Loader (Korman), 83
Tooth Book, The (Lesieg), 169
Tooth Fairy (Wood), 47
Tops and Bottoms (Stevens), 7
Torch Fishing with the Sun (Williams), 115
Tortillas Para Mama and Other Nursery Rhymes: Spanish and English (Griego), 159
Touch the Poem (Adoff), 66
Tough Boris (Brown), 11
Tough Cookie (Wisniewski), 48
Travels of Babar, The (de Brunhoff), 203
Tree, The (Lyons), 209
Tree for All Seasons, A (Bernard), 209
Tree for Me, A (Van Laan), 192
Tree Is a Plant, A (Bulla), 209
Tree Is Nice, A (Udry), 209
Trees of the Dancing Goats, The (Polacco), 206
Tremendous Tree Book, The (Brenner and Garelick), 71, 209
Trial of the Stone, The: A Folk Tale (Douglas), 7
Triceratops: The Last Dinosaur (Sandell), 177
Troll-Bridge Toll, The (Wolff), 47
Troodon (Cohen), 177
Trouble with Trolls (Brett), 202
Trucks: Giants of the Highways (Robbins), 87
True Story of the Three Little Pigs, The (Scieszka), 39, 152
Trupp: A Fuzzhead Tale (Cannon), 185
Tuesday (Wiesner), 23
Tutankhamen's Gift (Sabuda), 41
Twelve Dancing Princesses, The (Sanderson), 193
12 Days of Christmas, The (Knight), 184
12 Ways to Get to 11 (Merriam), 61

Twister (Beard), 43
Two Bad Ants (Van Allsburg), 151
Two Cool Cows (Speed), 97
Two Greedy Bears: Adapted from a Hungarian Folk Tale (Ginsburg), 7
Two of Everything: A Chinese Folktale (Hong), 75

Ugly Duckling, The (Andersen), 58
Umbrella Thief, The (Wettasinghe and Hirano), 37
Uncle Pete's Pirate Adventure (Leigh), 11
Under One Rock: Bugs, Slugs, and Other Ugs (Fredericks), 151
Up, Up, Up! Apple-Picking Time (Shapiro), 147

Valentine's Day (Gibbons), 30
Verdi (Cannon), 185
Very Busy Spider, The (Carle), 106
Very First Americans, The (Ashrose), 105
Very Hungry Caterpillar, The (Carle), 106
Very Important Day, A (Herold), 195
Very Last First Time (Wallace), 3
Vietnamese Americans (Fitterer), 73
Vincent Van Gogh: Sunflowers and Swirly Stars (Holub), 53
Virgie Goes to School with Us Boys (Howard), 21
Visit from St. Nicholas, A (Moore), 203
Voice of Her Own, A: The Story of Phillis Wheatley, Slave Poet (Lasky), 21

Wagons West! (Gerrard), 213
Wait Till the Moon Is Full (Brown), 119
Waiting for Wings (Ehlert), 141
Wake Up, City (Verlander), 191
Wake Up House! Rooms Full of Poems (Lillegard), 69
Walking with Maga (Biro), 147
Walt Disney: A Photo-Illustrated Biography (Preszler), 202
Walter the Baker (Carle), 155
Washington Monument, The (Nelson), 34, 203
Watch the Stars Come Out (Levinson), 4
Water Hole, The (Base), 62
We Are Best Friends (Aliki), 25
We Are the Many: A Picture Book of American Indians (Rapaport), 105
We Had a Picnic This Sunday Past (Woodson), 27
We Lie Here Too! Kids Talk About Good Citizenship (Loewen), 111
We Love Baseball! (Harrison), 91, 123
We the Kids: The Preamble to the Constitution of the United States (Catrow), 111
Weather Forecasting (Gibbons), 24, 43
Weather Words and What They Mean (Gibbons), 43
Wednesday Surprise, The (Bunting), 147, 184, 207
Weed Is a Flower, A: The Life of George Washington Carver (Aliki), 5
Weekend in the City, A (Lorenz), 191
Wemberly Worried (Henkes), 205
Whale Snow (Edwardson and Gill), 3
What a Hat! (Keller), 201
What Are You So Grumpy About? (Lichtenheld), 57

What Can You Do with a Shoe? (Sendak), 138
What Dads Can't Do (Wood), 101
What Do Authors Do? (Christlow), 184
What Do Illustrators Do? (Christelow), 49
What Do the Fairies Do with All Those Teeth? (Luppens), 169
What Do You Do with a Kangaroo? (Mayer), 215
What Do You Know About Manners? (MacGregor), 179
What Do You Say, Dear? (Joslin), 179
What Good Is a Tree? (Brimner), 209
What Grandmas Do Best (Numeroff), 147
What Grandpas Do Best (Numeroff), 147
What Happened to the Dinosaurs? (Branley), 177
What Makes a Bird a Bird? (Garelick), 29
What Moms Can't Do (Wood), 79
What the Dinosaurs Saw: Animals Living Then and Now (Schlein), 177
What the Moon Is Like (Branley), 118
What Time Is It? (Keenan), 61
What Would You Do If You Lived at the Zoo? (Carlstrom), 131
What You Never Knew About Fingers, Fords, and Chopsticks (Lauber), 30
What's in Aunt Mary's Room? (Howard), 214
Wheels on the Bus (Raffi), 116
When Bluebell Sang (Ernst), 97
When Cows Come Home (Harrison), 97
When I Am Old with You (Johnson), 147
When Pigasso Met Mootisse (Laden), 37
When Spring Comes (Maass), 48
When the Moon Is Full: A Lunar Year (Pollock), 119
When This World Was New (Figueredo), 195
When We Were Very Young (Milne), 9
When Winter Comes (Van Laan), 192
Where Are You Going? To See My Friend! (Iwamura), 25
Where Did Bunny Go? (Tafuri), 189
Where Did the Butterfly Get Its Name? (Berger), 141
Where Do Balloons Go? An Uplifting Mystery (Curtis), 173
Where Do I Live? (Chesanow), 187
Where Does the Butterfly Go When It Rains? (Garelick), 141
Where Does the Wind Blow? (Rink), 43
Where People Live (Royston), 187
Where the Forest Meets the Sea (Baker), 184
Where the Sidewalk Ends (Silverstein), 171
Where the Wild Things Are (Sendak), 51, 98
Where to Look for a Dinosaur (Most), 177
Where's Spot? (Hill), 152
Where's Waldo? (Handford), 161
Where's Wallace? (Knight), 184
Whistling (Partridge), 101
White Snow, Bright Snow (Tresselt), 143
Who Settled the West? (Kalman), 213
Who Took Cookies from the Cookie Jar? (Lass), 155
Who Took the Farmer's Hat? (Nodset), 201
Whooping Crane (Graves), 156
Whose Hat? (Miller), 201
Why Do Leaves Change Color? (Maestro), 209

Why Mexican Immigrants Came to America (Parker), 195
Why Mosquitoes Buzz in People's Ears: A West African Tale (Aardema), 40, 95
Why the Sun and the Moon Live in the Sky (Dayrell), 13, 119
Why Vietnamese Immigrants Came to America (Parker), 195
Wild Birds (Ryder), 5
Wild Christmas Reindeer, The (Brett), 202
Will I Have a Friend? (Cohen), 25
Will We Miss Them? (Peck), 214
Will You Sign Here, John Hancock? (Fritz), 13
William's Doll (Zolotow), 107
Wings of Change (Hill), 141
Wolf's Chicken Stew, The (Kasza), 155
Wonderful Words (Hopkins), 66
Woodpeckers (Stone), 29
Work We Do, The (Conrad), 81
Working Cotton (Williams), 21
World of Baseball, The (Buckley), 123
World Turns Round and Round, The (Weiss), 165

Wright Brothers, The (Edwards), 137, 139
Wright Brothers for Kids, The: How They Invented the Airplane (Carson), 139
Wright Vs. Wrong: The True and Not-So-True Story of the Airplane (Tegge), 183
Wynton Marsalis: Gifted Trumpet Player (Awmiller), 171

Year at Maple Hill Farm (Provensen and Provensen), 44, 191
Year of the Perfect Christmas Tree, The (Houston), 206
Yippee-Yay! A Book About Cowboys and Cowgirls (Gibbons), 83
Yo! Yes? (Raschka), 41, 51
Yoko (Wells), 17
You Be Good and I'll Be Night (Merriam), 121
You Wouldn't Want to Be an American Pioneer! (Morley), 213
You'll Soon Grow into Them, Titch (Radunsky), 133

Young Cam Jansen and the Ice Skate Mystery (Adler), 173
Young Cam Jansen and the Lost Tooth (Adler), 173
Young Cam Jansen and the Missing Cookie (Adler), 173
Young Cam Jansen and the Pizza Shop Mystery (Adler), 173
Young Teddy Roosevelt (Harness), 178
Young Thurgood Marshall: Fighter for Equality (Carpenter), 21
You're Aboard Spaceship Earth (Luaber), 23

Zachary's Ball (Tavares), 123
Zack in the Middle (Michels), 133
Zanzibar Zoo (Prediletto), 65
Zara's Hats (Meisel), 201
Zelda and Ivy (Kvasnosky), 16
Zero Grandparents (Edwards), 147
Ziggy Piggy and the Three Little Pigs (Asch), 134
Zin! Zin! Zin! A Violin (Moss), 69
Zoo (Gibbons), 65
Zoo-Looking (Fox), 65

Index of Themes by Subject

Aardema, Verna, 40, 95
Ada, Alma Flor, 4
Adams, Ansel, 31
Alaska, 2–3, 4, 52
Alborough, Jez, 189
Aliki, 149
Allard, Harry, 16
Aloha! (Sweeney), 114
"America the Beautiful," 112
American Artist Appreciation Month, 127
Andersen, Hans Christian, 58
Anglund, Joan Walsh, 4
Animal Cruelty Prevention Month, 55
Anno, Mitsumasa, 48
Answer Your Cat's Question Day, 13
Anthony, Susan B., 31
April: highlights, 55; reading strategy for, 72; reading tip for, 55; special events in, 55
April weekly themes: humor, 56–57; numbers, 60–61; poetry, 68–69; zoo animals, 64–65
April Fool's Day, 58
Aquarium Month, 55
Arbor Day, 71
Armed Forces Day, 84
Arnosky, Jim, 148
Asch, Frank, 134
Asian/Pacific American Heritage Month, 73
Auch, Mary Jane, 193

August: highlights, 127; reading strategy for, 144; reading tip for, 127; special events in, 127
August weekly themes: butterflies, 140–41; circus, 128–29; inventors, 136–37; siblings, 132–33
Aviation, history of, 182–83

Bach, Johann Sebastian, 48
Baker, Jeannie, 184
Banks, 215
Banneker, Benjamin, 188
Barnum, Phineas T., 113
Barracca, Debra, 211
Base, Graeme, 62
Baseball, 122–23
Basketball, 32, 202
Beethoven, Ludwig van, 207
Bemelmans, Ludwig, 71
Berenstain, Jan, 124
Bill of Rights Day, 206
Bird Day, 5
Birds, 28–29
Black History Month, 19, 20–21
Bond, Michael, 8
Boone, Daniel, 184
Boston Tea Party, 207
Brahms, Johannes, 80
Braille, Louis, 5
Brett, Jan, 202
Bridwell, Norman, 31
Brown, Marc, 196

Brown, Marcia, 117
Brown, Margaret Wise, 88
Bryan, Ashley, 117
Bunting, Eve, 207
Burningham, John, 71
Burton, Virginia Lee, 143
Butterflies, 140–41, 142

Caldecott, Randolph, 49
Caldecott Award winners, 50–51
Calmenson, Stephanie, 197
Cannon, Janell, 185
Carle, Eric, 106
Carlstrom, Nancy White, 131
Carson, Christopher (Kit), 211
Carver, George Washington, 5
Cavoukian, Raffi, 116
Celebration USA, 157
Cézanne, Paul, 12
Cherry, Lynn, 5
Chess, Victoria, 192
Child Magazine Month, 163
Children's Day—Japan and Korea, 80
Children's Vision and Learning Month, 127
Christmas, 211
Christmas trees, 206
Cinco de Mayo, 77
Circus, 128–29
Citizenship for Native Americans, 99
City/Farm life, 190–91
Civil rights march on Washington, 143

Climo, Shirley, 196
Cody, William "Buffalo Bill," 35
Cole, Joanna, 135
Columbus Day, 170
Cooney, Barbara, 134
Cousteau, Jacques, 98
Cowley, Joy, 134
Cows, 96–97
Craig, Helen, 143
Crews, Donald, 143
Crockett, David (Davy), 139

da Vinci, Leonardo, 76
Day, Alexandra, 151
De Brunhoff, Jean, 203
De Regniers, Beatrice Schenk, 138
Deaf Awareness Week, 145
Deaf History Month, 37
Deaf-Blind Awareness Week, 107
Debussy, Claude, 142
December: highlights, 199; reading
    strategy for, 216; reading tip for,
    199; special events in, 199
December weekly themes: hats,
    200–201; mice, 204–5;
    pioneers, 212–13; trees,
    208–9
Degen, Bruce, 99
Delacre, Lulu, 210
Demi, 148
dePaola, Tomi, 156
Dillon, Leo, 40
Dinosaurs, 176–77
Disney, Walt, 202
Douglass, Frederick, 31
Duvoisin, Roger, 143

Earhart, Amelia, 124
Earthquakes, 52
Eastman, P. D., 196
Edison, Thomas Alva, 27
Ehlert, Lois, 188
Elephant Appreciation Day, 160
Elephants, 14–15
Ellis Island, 4
Emberley, Ed, 174
Endangered Species Act (1973), 214

Fair tales, 6–7
Farm/City life, 190–91
Father's Day, 102
February: highlights, 19; reading strategy
    for, 36; reading tip for, 19; special
    events in, 19
February weekly themes: birds, 28–29;
    Black History Month, 20–21;
    friendship, 24–25; sports, 32–33
Fire Prevention Month, 163
First american automobile race, 197
Fleming, Denise, 17
Florian, Douglas, 45
Folktales, 6–7
Food, 154–55
Football, 32–33
Fourth of July. *See* Independence Day
Fox, Merrion Frances (Mem), 40
Franklin, Benjamin, 9
Freeman, Don, 135
Friedman, Ina, 8
Friendship, 24–25
Fritz, Jean, 192

Gag, Wanda, 44
Galdone, Paul, 93
Galilei, Galileo, 31
Gauguin, Paul, 95
Geisel, Theodor "Dr. Seuss," 40
Geography, 186–87
Geography Week, 192
Gesert, Arthur, 160
Gibbons, Gail, 130
Goble, Paul, 157
Gorillas, 210
Grand Canyon National Park Anniversary,
    35
Grandparents, 146–47
Grimm, Jacob, 5
Grimm, Wilhelm Carl, 34
Groundhog Day, 22
Gruelle, Johnny, 211

Halloween, 179
Hancock, John, 13
Handford, Martin, 161
Hanukkah, 210
Hats, 200–201
Hawaii: annexation of, 113, 114–15;
    statehood of, 142
Haydn, Franz Joseph, 53
Hays, Mary (Molly Pitcher), 170
Helen Keller Deaf-Blind Awareness Week,
    91
Hill, Eric, 151
Hispanic Heritage Month, 157, 158–59
Hissey, Jane, 148
Hoban, Lillian, 85
Hoban, Russell, 23
Hoberman, Mary Ann, 138
Hoff, Syd, 149
Holabird, Katharine, 13
Hopkins, Lee Bennett, 66
Houdini, Harry, 49
Howard, Elizabeth, 214
Hughes, Langston, 22
Humor, 56–57
Hurd, Thacher, 40
Hutchins, Hazel, 135
Hutchins, Pat, 102
Hyman, Trina Schart, 63

Immigrants, 194–95
Independence Day, 109, 112
Insects, 150–51
International children, 164–65
International Clown Week, 127, 130
International Day of Peace, 145
International Dinosaur Month, 178
International Table Manners Week, 30
International Youth Day, United Nations,
    138
Inventors, 136–37
Irish-American Heritage Month, 37
Irving, Washington, 59

January: highlights, 1; reading strategy
    for, 18; reading tip for, 1; special
    events in, 1
January weekly themes: Alaska, 2–3;
    elephants, 14–15; fairy
    tales/folktales, 6–7; pirates,
    10–11
Jefferson, Thomas A., 66
Jones, Casey, 44

July: highlights, 109; reading strategy for,
    126; reading tip for, 109; special
    events in, 109
July weekly themes: baseball, 122–23;
    Hawaii, 114–15; moon, 118–19;
    patriotism, 110–11
June: highlights, 91; reading strategy for,
    108; reading tip for, 91; special
    events in, 91
June weekly themes: cows, 96–97; fathers,
    100–101; Native Americans,
    104–5; Wordplay/National Spelling
    Bee finals, 92–93

Keats, Ezra Jack, 43
Keep America Beautiful Month, 55
Keller, Helen, 107
Kellogg, Steven, 175
Key, Francis Scott, 130
Kids Love a Mystery Month, 163, 170
Kimmel, Eric, 179
Kindergarten Day, 70
King, Martin Luther, Jr., 9
Kinsey-Warnock, Natalie, 184
Kipling, Rudyard, 215
Knight, Hilary, 184
Kraus, Robert, 103
Kuskin, Karla, 120
Kvasnosky, Laura, 16
Kwanzaa, 214

Labor Day, 148
Language arts, 172–73
Lauber, Patricia, 23
Lear, Edward, 81
Lent, Blair, 13
Lewis and Clark Expedition, 81
Library Card Sign-Up Month, 145
Library Lover's Month, 19
Lincoln, Abraham, 27
Lindbergh, Charles, 23
Lionni, Leo, 80
Livingston, Myra Cohn, 139
Lobel, Anita, 94
Lobel, Arnold, 88
Lodge, Bernard, 174
Luenn, Nancy, 214

Magical people, 46–47
Marcellino, Fred, 175
March: highlights, 37; reading strategy
    for, 53; reading tip for, 37; special
    events in, 37
March weekly themes: Caldecott Award
    winners, 50–51; magical people,
    46–47; pigs, 38–39; weather,
    42–43
Mardi Gras, 26
Marsalis, Wynton, 171
Matisse, Henri, 215
May: highlights, 73; reading strategy for,
    90; reading tip for, 73; special
    events in, 73;
May Day, 76
May weekly themes: Asian/Pacific
    American heritage, 74–75; mothers,
    78–79; vehicles/transportation,
    86–87; world of work, 82–83
Mayer, Mercer, 215
McClosky, Robert, 156
McCully, Emily Arnold, 112

McDermott, Gerald, 17
McDonald, Megan, 35
McKissack, Patricia, 135
Meddaugh, Susan, 166
Medearis, Angela Shelf, 192
Memorial Day, 89
Merriam, Eve, 121
Mice, 204–5
Michelangelo, 41
Milne, A. A., 12
Minarik, Else, 153
Monarch butterflies fall migration, 127, 142
Monet, Claude, 189
Month of the Young Child, 55
Moon, man landing on, 121
Mora, Pat, 12
Morris, Ann, 166
Most, Bernard, 148
Mothers, 78–79
Mother's Day, 73
Mozart, Wolfgang Amadeus, 16
Munsch, Robert, 98
Munsinger, Lynn, 211
Music in Our School Month, 37

Napoli, Donna Jo, 35
National 911 Day, 153
National Adoption Month, 181
National Adoption Week, 193
National Agriculture Week, 44
National Author Day, 184
National Aviation Day, 139
National Aviation History Month, 185
National Baked Bean Month, 109
National Bike Month, 73
National Bird Feeding Month, 19
National Book Month, 73
National Child Abuse Prevention Week, 55
National Coin Week, 70
National Compliment Day, 16
National Craft Month, 37
National Dairy Month, 91, 95
National Dental Hygiene Month, 167
National Dinosaur Month, 163
National Dog Week, 145, 160
National Family Literacy Day, 184
National Farm Animals Awareness Week, 160
National Farm/City Week, 181, 193
National Flag Day, 99
National Flag Week, 99
National Geography Awareness Week, 181
National Grandparents Day, 149
National Hispanic Heritage Month, 145
National Honey Month, 145, 149
National Hot Dog Month, 109
National Hot Tea Month, 1
National Humor Month, 55
National Ice Cream Day (third Sunday in July), 109
National Inventors' Month, 127, 138
National Little League Baseball Week, 91
National Magic Day, 179
National Mentoring Month, 1
National Mustard Day, 131
National Nurses Week, 73
National Pasta Month, 163
National Poetry Month, 66
National Poinsettia Day, 206

National Reading a Road Map Week, 59
National Rivers Month, 91
National Roller-Skating Month, 174
National Rose Month, 91
National Safety Month, 91
National Sandwich Day, 185
National Spelling Bee finals, 92–93, 94
National Teacher Day, 77
National Transportation Week, 85
National Umbrella Month, 37
National UNICEF Day, 179
National Week of the Ocean, 62
National Whiners Day, 214
Native Americans, 106–7; citizenship for, 99
New Year's Eve, 215
November: celebrating, 197; highlights, 181; reading strategy for, 197; reading tip for, 181; special events in, 181
November weekly themes: aviation, history of, 182–83; farm/city life, 190–91; geography, 186–87; pilgrims and immigrants, 194–95
Numbers, 60–61
Numeroff, Laura Joffe, 117

Oatmeal Month, 1
O'Connor, Sandra Day, 52
October: highlights, 163; reading strategy for, 180; reading tip for, 163; special events in, 163
October weekly themes: dinosaurs, 176–77; international children, 164–65; language arts, 172–73; teeth, 168–69
Older American Month, 73
100 Billionth Crayola Crayon Anniversary, 26

Pan American Day, 67
Parks, Rosa, 202
Parrish, Peggy, 117
Patriot Day, 153
Patriotism, 110–11
Peanut Butter Lover's Month, 181
Picasso, Pablo, 175
Pickett, Bill, 202
Pigs, 38–39
Pilgrims, 194–95
Pinkney, Jerry, 210
Pioneers, 212–13
Pirates, 10–11
Pitcher, Molly (Mary Hays), 170
Poetry, 68–69
Polacco, Patricia, 116
Police Officer Memorial Day, 84
Post, Emily, 179
Potter, Beatrix, 125
Prediction, skill of, 126
Prelutsky, Jack, 152
Presidents' Day, 19, 31
Pryor, Bonnie, 210

Questioning, art of, 72

Ransome, Arthur, 12
Raschka, Chris, 41
"Reading Rainbow," 112
References, using, 197
Rembrandt, 120

Revere, Paul, 4
Rey, H. A., 156
Rey, Margaret, 84
Ride, Sally, 89
Robinson, Jackie, 17
Rockwell, Anne, 26
Rohmann, Eric, 175
Roosevelt, Eleanor, 167
Roosevelt, Theodore, 178
Root, Phyllis, 30
Rosa Parks Day, 202
Ross, Betsy, 4
Rowling, J. K., 125
Rudoph, Wilma, 106
Rule of five, 162
Ruth, George Herman "Babe," 26

Sabuda, Robert, 41
Sacagawea, 210
Saint Nicholas Day, 203
Saint Patrick's Day, 45
Salk, Jonas, 178
Sandburg, Carl, 7
Sanderson, Ruth, 193
Say, Allen, 143
School Library Media Month, 55
Sendak, Maurice, 98
September: highlights, 145; reading strategy for, 161; reading tip for, 145; special events in, 145
September weekly themes: food, 154–55; grandparents, 146–47; Hispanic heritage, 158–59; science, 150–51
Seuss, Dr. (Theodor Geisel), 40
Siblings, 132–33
Silverstein, Shel, 171
Simon, Seymour, 135
Sister's Day, 131
Sitting Bull, 206
Small, David, 27
Smile Week, 127
Soccer, 33
Soup Month, 1
Sousa, John Philip, 185
Sports, 32–33
Spring, 48
Statue of Liberty, 178
Steig, William, 189
Stevenson, James, 116
Stevenson, Robert Louis, 189
Summer solstice, 103

Taback, Simms, 30
Tafuri, Nancy, 189
Tallarico, Tony, 160
Tchaikovsky, Peter Ilich, 80
Teeth, 168–69
Thank Your School Librarian Day, 70
Transportation, 86–87
Trees, 208–9

United Nations Day, 174
United Nations International Youth Day, 138
Universal Children's Week, 166

Valentine's Day, 19, 30
Van Allsburg, Chris, 102
Van Gogh, Vincent, 53
Van Laan, Nancy, 192
Van Leeuwen, Jean, 214

Vehicles, 86–87
Venn diagrams, 53
Veterans Day, 188
Viorst, Judith, 22
Vocabulary development, 180

Waber, Bernard, 161
Walk Your Pet Month, 1
Wallace, Karen, 58
Walsh, Ellen Stoll, 148
Washington, George, 34
Washington Monument, 203
Weather, 42–43
Weather Forecasters' Day, 23
Webster, Noah, 171

Wells, Rosemary, 17
Whooping cranes, fall migration of, 156
Wiesner, David, 23
Williams, Garth, 67
Williams, Vera, 16
Winter solstice, 210
Wisniewski, David, 48
Women's History Month, 37
Wood, Don, 77
Wood, Grant, 30
Woodson, Jacqueline, 27
Word classes, 216
Wordplay, 92–93
Work, world of, 82–83

World Food Day, 171
Wright, Orville, 139

Yolen, Jane, 27
Yorinks, Arthur, 142
Young, Ed, 197
Youth Art Month, 37

Zelinsky, Paul O., 30
Zemach, Margot, 197
Ziefert, Harriet, 113
Zion, Gene, 167
Zolotow, Charlotte, 107
Zoo animals, 64–65
Zoos, 112